D1596326

Ernest Newman

Music in Britain, 1600–2000

ISSN 2053-3217

Series Editors:
BYRON ADAMS, RACHEL COWGILL AND PETER HOLMAN

This series provides a forum for the best new work in the field of British music studies, placing music from the early seventeenth to the late twentieth centuries in its social, cultural, and historical contexts. Its approach is deliberately inclusive, covering immigrants and emigrants as well as native musicians, and explores Britain's musical links both within and beyond Europe. The series celebrates the vitality and diversity of music-making across Britain in whatever form it took and wherever it was found, exploring its aesthetic dimensions alongside its meaning for contemporaries, its place in the global market, and its use in the promotion of political and social agendas.

Proposals or queries should be sent in the first instance to Professors Byron Adams, Rachel Cowgill, Peter Holman or Boydell & Brewer at the addresses shown below. All submissions will receive prompt and informed consideration.

Professor Byron Adams,
Department of Music – 061, University of California, Riverside, CA 92521–0325
email: byronadams@earthlink.net

Professor Rachel Cowgill MBE,
School of Music, Humanities and Media, University of Huddersfield,
Queensgate, Huddersfield, HD1 3DH
email: r.e.cowgill@hud.ac.uk

Professor Peter Holman,
School of Music, University of Leeds, Leeds, LS2 9JT
email: p.k.holman@leeds.ac.uk

Boydell & Brewer, PO Box 9, Woodbridge, Suffolk, IP12 3DF
email: editorial@boydell.co.uk

Previously published volumes in this series are listed at the back of this volume.

Ernest Newman

A Critical Biography

Paul Watt

THE BOYDELL PRESS

First published 2017
The Boydell Press, Woodbridge

ISBN 978 1 78327 190 0

The Boydell Press is an imprint of Boydell & Brewer Ltd
PO Box 9, Woodbridge, Suffolk IP12 3DF, UK
and of Boydell & Brewer Inc.
668 Mt Hope Avenue, Rochester, NY 14620–2731, USA
website: www.boydellandbrewer.com

The publisher has no responsibility for the continued existence
or accuracy of URLs for external or third-party internet websites
referred to in this book, and does not guarantee that any content on
such websites is, or will remain, accurate or appropriate

A CIP catalogue record for this book is available
from the British Library

This publication is printed on acid-free paper

Frontispiece Newman, c. 1908. Photographer unknown.
Reproduced by kind permission of the Estate of Ernest Newman.

'Have you read about music in the newspapers and periodicals of the last thirty and more years—in the *Manchester Guardian*, the *Birmingham Post*, the *Observer*, the *Sunday Times*, and the great weeklies and monthlies? Or have you read all the good books on musical subjects published in England since the year 1895? If you have, you will know the work of Ernest Newman and will need no introduction to it. But you will know little or nothing of the man himself and his history; and ignorance of this kind is, I think, to be regretted and, if possible, removed.'

Eva Mary Grew, 'Ernest Newman: English Music Critic',
The Sackbut, November 1928, 113.

'I should like to emphasize the fact that Mr Newman has exercised a dominating influence over musical taste in this country. His articles and books have been read assiduously by almost every intelligent amateur and professional musician for the past thirty years.'

Ralph Hill, *Challenges: A Series of Controversial Essays on Music*.
London: John Williams, 1943, 9.

'Ernest Newman was perhaps the first writer truly to Europeanise our music and our humane responses to music. He quickened our antennae, opened doors for us.'

Neville Cardus, 'Ernest Newman', in *Fanfare for Ernest Newman*,
ed. Herbert van Thal. London: Arthur Baker, 1955, 29–37; 31.

'So, when we have said that he [Newman] was a great scholar, a great writer, and a great wit, and admired his books, we have not done with him. He left one of the great tasks of his life undone; and this can still be done for him, if someone will study hard everything that he had to say, in his ephemeral essays as well as in his published works, and produce a much-needed book synthesizing his whole theory of musical aesthetics.'

Deryck Cooke, 'Ernest Newman (1868–1959)', *Tempo* 52 (Autumn 1959), 3.

To my parents, Heather and Laurence

❧ Contents

Figures

Preface and Acknowledgements

THE idea for this book presented itself in the early 1990s. I was a post-graduate student at Monash University writing a dissertation on Berlioz, which inevitably led me to Newman's essays on the composer. Shortly there-after—on a visit to the Grub Street Bookstore in Brunswick, an inner suburb of Melbourne—I chanced upon Newman's 1895 biography of Gluck. I read the introduction while standing in one of the bookshop's narrow passages, and was transfixed: his introductory essay on the necessity for historical method in musical criticism intrigued me. I wondered why a British writer on music was taking up the cause for this kind of history so late in the century and why no one had made much of it in the literature I had read on the history of musicology. I knew then that I wanted to find out more about Newman and what made him tick. And so I set to work.

For access to archives relating to Ernest Newman I would like to thank staff at the following libraries and archives: Bodleian Library, Oxford; British Library, London; Cadbury Research Library, University of Birmingham; National Library of Scotland; Harry Ransom Center, University of Texas at Austin; Houghton Library and Isham Memorial Library, Harvard University; Irving S. Gilmore Music Library, Yale University; Juilliard School Library, New York; King's College Library, Cambridge; Rauner Special Collections, Dartmouth College; and Special Collections at the universities of Glasgow, Liverpool and Cambridge.

Thanks are due to Odin Dekkers at Radboud Universiteit in Nijmegen who provided access to the personal research papers of various scholars in the Department of English Literature and Culture relating to the Dobell col-lection at the University of Oxford. Nigel Scaife kindly loaned his personal notes relating to the research he undertook on Newman for his 1994 doctoral dissertation.

Thanks to the University of Melbourne for permission to reproduce a part of the following article in chapter 8, 'Ernest Newman's *The Man Liszt* of 1934: reading its freethought agenda', *Context: A Journal of Music Research* 31 (2006): 193–205.'

I am grateful to the universities of Glasgow, Oxford and Texas at Austin, and the National Library of Scotland, for permission to reproduce copyright mate-rial in their collections. I am deeply indebted to Mary Parkin, Vera Newman's neice and the executor of the Newman Estate, who has given permission to reproduce all copyright material in this book. I am also grateful to Mary for generously sharing her memories of the Newmans and for providing most of the photographs reproduced in this book.

There are two collections relating to Newman that elude us. The first being the personal papers that were once in the stewardship of Walter Legge and Elisabeth Schwarzkopf. It is believed this collection contains some of Newman's research notes and correspondence relating to his work on Richard Strauss and Hugo Wolf. If this collection comes to light it will provide us with valuable information on Newman's working life in the early 1900s when he was working on these composers' biographies. These papers might also contain valuable material relating to the role that Newman, Legge and Schwarzkopf played, collectively, in the promotion of Wolf's music in Britain and North America. The second archive is a set of letters from John M. Robertson to Newman that, at the time of writing, are understood to be in a private collection and not yet available to scholars. If and when this correspondence is made public, it will add depth to what we know about Newman's relationship with his most important mentor and friend.

I am grateful to the following organizations that provided funding for this research. The University of Sydney provided a full scholarship for my PhD (2004–2007) that examined Newman's intellectual life in the 1890s, and the university further funded a research trip to the UK in 2005 as well as the purchase of microfilms and photocopies. Monash University, where I now work, has been generous through grants and research leave. In 2008 I was awarded a European Travel Grant that enabled me to take up a visiting fellowship in the Institute of Musical Research at the School of Advanced Studies, University of London, and facilitated just over two months' research at the British Library. In 2011 I was awarded an Alfred A. Knopf and Blanche Knopf Fellowship to the Harry Ransom Center, University of Texas at Austin, where I read correspondence between the Knopfs and the Newmans relating to various business and personal matters. A grant from the Australian Research Council (2012–2015) enabled me to complete the book.

On a personal level I owe a great deal of thanks to friends and colleagues over many years for their help, advice and encouragement. This book would never have been written were it not for the unflagging support, over many years, of Kerry Murphy, Margaret Kartomi, Sandra McColl and Rachel Segal. Other friends and colleagues who have helped in many different ways include Michael Allis, Megan Burslem, Sarah Collins, Odin Dekkers, Katrina Dowling, Trevor Clarke, Rachel Cowgill, Mark Davis, Bronia Kornhauser, David Larkin, Caroline Murray, Derek B. Scott, Jennie Shaw and Peter Tregear. Thanks go to Megan Milan, Rohais Haughton, Catherine Larner and Michael Middeke who have seen this book through to production.

Last, but by no means least, I thank my parents, Laurence Watt and Heather Watt, to whom this book is dedicated. They have nurtured my musical and scholarly aspirations from childhood and have supported my education in the many ways that have made this enterprise possible.

Chronology of Newman's Life and Works

1868 Born and named William Roberts on 30 November 1868 in Lancaster

1884 Begins five years of composition, including a 100-page draft for an opera-symphony based on Shelley's 'Prometheus Unbound'

1885 Enters University College, Liverpool

1886 Leaves University College, Liverpool; makes the personal acquaintance of John M. Robertson

1889 Works as a bank clerk; debut as published author in the September issue of *National Reformer* writing under his pseudonym Ernest Newman; research on *Gluck and the Opera* underway

1890 Typescript of *Gluck and the Opera* finished but attempts to find a publisher are unsuccessful until 1895

1891 Writes his one and only article for *University College Magazine*, Liverpool, under his birth name, William Roberts

1893 Regular contributor to Robertson's newly founded *Free Review*

1894 Marries his first wife, Kate Eleanor Woolett, on 3 February; installed as President of the Liverpool Branch of the National Secular Society

1895 Publication of *Gluck and the Opera* by Bertram Dobell; first article published in *Fortnightly Review*

1896 First articles published in *Truth Seeker*; work on *A Study of Wagner* begins around this time and is published in 1899

1897 Publication by the University Press, Watford, of *Pseudo-Philosophy at the end of the Nineteenth Century* under the pseudonym Hugh Mortimer Cecil, a pseudonym he was to use for some articles published in *University Magazine and Free Review*; first articles published in *Musician*

1898 First articles published in *Monthly Musical Record*; first essay published in *Fortnightly Review*

1899 Publication of *A Study of Wagner* by Bertram Dobell; writes programme notes for Granville Bantock's concerts at New Brighton; wins the Bankers' Institute prize for an essay, 'The literature of banking'; declines a commission to write a book on Edward FitzGerald

1900 First article in *Contemporary Review*

1904 Joins the staff of the Midland School of Music at the invitation of Granville Bantock; publication of *Wagner* in 'Music of the Masters' series

1905   Appointed music critic to the *Manchester Guardian;* publication of
       Musical Studies, comprising updated and previously published essays,
       each dedicated to friends and colleagues including John M. Robertson
       and Bertram Dobell

1906   Appointed music critic to the *Birmingham Daily Post*, a position he
       holds until 1919; publication of *Elgar*

1907   Publication of *Hugo Wolf*

1908   Publication of *Richard Strauss*

1914   Publication of *Wagner as Man and Artist*

1918   Death of Newman's first wife, Kate Eleanor Woolett. Joins the *Observer*
       in March until January 1920 when he begins work for the *Sunday Times*

1919   Publication of *A Musical Motley*, a collection of previously published
       essays; marries his second wife, Vera Hands

1920   Publication of *The Piano-Player and its Music*; joins the *Sunday Times*,
       a position he holds until 1958, a year before his death

1923   Publication of *Solo Singing*

1924   Guest editor, *New York Evening Post* (to 1925)

1925   Publication of *A Musical Critic's Holiday*, a reflective work on the
       problems of criticism; made an Honorary Associate of the Rationalist
       Press Association (the same award was made to Albert Einstein in 1934
       and Sigmund Freud in 1938)

1927   Publication of *The Unconscious Beethoven*

1928   Publication of *What to Read on the Evolution of Music*

1931   Publication of *Fact and Fiction about Wagner*

1933   Beginning of the publication of *The Life of Richard Wagner*, 4 volumes,
       1933, 1937, 1941, 1946; Cambridge University Press inaugurated its
       Music list in 1976 with a paperback edition

1934   Publication of *The Man Liszt: A Study of the Tragi-Comedy of a Soul
       Divided Against Itself* to severe critical reception

1940   Publication of *Wagner* (Novello edition)

1954   Publication of *More Opera Nights*

1958   Retires from the *Sunday Times* after 38 years; admitted to the Order of
       Merit of the Federal Republic of Germany (Commander Class) by the
       President of the Federal Republic, Theodor Heuss

1959   Made a Doctor of Letters, *honoris causa* in the University of Exeter on
       17 March; died on 7 July

Abbreviations

'Confessions' Ernest Newman, 'Confessions of a musical critic' first published in fifteen instalments between 21 March and 16 June 1923 in *Cassell's Weekly*; Reproduced in *Testament of Music*, ed. Herbert Van Thal (London: Putnam, 1962): 1–41

CR *Contemporary Review*

Essays *Essays Towards a Critical Method* by John M. Robertson (1889)

FoR *Fortnightly Review*

FR *Free Review*

Grove *The New Grove Dictionary of Music and Musicians*, ed. S. Sadie and J. Tyrrell (London: Macmillan, 2001)

Knopf Papers Alfred A. Knopf and Blanche W. Knopf Papers, Harry Ransom Center, University of Texas, Austin

MG *Manchester Guardian*

MH *Musical Herald*

ML *Music & Letters*

MMR *Monthly Musical Record*

MOMTR *Musical Opinion and Music Trade Review*

MQ *Musical Quarterly*

MR *Music Review*

MS Farmer Henry George Farmer Papers, University of Glasgow

MSS Dobell Dobell Papers, Bodleian Library, Oxford

MT *Musical Times*

Mus *Musician*

New Essays *New Essays Towards a Critical Method* by John M. Robertson (1897)

NQMR *New Quarterly Musical Review*

NR *National Reformer*

NW *New Witness*

ODNB *Oxford Dictionary of National Biography*

Parker Papers D.C. Parker Papers, National Library of Scotland

S *Sackbut*

Sp *Speaker*

SR *Saturday Review*

ST *Sunday Times*

TS *Truth Seeker*

UMFR *University Magazine and Free Review*

CHAPTER 1

Ernest Newman and the Challenge of Critical Biography

J EAN Sibelius once facetiously remarked that a monument had never been erected in honour of a music critic, implying that critics were irascible and unworthy hacks whose opinions were best ignored.[1] Yet a monument—of sorts—was erected for Ernest Newman. It was not of the bricks and mortar variety, but of the literary kind, a clerihew:

> Ernest Newman said
> 'next week, Schumann'
> But, when next week came
> It was Wagner just the same.[2]

Monuments, of course, are not always accurate representations of their subject. Rodin's controversial sculpture of Balzac, first displayed in 1898, is a case in point. Although Rodin believed the artwork accurately captured the writer's persona, the critics and public, expecting a true likeness of Balzac, were let down.[3] The same is true for what this clerihew tells us about Newman. Its suggestion that Newman was preoccupied with Wagner is rather wide of the mark, as this book will show.

Although Newman's work was at times dominated by writings on Wagner, it was not his sole focus. His essays and books spanned a wide spectrum of national literatures (novels, poetry and plays) and biographies (or biographical-style books) on composers including Gluck, Elgar, Strauss, Wolf, Beethoven and Liszt. He wrote extensively on rationalism and evolutionary theory, the reception of Russian and English music, and a host of other literary, social and musical topics. Underpinning most of Newman's writings was a commitment to critical and historical method derived from British and European critics,

---

[1] Bengt de Törne, *Sibelius: A Close-Up* (Boston: Houghton Mifflin Co, 1937): 27.

[2] The clerihew is cited in 'Editor's choice', *British Medical Journal* 299 (22 July 1989), n.p. A slightly different rendering of the clerihew is given by John Steane in 'English opera criticism between the wars 3: Newman of the "Sunday Times"', *Opera* 33/6 (June 1982): 582–9. The author of the clerihew is unknown, but is possibly Fritz Spiegel (1926–2003). Personal communication, Julian Rushton, 29 October 2014.

[3] See Albert E. Elsen, *Rodin* (New York: Museum of Modern Art, 1967): 93–7.

2 ERNEST NEWMAN: A CRITICAL BIOGRAPHY

historians and biographers, though such methods were not always faithfully applied.

This book explores the wide-ranging intellectual influences that affected Newman's life work as exemplified in a broad selection of essays and books that I think best represent his work as a music historian, critic and biographer. It is not a book about Newman the great Wagnerian (though his work on the composer occupies parts of chapters 3 and 7 and all of chapter 9). Nor is it a book that merely records his critical responses to particular composers on whom he wrote extensively, such as Berlioz. Rather, this critical biography is concerned with the motivations—intellectual, personal and economic— behind Newman's work. It examines the circumstances that gave rise to particular books and articles and the reasons for their creation. I show that a cast of European intellectual writers influenced Newman's work, although this influence is not always apparent. His pan-European breadth of knowledge about the methods of history, and his interest in critical theory, set Newman apart from many of his British contemporaries.

Biographers of any subject face the challenge of emphasis and this proved especially problematic for two of Newman's previous biographers, Henry Farmer and Vera Newman.[4] Their biographies were highly selective and therefore unattractive propositions for publishers. Farmer's book, 'Ernest Newman as I saw him', only covered the 1880s and 1890s, the years of Newman's involvement with the freethought movement.[5] By contrast, Vera Newman's *Ernest Newman: A Memoir by his Wife* concentrated on the time of their courtship and marriage (from around 1914), paying only perfunctory attention to the first forty or so years of her husband's life. Some background to the reasons why Farmer and Vera Newman were compelled to write these accounts, and the subsequent falling-out that came between them, helps position my biography and the slant I have chosen to give it.

Farmer completed his biography of Newman in the early 1960s. He had worked on the project on and off for over thirty years, and Newman had supplied him with material for it. Farmer's work was concerned with Newman's earliest works for the freethought press, including an analysis—albeit a particularly superficial one—of Newman's literary criticism. Moreover, Farmer's typescript was incomplete: it dealt only with Newman's life up to 1899, the year

---

[4] Henry George Farmer, 'Ernest Newman as I saw him', unpublished typescript, MS Farmer 44. (Drafts and additions of this unpublished typescript are at MS Farmer 42, 43/7–8, and 43/9.) Vera Newman, *Ernest Newman: A Memoir by his Wife* (London: Putnam, 1963).

[5] For more on Farmer's career see Israel J. Katz, *Henry George Farmer and the First International Congress of Arab Music (Cairo 1932)* (Leiden: Brill, 2015).

in which *A Study of Wagner* was published. Newman was then only thirty-one years old. His literary life had barely begun.

The publishers showed little interest in Farmer's hagiographical biography, and various editorial and commercial reasons were given for its rejection.[6] Farmer had initially given his book the title 'Ernest Newman as a Rationalist' and was partly right in predicting that its lack of attention to music 'might militate against its selling success'.[7] Roger Lubbock of Putnam's rejected the typescript on commercial grounds because it 'would overlap too far on to Mrs Newman's own book'.[8] Publishers Barrie and Rockliff found the book 'addressed too limited an audience'[9] and Constable and Co. supposed the manuscript better off with a music book publisher due to Newman's reputation as a writer on music.[10]

Like these publishers, Vera Newman was far from enthusiastic about Farmer's project. In March 1960 Farmer sent Vera a copy of his typescript which, at this point, was called 'Ernest Newman: Music Critic and Philosopher'.[11] Vera disliked it intensely for its coverage of Newman's connections with freethinkers such as Charles Bradlaugh and John M. Robertson. In her reply to Farmer she wrote of her displeasure at this angle: 'music and the arts and literature were his passion … and religion and rationalism were comparatively unimportant, or at any rate they were during our life together'.[12]

The prospect of seeing Farmer's biography in print, with its emphasis on the freethinkers, horrified Vera and she wrote to her friend D.C. Parker about it:

> I have now read Dr Farmer's book and I have not hidden from him the comments for which he asked, that I am very disappointed there are nine chapters in the book and the first six deal almost entirely with Ernest's very early years and his writings and lectures about atheism and freethought. This, as you can imagine, is not very agreeable to me. Farmer insists that this was a very important part of Ernest. I do not agree. Ernest's passion all his life was music, and since I first knew him forty years ago, freethought and writing about it, or even

[6] MS Farmer 46/1–44 contains Farmer's correspondence with publishers.

[7] Correspondence from Farmer to Hector Hawton, managing director of the Rationalist Press Association, 27 December 1962, MS Farmer 46/22.

[8] Correspondence from Roger Lubbock, chairman of Putnam's, 18 September 1961, MS Farmer 46/28.

[9] Correspondence from John M. Bunting to Farmer, 17 June 1963, MS Farmer 46/18.

[10] Correspondence from Constable and Company Ltd, 28 January 1960, MS Farmer 46/14.

[11] Correspondence from Vera Newman to Farmer, 28 April 1960, MS Farmer 47/67.

[12] Correspondence from Vera Newman to Farmer, 28 April 1960, MS Farmer 47/67.

discussing it, had no more part in his life … I can't say I shall be very sorry if no one wants to publish it.[13]

As relations with Farmer broke down irretrievably, Vera relayed her anxiety about the possible publication of Farmer's book to Parker writing that, 'Confidentially, and absolutely between ourselves, I hope nobody will publish it'.[14] Vera then took matters into her own hands: three months later, in August 1960, she wrote to Parker outlining her plan for a book of her own but asked 'don't tell anyone'.[15] Then, on noting that Farmer was still having trouble placing his typescript with a publisher she exclaimed 'three rousing cheers!'[16]

Vera's motivation for her own book was not only to rescue Newman from the taint of freethought but to repair his coloured reputation in musical circles. As Vera noted in her preface, 'I had often heard E.N. referred to as a "soured old cynic", often unkind and even cruel. I knew him better than anyone, and he was none of these things'.[17] Drawing on letters and diaries, Vera wrote about Newman in his post-freethought years. She warmly recounted their life together, first in London, then in Tadworth, Surrey, and discussed the friendships they cultivated over the years with such well-known musicians as the conductor Serge Koussevitzky, the record producer Walter Legge and the soprano Elisabeth Schwarzkopf, who was also Legge's wife. Vera detailed the workaday Newman in considerable depth including his writing habits, relations with publishers, and his views on the successes and failures of his work. She related minor domestic details such as her husband's love of cats, his indifference to children and sensitivity to noise, as well as his episodes of melancholy and depression. Together, these details paint an all-round, personal portrait of the man. By Vera's own admission, the book was not intended as a study of his works, but it is a useful source that identifies many people with whom he and Vera associated. A major frustration of Vera's memoir is its unclear chronology. But that was to be the least of the publisher's concerns.

When Vera finished writing the book in 1963, she posted the typescript to Roger Lubbock at Putman's, with whom she had been in contact; he then

---

[13] Correspondence from Vera Newman to D.C. Parker, 6 May 1960. *Parker Papers* MS 22513.

[14] Correspondence from Vera Newman to D.C. Parker, 26 May 1960. *Parker Papers* MS25513.

[15] Correspondence from Vera Newman to D.C. Parker, 20 August 1960. *Parker Papers* MS25513.

[16] Correspondence from Vera Newman to D.C Parker, 20 August 1960. *Parker Papers* MS25513.

[17] Vera Newman, *Ernest Newman: A Memoir*, v.

forwarded it to Knopf in New York, where it was met with a frosty reception by William A. Koshland, one of Knopf's editors:

> I think Vera Newman's book is really pretty bad. Nothing in it is really good except the quotations from Ernest ... But chiefly, the record is just too trivial, and Vera hardly ever tells you enough about a person or an event to make the story interesting. On the other hand, there are endless descriptions of domestic household difficulties, illnesses and so forth. Someone simply did an atrociously bad job. I don't know what we can do with the book—certainly it isn't worth editing and setting up.[18]

The responsibility of delivering this bad news to Vera fell to Alfred Knopf who, along with his wife, Blanche, was a long-time friend of the Newmans. Knopf was blunt, writing to Vera on 16 April 1963 that: '[W]hat I think weakens the book is that it represents a blow-by-blow account of your life together. The result is—and I must be quite frank—an overwhelming amount of the trivial which tends to swamp the story'.[19]

Vera usually replied to letters promptly, but she took six weeks to calm herself to compose a measured reply to Alfred Knopf:

> Your letter ... was rather like having a bucket of ice water thrown over me. ... I am disappointed that you find my literary efforts so bad, and if you can find the time to send me particulars of anything especially disgraceful I shall be only too happy to put it right, if possible. [D]ear Alfred, I shall be very sorry if you don't publish my book in America, but there is no compulsion on you to publish any book that you do not consider worthy, and I can assure you that it would make absolutely no difference to our personal relations after so many years of friendship.[20]

Knopf was far from convinced that Vera's book was worthy of publication, but he reluctantly agreed to publish it in North America: what swayed him was a sense of duty, as he relayed to Koshland: 'the book presents a natural problem to us. In view of our ancient relationship with the Newmans, I feel that we must publish it, but the very nature of the work precludes, in our opinion, the possibility of any large sale over here'.[21]

---

[18] Memo from William A. Koshland to Alfred A. Knopf, 8 April 1963. Knopf Papers, File 294.7.

[19] Letter from Alfred A. Knopf to Vera Newman, 16 April 1963. Knopf Papers, File 294.7.

[20] Letter from Vera Newman to Alfred A. Knopf, 21 April 1963. Knopf Papers, File 294.7.

[21] Memo from Alfred A. Knopf to William. A. Koshland, 25 April, 1963. Knopf Papers, File 392.4.

The biographies by Farmer and Vera Newman provide an outline of Ernest Newman's life (and sometimes his works) from cradle to grave, but there are significant gaps. Both biographers were eager to promote and preserve a certain reputation in their subject, but the two books were problematic for their respective publishers. A larger and more complete biographical study has not been made since Vera's book was published, and a close and critical reading of Newman's work has also remained unexplored until now.[22]

﹩ Context for a Critical Biography

The aim of this book is to examine the formation of—and influences on—Newman's intellectual life. I am concerned neither with writing a blow-by-blow account of Newman's daily affairs nor to comment upon everything he wrote, not least because there is considerable repetition and duplication in Newman's oeuvre, and appraising all the essays and books he wrote on a particular subject would be repetitive. As far as possible, Newman is placed in the context of other writers of the period to illustrate the literary and musical milieu in which he worked.

---

[22] A number of studies cover only parts of Newman's work and career. See, for example, Sydney Grew, 'Mr Ernest Newman', *Edgbastonia* 31 (1 July 1911): 121–30; an unsigned article: 'Mr Ernest Newman', *MH*, 1 May 1912: 131–4; Eva Mary Grew, 'Ernest Newman, English music critic', *S*, November 1928: 113–21; Basil Maine, 'Personalities among music critics. IX. Ernest Newman', *MT*, 68/1007 (1 January 1927): 27–8; Sydney Grew, 'Ernest Newman: Twenty-five years of reading his writings', *British Musician*, July 1931: 154–6; August 1931: 167–8; September 1931: 192–7; October 1931: 208–10; November 1931: 232–4; July 1932: 151–5; Ralph Hill, 'On Wagner, Hanslick, and Mr Newman', *S*, October 1931: 18–24; Eva Mary Grew, 'Ernest Newman: His life and opinions', *British Musician*, January 1934: 4–6; February 1934: 36–8; March 1934: 54–6; April 1934: 86–8; May 1934: 108–10; June 1934: 126–8; July 1934: 153–4; August 1934: 176–8; September 1934: 203–5; October 1934: 230–1; November 1934: 248–52; December 1934: 275–7; William Blissett, 'Ernest Newman and English Wagnerism', *ML* 40/10 (1959): 311–23; Roger Hollinrake, 'Nietzsche, Wagner and Ernest Newman', *ML* 41/3 (1960): 245–55; Henry Raynor, 'Ernest Newman and the science of criticism', *MMR*, January–February 1960: 19–27; and Henry Farmer, 'Ernest Newman', *Freethinker*, 16 June 1961: 95–7. Dissertations on Newman (or that deal substantially with his work) are Siobhan McDonnell, 'Ernest Newman's philosophy of music criticism', MA thesis, McMaster University (1989); Ruth E. Easter, 'Music criticism: a study of the criteria and techniques of the journalistic critic, as seen in the critiques of G.B. Shaw, Ernest Newman, and Neville Cardus', MA thesis, State University College, Potsdam, New York (1972); Nigel Scaife, 'British music criticism in a new era: studies in critical thought, 1894–1954', DPhil thesis, University of Oxford (1994); and Paul Watt, 'The intellectual life of Ernest Newman in the 1890s', PhD thesis, University of Sydney (2009).

Since this is a critical biography, my focus is on Newman's work as a writer and therefore precludes a wider investigation of his other activities as a BBC broadcaster and work as a translator, editor and festival adjudicator. The book could be called a literary biography because of its emphasis on his relationship with his publishers and readers. His books and articles are, in my view, the most tangible expressions of his critical persona.[23] As in the case of any biographer, my choice of what to include in the book is inevitably personal, but the literature I have selected I consider best represents Newman's methods, most evident in his work on Gluck, Wagner, Beethoven and Liszt. Some of this literature may not be his best or his most popular work, but it illustrates a very wide intellectual compass. I have not dwelt much on Newman's work as an advocate for the performance of the music of composers such as Berlioz, Wolf and Sibelius. While important, it has been documented by previous writers.[24] In the case of Berlioz, Peter Heyworth's collection of Newman's Berlioz essays fills part of the gap.[25] Regarding Wolf, on whom Newman published four significant works—an article in the *Contemporary Review*, a monograph, an edition and liner notes for a landmark recording that sought to rehabilitate Wolf's works through the Gramophone Company—this literature is not first and foremost concerned with historical method to the same extent as his other work.[26] By founding the Sibelius Society in 1932 Newman helped raise

---

[23] Newman's career at the BBC is documented in Jennifer Doctor, *The BBC and Ultra-Modern Music, 1922–1936: Shaping a Nation's Taste* (Cambridge: Cambridge University Press, 1999). At the time of writing (April 2017) I am aware of other scholars looking at aspects of Newman's life and works, including a study of his rivalry with Edwin Evans (in the late 1910s into the 1920s), the role he played in the development of Dorothy Silk's operatic career, his interest in Schenkerian analysis and his influence on the career of Neville Cardus.

[24] In the case of Wolf, especially Walter Legge's association with Newman, see Ernest Newman, *Hugo Wolf* (with an introduction by Walter Legge) (New York: Dover, 1966); Elisabeth Schwarzkopf, *On and Off the Record: A Memoir of Walter Legge* (London: Faber and Faber, 1982); and Alan Sanders (ed.), *Walter Legge: Words and Music* (London: Duckworth, 1998). In 2012 Dover re-issued *Hugo Wolf* with a foreword by Roelof Oostwoud.

[25] Peter Heyworth, *Berlioz, Romantic and Classic: Writings by Ernest Newman* (London: Victor Gollancz Ltd., 1972).

[26] Ernest Newman, 'Hugo Wolf, *CR*, January 1904: 707–20; *Hugo Wolf* (London: Methuen & Co. Limited, 1907); Ernest Newman (ed.), *Fifty Songs by Hugo Wolf* (Boston: Oliver Ditson Company, 1909) and Hugo Wolf Society, *The Complete Edition*, 1931–1938, RLS 759. EMI: His Master's Voice 1981. Newman occasionally wrote on Wolf in other journals, for example, 'Hugo Wolf as a song-writer', *New Music Review and Church Music Review* 6/64 (1907): 234–7 and 6/65 (1907): 307–10.

an awareness of the composer in England, not least through the establishment of a newsletter.[27]

Deciding what to include in this book has involved a certain amount of value judgement. For example, while Newman wrote a little on Russian music in the *Musical Times* from 1900 to 1920, his work on the same subject in the *New Witness* between 1915 and 1918 is, in my view, more compelling and interesting, not least because it illustrates fierce discussion at the time on nationalism and war-time music-making. Similarly, in some chapters I have drawn on Newman's work in the *Manchester Guardian* (in 1905 and 1906, and again in 1919–23) rather than the *Birmingham Daily Post* (in the years 1906–19), because his writing for his Manchester readers was, on balance, more insightful than the articles of largely local interest in Birmingham. I have devoted complete chapters to four of his books or book series: *Gluck and the Opera* (1895); *Pseudo-Philosophy at the end of the Nineteenth Century* (1897); *The Man Liszt* (1934); and his five books on Wagner. I see these books to be representative of Newman's critical abilities (or lack of them, in the case of *The Man Liszt*). Some of these chapters (e.g. chapter 4, on *Pseudo-Philosophy*) are snapshots of Newman's work at a particular time—1897—while other chapters (e.g. chapter 7, on essays in the *Sunday Times*) consider his work over a much larger time-scale. Other chapters (e.g. chapter 9, on his Wagner biographies) do both. I have not included much discussion of Newman's biographies of Elgar (1906) or Strauss (1908), because they wear their biographical method all too lightly in contrast to Newman's other biographies. Similarly, Newman's many books on opera appreciation and performance, as well as *The Piano-Player and its Music* (1920), are not considered because they fall outside the purview of my focus on his historical and biographical work.[28]

I have not assumed that readers will be familiar with Newman's books and articles so I have described their contents, sometimes in depth, to explain their purpose and outline their scope. I have used direct quotation to give the reader

[27] The Sibelius Society *Newsletters* vols 1–6, *c.* 1932. For more on Newman's work on Sibelius see Peter Franklin, 'Sibelius in Britain', in Daniel M. Grimley (ed.), *The Cambridge Companion to Sibelius* (Cambridge: Cambridge University Press, 2004): 182–95 and Byron Adams, 'Thor's Hammer: Sibelius and British Music Critcs', in Daniel M. Grimley (ed.), *Jean Sibelius and his World* (Princeton: Princeton University Press, 2011): 125–57. For more on Sibelius's reception in Britain see Philip Ross Bullock (ed. and trans.), *The Correspondence of Jean Sibelius and Rosa Newmarch, 1906–39* (Woodbridge, Suffolk: The Boydell Press, 2011).

[28] For Newman's contribution to the literature about the player-piano see Timothy D. Taylor, 'The commodification of music at the dawn of the era of "mechanical music"', *Ethnomusicology* 5/2 (2007): 281–305.

a feel for Newman's voice, style and personality. Much of his tone is lost when paraphrased.

Pinpointing Newman's intellectual influences is tricky. He only once disclosed specific influences, in the *Sunday Times* on 26 June 1932:

> My own reading in criticism, in my first youth, was confined to writers like Sainte-Beuve, Hennequin, Taine, Brunetière, Lessing, Matthew Arnold, Leslie Stephen, Walter Pater, and so on, none of whom, of course, ever specialised in music. I studied music, and read histories of music and other books on the subject; but of musical journalism I knew next to nothing until I was foolish enough to become a musical journalist myself.[29]

This list is problematic and misleading because of who Newman left off it. Newman was well acquainted with (and largely influenced by) the works of Charles Darwin, Auguste Comte and Henry Thomas Buckle, indicating that his intellectual range was much greater than he admitted, at least in this excerpt. And the list does not yet account for some of Newman's later intellectual interests, for example, books and essays by André Maurois, Guido Adler, Heinrich Schenker and Paul Bekker.

In this biography, I look upon all of Newman's prose—his books, essays and journalism—as criticism. While there are large tranches of banal reporting of musical news in many publications in the nineteenth century, journalism—the work of the reporter—can still be a vehicle through which intellectual ideas are disseminated. In the late nineteenth century especially, the terms 'essayist', 'man of letters', 'sage' and 'belletrist' were employed to describe the profession of a number of writers.[30] Labelling Newman a 'critic' is a pragmatic description

---

[29] Ernest Newman, 'Mr Bernard Shaw as Musical Critic', *ST*, 26 June 1932, 7. The only detailed study on any of these writers' influence on Newman is Paul Watt, 'Ernest Newman's draft of a Berlioz biography (1899) and its appropriation of Emile Hennequin's style theory', *Nineteenth-Century Music Review* 10/1 (2013): 151–68.

[30] For literature on the cultural identity of these labels see, for example, John Holloway, *The Victorian Sage: Studies in Argument,* 2nd edn (New York: W.W. Norton, 1965); John Gross, *The Rise and Fall of the Man of Letters: Aspects of English Literary Life since 1800* (London: Weidenfeld and Nicolson, 1969); T.W. Heyck, *The Transformation of Intellectual Life in Victorian England* (London: Croom Helm, 1982); Stefan Collini, *Public Moralists: Political Thought and Intellectual Life in Britain, 1850–1930* (Oxford: Clarendon, 1991); Terry Eagleton, *The Function of Criticism: From 'The Spectator' to Post-Structuralism* (London and New York: Verso, 1996); Linda H. Peterson, 'Sage writing', in Herbert F. Tucker (ed.), *A Companion to Victorian Literature and Culture* (Oxford: Blackwell, 1999): 373–87; Denise Gigante (ed.), *The Great Age of the English Essay* (New Haven: Yale University Press, 2008); and Paul Poplawski, *English Literature in Context* (New York: Cambridge University Press, 2008).

Figure 1 Newman, c. 1900. Photographer unknown.
Reproduced by kind permission of the Estate of Ernest Newman.

of his work across the genres in which he wrote. It is also the term he most frequently used to describe himself.

Like many critics of his age, Newman wrote under different names. Though he was born William Roberts (see chapter 2) he used two pseudonyms: Ernest Newman and Hugh Mortimer Cecil. Newman never explained why he changed his name (in fact, he never legally ratified it) but others have guessed. A common anecdote in the secondary literature is that Newman was perceived as a 'new man in earnest' and he chose to play on this phrase.

Given Newman's well-known sense of humour, it is possible that he adopted 'Ernest Newman' in jest. Or it may have been more calculated; 'Ernest' (also spelt Earnest) was a common name in the nineteenth century so he may have thought it had popular appeal. With 'Newman' he could have been seeking to parody Cardinal John Henry Newman (1801–90) as his atheism was in opposition to the churchman's theology. By combining a common first name and a well-recognised and controversial last name, Newman's pseudonym would

Figure 2 Newman at leisure, c. 1904. Photographer unknown.
Reproduced by kind permission of the Estate of Ernest Newman.

have had a ring of familiarity about it.[31] The same principle might also be applied to Newman's second pseudonym, Hugh Mortimer Cecil, which he reserved largely for writing in publications operated by the University Press, London Ltd, but it was a collective pseudonym (see chapter 4).[32] If 'Hugh Mortimer Cecil' was a name coined by Newman it may have had a connection to boxing (Newman's favourite sport), and so the names 'Hugh Cecil' may have been borrowed from Hugh Cecil Lowther, the fifth Earl of Lonsdale, who was president of the National Sporting Club that governed boxing in England from

[31] Karl Beckson has written on the semantics of the name 'Earnest' in relation to its meaning in Oscar Wilde's *The Importance of Being Earnest*; see Beckson, *London in the 1890s: A Cultural History* (New York: Norton, 1992): 186–9.

[32] Hugh Mortimer Cecil has been erroneously attributed to John M. Robertson; see T.J. Carty, *A Dictionary of Literary Pseudonyms in the English Language* (London: Mansell Publishing, 1995): 27.

1891 to 1929.[33] 'Mortimer' could have been borrowed from a contemporary freethought writer named Geoffrey Mortimer.

More pragmatically, Stainton de B. Taylor suggests that because Newman's employer, the Bank of Liverpool, was, like all banks at that time, 'paternalistic in their attitude to employees' spare-time activities', he adopted a pseudonym to avoid drawing attention to his extra-curricular interests.[34] There was also a practical need for it: another William Roberts was writing in the 1890s and Newman was probably keen to avoid confusion with him.[35] But did Newman want to cover his past, erase his tracks? Writing under his real name in radical publications could have been an association frowned upon by mainstream employees, thereby compromising his future employment prospects.

In the absence of any evidence, we can only guess at the reasons why Newman adopted these pseudonyms, but I wager they were chosen in a conscious effort to layer them with particular associations.

❧ *Organization of the Book*

This book is divided into the two parts in which Newman's work was largely pitched: the freethought movement (up to 1899) and, for want of a better word, the mainstream (from 1900 onwards). Freethought publications were niche because they were aimed at a relatively small market with clearly defined and marginal interests that were rarely commercially viable. These publications were political and required an agitated and aggressive tone for maximum rhetorical affect. By contrast, Newman's mainstream career involved writing for well-established newspapers and journals with a large middle-class readership in the music and the arts that required a much more sober tone. Although they are clearly demarcated parts of his life, they were not mutually exclusive periods. For example, some of Newman's literary criticism from the freethought period is considered serious scholarship, and his sometime dialectical writing in the *Sunday Times* is a rhetorical skill he adapted from his first career.

Part I covers Newman's association with the freethought movement and the intellectual and practical influences that John M. Robertson (as mentor) and Bertram Dobell (as publisher) exercised on his career. Chapter 2 examines Newman's youth, adolescence and early adulthood, and outlines the

---

[33] James B. Roberts and Alexander G. Skutt, *The Boxing Register* (London: McBooks Press, 1999), 13.

[34] Stainton de B. Taylor, *Two Centuries of Music in Liverpool: A Scrap-book of Information Concerning Musical Activities both Professional and Amateur* (Liverpool: Rockliff Brothers Limited, *c.* 1974): 113.

[35] The other William Roberts was the author of many publications, chief among them being *The Book-hunter in London* (London: Elliot Stock, 1895).

crosscurrents in rationalism, history and scientific method that shaped his critical outlook and stayed with him for the rest of his life. Chapter 3 is an analysis of some of Newman's earliest essays on literature, science and music that invariably drew on pressing topics germane to the 1890s, such as tensions between naturalism and realism in literature and the impetus to interpret literature and music in evolutionary terms. Chapter 4 intentionally appears out of chronological order so that readers can consider Newman's social and literary works in the freethought press alongside each other, and examines Newman's classic freethought work, *Pseudo-Philosophy at the end of the Nineteenth Century*. Written under the pseudonym Hugh Mortimer Cecil in 1897, this work became a freethought classic as it illustrates Newman's skill at argument and his powerful rejection of the anti-Darwinists in favour of scientific history. In Chapter 5 Newman's *Gluck and the Opera* (1895) is considered as one of his finest attempts for music history to be undertaken in the mould of comparative history.

Following the publication of *A Study of Wagner* in 1899, Newman not only distanced himself from the freethought movement but sought a more mainstream audience. Chapters 6 and 7 explore Newman's journalism and essays and his pursuit of specific musical, economic and social causes. Chapter 6 examines Newman's earliest musical criticism. It looks principally at essays in the *Speaker, New Witness* and *Manchester Guardian* that illustrate his interests in a number of topics including British and Russian music. Chapter 7 examines Newman's work in the *Sunday Times* from 1920 to 1958 on a variety of subjects including his qualified support for British music, his quest to improve the standard of opera production, and the advocacy of scientific history and criticism. The chapter also explores Newman's advocacy of German-language musicology and his observations on the politics of the Bayreuth Festival after it reopened in 1951 after the Second World War. Chapter 7 also charts Newman's defence of the value of Wagner's music and explanations of the composer's anti-Semitism, which came under close scrutiny in the British press. Chapter 8 studies Newman's biggest failure: his 1934 biography of Liszt and the way it compromised his ideals of scientific biography. The critical reception of this book also betrays significant hostility to works approaching psychoanalytic biography by musicologists of the time. The final chapter analyses Newman's books on Wagner from 1899 to 1946 examining his shifts in attitude towards the composer and the different historical and biographical methods used in the process. The critical reception of his final Wagner work, his four-volume *Life of Wagner*, published between 1933 and 1946, has caricatured Newman as a particularly devoted Wagnerian and has tended to overshadow the value of his other writings and achievements. This chapter concludes with an appraisal of Newman's Wagner career from an unlikely source, Theodor W. Adorno, and reflects on the impact that this body of works had on twentieth-century cultural history.

Within a decade of starting work on the *Sunday Times* in 1920, Newman was regarded as a significant cultural and intellectual figure. Basil Maine regarded Newman as a British institution, much like the Anglican Church and parliamentary government, while much later, after the critic's death, Geoffrey Sharp and Frank Howes went so far as to claim Newman to be one the greatest music critics to have lived.[36] But Newman was neither saint nor hero: Cecil Gray, for example, sparred with Newman in the early 1920s over Newman's apparently old-fashioned approach to criticism and, in the early 1930s, Carl Engel wrote of Newman's shortcomings as a musicologist in his biography of Franz Liszt.[37] Yet, despite these criticisms, it is no exaggeration to claim that Newman was one of the most significant—and controversial—music critics and biographers of his generation.

Neville Cardus once remarked that Newman's greatest gift to posterity was saving Britain from a musical culture characterised by 'provincial stiffness' and 'narrowness of vision'.[38] In Cardus's opinion, Newman 'was perhaps the first writer truly to Europeanise our music and our humane responses to music. He quickened our antennae, opened doors for us'.[39] In the chapters that follow, my aim is to see this European intellect at work.

---

[36] Basil Maine, *Behold These Daniels, Being Studies of Contemporary Music Critics* (London: H. & W. Brown, 1928): 15; Geoffrey Sharp, 'Ernest Newman', *MR* 21/3 (February 1960): 77–8; and Frank Howes, *The English Musical Renaissance* (London: Secker & Warburg, 1966): 351.

[37] For the clash between Gray and Newman, see Cecil Gray, 'The task of criticism', *S*, 1/1 (1920): 9–13; Ernest Newman, 'A note on musical criticism', *ST*, 30 May 1920, 6; and Cecil Gray, 'A critique of pure cant: being an earnest enquiry into the nature of the new man', *S*, 1/3 (1920): 112–15. The politics and fallout of this exchange are discussed in Sarah Collins, '"Never out of date and never modern": Aesthetic democracy, radical music criticism and *The Sackbut*', *ML* 95/3 (2014): 404–28. On Engel's reaction to Newman's Liszt book see chapter 8.

[38] Neville Cardus, 'Ernest Newman', in Herbert van Thal (ed.), *Fanfare for Ernest Newman* (London: Arthur Baker, 1955): 29–37; 31.

[39] Neville Cardus, 'Ernest Newman', 31.

PART I

The Freethought Years

CHAPTER 2

Formation of a Critical Sensibility: The 1880s and 1890s

NEWMAN'S early reading and book-buying habits focused on musical history, literature, philosophy and fine arts.[1] From a young age he developed a love of music, especially opera, and as a student at University College Liverpool in the 1880s, Newman immersed himself in studies of literature and languages. While living in Liverpool he encountered rationalism through his college lecturers as well as the speeches and literature by freethought radicals such as Charles Bradlaugh and John M. Robertson. The ways in which Newman's writings on music in particular reflect the rationalist agenda were complex, and they provided a critical framework that set Newman apart from most of his contemporaries. By the 1890s Newman had positioned himself as a key figure in an emerging new school of music criticism.

☙ Childhood and Early Schooling

The only account of Newman's upbringing comes from his second wife, Vera:

> He [William Roberts] was born on November 30th, 1868, at 16 Waterhouse Street, Lancaster. His father was a Welshman named Seth Roberts; a master tailor by trade, and his mother was born Harriet Sparks. He was the only child of a late second marriage by both his parents, and he was christened William. He had half-brothers and sisters, but he never spoke of them.[2]

Newman's parents were Anglican although the extent to which they practised their religion is unknown. He wrote little about his life except for a series of articles he labelled 'Confessions' in the early 1920s, from which a portrait of his youth can be discerned.[3]

Newman attended St Saviour's School in Everton, then the Middle School of Liverpool, in the late 1870s and early 1880s. In 1885, aged seventeen, he entered

[1] For details on Newman's extensive library containing editions and books on music, literature and science see Paul Watt, 'The catalogue of Ernest Newman's library: Revelations about his intellectual life in the 1890s', *Script and Print* 31/2 (2007): 81–103.
[2] Vera Newman, *Ernest Newman: A Memoir by his Wife* (London: Putnam, 1963): 3.
[3] Newman, 'Confessions', 1–41.

17

University College Liverpool on a scholarship and left the following year, without matriculating.[4] Formal institutional instruction was not Newman's only avenue of learning: he taught himself musical composition until about 1889, aged twenty-one, when his first articles were published.[5] He was a voracious reader: in his early twenties he had acquired a good knowledge of literature, philosophy and biology, and a working knowledge of many languages including German, Russian, Greek, Swedish and Hebrew.[6]

As a child Newman learned piano, but he apparently taught himself. He recalled having only one music lesson in his life: aged seventeen, Newman claims he took a theory lesson at college from which no benefit was derived, but clearly, as we shall see below, he must have had some instruction in elementary theory and counterpoint to be able to read scores and to compose.[7] His knowledge of music was vast and by his late teens Newman claimed that:

> I had dozens of scores in my head. I knew most of them by heart—all the pianoforte sonatas and the symphonies of Beethoven and the forty-eight preludes of Bach, many of Mozart's piano sonatas and piano duets, practically the whole of Wagner, Beethoven's *Fidelio*, all of Gluck's operas that are obtainable in modern editions ... thirty or forty other operas of all schools ... one or two of the oratorios and a few of the clavier works of Handel, a few specimens of the older music ... a few old English and Italian madrigals, and a good deal of Schubert, Schumann, Mendelssohn and Chopin ... and a heap of other music of all sorts, all periods, all schools ... For years I had been reading music daily, with the ardour with which schoolgirls used to read novelettes, or schoolboys adventure stories.[8]

Newman's self-education was extensive and continued even while a student at University College, Liverpool.

---

[4] The scholarship is mentioned in Nigel Scaife, 'British music criticism in a new era: studies in critical thought, 1894–1945', DPhil thesis, University of Oxford (1994): 137. I am grateful to Adrian Allan, Archivist, University of Liverpool and Richard Temple, Archivist, Senate House, University of London, for checking the enrolment records and for providing some additional background information. Personal communication, 4–5 January 2007.

[5] Ernest Newman, 'Morality and belief', *NR*, 15 September 1889, 170; 22 September 1889, 188–9; and 'The doctrine of evolution in modern poetry', *NR*, 27 October 1889, 260–2.

[6] Newman, 'Confessions', xiii.

[7] Newman, 'Confessions', 10–11.

[8] Newman, 'Confessions', 11.

❧ College Education

Newman's memories of his time at college in 1885 and 1886 are generally positive: 'those were happy, irresponsible days. The future had no worries for me',
he wrote.[9] This irresponsibility led to Newman playing truant from Sir Oliver
Lodge's science lectures, absconding to the college library to indulge his passion for Elizabethan poets and dramatists. 'English literature and art, indeed,
were the only things that interested me at the University', he wrote.[10] Only one
of Newman's lecturers managed to irk him: Professor Strong, a Latinist, whom
Newman described as 'a rather bad-tempered man'.[11]

Three particular lecturers excited Newman's mind: 'I still have the liveliest
recollections of the joy I used to get from Professor A.C. Bradley and Professor
(later Sir Walter) Raleigh, and I think Sir Martin Conway used also to lecture
in my time'.[12] A.C. Bradley, who was appointed Professor of Modern Literature
and History at University College upon its inauguration, was a noted literary
scholar, formerly of Balliol College, Oxford.[13] His published work included
Aristotle, Elizabethan literature and Romantic poetry, and he probably intro-
duced Newman to the Elizabethan dramatists, or fostered his already acquired
interest in them.[14] By 1905 Newman had acquired such considerable expertise in Elizabethan literature that he provided significant assistance to a book
on the subject by John M. Robertson entitled *Did Shakespeare Write 'Titus
Andronicus'?: A Study in Elizabethan Literature* (1905).[15] Details of Newman's
association with Raleigh are not known, though Raleigh was a subscriber to
Newman's first book, *Gluck and the Opera* (1895).[16] Sir Martin Conway may

---

[9] Newman, 'Confessions', 27–8.

[10] Newman, 'Confessions', 27–8.

[11] Newman, 'Confessions', 27–8.

[12] Newman, 'Confessions', 27. Newman's memory is not reliable, here: Raleigh did not
teach at University College until 1900.

[13] See G.K. Hunter, 'Andrew Cecil Bradley', in *ODNB*, accessed 20 February 2016.

[14] See, for example, A.C. Bradley, *Aristotle and the State* (London: Abbott Hellenica,
1898); *Commentary on Tennyson's 'In memoriam'* (London: Macmillan and Co.,
1901) and *Shakespearean Tragedy: Lectures on Hamlet, Othello, King Lear and
Macbeth* (London: Macmillan and Co. Ltd., 1904).

[15] *Did Shakespeare write 'Titus Andronicus'?: A Study in Elizabethan Literature*
(London: Watts and Co., 1905). On page xi, Robertson wrote 'In addition, I have to
acknowledge another debt of thanks to my friend Mr Ernest Newman, who, going
watchfully over part of the ground in sympathy with my thesis, detected some
important evidence which I had overlooked'.

[16] See Robertson to Dobell, 23 October 1895, MS Dobell. Newman also sent Raleigh
what appears to be a complimentary copy of his *Study of Wagner* suggesting they
knew each other—see MS Dobell, 23 January 1899.

also have been an influence on Newman; he joined University College in 1885 as Roscoe Professor of Art and could have fostered Newman's love of architecture and fine arts.[17]

Henry Farmer has suggested that John MacCunn's lectures on Spinoza, Kant and Herbert Spencer would have been influential on the young college student.[18] MacCunn was a rationalist: in 1907 he published a book on the subject, which examined the works of John Stuart Mill, Thomas Carlyle, Joseph Mazzini and T.H. Green.[19] This text—and MacCunn's lectures—may well have played a significant part in Newman's interest in social theory and rationalism.

Whatever the influence of individual personalities, the secularist intellectual culture of University College would have played a vital part in nourishing Newman's early interest in freethought. As Oliver Lodge observed about the college: '[it] was founded on an unsectarian basis, to be open to all comers; and this in those days excited rather rabid opposition so that it was frequently spoken of as a godless institution; and one of the vicars of a city church (now pulled down) at the top of Lord Street used to fulminate against it'.[20] Newman cultivated further 'godless' networks outside the college: in 1888 he joined the Liverpool Branch of the National Secular Society where he came into contact with some of Britain's leading rationalists and freethinkers who would help establish his career as a writer.

✌ *Freethought Connections*

Freethought, like many other political and intellectual movements, is characterised by competing claims of leadership and authenticity. The movement is still known today by various names and labels and it intersects with a range of social, scientific, intellectual and political agendas.[21] The freethought

---

[17] Some of Conway's books included *The Woodcutters of the Netherlands in the Fifteenth Century* (Cambridge: Cambridge University Press, 1884) and *Dawn of Art in the Ancient World: An Archaeological Sketch* (London: Percival, 1891).

[18] Henry George Farmer, 'Ernest Newman as I saw Him', MS Farmer 42/17.

[19] John MacCunn, *Six Radical Thinkers* (London: Edward Arnold, 1907).

[20] Oliver Lodge, *Past Years: An Autobiography* (London: Hodder and Stoughton, 1931): 160–1.

[21] The literature on freethought history includes John M. Robertson, *A History of Freethought Ancient and Modern to the Period of the French Revolution*, 2 vols (London: Watts and Co., 1929); David Tribe, *100 Years of Freethought* (London: Elek Books, 1967); Edward Royle, *Victorian Infidels: The Origin of the British Secularist Movement, 1791–1866* (Manchester University Press and Totowa, NJ: Rowman & Littlefield Publishers, 1974) and *Radicals, Secularists and Republicans: Popular Freethought in Britain, 1866–1915* (Manchester University Press and Totowa, NJ: Rowman & Littlefield Publishers, 1980). Some specialised studies include

movement of the late nineteenth century bore all the signs of an eclectic and diverse concern and its followers included agnostics, republicans, socialists, humanists, positivists and atheists. The freethinkers' heroes included Auguste Comte, Charles Darwin and Herbert Spencer, and Newman came into contact with their work through the publications of the National Secular Society (NSS). Indeed, the freethought press, particularly the *National Reformer,* was pre-occupied with the writings of their intellectual role models and dozens of articles were written explaining and analysing theories of positivism, evolution and the nascent discipline of sociology.

Newman joined the Liverpool Branch of the National Secular Society after hearing a lecture by a visiting London-based freethinker, G.W. Foote. One of Newman's friends, Francis Woolett, a writer for the *Freethinker* under the pseudonym of George Underwood, joined the NSS at the same time. In 1894, Newman and Woolett were elected onto the committee of the Liverpool Branch and Newman took up the president's role later in the year. He delivered thirty-eight lectures to audiences in Liverpool, Manchester, Chester and Leicester from 7 January 1894 until 10 May 1896, at which point he stood down as president (see Appendix: Freethought Lectures by Newman). These lectures typically reflect freethought issues: moral philosophy, religion, atheism, literature, history and rationalism but copies have not survived.

Charles Bradlaugh—who Newman first heard give a speech in August 1899—was a particularly important role model. Newman wrote to Henry Farmer about Bradlaugh reporting that 'I had read many of his pamphlets. What did appeal to me was his skill in dialectics, especially his superb handling of the arguments for the existence of God'.[22] Bradlaugh, once described as 'undoubtedly the greatest leader' of the freethought movement, formed the National Secular Society in 1866, installing himself as president and as editor of the *National Reformer.*[23] Like many freethinkers, Bradlaugh toured Britain, proselytising for the freethought cause. Newman's beliefs may have

David Nash, *Secularism, Art and Freedom* (Leicester University Press, 1992) and Bill Cooke, *The Gathering of Infidels: A Hundred Years of the Rationalist Press Association* (Amherst, NY: Prometheus Books, 2004).

[22] Henry George Farmer, citing an undated letter from Newman to Farmer in 'Ernest Newman as I saw Him', 32. Information in these paragraphs is sourced from Henry Farmer, 'Ernest Newman', *Freethinker,* 16 June 1961, 32.

[23] Royle, *Radicals, Secularists and Republicans,* 88. Bradlaugh had previously edited the *National Reformer* in 1860–4. For a more recent account of Bradlaugh's milieu see Michael Rectenwald, *Nineteenth-Century British Secularism: Science, Religion, and Literature* (Basingstoke, Hants: Palgrave Macmillan, 2016).

been influenced by Bradlaugh's 1864 pamphlet, 'A plea for atheism'.[24] This work
aimed to dispel prevailing stereotypes about atheism and in it Bradlaugh put
forward an uncompromisingly secular ideology.[25]

Newman's wide reading would have put him in touch with a substantial
literature on the politics of atheism and agnosticism but it is worth considering
an earlier influence. Newman wrote an opera in his teens based on Shelley's
'Prometheus Unbound', which combined a secularist theme with music.[26]
Newman described this undertaking as 'a big work—big I mean, in that it ran
to some hundreds of pages of score … inspired, I should now imagine, by
Schumann's *Manfred*'.[27] Newman also composed a song, 'Green Apples'. It is
possible Newman wrote other songs and vocal works but these compositions,
like his opera, are lost.[28]

College lecturers and leading freethinkers were major sources of inspiration for Newman but no event would influence him more than meeting the
polymath John M. Robertson.

๔ Meeting John M. Robertson

Robertson (1856–1933) was the author of dozens of books and hundreds of essays
and pamphlets. He was also one of the most prominent freethought activists
of the 1890s. Some of his best-known early works include *Essays Towards a
Critical Method* (1887), *Modern Humanists* (1891) and *Buckle and his Critics:
A Study in Sociology* (1895). Later works included *The Economics of Progress*
(1918) and *A History of Freethought in the Nineteenth Century* (published in 2
volumes in 1929). He published widely on the subjects of Elizabethan literature
(especially Marlowe and Shakespeare), economics, politics and social theory.[29]

---

[24] Charles Bradlaugh, 'A plea for atheism' was first published in London in 1867
(publisher unknown). It was subsequently reprinted by the Freethought Publishing
Company at various times, including its republication, along with some other
Bradlaugh pamphlets, in *Theological Essays* (London: Freethought Publishing
Company, 1898).

[25] The nuances of Bradlaugh's atheism in context of its period is detailed in David
Berman, *A History of Atheism in Britain: From Hobbes to Russell* (London: Croom
Helm, 1988): 214–17.

[26] Newman, 'Confessions', 10, 19.

[27] Newman, 'Confessions', 10, 19. Newman's music education included piano lessons
and composition. See 'Confessions', 6, 16 and 20.

[28] A copy was received by the British Library in 1923 but has since been misplaced. I
am grateful to Robert Balchin, Curator, Music Collections at the British Library, for
following this trail: personal communication, 4 October 2004.

[29] For the most recent and comprehensive study of Robertson see Odin Dekkers,
J.M. Robertson: Rationalist and Literary Critic (Aldershot: Ashgate, 1998). An

Robertson's influence was also evident in the leading radical periodicals of his time. He succeeded William Archer on the *Edinburgh Evening News* in 1878. In the same year he joined the freethought movement and in 1884 moved to London to become an assistant editor on Bradlaugh's *National Reformer*. When the *National Reformer* went out of business in 1893, Robertson founded the *Free Review* in its place, but set about making it a much more intellectually robust journal than its predecessor.

Newman explained the influence of Robertson in his life in the preface to a new edition of Robertson's *A History of Freethought in the Nineteenth Century* (1936):

> I cannot remember now when my personal acquaintance with John M. Robertson began, but it must have been some time before 1889, for in that year he sent me an inscribed copy of his *Essays Towards a Critical Method* at the time of publication of that volume. Nor can I remember precisely how the acquaintance ripened into friendship, though I should imagine that after two or three articles of mine had appeared in the *National Reformer* under his editorship he sought me out, with his usual kindness to eager young students, during one of his visits, for lecturing purposes, to Liverpool, where I lived at that time. ... He would in any case, by virtue of his books alone, have become the greatest influence my own intellectual life has ever experienced. But my personal intercourse with him from those distant days to the time of his lamented death deepened that influence enormously. Year by year the conviction grew upon me that he was not only intellectually the greatest, but in character the best, man I have ever known or am ever likely to know.[30]

Robertson facilitated the publication of Newman's first three books, *Gluck and the Opera* (1895), *Pseudo-Philosophy at the end of the Nineteenth Century* (1897, written under the pseudonym Hugh Mortimer Cecil) and *A Study of Wagner* (1899). Two other critics of the period came into contact with Robertson's work. George Bernard Shaw knew Robertson well but vehemently rejected the rationalist agenda.[31] Neville Cardus was not acquainted with Robertson personally but exhibited some knowledge of his work.[32] Like Newman the routes to music criticism taken by Shaw and Cardus came about after they

earlier study of Robertson was G.A. Wells (ed.), *J.M. Robertson (1856–1933): Liberal, Rationalist and Scholar* (London: Pemberton, 1987).

[30] Ernest Newman, 'Appreciation', in John M. Robertson, *A History of Freethought*, xxii.

[31] See further Odin Dekkers, 'Robertson and Shaw: "An unreasonable friendship"', *English Literature in Transition* 39/4 (1996): 431–9.

[32] See, for example, Cardus, *Autobiography* (London: Collins, 1947) and 'Ernest Newman', *Opera* 10, no. 10 (October 1959): 668–71.

had established themselves experts in other fields; for Shaw it was literary and social criticism, for Cardus it was cricket. Newman's career flourished under Robertson, as did his interest in rationalism and its potential as a model for interpreting works of history, criticism and biography. It was these interests in method in criticism that set Newman apart from many of his musical peers.

♪ Robertson and Nineteenth-Century Rationalism

Rationalism is often characterised as a seventeenth- and eighteenth-century school of thought associated with the works of Descartes, Leibniz, Kant and Spinoza, but Newman's rationalist ideology was couched in a particular nine-teenth-century vein. Specifically, it was the rationalist ideology of Robertson, to which Newman was aligned.

Robertson's brand of rationalism was borne of a wide engagement with European liberal thought of the later nineteenth century. Joseph McCabe, writing in 1909, defined this kind of rationalism as 'a critical action of reason on authoritative religious tradition, which leads to its partial or entire rejection'.[33] Similarly, John Russell in his book *The Task of Rationalism* (1910) defined rationalism as 'the mental attitude which unreservedly accepts the supremacy of reason and aims at establishing a system of philosophy and ethics verifiable by experience and independent of all arbitrary assumptions or authority'.[34] McCabe and Russell—and of course Robertson and Newman— saw rationalism as an umbrella term under which more specialised intellectual frameworks sat, such as Darwinism and positivism.

The 'critical action of reason' described by McCabe was central to Robertson's application of a rationalist ideology and was defined in Robertson's book *Letters on Reasoning* (1902).[35] Addressed to 'My dear Children', Robertson outlined the reasoning process as a first step towards criticism:

> All argument, every attempt to influence opinion or conduct by presenting a 'because', is a process of reasoning ... I want you therefore to grasp first the truth that *all* attempts to persuade are processes of reasoning. Some, we say, are good or 'logical' or 'valid'; by which we mean that on analysis their parts or stages are consistent. A good reasoner is one who does not contradict himself in the course of his argument, and who further takes intelligent account of all the important facts of the case he is dealing with. A 'bad reasoner' is one who, in seeking to

---

[33] Joseph McCabe, *Modern Rationalism: Being a Sketch of the Progress of the Rationalistic Spirit in the Nineteenth Century* (London: Watts and Co., 1909): 8.

[34] John Russell, *The Task of Rationalism* (London: Watts & Co., 1919).

[35] John M. Robertson, *Letters on Reasoning* (London: Watts & Co., 1902).

prove or convince, takes up ... contradictory positions, whether or not he has the main facts of his case before him.[36]

Robertson argued that reasoning was an ethical, utilitarian and rhetorical process that made for 'being a good citizen'.[37] He warned his readers that reason was often criticised for being 'cold' and urged rationalists not to be deterred by their antagonists.[38] Moreover, Robertson counselled that merely exercising one's reasoning power was not the same thing as acquiring wisdom, and he told his followers: 'I would have you realise very clearly that all discussion, all criticism, whether wise or unwise, is reasoning'.[39] His emphasis was on wide and critical reading as the foundation of judgement.

In 1912, Robertson gave a less paternalistic account of rationalism in his book *Letters of Reasoning*. The book began with a brief overview of the history of rationalism in works by Aristotle, Bacon, Kant and Hegel as precursors to late nineteenth-century rationalism.[40] After this background, Robertson provided his own definition of rationalism for contemporary readers:

> The name 'rationalist', in short, has come to mean for most people in this country very much what 'freethinker' used to mean for those who did not employ it as a mere term of abuse. It stands, that is to say, for one who rejects the claims of 'revelation', the idea of a personal God, the belief in personal immortality, and in general the conceptions logically occurring to the practices of prayer or worship.[41]

Robertson ended the overview by waving the flag of rationalist propaganda, linking the cause to their positivist heroes:

> Of such [rationalist] thinkers the number is daily increasing. There are now, probably, tens of thousands of more or less instructed men and women in this country who would call themselves rationalists ... They are all, probably, Darwinians, evolutionists, mostly 'monists' in Spencer's way, 'determinists' in

---

[36] John M. Robertson, *Letters on Reasoning*, 4–5. Robertson singled out Benjamin Kidd's *Social Evolution* (London: Macmillan and Co., 1894) as an example of bad reasoning. Newman was to take up the case against Kidd in his *Pseudo-Philosophy at the end of the Nineteenth Century* (London: University Press, 1897) and this is discussed in full in chapter 4.

[37] Robertson, *Letters on Reasoning*, 6–7.

[38] Robertson, *Letters on Reasoning*, 3, 15.

[39] Robertson, *Letters on Reasoning*, 14.

[40] Robertson, *Rationalism* (London: Constable and Company Ltd, 1912).

[41] Robertson, *Rationalism*, 4.

the philosophic sense of that term if they have worked at the 'free-will' problem at all, and non-believers in personal immortality.[42]

This readership would have been familiar with the writings of a number of nineteenth-century authors including Auguste Comte and J.S. Mill. But theory was one thing: turning rationalism into practice—by exercising sound judgement and writing quality criticism—was quite another.

✿ Rationalism: Links to History and Criticism

The freethinkers regarded theories of natural selection, evolution and heredity—and Comte's positive philosophy in particular—as intrinsically rational and objective, and therefore critical. These theories occupied huge portions of the freethought press, especially those publications controlled by Robertson. Furthermore, the ideal of rational and objective thought as the basis for criticism underpinned much of Robertson's literary writings. Personal opinion alone held no place in Robertson's rationalist scheme; rather, he advocated the adoption of method to rid criticism of what was widely referred to as the 'personal equation'. The scientific method, according to Robertson and a host of writers, would distinguish higher criticism (or scholarship) from lower criticism (mere journalism). Newman would take up this mantle of reform in music criticism, as we will soon see.

Scientific method in its nineteenth-century context has been described as an intellectual process that 'secularised the European mind' affecting all branches of knowledge; it was also known as the inductive, historical and comparative method.[43] Leopold von Ranke's *History of the Popes* (1842) and Henry Buckle's *History of Civilization in England* (1857) were representative of this new-fashioned history. Modern historiographers consider Ranke the founder of the scientific method of history for its emphasis on utilizing primary sources. Buckle's work is also regarded as one of the finest exemplars of scientific history in Britain for its emphasis on social history.[44]

[42] Robertson, *Rationalism*, 8–9.

[43] Heinrich Hermelink, *Das Christentum in der Menschheitsgeschichte* (Stuttgart, 1955): vol II, ix. A variation of this term is used and cited by Owen Chadwick as the title of his book, *The Secularization of the European Mind in the Nineteenth Century* (Cambridge: Cambridge University Press, 1975). Chadwick quotes Hermelink on p. 11.

[44] On the contribution of Ranke to the cultivation of scientific method see G.P. Gooch, *History and Historians in the Nineteenth Century* (Boston: Beacon Hill, 1965): 72–97; Georg G. Iggers, *The German Conception of History* (Middletown, CT: Wesleyan University Press, 1966): 64–89; Georg G. Iggers, *Historiography in the Twentieth Century: From Scientific Objectivity to the Postmodern Challenge*

The idea of history as a science was well established across Europe by the time Robertson and Newman were writing. So ubiquitous was this commitment to scientific method that scholars embraced what the historian Michael Bentley called the 'cult of objectivity', in which writers were preoccupied with 'what really happened'.[45] For this new generation of historians, evidence and objectivity were paramount no matter how simplistic some of these narratives seem to us today.

Robertson was aware that anyone claiming to know 'what really happened' or to have a definitive interpretation of an artistic object would be hard pressed to defend himself from allegations of bias or intellectual superiority. But Robertson was convinced that a critic, by virtue of his learning and carefully cultivated intellectual sensibilities, would possess the knowledge and high-level rhetorical abilities to persuade the reader to his point of view. For Robertson, this skill could only be achieved through 'careful, critical, [and] reflective' writing.[46] He firmly believed that most contemporary British literary criticism failed in this regard, and he sought to reform it.

But neither Robertson nor the freethinkers held a monopoly on trying to reform literary criticism in Britain: it had irked a range of writers for decades. In the 1860s, for example, Matthew Arnold, Anthony Trollope and Grant Allen had articulated serious problems in the theory and practice of British literary criticism and, in the 1880s, Walter Besant and Arthur Conan Doyle were still insistent that more needed to be done to professionalize it.

Matthew Arnold articulated a problem with nineteenth-century English criticism in his renowned 1864 essay 'The function of criticism at the present time', in which he described his contemporaries' works of criticism as 'polemical and controversial.'[47] He advocated an environment in which 'criticism must be sincere, simple, flexible, ardent, ever-widening in its knowledge'

(Hanover: University Press of New England, 1997): 23–30; and Patrick Bahners, "'A Place Among the English Classics": Ranke's *History of the Popes* and its British Readers', in Benedikt Stuchtey and Peter Wende (eds), *British and German Historiography, 1750–1950: Traditions, Perceptions, and Transfers* (Oxford: Oxford University Press, 2000): 123–57. For literature on Buckle see John Kenyon, *The History Men: The Historical Profession in England since the Renaissance* (London: Weidenfeld and Nicolson, 1983): 97–114 and Ian Hesketh, *The Science of History in Victorian Britain: Making the Past Speak* (London: Pickering & Chatto, 2011): 13–33.

[45] Michael Bentley, *Modern Historiography: An Introduction* (London: Routledge, 1999): 39.

[46] John M. Robertson, 'Criticism and science', *North American Review* 209/762 (May 1919): 690–6; 693.

[47] Matthew Arnold, 'The function of criticism at the present time' *National Review* 2/1 (1864): 280–307.

and argued that it should not be a platform for peddling personal agendas.[48] Arnold favoured a more detached style of criticism and asserted that English critics should look for inspiration in certain French and German critics, whom he deemed to be more ethical and objective.[49]

Chief among the many complaints about critics made by Anthony Trollope and Grant Allen was anonymous criticism (as well as pseudonymous criticism). They asserted this gave the critic a *carte blanche* to be unjustly cruel. They also complained about nepotism in the press and the alleged prevalence of bribes and kickbacks offered to critics for writing sycophantic articles. The bias fostered by anonymous criticism was thought by many readers to be the most significant problem of all in contemporary criticism. For example, in his autobiography published posthumously in 1883, Anthony Trollope devoted an entire chapter to the 'sin in modern English criticism', despairing that anonymous writing had become 'the custom of the trade' that enabled critics to write out of friendship or animosity, and to accept gifts from authors in return for 'hospitable favours'.[50] Trollope also used short stories and other works of fiction to advocate critical reform, and led by example in establishing the *Fortnightly Review*, which aimed to be unbiased. In an especially negative article in this journal in 1882, Grant Allen lamented that criticism had turned the reviewer into 'a kind of improvisatore, instead of a careful and deliberate critic' and further complained that the English were slow and philistine.[51] Arthur Conan Doyle was more scathing about the profession of the literary critic. In 1893, for instance, he accused some critics of 'obtaining money under false pretences' and alleged their work was infused with 'laziness', 'petty larceny', 'aggravated assault' and 'impersonation', rather than thoughtful criticism.[52]

Meanwhile, music critics had identified a similar problem and solutions were proposed for the reform of musical criticism, particularly in rescuing the profession from accusations of bias, favouritism and anti-intellectualism.

[48] Arnold, 'The function of criticism at the present time', 40.
[49] This point is explored in particular detail in Robert A. Donovan, 'The method of Arnold's Essays in Criticism', *Proceedings of the Modern Language Association* 17, no. 5 (1956), 922–31.
[50] Anthony Trollope, *An Autobiography* with an introduction by Charles Morgan (London: Williams and Norgate Ltd, 1946 [1883]). See especially chapter 14, 'On Criticism', 232–9; Trollope, *An Autobiography*, 233, 233, 234.
[51] Grant Allen, 'The decay of criticism', *FoR*, March 1882, 339–51; 344; 349.
[52] Arthur Conan Doyle in *Morning Leader*, 1893, quoted in Richard Findlater (ed.), *Author! Author! A Selection from The Author, the Journal of the Society of Authors since 1890* (London: Faber & Faber, 1984): 184. The date of publication and its pagination are not cited.

These problems came to exercise the minds of many critics, periodicals and institutions, and Newman would soon enter the thick of these discussions.

﴾ The Reform of Musical Criticism: Old versus New

Like their literary counterparts, some music critics and musicians were dissatisfied with the state of affairs in music criticism and set about reforming it. The pianist and composer, Charles Kensington Salaman, was one such reformer. On 1 November 1875, he addressed the Musical Association, which had been established the year before, on the need for criticism to be governed by a set of standards. He argued that the critic 'should possess many and various qualifications, which are rarely met with in combination'.[53] When these skills (which Salaman outlined later in the address) were 'exercised with ability, justice, and earnestness, it [the office of music critic] is an honourable profession'.[54] Essential to good criticism, according to Salaman, is 'long and patient study' of music, with the critic possessing 'mental facility of analysis, investigation, comparison and discrimination'.[55] Salaman also desired critics to think logically.[56] They should value novelty, be able to distinguish between a genius and a pioneer, and avoid conflicts of interests with publishers and friends. Salaman singled out George Hogarth (1783–1870) and Henry Chorley (1808–72) as 'the best modern musical critics'.[57] He was especially impressed by Hogarth's 'well-expressed opinions, based on sound musical knowledge and expression'.[58]

The composer John Stainer was another early advocate for the reform of musical criticism. Like Salaman, he delivered a speech to the Musical Association, in 1880, entitled 'The principles of musical criticism'.[59] In this speech Stainer observed that 'musical criticism at the present moment is oscillating dangerously between the two extremes of dogmatic conventionalism and unblushing nihilism. I think it is the duty of all of us to try and steady it'.[60] Given so many ill-considered judgements from critics, Stainer asserted

---

[53] Charles Kensington Salaman, 'On musical criticism', *Proceedings of the Musical Association*, second session, 1875–1876, 1–15.

[54] Salaman, 'On musical criticism', 1

[55] Salaman, 'On musical criticism', 2–3.

[56] Salaman, 'On musical criticism', 3.

[57] Salaman, 'On musical criticism', 8.

[58] Salaman, 'On musical criticism', 8.

[59] John Stainer, 'The principles of musical criticism', *Proceedings of the Royal Musical Association*, seventh session, 1880–1, 35–52.

[60] Stainer, 'The principles of musical criticism', 37.

they had become 'unjust judges and false prophets'.[61] He viewed the reporting of personal opinion without 'intellectual and emotional training' as a major cause for concern and was convinced it needed to be fixed.[62]

A similarly bleak picture of contemporary musical criticism was painted by Frederick J. Crowest in his 1880 book *Phases of Musical England*:

> The present condition of Musical Criticism in England cannot be said to be remarkable either for its quantity or genuine quality. At the most, our fund of criticism is only represented by an occasional notice in one or more of the daily journals, and by a few class papers ... For instance, what good is served by the untutored splutterings of the anonymous writers in our weekly and biweekly prints—writers who, under the garb of some high-flown *nom-de-plume*, regale their readers with flippant notes upon a subject of which such writers know comparatively nothing. Why should the public lend itself to such a prostitution of good ink and paper? Scraps of personal gossip and bits of scandal and slander cannot be called criticism, *malgré* newspaper proprietors permit their columns to be lowered with the insertion of such rubbish.[63]

Over the next thirteen years, the situation had not changed, according to W.H. Hadow in his *Studies in Modern Music* (1893). He argued that musical criticism lacked authority and maturity and critics were often heavy-handed and cavalier.[64] To counter musical criticism of this type, Hadow identified three grounds on which authority could be established: writing about music with 'clearness and certainty'; finding suitable words; and using parameters, such as harmony and counterpoint, to understand and interpret music objectively.

Hadow proposed a set of principles that he argued ought to be adopted to assess the most important value of a musical work. The first of these concerned originality. The extent to which a composer quoted from the compositions of others or adapted their musical structures, would be a measure against which originality could be determined. He then put forward an additional principle of musical judgement, 'the "principle of proportion", that measured compositions in terms of the sum of its parts'.[65] Using frequent analogies to literature, Hadow explained that 'A great work must not be a congeries of unconnected beauties, like those out of which the Greek artist is incredibly said to have constructed his Aphrodite: it must be marked by a sense of propriety and

---

[61] Stainer, 'The principles of musical criticism', 42.

[62] Stainer, 'The principles of musical criticism', 42.

[63] Frederick J. Crowest, *Phases of Musical England* (London: Remington and Co., 1881): 9–10.

[64] W.H. Hadow, *Studies in Modern Music* (London: Seeley, 1893): 4.

[65] Hadow, *Studies in Modern Music*, 40.

subordination, by wise reticence and provident self-control.'[66] On the other hand, Hadow did not insist that a work be seen as inferior simply because it failed to adhere to a strict structure such as sonata form. He then outlined his 'Principle of fitness', explaining that a musical work should adopt a form or expression suited to its purpose.

Hadow admitted that his set of principles was not fully fleshed out, that it was a mere 'bare sketch of a critical method', but reaffirmed a view, well-worn by now, that English musical criticism exhibited too much 'personal predilection'.[67] In the next part of his essay, 'Securus judicat orbis', Hadow was deeply critical of the dogmatic and pedantic critic and went on to give some specific (though unidentified) examples of what he thought to be ill-informed Beethoven criticism from the *Harmonicon*. He heavily criticised Chorley on the *Athenaeum* for his failure to engage with new music, especially Wagner. A clearly exasperated Hadow exclaimed, 'these are the men in whom we are expected to put our trust'.[68]

In concluding his article, Hadow accused contemporary critics of careless-ness that exhibited hallmarks of 'the lower journalism'.[69] He even went so far as to suggest that the public would be better off without critics: he believed people could make up their own minds about musical value. Still, Hadow was hopeful that 'we have a growing and extending interest in musical science' and asserted that a more judicious sort of musical criticism was possible.[70]

A flurry of articles on the state of musical criticism in England was published following the release of Hadow's book. In 1894, Charles V. Stanford and John Runciman took up the subject in the *Fortnightly Review*.[71] Stanford's article, 'Some aspects of musical criticism in England', was concerned with practical matters, describing 'two baneful oppressions under which musical criticism in England is now groaning'.[72] The first complaint argued that criticism was written in a rush; the second complaint concerned anonymity. Hurried criti-

---

[66] Hadow, *Studies in Modern Music*, 40.

[67] Hadow, *Studies in Modern Music*, 53.

[68] Hadow, *Studies in Modern Music*, 60.

[69] Hadow, *Studies in Modern Music*, 60.

[70] Hadow, *Studies in Modern Music*, 67.

[71] C.V. Stanford, 'Some aspects of musical criticism in England', *FoR*, June 1894, 826–31 and John F. Runciman, 'Musical criticism and the critics', *FoR*, August 1894, 170–83. Runciman published a further essay on the topic of critical reform called 'The gentle art of musical criticism', in *New Review* 12 (January–June 1895): 612–24. See also 'Musical writing and Paterian aestheticism, or, the "ravished pen" and the "temperamental critic"' read at the international conference on Music in Nineteenth-Century Britain, University of Nottingham (8 July 2005).

[72] Stanford, 'Some aspects of musical criticism in England', 826.

cism, according to Stainer, produced badly composed copy, while anonymity allowed a critic to write several negative reviews in more than one paper, and this could damage a composer's reputation when the criticism was wrong or misguided. To remedy these situations, Stanford called for the adoption of the French method of writing *feuilletons*, whereby a brief notice was given of a performance immediately after the event, while a fuller, reflective review was printed a few days later. Stanford went on to denounce much of the musical criticism in the daily press for its anti-intellectualism, describing it as merely for 'ephemeral consumption', and urged newspaper editors to employ literary talents who were knowledgeable about music.[73]

Meanwhile, John F. Runciman's article in the *Fortnightly Review*, which was a reply to Stanford, was published two months later, in July. In it, he announced a new era of musical criticism in England. According to Runciman, the worst critic of the 'old' school was J.W. Davison (1813–1885).[74] Runciman dismissed Davison's dogmatic criticism as 'beneath contempt' and described the old school for its 'ignorance, petty spite, stupid obstinacy, besides a lack of artistic susceptibility, that are almost inconceivable to the modern person. For thirty years this, the "old criticism", hung like a millstone round the neck of English music'.[75] For Runciman, the new critic required 'a distrust of the anonymous writer that must force him to display his credentials ... if his criticism is to carry weight, it thus forces the capable man to adopt the new or personal method, which is the only one that can produce results of value, and it forces the incapable man out of the field altogether'.[76]

Runciman identified many able new and contemporary critics, including J.S. Shedlock (1843–1919), E.J. Jacques (1850–1906) and J.A. Fuller Maitland (1856–1936). But he heaped most praise of all on George Bernard Shaw (1856–1916): 'Mr Bernard Shaw's column in the *Star* did most of all to send the old criticism out of date, and with his appointment to *The World* the fact that the new criticism has "come to stay" may be taken as recognised'.[77] Indeed, in a column on critical reform for the *Saturday Review* in 1899, Runciman argued, like many before him, that a solid music education and a highly polished,

---

[73] Stanford, 'Some aspects of musical criticism in England', 829.

[74] James William Davison was critic of the *Times* from 1846–78. For a study of some of his works see Charles Reid, *The Music Monster: A Biography of James William Davison* (London: Quartet Books, 1984).

[75] Runciman, 'Musical criticism and the critics', 171.

[76] Runciman, 'Musical criticism and the critics', 176.

[77] Runciman, 'Musical criticism and the critics', 173.

engaging and individual writing style were paramount to good criticism, and in his view, Shaw was its best exponent.[78]

Technical criticism was another style of writing that Runciman turned upon. In 'The gentle art of musical criticism' in 1895, Runciman disparaged this unimaginative kind of writing:

> Unless you turn out the old, old clichés; unless you fill your columns with profound references to consecutive fifths, and the birth- and death-dates of composers and popular singers, the Old Critics and the Academics of this land (who should have read their Schumann, their Berlioz, and their Wagner, and so know better) at once assume that you are ignorant, that is, of the technique of music.[79]

Runciman argued that this kind of criticism patronised readers and asserted that critics writing in this technical vein 'have no more than just such a textbook acquaintance with musical technique as they might get by a course of evening classes at Trinity College; and often not even that'.[80] Runciman also complained about the poor writing style of some critics, chastising them for producing 'gems of inexpressiveness'.[81]

Newman entered the discussion on poorly crafted criticism in November 1894 with an article in the *New Quarterly Musical Review* (a journal founded by Granville Bantock that ran from 1893–96 and published essays on musical history, contemporary music as well as reviews of books and concerts). Ostensibly, Newman's article was a review of Hadow's *Studies in Modern Music*.[82] Although Newman described the work as 'one of the ablest books on music that has ever appeared in England', he disagreed with Hadow that the public did not need critics.[83] He argued that a psychological or physiological explanation of composers' intentions was required (a point Newman takes up again, as we will see in later chapters). But Newman was optimistic about the future: 'truly, there is much to be done in musical criticism; and the main necessity at present seems to be to clear away the obscurities from the subject, and to get critics to see the difficulties that lie in the very nature of criticism in general, and of musical criticism in particular'.[84]

---

[78] Runciman, 'Concerning musical criticism', *SR*, 28 January 1899, 108–9.

[79] Runciman, 'The gentle art of musical criticism', 617.

[80] Runciman, 'The gentle art of musical criticism', 619.

[81] Runciman, 'The gentle art of musical criticism', 623.

[82] Ernest Newman, 'The difficulties of musical criticism', *NQMR*, November 1894, 105–12.

[83] Newman, 'The difficulties of musical criticism', 105.

[84] Newman, 'The difficulties of musical criticism', 112.

Newman wrote again on the topic of reporting (as opposed to criticism) seven years later, in November 1901. In 'English music and musical criticism' Newman was pessimistic: 'the public is becoming rather tired of the daily or weekly columns that tells it, for the thousandth time, that Paderewski played or Albani sang at this, that, or the other concert in London'.[85] He wanted critics to aspire to a more 'poetical criticism':

> Artists and singers are no doubt a necessary evil, and we need to be kept abreast of what is going on in the world of music; but to cultivate mere reporting at the expense of genuine criticism is to transpose the real value of things. One or two musical critics do make a gallant effort to lift the discussion of the art to a higher plane; and one of them at least—Mr Runciman of the 'Saturday Review'—deserves to be in somewhat better company.[86]

In the remainder of the article, Newman went on to suppose that British musical criticism was 'really only in its infancy' and that quality musical criticism takes time and perseverance:

> The criticism of music presents special difficulties that are unknown to any of the other arts. We can read a play or a story through in an hour or two, and then be quite able to discuss its main features. But to be able to speak with authority on a complex piece of music, like a Strauss symphonic poem or a Wagner opera, we need either to have heard it half-a-dozen times—or to have devoted hour after hour to a study of the score. If a critic has heard the same symphony very often, even if he has never seen the score, he is perhaps in a position to pass an opinion upon it.[87]

In the many discussions and debates over the ills of British musical criticism, some common threads emerged: the need for principles, method and training, all of which would cultivate an intellectually rigorous mind and erudite style of writing. To achieve these goals, reform in both the practice and theory of criticism was needed. As Newman put it in his article in the *Contemporary Review*, '[I]n a word, our critics need to take the profession of music criticism more seriously than most of them do at present. For one thing, readers require it'.[88]

---

[85] Ernest Newman, 'English music and musical criticism', *CR*, November 1901, 734–48; 744.

[86] Newman, 'English music and musical criticism', 745.

[87] Newman, 'English music and musical criticism', 747.

[88] Newman, 'English music and musical criticism', 748.

❧ Newman and a New Critical Spirit

By the end of the nineteenth century, a new critical spirit was in the ascendant:

> The temper and conditions of the age encourage the critical habit. Literature is no longer the affair of patron or coterie, but of the public. The public reads for itself and estimates. It is not the scholar alone but the artisan who judges the latest novel, satire, or barrack-room ballad. He weighs, compares, and pronounces judgment. And from the multitude of men that are critics unto themselves, and out of the confusion of conflicting opinions, arises the demand for system and principle.[89]

The problem with criticism, however, was its 'mode of self-expression', which had preoccupied many writers on criticism in mid- and late nineteenth-century England.[90] Commentators on criticism wanted an end to criticism that was inductive: the new era of criticism was to be based on reason, deduction and method in the same way that Ranke and Buckle had constructed their famous histories and on which Robertson's rationalism was predicated.

The link between criticism and method was not articulated in much depth in the late nineteenth century, for the connections were often assumed. However, there were some particularly striking works in which the relationships were cogently integrated. For example, the dramatic critic, William Archer, synthesised these elements in an article entitled 'Criticism as an inductive science' in 1886.[91] In reviewing a recent book on Shakespeare, in which its author, Richard G. Moulton, had argued the case for inductive criticism based on archival research and considerations of social and cultural context, Archer supposed that the modern critic:

> is not a 'judge' but an 'investigator'. He must come down from the bench and find his place in the laboratory. He is not to praise or dispraise, to accept or reject; but to note, register, classify. He has nothing whatever to do with taste; when garbage comes under his notice, he must simply hold his nose and study it as an instance of the laws of putrescence.[92]

Yet Archer was realistic enough to see that, although this was a sound theory for criticism, in practice it was a problem:

[89] Charles Mill Gayley and Fred Newton Scott, *An Introduction to the Methods and Materials of Literary Criticism* (Boston: Ginn & Company, 1899), iii.

[90] The term 'mode of self-expression' is from A.B. Walkley, *Dramatic Criticism: Three Lectures Delivered at the Royal Institution* (London: John Murray, 1903), 52.

[91] William Archer, 'Criticism as an inductive science', *Macmillan's Magazine*, May–October 1886, 45–54.

[92] Archer, 'Criticism as an inductive science', 45.

Criticism, then, is and will continue to be, so long as human faculties remain as they are, the utterance of individual judgments resulting from the application of individual standards to works of art, the very perception of which is affected by a 'personal equation' by no means to be eliminated. It is to be held good, bad, or indifferent according to the degree in which it commands the assent of men of culture and intelligence in the critic's own time and in subsequent generations. So far from having to do with induction, its methods are mainly deductive.[93]

The nexus between rationalism, history, criticism and method is also evident in a widely read book of the early twentieth century, *Introduction to the Study of History* by Charles V. Langlois and Charles Seignobos. For Langlois and Seignobos, 'instinctive methods are irrational' and that 'all historical work is ... pre-eminently critical'.[94] In their view of history as a rational and critical exercise, they asserted in particularly strong terms that 'the detailed analysis of the reasonings which lead from the inspection of documents to the knowledge of facts is one of the chief parts of Historical Methodology. It is the domain of criticism'.[95]

Inductive criticism, also termed personal or aesthetic criticism, was, for Archer, as well as Langlois and Seignobos, a thing of the past. A new era of criticism was in the ascendant and Newman's work throughout his career was defined by it. Newman positioned himself as a critic in this so-called new school of criticism, eschewing dilettantism and impressionist criticism as the work of the hack journalist. Newman belonged to that coterie of writers who had formed an obsession for objectivity, impartiality and distance from the object of criticism in all genres of their writing. Although some rationalists were partly sympathetic to aestheticism, they largely ignored and sometimes belittled it for its personal, self-conscious and subjective position. The rationalists assumed the high moral ground over the aesthetic critics. This was especially true of Newman in the context of musical criticism, and the rationalist vantage point was one from which he never wavered, no matter how many times this scientific approach to criticism was called into question.

[93] Archer, 'Criticism as an inductive science', 49.

[94] Ch. V. Langlois and Ch. Seignobos, *Introduction to the Study of History,* trans. G.G. Berry (London: Duckworth & Co., 1925): 8, 69.

[95] Langlois and Seignobos, *Introduction to the Study of History*, 65.

CHAPTER 3

Social, Literary and Musical Criticism: 1893–1897

I N the 1880s and 1890s Newman wrote on a broad range of subjects in the freethought press including religion and society, science and scientific method, literary criticism and music. With the exception of music, the free-thinkers regarded these topics as the most pressing of the time. Newman's essays on religion and society, as well as science and scientific method, were infused with the parlance of positivism and evolutionary theory. These con-nections were also made in his literary criticism, though Newman's emphasis was to analyse plot, narrative and character. His musical criticism, showing a strong interest in Wagner, aesthetics and opera, brought Newman high praise. However, his talent as a literary critic was called into question, and this resulted in an ugly and dramatic confrontation with his employer and mentor John M. Robertson.

Newman got his break as a writer in September 1889 in the *National Reformer*, the leading intellectual freethought journal of its time. He had met the journal's editor, Charles Bradlaugh, the month before. Newman proceeded to write about twenty pieces for the *National Reformer* (and related periodi-cals) over the next four years.

❧ Essays for the National Reformer, 1889–1894

The *National Reformer* was first published on 14 April 1860. It focused on pol-itics and government 'which it discussed in the sober terms of a respectable review'.[1] John M. Robertson became one of its assistant editors in 1884 and, on the death of Bradlaugh in January 1891, was elevated to editor.[2] He took Newman under his wing and provided him with opportunities for publication.

---

[1] Edward Royle, *Radicals, Secularists and Republicans* (Manchester: Manchester University Press; Totowa, NJ: Rowman & Littlefield, 1980), 34. Here Royle is prob-ably thinking of the more famous reviews of the period including the *Westminster Review*, *Fortnightly Review* and *Contemporary Review*.

[2] Odin Dekkers, *J.M. Robertson: Rationalist and Literary Critic* (Aldershot: Ashgate, 1998), 8. It is likely Robertson had been acting editor for at least twelve months as Bradlaugh had been preoccupied with his parliamentary duties and had been ill. See Dekkers, *J.M. Robertson*, 25.

During his term, Robertson did much to turn the *National Reformer* into a high-end journal rivalling such publications as the *Westminster Review* but, with increased competition and declining subscriptions, it ceased trading in 1893. Originally pitched to a working-class readership, by the time of its demise the *National Reformer* had become a heady and intellectual publication that claimed to attract the 'pick' and 'elite' of the working classes.[3]

The *National Reformer* gave Newman a platform on which he could push the freethought agenda, though most of his writings were preaching to the converted. Nevertheless, a study of some of these early essays reveals that Newman was exceptionally well read and had developed a capacity for a direct and sometimes combative turn of phrase, which was a hallmark of much of his later work.[4] Newman's unique contribution to the journal was in articles on music and music criticism, as the *National Reformer* did not usually publish articles on these topics, or on the arts in general. The periodical did, however, publish extensively on social issues with frequent references to works by Auguste Comte, Herbert Spencer and J.S. Mill whose works were directly and indirectly invoked in Newman's essays.

RELIGION AND SOCIETY

In his book, *London in the 1890s: A Cultural History*, Karl Beckson observed that:

> At the end of the nineteenth century, many intellectuals, having abandoned their religious faith but inspired by utopian dreams, envisioned a new age in the next century, convinced that the past—with its failures and disappointments—was a burden to be abandoned.[5]

---

[3] These two quotations are from, respectively, the *National Reformer* in 1892; *The Freethinker* in 1888. Cited in Royle, *Radicals, Secularists and Republicans*, 126. Royle does not give specific issue numbers or page numbers.

[4] Newman's articles were 'The meaning of science', *NR*, 24 July 1892, 52–3; 'The coming menace', *NR*, 14 August 1892, 99–100; 'Crucifixion: To the Editor of the "NR" ' [Letter to the editor signed 'W. Roberts' attrib. Newman], *NR*, 28 August 1892, 139; 'A note on death', *NR*, 4 September 1892, 146–8; 'Mr Harrison and Mr Huxley', *NR*, 23 October 1892, 259–60; 'Poetry and music', *NR*, 30 October 1892, 277; 'Marriage as a science', *NR*, 13 November 1892, 309–11; 'Poetry and music: a reply', *NR*, 4 December 1892, 355–7; 11 December, 373–5; 'Wagner and the music-drama', *NR*, 1 January 1893, 11–12; 'A note on Amiel', *NR*, 26 February 1893, 136; 5 March, 147–8; 12 March, 163–4; 19 March, 180–1; 26 March, 200; 'Our morality', *NR*, 4 June 1893, 355–7; 'Mr Meredith and the eternal-feminine', *NR*, 23 July 1893, 54–5; and 'Some thoughts on Weismann', *NR*, 6 August 1893, 84–5; 13 August, 102–3; 20 August, 116–17.

[5] Karl Beckson, *London in the 1890s: A Cultural History* (New York and London: W.W. Norton & Co., 1992): xi.

Newman was a good example of this kind of intellectual. He loathed religion, and his first article in the *National Reformer*, 'Morality and belief', articulated the commonplace secular attitude that religious thought was a barrier to 'enlightenment'.[6] In Newman's view, religion was a stifling social construction and out of place in the contemporary world: 'In no sphere of life does the dead past live on so long as in the ecclesiastical. Ecclesiastical music, ecclesiastical art, ecclesiastical printing, ecclesiastical dress even, bear the stamp of an age other than the present'.[7] However, Newman was confident that the age of science would unfetter society from the trappings of religion:

> Thus modern science has rent us away from the ideals of the past, destroying both our intellectual belief in the activity, and our emotional reverence for the goodness of the deity ... But grant a wider knowledge of the universe, a closer relation between nations past and present, and between nations near and far in the world, a greater acquaintance with the nature of man's moral system, and the origin and development of his ideas, and the narrow conception of an anthropomorphic God becomes merged in the infinitely grander conception of humanity.[8]

Newman's concept of utopia was not merely an abstraction: he gave considerable thought to its utility in which 'strong love and fellowship ... [will be] our great happiness and our true satisfaction'.[9] This was not a new idea. In Auguste Comte's *General View of Positivism*, for example, the necessity of society 'totally abandoning the theological principle' is spelt out.[10] Indeed, Comte saw the cultivation of love as humanity's driving principle.[11] J.S. Mill described it more succinctly as the 'Greatest Happiness Principle'.[12] The parlance of positivism was clearly etched in Newman's work.

---

[6] Newman, 'Morality and belief', 170.

[7] Newman, 'Morality and belief', 170.

[8] Newman, 'Morality and belief', 170.

[9] Newman, 'Morality and belief', 170.

[10] Auguste Comte, *General View of Positivism* [being the Preface to Part III of the Second system, *Système de Politique Positive*] (Paris: Republic of the West Order of Progress, 1848): 19–20.

[11] Comte, *General View of Positivism*, 40.

[12] Henry R. West, *The Blackwell Guide to Mill's Utilitarianism* (Maldon: MA, Blackwell, 2006): 68. See also Herbert Spencer, *Social Statics or The Conditions Essential to Human Happiness, Specified, and the First of them Developed* (London: John Chapman, 1851) and John Stuart Mill, *On Liberty* (London: John W. Parker, 1859).

SCIENCE

After positivism, science—and scientific method—was another of Newman's earliest intellectual preoccupations. He regarded scientists (as well as positivists) as the harbingers of new knowledge that privileged method over metaphysics. In 'The meaning of science', Newman attempted a definition of science and its purpose:

> What is science? We are familiar with the definition of it as 'organised knowledge'—knowledge of a high degree of generalisation. This being so, it is the extremity of ignorance to assert that science is only concerned with objective description of things, or—a still greater folly—that its province lies only in the material amelioration of mankind. The very essence of science is that it is *not* concerned with facts in themselves, but with facts in their implications with other facts. It ever presses on from the particular to the general, from the many to the one—that is, the goal to which it constantly tends is that of the unification of knowledge.[13]

Newman regarded the scientist as a hero, as one 'above all men, who leads us from chaos to cosmos, who clears our vision and broadens our horizon, and so takes us, step by step, to intellectual planes whence we view the world in truer and juster proportion'.[14] He was drawn to scientific method as a 'synthetic and generalising' process that enabled categorisation and order.[15] Newman's use of the phrase 'synthetic philosophy' is probably made in reference to Herbert Spencer's magisterial work by the same name, a series of ten volumes published between 1864 and 1897 in which Spencer proposed 'principles' or patterns of acquiring knowledge in biology, psychology, sociology and ethics.[16]

However, Newman did not revere all the scientists of his generation. He was extremely sceptical of pseudo-science, which he believed characterised August Weismann's book *The Germ-Plasm: A Theory of Heredity* published in England in 1893. This book was controversial because Weismann argued that only the reproductive cells, the germ plasm, contained hereditary material, a theory at odds with Lamarck's theory of heredity arising from acquired characteristics.[17]

---

[13] Newman, 'The meaning of science', 52–3.

[14] Newman, 'The meaning of science', 53.

[15] Newman, 'The meaning of science', 53.

[16] Herbert Spencer, *First Principles* (London: Williams and Norgate, 1862); *Principles of Biology*, 2 vols (London: Appleton, 1864); *Principles of Psychology*, 2 vols (London: Williams and Norgate, 1870); *Principles of Sociology*, 3 vols (London: Appleton, 1874–5) and *Principles of Ethics*, 2 vols (London: Appleton, 1897).

[17] August Weismann, *The Germ-Plasm: A Theory of Heredity* (London: Charles Scribner's, 1893), first published the year before in Germany as *Das Keimplasma*. Weismann's book attracted a great degree of discussion in the press, including the

Newman was convinced that Weismann was wrong on one particular case study: his hypothesis that if Mozart was born in Samoa, he would have composed Samoan music, but with a discernible classical and European flavour.[18] Indeed, Newman thought Weismann's reasoning was totally flawed:

> The expression 'Samoan Mozart' is meaningless on the face of it. A Mozart is an individual descended from generations of ancestors whose mental organisation had been continually increasing in complexity, and he himself is born with a brain of a complexity equal to, if not greater than, that of the average European of his time. Does Weismann mean that such an individual could be born in Samoa? If so, then obviously he would not be a Samoan, in the sense in which the word applies to Samoans in general, as a race of a certain organization: he would, in fact, be a European. So that a Samoan Mozart is equivalent to a Samoan European, which is meaningless. We might as rationally talk of a mammalian amphioxus.[19]

In Newman's view, Weismann's process of explaining the musical potentials of the Samoan-born Mozart further confused the nature versus nurture debate. Moreover, Newman simply did not accept, like Weismann's many other critics had, that the germ plasm was the sole carrier and determiner of hereditary features. But Newman further felt that the nature–nurture debate could not rely only on questions of heredity and environment: 'more service would be done to sociology if physical characteristics were left alone and an examination of mental characteristics taken up'.[20]

National Reformer; see especially Spencer, 'The inadequacy of natural selection', *CR*, February 1893, 153–66 and March 1893, 434–56; August Weismann, 'All sufficiency of natural selection', *CR*, September 1893, 309–38; October 1893, 596–610; and Herbert Spencer, 'A rejoinder to Professor Weismann', *CR*, December 1893, 893–912. Essays on the subject in the *National Reformer* were H. Croft Hiller, 'Spencer or Weismann?', *NR*, 30 April 1893, 277–9; H. Croft Hiller, 'Weismannism and its adversaries', *NR*, 28 May 1883, 339–41; John M. Robertson, 'Weismannism and sociology', *NR*, 4 June 1893, 353–4, 11 June, 371–3; H. Croft Hiller, 'Weismannism and sociology: a reply', *NR*, 18 June 1893, 388–90; W.P. Ball, 'Weismann's views', *NR*, 25 June 1893, 403–4; H. Croft Hiller, 'Weismannism and sociology: a further reply', *NR*, 2 July 1893, 10–11; John M. Robertson, 'Weismann's views', *NR*, 9 July 1893, 20–1; W.P. Ball, 'Weismann's views', *NR*, 16 July 1893, 35–6; John M. Robertson, 'Reply to the foregoing', *NR*, 16 July 1893, 36–7; H. Croft Hiller, 'Weismannism and sociology: a further reply', *NR*, 23 July 1893, 58–9; and W.P. Ball, 'Weismann's views', *NR*, 23 July 1983, 60–1.

[18] Newman, 'Some thoughts on Weismann', *NR* 6 August 1893, 84–5; 13 August, 102–3; 20 August, 116–17.

[19] Newman, 'Some thoughts on Weismann', 102.

[20] Newman, 'Some thoughts on Weismann', 84. Newman's work on Weismann was greatly criticised in H. Croft Hiller, *Against Dogma and Free-Will and for Weismann* (London: Williams and Norgate), *c.* 1893.

LITERARY CRITICISM

Newman was an avid reader of fiction and poetry—he even once attempted writing a short story—but his reading was not undertaken for mere enjoyment, because Newman fancied himself as a literary critic.[21] Three essays by Newman in the *National Reformer*—'The doctrine of evolution in modern poetry', 'Mr Meredith and the eternal-feminine' and 'A note on Amiel'—interpret works of literature along evolutionary, psychological and stylistic lines.

In 'The doctrine of evolution in modern poetry' Newman identified tropes of evolution in the poetry of Wordsworth, Tennyson, Browning and Swinburne, and quoted a considerable amount of text from some representative poems to prove his point. Through a close reading of each of the poems, Newman suggested that in the Wordsworth extract (from the 1814 work, *The Excursion*) the poet was alert to the 'idea of the silent progression of society from the life of the past through ever-improving forms'.[22] In Newman's eyes, these poets had become champions of progress and were, as a consequence, freethought role models.[23] He also saw poetry as a particularly evolved and altruistic genre: 'modern poetry has linked itself strongly with this great idea of the evolution of man, gradual but certain, to a higher plane of being'.[24]

Next, Newman turned to novelists. In 'Mr Meredith and the eternal-feminine', Newman analysed three of George Meredith's novels: *Diana of the Crossways* (1885), *Sandra Belloni* (1887, formerly published in 1864 as *Emilia in England*) and *The Ordeal of Richard Feveral* (1859), all of which left him cold and critical of Meredith's writing style and characterisation. Newman argued that Meredith had over-sensualised both the female and male protagonists, typecasting them to the point of over-refinement: 'for Mr Meredith is so feminine, and knows so much about the feelings of women, that he reproduces their talk too realistically; so realistically as to be inartistic and disgusting ... Mr Meredith has almost a ghoul-like delight in the nauseous at times'.[25]

---

[21] The short story was called 'Nancy', *UMFR*, June 1897, 299–322. In correspondence to Bertram Dobell on 27 June 1897 (MSS Dobell 38484–5), Newman had written: 'However, I mean to go on a little longer in that [fiction] line, just for the fun of the thing. I don't mind people telling me I can't write fiction. I know that myself; but it's a little change and amusement for me'.

[22] Newman, 'The doctrine of evolution in modern poetry', 261.

[23] A good overview of tropes of evolution in romantic poetry can be found D.R. Oldroyd, *Darwinian Impacts: An Introduction to the Darwinian Revolution* (Sydney: University of New South Wales Press, 1980): 309–20.

[24] Oldroyd, *Darwinian Impacts*, 262.

[25] Newman, 'Mr. Meredith and the eternal-feminine', 54.

Newman also criticised Meredith's realist and historical novels for their farcical plots and characters; or, as another scholar has suggested, their 'artificial behaviour'.[26] Newman was particularly scathing of the 'Philosopher' in *Sandra Belloni*, used by Meredith for the narrative voice, because he found it contrived. But freethought politics may have had something to do with Newman's review. G.W. Foote, then president of the National Secular Society, and editor of the rival freethought journal, the *Freethinker*, was a close friend of Meredith's, and it is possible that Newman took advantage of this connection—as well as Meredith's then 'fashionable vogue'—in a bid to pepper his essay with controversy.[27] As we will soon see, Newman relished debunking popular literary figures.

Apart from interpreting literature from the standpoint of evolution, and of plot, narrative and character, Newman was also interested in a writer's psychology, evident in his essay on Henri-Frédéric Amiel's *Journal Intime*. The *Journal* was an introspective work *par excellence* that was published in English translation in 1885 to a huge and largely favourable critical reception.[28] Amiel's work was already well known in some British quarters as Matthew Arnold had written about him at length in his *Essays in Criticism*. He described the Swiss professor of aesthetics and philosophy as a writer of 'cultivation, refinement and high feeling'.[29] Newman was similarly positive about Amiel's psychology describing it as 'perhaps the most complete picture we have of any individual mind, and the interest of it is varied'.[30] It was by far Newman's longest essay for the *National Reformer*, which suggests he was particularly keen on this topic. Newman saw many dualities at play in Amiel's life describing the diarist as 'hovering between Buddhism and asceticism, between absorption and duty, between hope and fear'.[31] Newman was drawn to the diarist, writing once

[26] Robert W. Watson, 'George Meredith's *Sandra Belloni*: The "Philosopher" on the sentimentalists', *English Literary History* 24/4 (1957): 321–35; 334.

[27] L.T. Hergenham, 'The reception of George Meredith's early novels', *Nineteenth-Century Fiction* 19/3 (1964): 214. Foote's connection to Meredith is discussed extensively in Joss Lutz Marsh, '"Bibliolatry" and "bible-smashing": G.W. Foote, George Meredith and the heretic trope of the book', *Victorian Studies* 34/3 (1991): 315–36.

[28] Henri-Frédéric Amiel's *Journal Intime* was first published in Geneva in 1882. Mrs Humphrey Ward was the book's English translator, the first edition of which was published by Macmillan in 1885. A second edition was published, and then reprinted, in 1889. It was reprinted twice in 1890, twice in 1891 and thirteen times between 1892 and 1933. Source: *Amiel's Journal*, trans. Mrs Humphrey Ward (London: Macmillan and Co., 1933): iv.

[29] Matthew Arnold, *Essays in Criticism*. 2nd series. (London and New York: Macmillan and Co., 1888): 300–31; 301.

[30] Newman, 'A note on Amiel', 148.

[31] Newman, 'A note on Amiel', 180.

more in the language of the positivists and utilitarians, that 'Amiel is certainly modern in his synthetic power, and in his desire for a philosophy that shall be the unification of all orders of existence'.[32]

Newman argued that Amiel had the potential to be the next C.A. Sainte-Beuve, widely regarded as France's foremost literary critic. As Newman explained: 'some of the short studies of men and books in the Journal are remarkably fine and true … Amiel had a potentiality of a fine critic in him'.[33] But while Newman was enthusiastic about Amiel's quest for enlightenment, he saw it as a poor effort in relation to Spencer's work:

> to assert that Amiel is a true picture of the modern mind is a fallacy that becomes evident as soon as we point to men like Mr. Spencer, who contain a synthetic power probably ten times as great as Amiel with a juster sense of their place in the universe, and so manage to extract some hours of happiness from threescore years and ten without making a Calvary and a Gethsemane for themselves.[34]

Newman had no time for Amiel's morbid introspection and vanity. When viewed alongside the intellectual clout of Spencer, Amiel simply did not compare.

MUSIC CRITICISM

Newman's writings on music for the *National Reformer* came about more by accident than design, motivated by a series of exchanges between Robertson and the journal's readers—via the letters to the editor column—over questions of evolutionary theory, aesthetics and Wagner.[35] The letters and articles were dominated initially by arguments concerning claims of the superiority of Wagner's opera dramas over Beethoven's symphonies, especially the Ninth. The debate then moved to a broader discussion of text–music relationships and music of the future.

A writer by the name of H.D. facilitated this tussle in an article entitled 'Poetry and music':

---

[32] Newman, 'A note on Amiel', 180.

[33] Newman, 'A note on Amiel', 180.

[34] Newman, 'A note on Amiel', 200.

[35] John M. Robertson, 'Tennyson', *NR*, 16 October 1892, 241–2. The rejoinders facilitated by this piece are: H.D., 'Poetry and music', *NR*, 23 October 1892, 270; Ernest Newman, 'Poetry and music', *NR*, 30 October 1892, 277; H.D., 'Poetry and music: a rejoinder', *NR*, 13 November 1892, 309; Melody, 'Poetry and music', *NR*, 20 November 1892, 362; John M. Robertson [editorial note to Melody's 'Poetry and music', above], 362; Ernest Newman, 'Poetry and music: a reply', *NR*, 4 December, 355–7; 11 December, 373–5 and Newman, 'Wagner and the music drama', *NR*, January, 11–12.

I suggest that music as a separate art probably reached its highest development in the genius of Beethoven, who brought his masterpieces into being by a painstaking care suggested by Mother Nature … [I]f modern music has reached its highest development, then it may get more and more diffuse. There are signs that this is happening already.[36]

H.D. (who was clearly an ambivalent Wagnerian) proposed that it was too soon for anyone to consider Wagner a genius, arguing that this would only be possible if interest in the composer could be sustained for at least another fifty years.[37] But Newman was having none of it:

I believe Wagner to be, not only the deepest and clearest thinker, but also the most consummate and potent artist that ever expressed himself in music … I do not refer to his union of poet, musician, dramatist, scene artist, philosopher, and analyst, although that in itself is wonderful. I refer rather to the unique balance in him between poetry and music, and again, within the inner sphere of each of these, between the more abstract and the more concrete elements of each.[38]

The rest of Newman's response focused on the aesthetics of text–music relationships with some homespun philosophizing propping up his admiration of the Wagner music dramas. Newman proposed that poetry and music, although separate entities, contained elements of the abstract and the concrete in their inner spheres and that Wagner's greatness rested on the unique way in which these spheres were blended:

Poetry *per se* and music *per se* exist separately, each working in its own sphere. As soon as they are properly combined, individual distinctions must disappear; each must sacrifice something if it is to become one with the other; and the true musical-dramatic expression must come from the mental mood that is a compromise between these two diverse ways of looking at life. This mood of compromise Wagner alone has achieved, and that through a lucky hit of Nature. It may be ages before such a mind comes again. Thus, supreme as Wagner is, the future course of opera will not go on the lines laid down by him. It will have to begin its development afresh.[39]

Newman then suggested ways in which music could evolve in the post-Wagner age, with reference to the form and function of contemporary poetry. He considered such poetry to be restricted in matter but growing in form. For

[36] H.D., 'Poetry and music', 270.
[37] H.D., 'Poetry and music', 270.
[38] Newman, 'Poetry and music', 277.
[39] Newman, 'Poetry and music', 277.

Newman, poetry was 'a flower of thought'.[40] He then reasoned that if 'poetry is the flower of thought, music is in many respects the flower of poetry' and that instrumental music had evolved to be the supreme art form and that 'from the symphony in the new shapes it will assume in the future, we may expect the most perfect emotional expression of what life really means'.[41]

H.D. and Newman were clearly at odds on the question of Wagner but they both concurred that the time was ripe for new study of Wagner's prose works. Newman put the case in an article on 1 January 1893, 'Wagner and the music-drama':

> I agree with 'H.D.' that there should be greater study given to Wagner's prose works. If he had done nothing in the way of creation, his claim to immortality could be grounded on the uniqueness of his position. He has given a wealth of new data to the student of aesthetics.[42]

By 1899 Newman would undertake this task himself in his *A Study of Wagner*.

During the debate over Wagner in the *National Reformer*, Newman took the opportunity to comment on the composer's unfavourable critical reception in England. Disparaging remarks from a writer named 'Melody' had culminated in an article of November 1892 called 'Poetry and music' in which the writer asserted: 'I should venture to allege that a small minority, comparatively, have gone over to Wagner, and that not the truly music loving'.[43] Newman was incensed:

> I am not a hero-worshipper, and my admiration for Wagner is, I hope, a ration-ally tempered one, but I must confess to a slight stirring of bile at the remarks ... of 'Melody' about Wagner. ... English musical criticism never was particu-larly brilliant, but [John] Hullah and [George Alexander] Macfarren represent the most stupid and most commonplace side of it. Macfarren especially was so grossly ignorant of anything that is necessary for the criticism of music—above all, new music—that it is only in such a country as this that he would be listened to. I do not say this of him because he did not like Wagner's music, but because he gives no sensible reasons for disliking it, because he was never anything more than a narrow musical theorist, suffering from the one great curse of English

[40] Newman, 'Poetry and music', 277.

[41] Newman, 'Poetry and music', 277. In two further articles Newman continued to argue his point about the supremacy of instrumental music without adding signifi-cantly new material or thought to his previous articles.

[42] Newman, 'Wagner and the music-drama', 1 January 1893, 12.

[43] Melody, 'Poetry and music', 20 November, 362.

music—the devotion to dull religious music, and the unintelligent slavishness toward the most conservative sides of Handel and Mendelssohn—and because everything he says in the way of musical criticism, even on such idols as Bach and Handel, is marked with the same dullness and stupidity. It is no wonder that English music and English criticism are so backward when unintelligent men like these are a power in the land.[44]

There was no rejoinder to this tirade. Newman had provided the last word and the sparring over Wagner in the *National Reformer* was drawn to a close.

Newman's career as a literary critic almost came to an end at about the same time because the *National Reformer* could not pay its way and ceased trading. However, its editor, John M. Robertson, established the *Free Review*, and Newman was recruited to write for it. Despite the optimism around this new venture, trouble was brewing. Newman's ability as a literary critic was called into question, and he reacted badly.

❧ Essays in the Free Review, 1893–1898

The first issue of the *Free Review* was published in October 1893 and opened with an essay by Robertson entitled 'Concerning magazines in general and this one in particular'.[45] In it, Robertson provided a rich overview of contemporary journal publishing and outlined the aims and uniqueness of his new enterprise. In justifying the establishment of another publication in an already crowded literary marketplace—one that already contained successful reviews, including the well-known periodicals *Contemporary*, *Fortnightly*, *Westminster* and *New Review*—Robertson argued that the reviews genre was tainted by editorial and political bias. He proposed that the *Free Review* would not present such prejudices. In terms of its scope and relation to other journals of its genre, Robertson announced that the *Free Review*:

> … makes no claim to being a good advertising medium, save for high-class publishers, and which has no capital behind it whatever. It is primarily an attempt to make a platform for opinions which are more or less unlikely to get a hearing in even the more balanced of the established reviews, with perhaps the exception of the *Westminster* … Even the so-called *Fortnightly Review*, good work as it has done for progressive thought, is now obviously managed with an eye to respectable or average prejudices, and cannot be regarded as the platform for new ideas

---

[44] Melody, 'Poetry and music', *NR*, 20 November 1892, 362; Newman, 'Poetry and music: a reply', 356.

[45] John M. Robertson, 'Concerning magazines in general and this one in particular', *FR*, October 1893, 1–10.

any more than for safe ones. No review whatever is conducted with a view to getting a hearing for good independent criticism all round.[46]

In terms of democratic editorial practices and policy, Robertson explained that:

> [N]o attempt will be made by the editor to secure conformity to any fixed set of doctrines, or to tie down contributors to any one creed. Each contributor is to be considered responsible for his own articles only; and it may be taken for granted that, though as a rule the writers will be broadly in sympathy with each other, they will often differ on particular issues.[47]

This was a high-risk venture. The *Free Review* was established in an already saturated market, without an underwriter, and without remuneration for some of its authors. Moreover, Robertson's aim of cultivating 'higher litera-ture' seemed perilously at odds with his observation that the 'whole economic conditions of the time are against the spread of hard reading'.[48] In these cir-cumstances, the *Free Review* was launched, but its short life was an unstable one. Robertson oversaw the production of four volumes from October 1893 to September 1895; G.A. Singer then took over the journal for three volumes from October 1895 to March 1896; and from April 1897 to 1900 'Democritus' edited the *Free Review*.[49] In 1896 the journal was sold to Swan Sonnenschein and its name was changed to *University Magazine and Free Review* (UMFR). Newman was to have a close but uneasy relationship with these periodicals and their publishers.

The topics on which Newman wrote for the *National Reformer* were largely replicated in the *Free Review*: religion and society; science and pseudo-science; literary criticism; and music. Indeed, some of Newman's articles were on exactly the same topics as previously published in the *National Reformer*— one article each on Meredith and Weismann, and an article on Amiel, spread over two issues. Newman's views on these topics remained the same, although the content was greatly augmented.[50] However, there were topics on which

---

[46] Robertson, 'Concerning magazines', 2–3.

[47] Robertson, 'Concerning magazines', 9–10.

[48] Robertson, 'Concerning magazines', 5.

[49] There is no specific date on the bound publisher's copy for the 1900 issues. 'Democritus' was a pseudonym of Matthew Gallichan. See Odin Dekkers, 'Walter Matthew Gallichan: fiction and freethought in the 1890s', *English Studies* 5 (2002): 407–22.

[50] Ernest Newman, 'George Meredith', *FR*, August 1894, 398–418; 'Concerning Weismann', *FR*, December 1894, 210–38; and 'Amiel', *FR*, October 1895, 44–57; November, 197–205.

Newman wrote for the first time: Ibsen, Kipling, Oscar Wilde and Nietzsche.[51] Though these articles were compelling and well written, they failed to be innovative, and Robertson required this of writers in his journal. Analyses of some of Newman's articles give an insight into why they were considered to be derivative and why he was criticised for writing them.

'The Real Ibsen' was Newman's first article for the *Free Review*, published in October 1893. In this article, Newman set out to give what he considered a more balanced interpretation of Ibsen's life and works against claims of the playwright's immorality by other critics. Newman refrained from naming these critics though he was probably referring to three of Ibsen's greatest English admirers George Bernard Shaw, William Archer and J.T. Green.[52] Newman wanted to clear up what he considered to be some misunderstandings about Ibsen and to find a middle path between extremes of appreciation. But he was not the first writer to touch on this topic. As Shaw had already noted two years previously, opinion was already divided: on the one hand, Ibsen was hailed as 'the greatest living poet'; on the other, he was described as 'obscene'.[53] Not content with these observations, Newman delivered a stinging missive to his fellow critics and the public:

> Nine-tenths of the current ideas concerning him [Ibsen], indeed, are so gro-
> tesquely stupid, and so painfully wide of the mark, that only the universal dis-
> position to believe and repeat unthinkingly any foolish or damaging opinion
> of a person one does not like would make these ideals at all conceivable ... and
> students of Ibsen may well smile at the grotesque misunderstanding of him that
> exists in the mind of that precious product of nineteenth-century civilisation—
> the average person.[54]

Newman did not regard Ibsen, or his plays, as immoral. Rather, he argued that, like the novels of George Meredith, Ibsen's plays lacked character

---

[51] 'The Real Ibsen', *FR*, October 1893, 20–37; 'Mr Kipling's stories', *FR*, December 1893, 236–48; 'Oscar Wilde: A Literary Appreciation', *FR*, June 1895, 193–206; 'Friedrich Nietzsche', *FR*, May 1896, 113–22.

[52] See 'The higher drama', in Holbrook Jackson, *The Eighteen Nineties: A Review of Art and Ideas at the Close of the Nineteenth Century* (London: Cressett, 1988 [1913]): 249–60.

[53] George Bernard Shaw, *The Quintessence of Ibsenism* 3rd edn (London: Constable, 1926 [1891]): 5. Shaw named many Ibsen detractors in this book, including theatre critic Clement Scott; see especially 1–6. The critical reception of Ibsen in England, France and Germany is discussed in Simon Williams, 'Ibsen and the theatre 1877–1900', in James McFarlane (ed.), *The Cambridge Companion to Ibsen* (Cambridge University Press, 1994): 165–82; especially 170–1.

[54] Newman, 'The Real Ibsen', 20.

development. They were also naively political. As Newman explained, Ibsen was 'too strenuous a propagandist to be an artistic dramatist or a convincing thinker'.[55] Newman argued that Ibsen's later works were better because they were 'more successful in keeping his own temperament in the background'.[56]

Newman then contradicted anyone who thought Ibsen was 'a great and wise thinker', declaring instead that Ibsen was 'a sombre Puritan turned dramatist'.[57] Despite his reservations over Ibsen's social milieu, intellectual clout and dramatic abilities, Newman appeared to enjoy the playwright's works, even though he thought the local critical reception was wanting: 'Surely it is time that the storm of stupid abuse and indecent epithet and vulgar innuendo died away, and the value and beauty of his work be recognised even here, where sanity in dramatic art finds it as difficult to make an opening for itself as sanity in science or theology'.[58]

The next subject to interest Newman was Rudyard Kipling. Newman considered his works to be over-rated and argued the case in a review of a recently published edition of Kipling's works.[59] When Kipling arrived in London in October 1889 he was something of a literary celebrity, but by the 1940s his reputation had declined. T.S. Eliot, for example, considered Kipling's work to be 'aesthetically disgusting'.[60] The tide of appreciation for Kipling had begun to change in the 1890s, and Newman's essay reflects that shift in appreciation.[61] While acknowledging Kipling's 'brilliancy of observation and his freshness of phrase and manner', Newman saw little talent in Kipling's 'superficial characters' and accused him of 'jingoism towards other nationalities'.[62] Newman continued: 'Mr Kipling's sentiments and emotions are mainly barbaric, and his treatment

---

[55] Newman, 'The Real Ibsen', 29.

[56] Newman, 'The Real Ibsen', 29.

[57] Newman, 'The Real Ibsen', 28.

[58] Newman, 'The Real Ibsen', 37.

[59] 'Mr Kipling's stories', FR, December 1893, 236–48. Newman does not specify the edition under review, though he noted, rather imprecisely, that it contained 'some seven or eight volumes of prose and verse' (p. 236). Given this information, the edition to which Newman most likely refers is the English version of the Indian Railway Library (published in India in 1888) and subsequently published in London by Sampson Low, Marston and Company in 1890–1.

[60] Both quotes are cited in Phillip Mallett (ed.), Kipling Considered (London: The Macmillan Press Ltd., 1989): vii.

[61] Richard Le Gallienne, for example, had supposed Kipling's celebrity status to have seriously declined by 1899, describing his work as jingoistic and chauvinistic. See Le Gallienne, Rudyard Kipling: A Criticism (London and New York: John Lane, The Bodley Head, 1900): 1–2, 128–9, 155–60. A general overview of Kipling's reception in the 1890s is in Jackson, The Eighteen Nineties, 280–96.

[62] Newman, 'Mr Kipling's stories', 238, 238, 242.

of the real emotions of our race is generally either sentimental or brutal'.[63]
Just as Newman criticised Meredith and Ibsen for failing to construct realistic
or authentic personalities in their characters, he similarly accused Kipling
of churning out 'wooden images'.[64] Newman's article on Kipling was hardly
original, however. It presented the same ideas as a previously published essay
by Robertson, who described Kipling and his work as 'an entire adaptation to
ordinary Philistine taste, and a plain incapacity to write a great novel'.[65] It is
hard to understand why Robertson, for the moment, turned a blind eye to the
second-hand work of his protégé. However, in due course—as we shall see—this
ruction over originality and innovation would come to a head. Meanwhile,
Newman turned his attention to writing about music and it was in this small
body of works that he was approaching a semblance of innovation.

Newman wrote three articles on music for the *Free Review*—'Mascagni and
the opera', 'Women and music' and 'The eighteenth-century view of opera'—all
reflecting, to some extent, the content of his articles for the *National Reformer*.
They continue to illustrate Newman's interest in the history of opera, aesthetics and social history. 'Mascagni and the opera' was an offshoot of Newman's
biography of Gluck, which he was writing at the time. The article began with
an explanation of how the fusion of music and poetry had been an age-old
problem for composers of opera, and Newman went on to praise the particularly skilful blending of words and music in Mascagni's opera, *Cavalleria
Rusticana*. He praised the libretto, though he later qualified this opinion.[66]
Newman found the work to be fresh and original and admired its dramatic
expression. He found himself in rare agreement with Eduard Hanslick who
thought that Mascagni, in this work, showed a 'good sense of theatre', especially in the chorus writing and the 'non-lyrical portions'.[67] But Newman was
critical of Mascagni, describing his use of leitmotifs as 'absurd' and condemn-
ing the overture as 'inconceivably ludicrous'.[68] In the remainder of the article
Newman discussed the art of blending poetry and music and once more took
the opportunity to praise Wagner for his 'curious balance' in fusing words with
music. The article ended with Newman describing Mascagni as a 'genius' for

---

[63] Newman, 'Mr Kipling's stories', 246.

[64] Newman, 'Mr Kipling's stories', 238, 244 respectively.

[65] John M. Robertson, 'Literature in 1890', NR, 28 December 1890, 402–3. This article
is discussed in Odin Dekkers, *J.M. Robertson: Rationalist and Literary Critic*, 211–12.

[66] Newman, 'Mascagni and the opera', FR, June 1894, 210–23; 214.

[67] Newman, 'Mascagni and the opera', 214. A brief excerpt detailing Hanslick's veiled
admiration for Mascagni can be found in context of a sarcastic 1894 review of
Engelbert Humperdinck's *Hansel and Gretel* in *Hanslick's Music Criticisms,* ed. and
trans. Henry Pleasants (New York: Dover Publications, Inc., 1978): 296.

[68] Newman, 'Mascagni and the opera', 217.

writing recitative with 'great efficiency', but despite this praise, Newman suggested Mascagni needed a better librettist.[69]

In 'Women and music' Newman argued for a progressive view of supporting the efforts of female composers. Newman was clear that any suggestion of women's inferiority to men was 'nonsense' and lamented the fact that women had been denied university education and the vote.[70] 'Women and music' discussed Havelock Ellis's recently published *Man and Woman*, in which Newman outlined that author's progressive ideas on sexual psychology, especially the argument for the recognition of equality of the sexes.[71] Newman then criticised other studies, including *Woman in Music* in which George Upton claimed music to be the highest expression of the emotions, to which women composers were unable to aspire.[72] Newman delighted in demolishing Upton's argument, describing it as a 'hodge podge of fallacies'.[73] And Newman was ever-hopeful and rational about the prospects for female composers: 'We must wait and see what the musical future will bring forth. We cannot say that women will produce a female Beethoven or Wagner; but we can say that there is scarcely any reason why they should not; and almost every reason why they should'.[74]

'The eighteenth century view of opera' was a continuation of Newman's article on Mascagni and was an extension of issues that were raised in his 1895 biography of Gluck, particularly on the use of recitative and operatic reform. In this article, Newman examined the various social, political and aesthetic conditions that gave rise to nineteenth-century opera (focusing mainly on Italy), but he also discussed a number of eighteenth-century treatises (or what he called 'aesthetic criticisms') by Antonio Planelli, Stefano Arteaga, Francesco Algarotti and John Brown.[75] These writers saw the need for operatic reform in some way or another, he said, and pointed out the ways in which Gluck took up these challenges in *Alceste*. In the second half of the article, Newman returned to the topic of 'Mascagni and the opera', writing in greater detail of

[69] Newman, 'Mascagni and the opera', 217.

[70] Newman, 'Women and music', *FR*, April 1895, 48–62; 48–9.

[71] Havelock Ellis, *Man and Woman: A Study of Human Secondary Sexual Characters* (London: W. Scott, 1894).

[72] George P. Upton, *Woman in Music* (Chicago: A.C. McClurg, 1886).

[73] Newman, 'Women and music', 52.

[74] Newman, 'Women and music', 62.

[75] Antonio Planelli, *Dell' Opera in Musica* (Naples: D. Campo, 1772); Stefano Arteaga, *Le Rivoluzioni del Teatro Musicale Italiano dalla sua origine fino al presente*, 3 vols (Bologna: per la stamperia di Carlo Trenti all'insegna di Sant'Antonio, 1783–8); Francesco Algarotti, *Saggio dell' Opera in Musica* (Livorno: Coltellini, 1763) and John Brown, *Letters Upon the Poetry and Music of the Italian Opera* (1789).

the difficulties faced by composers when balancing lyrical and non-lyrical components of opera. In the context of discussing M. Charles Beauquier's *La Musique et le drame*, 1884, he debated again that recitative ought to be abandoned in future operas.

In 'The eighteenth century view of opera', Newman once more commented about the future of music:

> In England, of course, the opera has been hindered by the forces that have hindered the development of our music as a whole—the enormous hold of Handel and the oratorio upon the musical public (followed by that of Mendelssohn), and the prevailing mediocrity of the ignoble epoch that followed Waterloo, when an uncultured, reactionary, religious middle-class was the main power of the land, loving mediocrity as we now love the abnormal. English opera of any freshness or originality could not well flourish in an atmosphere like this ... A nation that still has the *Messiah* every Christmas, and waits thirty years to hear *Tristan*, is somewhat too far removed from musical intelligence to give birth to new forms of musical art; and under conditions like these it is not surprising that we have either imitated foreign opera or been content with the more pecuniarily successful of its products.[76]

This article is the first that Newman devoted to the improvement of opera in England. His tactic of making sarcastic comments about the level of musical taste as a way of shaming and intimidating his critics and the public was to prevail in the rest of his career.

In most of Newman's articles in the *Free Review* he catalogued the shortcomings of prominent literary figures such as Ibsen and Kipling. But in an article entitled 'Oscar Wilde: a literary appreciation', he did the reverse.[77] While in the opening lines of the Wilde essay Newman said: 'to write down a man whom everyone else is praising is one of the holiest joys that the pursuit of literature can give', nevertheless he championed, rather than criticised, Wilde, who had recently been arrested on suspicion of sodomy.[78] Newman's focus was Wilde's use of paradox, for which the author had become particularly famous. These included 'the three qualifications of a great critic are unfairness, insincerity, and irrationality' and 'the remarkable increase in London fogs during the last ten years is entirely due to the impressionist painters'.[79] Newman was amused by these paradoxes, writing that 'I do not think I am overstating the case when

[76] Newman, 'The eighteenth century view of opera', *UMFR*, June 1898, 262–74; 262–3.

[77] Newman, 'Oscar Wilde', 193–206.

[78] Newman, 'Oscar Wilde', 193.

[79] Quoted in Newman, 'Oscar Wilde', 196–7.

I say that his is one of the clearest and soundest intellects in England to-day'.[80]
He wrote that his aim in the article was 'to call attention to lesser-known qualities of Mr Wilde's genius, and to show my readers, if I can, that he is not the
lackadaisical dandy they have always imagined him to be'.[81] As in many of his
essays for both the *Free Review* and the *National Reformer*, Newman liked to
attack stereotypes and the status quo.

Nietzsche was another figure Newman complained had fallen foul of public
appreciation.[82] Newman argued, in an extremely patronising way, that

> Lagging behind the intellectual movements of Europe in philosophy as in
> everything else, England is just now beginning to hear of the existence of
> Friedrich Nietzsche. A little while ago it was Ibsen who, after being well known
> on the Continent for many years, was treated by the English as if he had just
> begun his literary career ... the fact remains that nine hundred and ninety-nine
> out of every thousand Englishmen are just beginning to be aware of the exist-
> ence of a writer on philosophy who had a large following on the Continent.[83]

Indeed, on Nietzsche's death in 1900, the *Times* could only muster the
briefest of obituaries. This consisted largely of a potted biography and concluded that 'his works were certainly not taken very seriously in England'.[84]
Though Newman's article was designed as an introduction to Nietzsche's
work, it was also a scathing critique of Max Nordau's study of Nietzsche from
1892, *Degeneration*.[85] In this book, Nordau had written a long and hateful
appraisal of Nietzsche's philosophy, depicting him as 'a madman, with flash-
ing eyes, wild gestures, and foaming mouth'.[86] Nordau described Nietzsche's
philosophy as 'dogmatic' and his writing style as 'turgid', and was scornful that
Germany considered Nietzsche a philosopher.[87] Newman thought Nordau's
book was 'too serious, too irritable, too German', and criticised Nordau for
pushing Nietzsche 'to an absurd extreme'.[88] But Newman's article was equally

---

[80] Newman, 'Oscar Wilde', 200.

[81] Newman, 'Oscar Wilde', 198.

[82] Ernest Newman, 'Friedrich Nietzsche', 113–22.

[83] Newman, 'Friedrich Nietzsche', 113.

[84] 'Professor Nietzsche', Unsigned obituary, the *Times*, 27 August 1900, 4.

[85] Max Nordau, *Entartung* (Berlin: C. Duncker, 1892). The first English translation,
   Degeneration, was published in London in 1895 by Heinemann.

[86] Max Nordau, *Degeneration* trans. George L. Mosse (New York: Howard Fertig,
   1968): 416.

[87] Max Nordau, *Degeneration*, 461, 472.

[88] Newman, 'Friedrich Nietzsche', 114.

scurrilous, describing the philosopher as 'obviously an insane type' and 'naïve', especially in his lack of appreciation for Wagner.[89]

One of Newman's lifelong strategies as a critic was to mediate polarised opinion, to debunk one or both sides of the argument, and to then put forward his own interpretation, criticising his readers for their ignorance in the process. This technique was clearly operating in the articles in the *Free Review*. In particular, the essays on Ibsen, Kipling, Nietzsche and music either sneered at contemporary opinion and writers, or patronised and insulted the reader's literary and music taste (in the case of Ibsen, they did both). Moreover, in his work on Ibsen and Kipling, Newman's views were far from innovative.[90] For his grandstanding and supercilious writing, Newman was soon to land himself in hot water.

❧ *Newman* contra *Robertson: Disputes over Innovation*

The trouble brewing between Robertson and Newman in the early years of the *Free Review* eventually led to the pair's dramatic falling-out between late 1897 and April 1898. The dispute was fuelled by objections from some readers about the quality of Newman's articles. Robertson apparently agreed though he appears at first to have kept these criticisms to himself while continuing to publish the work of his protégé. Newman, though, had developed an inflated view of his critical abilities, setting him on a collision path with Robertson. Both men were to accuse each other's work of lacking insight and critical acuity.

The first sign of trouble between the men is evident in Newman's review of Robertson's book *Buckle and his Critics* in March 1896.[91] Henry Buckle's *Introduction to the History of Civilisation in England* (published in two volumes in 1857 and 1861) had received a mixed critical reception.[92] For the freethinkers it was a monument to, and a model of, modern history and sociology and

---

[89] Newman, 'Friedrich Nietzsche', 115, 122.

[90] On a brief history of Ibsen reception in England see Clarence R. Decker, *The Victorian Conscience* (Westport, CT: Greenwood Press, 1952): 115–29.

[91] Ernest Newman, 'Buckle and his critics', *FR*, March 1896, 600–15. Robertson's book was called *Buckle and his Critics: A Study in Sociology* (London: Swan Sonnenschein & Co., 1895).

[92] Henry Buckle, *History of Civilisation in England*, 2 vols (vol. I: London: John W. Parker & Son, 1857; vol. II: London: Parker, Son & Bourn, 1861).

Robertson had written in defence of it.[93] Newman began with a sympathetic reading of Robertson's book, but then he turned on its author:

> Mr Robertson hits hard and hits often … And I myself who, having evil passions of my own, like to see other people possessed with the same spirit, even I am compelled to admit that Mr Robertson might have done his literary murders more gracefully. Murder may be made a fine art if it is done beautifully, but wholesome clubbing and ripping of your victims offends the aesthetic eye, even if one has not the slightest sympathy with the murdered men. After reading two or three hundred pages of Mr Robertson's book I retired to rest, only to be haunted by the memory of the scenes I had passed through. The night air seemed red with blood; the groans of dying men filled my ears; I felt somewhat as a special correspondent might feel at the spectacle of the Armenian atrocities.[94]

Robertson let the criticism pass without comment.

Six months later, Newman took Robertson to task a second time, albeit in a rather indirect way, in an article entitled 'The philosopher at the music hall'.[95] Robertson deplored the music hall (as we will see below), but Newman loved it and exploited this difference of their social and aesthetic sensibilities in order to hurl yet more abuse in Robertson's direction:

> The evil reputation which the music-hall has acquired comes, of course, as in all similar cases, from the super-virtuous Puritans who have never been inside a music-hall in their lives; just as the outcry against alcohol comes from those who have never drunk, and the outcry against tobacco from those who have never smoked. Some of these have never been inside any theatrical building, while others are assiduous haunters of the 'legitimate' drama, though they turn up their noses at the music-hall.[96]

Newman continued to provoke Robertson, claiming that 'the music-hall is not respectable, and the Philistine dearly loves his respectability' and 'if our respectable Philistine would only allow one of his lady friends to take him to

---

[93] George Bernard Shaw, for example, was high in his praise of Buckle's book claiming it to be, alongside Marx's *Capital* and Ruskin's *Modern Painters*, 'mind-changing property'. Shaw's quote is from 'Beethoven's *Unsterbliche Geliebte*', *The World*, 1 November 1893, reproduced in Dan H. Laurence (ed.), *Shaw's Music: The Complete Musical Criticism of Bernard Shaw*, vol. III (London: The Bodley Head, 1981): 18. For further on the scope of Buckle's book see Ian Hesketh, *The Science of History in Victorian Britain: Making the Past Speak* (London: Pickering & Chatto, 2011).

[94] Newman, 'Buckle and his Critics', 600.

[95] Newman, 'The philosopher at the music hall', *FR*, September 1896, 653–8.

[96] Newman, 'The philosopher at the music hall', 653.

a music-hall some evening, he would really learn something about art'.[97] This was nasty criticism, but things were about to get much worse.

Newman's most ferocious attack on Robertson was published in *UMFR* in December 1897.[98] Entitled 'An open letter', the article was a review of Robertson's *New Essays Towards a Critical Method* (hereafter *New Essays*), published earlier that year.[99] *New Essays* was a follow-up to Robertson's book *Essays Towards a Critical Method* (hereafter *Essays*), published in 1889.[100] These books grew out of Robertson's dissatisfaction with the bias, subjective opinion and inconsistent judgement in contemporary literary criticism, especially book reviews. Both Robertson's books contained various chapters on individual writers, all previously published.

Robertson's aim, like that of many of his contemporaries mentioned in chapter 2, was to rescue criticism from 'the level of random self-expression', to arguments that reasoned 'from a common ground to a new ground, on a basis of fairly proved facts, and set up a basis for a certain amount of rational agreement'.[101] Moreover, Robertson wanted to comment on the unchecked and uncritical acceptance of personal opinion in criticism.[102] One of Robertson's biggest complaints in both *Essays* and *New Essays* was directed at the belletrist.[103] According to Robertson, the belletrist had become a specialist, who lived in a rarefied world:

> It [the *belles lettres* genre] grows enamoured not merely of art for art's sake, thus narrowing the critic's activity, but of all the waste matter which is a mere record of artistic failure, thus warping his judgment. Tenderly conning every vestige of old conventions, devoutly ready to take in earnest every new deliverance which assumes the old manner, he becomes a specialist in verbiage, a kind of artistic Talmudist, living in a world of word-begotten thoughts, the mere spectra of ideas.[104]

---

[97] Newman, 'The philosopher at the music hall', 653, 654. This criticism of Robertson might imply that he was a flirt.

[98] Ernest Newman, 'An open letter', *UMFR*, December 1897, 397–409.

[99] John M. Robertson, *New Essays Towards a Critical Method* (London: John Lane, 1897).

[100] John M. Robertson, *Essays Towards a Critical Method* (London: T. Fisher Unwin, 1889).

[101] Robertson, *New Essays*, vii, 21.

[102] Robertson, *New Essays*, 18.

[103] See Robertson, *Essays*, 39–41 for a more detailed exposition.

[104] Robertson, *Essays*, 87.

By the time Robertson had written the introductory chapter to *New Essays* he had less to say about the belletrists, but his commentary on their work remained harsh, describing them as insensitive, ignorant and incompetent.[105]

Robertson proposed that the wayward criticism of the belletrist needed method to stabilize it. He broadly conceived what this might entail:

> Assuming the general position that all literature is the expression of human rela-
> tions to or notions of things, then, we may say that it is discussible under three
> aspects: (1) its account of things actual or things imagined, this including all
> correction or impeachment of any kind of misstatement; (2) its presentation of
> the writer's mind; (3) the charm or merit of its expression in respect of language.
> Equivalent heads would be: What the writer sees or thinks; what he is; and how
> he speaks; or, yet again, (1) the objective import, (2) the subjective import, and
> (3) the medium ... Now, on each of the three heads of the division there is obvi-
> ous possibility of variation of opinion in terms of the three aforesaid forces of
> bias, expertness, and lessoning.[106]

Although Newman had 'nothing to say against the majority of the essays' he was nevertheless critical of the comments on Shelley and Poe, arguing they were tainted by Robertson's 'personal equation', or subjective opinion.[107] Newman was not an admirer of Shelley's poetry, but he could not accept Robertson's judgement that some of the work was 'weak', given the high esteem in which the poet was held.[108] Newman once more lashed out at his mentor:

> You assume far too readily that the Shelleyite is a hysterical emotionalist, and
> that 'the critic' objects to Shelley on the grounds of the higher reason. That is
> exactly the point to be proved. A great many people are no more crude emotion-
> alists than you are; and the real explanation of their liking a poet whom you do
> not like is, as I have already expressed it, that they are they and you are you.[109]

In Newman's opinion, Robertson was allowing personal taste to cloud his judgement on Shelley, and this was the kind of criticism Robertson's *Essays* and *New Essays* sought to combat. Newman went so far as to describe Robertson's essay on Shelley as 'the worst thing I ever read of yours', claiming it contained 'some very bad blunders of taste', and was therefore 'deplorable' and 'uncon-vincing'.[110] Newman found he could not take Robertson's method seriously

[105] Robertson, *New Essays*, 39.
[106] Robertson, *Essays*, 71–2.
[107] Newman, 'An open letter', 397.
[108] Newman, 'An open letter', 402–3.
[109] Newman, 'An open letter', 403.
[110] Newman, 'An open letter', 401, 401, 402 and 402 respectively.

because Robertson himself was as unscientific and irrational as the writers he criticised.

Newman was especially upset that Robertson disparaged the belletrist, and fell for Robertson's taunt, taking the criticism personally:

> Let me beg you to stop writing in terms of such contempt about the lover of belles letters ... What I protest against is your habit of using the terms belles letters and belletrist as if they were opprobrious epithets ... You say nasty things about the belletrist ... I want you to see that your contempt for belletrists is simply due to your peculiar temperament, which tends towards the real rather than the ideal ... So refrain, I implore you *cher maître*, from snapping at belletrists as if they were an inferior race.[111]

In his final swipe at Robertson's work, Newman ridiculed his mentor for claiming music's aesthetics properties were similar to poetry. While Newman was irritated by Edgar Allen Poe's practice of adding part-repeated lines to his poems, Robertson saw things differently: 'there are some of us ... who think the culminating music [of Poe's poems] is closely analogous to effects produced a hundred times by Mozart and Schubert and Beethoven'.[112] Newman was not convinced, claiming 'I really never heard a worse argument. The analogy with music is absurd' and continued, telling Robertson 'your rhythmical and musical sense in verse is satisfied by devices that appear to some of us merely childish'.[113] Fuelling the debate, Newman switched from anger to sarcasm, claiming, for instance, that 'France and myself have done much for you,' implying that he, Sainte-Beuve, Hippolyte Taine and Emile Hennequin—critics on which Robertson often wrote favourably—were intellectually superior.[114] But Newman saved his most pompous outburst until the very last sentence of his letter: 'all I hope in conclusion, is that you will dedicate your next volume of "Newest Essays Towards" to me, in gratitude for the *katharsis* of your method'.[115]

Robertson's reply to Newman was printed as an open letter the following March.[116] He defended his stance on Shelley, the belletrists, Poe and his music analogies, claiming that Newman had misunderstood him or misconstrued his ideas. Robertson's counter-attacks were concise and reasonable, but he

---

[111] Newman, 'An open letter', 398–401, passim.

[112] Robertson, 'Edgar Allen Poe [part 2]', *Our Corner* 6/4 (October 1885): 204–13; 211.

[113] Newman, 'An open letter', 405, 406.

[114] Newman, 'An open letter', 409.

[115] Newman, 'An open letter', 409.

[116] John M. Robertson, 'Concerning mares' nests': an open letter, *UMFR*, March 1898, 611–16.

also made some extremely critical comments about Newman, accusing him of writing 'shoddy satire' and for displaying a 'neurotic' personality.[117] Robertson chastised Newman for 'fluffing and shouting and kicking' and suggested Newman ought to be 'a little more French in his manner of criticism'.[118] Not done with criticising Newman's style, Robertson got personal. He accused Newman of 'music-hall-ism', describing his review of *New Essays* as having been 'delivered in your best music-hall manner'.[119] Further taunting Newman, he also asked, 'are they talking that way in the music-halls?'[120] To counter Newman's misplaced sense of intellectual superiority, Robertson addressed him sarcastically as 'most seraphical doctor' and 'O sage'.[121] To emphasise (or indeed, restore) the intellectual pecking order of the two men's relationship, Robertson then addressed Newman as '*cher élève*'.[122]

Robertson's open letter tells us more about his relationship with Newman. He indicated that he had received complaints about the quality of Newman's work in the *Free Review*, exclaiming that 'people have repeatedly held me responsible for your escapades; and when I have pleaded your youth and your wayward temperament in exculpation they have accused me of favouritism'.[123] Although Robertson praised Newman's knowledge of music as 'exceptional', he wrote 'you don't know much about poetry', and that 'you are only one of thousands who illustrate the fact that musical culture and poetical culture require different things'.[124] At the end of his rejoinder, Robertson failed to see any humour in Newman's letter, describing it as 'bad form'.[125] Newman's hostility to Robertson was possibly ignited by some recent and unwelcome advice Robertson had given him, which Robertson aired in his final sentence: 'remember, then, in conclusion, my recent advice to work your brain more equably, not in spurts of overwork alternating with hand-to-mouth composition. Do not give me the pain of seeing my ablest pupil turn out a muddle-head. I can forgive you anything save that'.[126] But forgiveness was not yet on the horizon.

---

[117] Robertson, 'Concerning mares' nests', 612.

[118] Robertson, 'Concerning mares' nests', 615.

[119] Robertson, 'Concerning mares' nests', 611.

[120] Robertson, 'Concerning mares' nests', 612.

[121] Robertson, 'Concerning mares' nests', 613, 614.

[122] Robertson, 'Concerning mares' nests', 611.

[123] Robertson, 'Concerning mares' nests', 612.

[124] Robertson, 'Concerning mares' nests', 614.

[125] Robertson, 'Concerning mares' nests', 616.

[126] Robertson, 'Concerning mares' nests', 616.

In February 1898 Newman had written to Bertram Dobell about his clash with Robertson exclaiming, 'I have seen a proof of Robertson's reply to my open letter. He has taken it all very seriously, lost his temper completely, and been rather insulting and personal'.[127] And so Newman planned a second letter that was published in the April 1898 issue of *UMFR*.[128] It began in strained humour: Newman suggested that the air in Boston (where Robertson was travelling at the time), and low quality American journalism, had infected Robertson's brain and was the cause of the ill-tempered reply to Newman's initial letter. After the first page of the letter, Newman abandoned his attempt at humour and gave a rambling defence of his original complaints. By and large this rejoinder is a squabble over minutiae, although there is a desperate outburst from Newman on the third and fourth page of his rejoinder:

> Why will you persist in this cocky assumption that if anyone differs from you on a question of poetry, *you* are the cool, impartial critic, and *he* a poor half-organised being, painfully stumbling towards the full critical light? ... You affect to teach me what the personal equation means in aesthetics—wasting your time, as usual, in very dreary *badinage*, instead of trying to understand my criticism ... If you go on like this you will have Nordau citing you in his next book as a type of egomania. I suppose in five years from now you will be alleging that you invented the atmosphere ... Really, my dear Robertson, don't you think you could advance culture a little more, and waste less of my time, your own, and the readers', if you allowed a slight measure of capacity to those who disagree with you?[129]

If Robertson was an overbearing and opinionated mentor it is no wonder Newman was so angry. Clearly, Newman felt stifled by Robertson, feeling forever destined to be the pupil of the relationship, never to be acknowledged by Robertson as an equal and gifted writer in his own right, and forever to dwell in Robertson's shadow. The frustration and hurt expressed by both men in the articles are palpable—Newman was angry with Robertson for his pig-headedness and self-righteousness, while Robertson clearly felt betrayed by his protégé. In Newman's closing remarks, he accused Robertson of pseudo-science—that most pejorative term—and severed their association:

> A few haphazard observations ... are quite insufficient to justify your printing your pseudo-scientific opinions about my purely personal affairs ... These things

---

[127] MSS Dobell 38484–5, 22 February 1898.

[128] Ernest Newman, 'The substance and the shadow, or the ethics of controversy: being a brief epistolary sermon suggested by a recent American blizzard', *UMFR*, April 1898, 82–90.

[129] Newman, 'The substance and the shadow', 85–6.

should be kept for private, not public, correspondence. However, the thermal conditions of Boston may account for some of the fault of your letter. The best of men have their lapses. *Au revoir*.[130]

It is remarkable that Newman chastised Robertson for publicly airing opinions on personal affairs when it was Newman who started it! Eventually the men brokered a truce and their friendship was restored. This episode, however, indicates a shift in their relationship. Newman was growing more independent of Robertson. He needed him less for intellectual stimulation and, from 1895, Newman did not need to rely on Robertson to get his work published. However, the significance of this intellectual duelling lies in Newman's struggle to find his own voice and niche. It also shows that Robertson was most likely doing Newman favours by publishing sub-standard work. The episode exposes Newman as a sometimes temperamental and insecure figure whose literary criticism was not as robust as he thought it to be.

❧ *Newman's Contribution to Freethought Literature*

Newman's writing in the *National Reformer* is not the stuff of the regular news-reporting journalist: these are serious-minded essays published in a journal that considered itself highbrow. Newman's essays on religion and society, as well as science and pseudo-science, were clearly from the pen of a zealous, and often angry, atheist and freethinker, who appeared troubled by the strangle-hold he feared religion still had on the world around him. Solace appears to have come from the works of Comte, Mill and Spencer, whose visions for the future constituted a secular utopia. Newman's literary criticism may not have been particularly searching, but he was viewing his subjects through the lens of Darwinism and other works on theories of heredity and evolution. His contempt for sentimentality in novels may imply a reaction against aestheticism, especially when he attempted a reading of Amiel's psychology that was critical of the poet's introspection and asceticism. His work on Weismann's germ-plasm theory was an opportunity for Newman to write about music, perhaps in an attempt to make his contribution to the *Free Review* unique. None of the other contributors wrote on the subject and he could ponder the possibility of further work in the area of psychology. On music, Newman provided confronting defences of Wagner and Wagnerism and confidently articulated his and others' positions on aesthetics, even when made from the comfort of his armchair. As in the case of the Weismann article, Newman spent considerable time and energy exploring other writers' efforts on particular subjects before launching his own views on the matter. His explanation of music and poetry

---

[130] Newman, 'The substance and the shadow', 90.

as different kinds of thought exhibited a clear, rational mind seeking to distil complex issues simply. Newman's attack on contemporary music critics sees his truculent tone in play as well as showing how his ideals of well-tempered criticism were at odds with the ideals that Robertson had propagated.

Newman's work in the *Free Review* was not as dogmatic as his work in the *National Reformer*; his adoration for Spencer and evolutionary theory were much less evident in the *Free Review* essays, and he barely referred to Comte and Mill. His writing style in the *Free Review* was clearer and more cogent than his essays for the *National Reformer*, though his tone and register sometimes left much to be desired. Newman was aware that he could be belligerent, at one point writing in 'Nietzsche and Wagner' that 'I do not, of course, try to disguise even from myself that the tone of my former article [on Nietzsche] was insufferably supercilious; I know that it was full of that flippant impertinence which is so characteristic of me and so unbecoming to anyone'.[131] Such expression also flies in the face of contemporary attempts for criticism to be less bellicose and more objective and rational. Perhaps Newman was trying to imitate, or parody, George Bernard Shaw's witty and urbane writing style, only to fall far short in doing so; unlike Shaw, Newman's writing was frequently patronizing and pompous.

In the eyes of Robertson, Newman's articles on music were his most innovative work. His article on Weismann, in particular, was unique, for Newman appears to have been the only writer in the long debate over germ-plasm theory to take Weismann to task over his Mozart hypothesis. Newman's entry into long-running debates over Wagner, musical evolution and aesthetics provided new copy for many freethought readers, looking into the relationship between music and poetry in operatic history, a theme that was taken up later in *Gluck and the Opera* (1895). Newman's writings on Nietzsche and women in music would have struck many readers as fresh, either because the topic was uncommon in English writing (as in Nietzsche reception) or because it was a subject of much contention (the championing of women composers). Newman's interest in opera, evident in his essays on Wagner and Mascagni (including his commentary on the fate and fortunes of English musical criticism and opera), was to stay with him all his life, especially relating to the quality of librettos and the ways in which composers used texts—especially English ones—when writing new national works.

The *Free Review* was the only freethought periodical in which music was discussed in any detail; it might even be suggested that music was one of the journal's strong points. Robertson himself had only published one article on music. 'The music of the future' (1884) expressed his surprise at the variety of

---

[131] Newman, 'Nietzsche and Wagner', *FR*, December 1896, 268–75; 268.

opinions in the musical press over Wagner and speculated on the composer's position in music in the future.[132] Of all the arts, the academic freethinkers appeared interested mostly in literature (or at least this was what Robertson promoted) and articles on music would have been a novelty for the readers of this journal.

It is easy to dismiss Newman's work in the freethought press for its over-zeal-ousness, and sometimes naive and homespun critical interpretations. However, Newman's early articles demonstrate a strong intellectual engagement with a large array of European literature, the ability to dissect others' work in exacting detail, and the dexterity of successfully casting an argument, even if it meant belittling his colleagues and readers in the process. All of these skills made Newman an erudite, convincing and sometimes fierce critic, especially when, in 1897, he wrote his most successful work as a freethinker, *Pseudo-Philosophy at the end of the Nineteenth Century*, the subject of the next chapter.

---

[132] John M. Robertson, 'The music of the future', *Progress* 4 (December 1884): 278–84.

CHAPTER 4

A Rationalist Manifesto:
Pseudo-Philosophy at the end of the Nineteenth Century, 1897

I N 1964, the music critic Philip Hope-Wallace committed to print some unsavoury rumours about Newman's past: 'I once met an owl who solemnly assured me that Newman was an ex-criminal with a "closed chapter" in his life'.[1] This closed chapter was the publication of *Pseudo-Philosophy at the end of the Nineteenth Century* (1897), which brought Newman into contact with a shady publisher and appears to have dashed his chances of receiving a British knighthood.[2] Not even lobbying by William Emrys Williams (chief editor at Penguin Books, 1936–1965) to have Newman admitted to the Order of the Companions of Honour on his eightieth birthday came to anything.[3] The stench of association from this controversial episode in Newman's life hung over the rest of his career.

Newman wrote *Pseudo-Philosophy* during his time on the *Free Review* (discussed in the previous chapter), under the pseudonym of Hugh Mortimer Cecil. In the course of the book's production, Newman unwittingly became associated with a criminal who owned the imprint under which the book was published, the University Press, Watford. There is no evidence that Newman broke the law or was a criminal. Nevertheless, the publication of *Pseudo-Philosophy* implicated Newman in a case of imprint theft and, indirectly, the suicide of a publisher.

Pseudo-Philosophy is an extreme example of Newman's rationalist ideology and capacity for hard-hitting criticism. Despite its overwhelmingly positive

---

[1] Philip Hope-Wallace, 'E.N.', *MT*, 104/1450 (1 December 1963): 870–1.

[2] Newman, however, was awarded many prestigious honours, including foreign knighthoods. He was made an honorary associate of the Rationalist Press Association in 1925 (other recipients included Albert Einstein in 1934 and Sigmund Freud in 1938) and was admitted to the Order of Merit of the Federal Republic of Germany (Commander Class) in 1958. In 1959 he was appointed to the Finnish Order of a Knight of the White Rose (First Class) and made an honorary Doctor of Letters in the University of Exeter.

[3] Harold Hobson, Phillip Knightley and Leonard Russell, *The Pearl of Days: An Intimate Memoir of The Sunday Times, 1822–1972* (London: Hamish Hamilton, 1972): 142.

critical reception, which brought Newman considerable respect in freethought circles, it was Newman's last major freethought work. The book was a fierce critique of three recently published, and hugely popular but conservative, books (discussed below) that, amongst other agendas, questioned evolutionary theory and the idea of progress.

G.A. Singer, the *Free Review*'s second editor, commissioned Newman to write *Pseudo-Philosophy* (John M. Robertson had bequeathed the journal to Singer in 1895 while he pursued a career in politics).[4] Singer's real name, however, was George Ferdinand Springmühl von Weissenfeld. He was a criminal who, under yet another name, Dr Roland de Villiers, was the proprietor of Watford University Press, which later changed its name to University Press Limited, London. By April 1897, Watford University Press had taken control of the *Free Review*, renaming it *University Magazine and Free Review*, and had announced the publication of Newman's *Pseudo-Philosophy*.

There are conflicting accounts over the establishment of Watford University Press whose address in 1897 was in Bedford Row, London. According to Vincent Broome, Watford University Press was to publish Havelock Ellis's *Sexual Inversion* under the name first proposed for the publishing house, Wilson & Macmillan, but Ellis was uneasy with this arrangement. It had the potential to be 'confused with that … well-known and existing company [Macmillan] whose reputation was irreproachable'.[5] According to Broome, the publisher changed its name to Watford University Press to make the enterprise appear more scholastic and less commercial, even though there was no university in Watford.[6]

The circumstances through which von Weissenfeld came into contact with the freethinkers are unknown.[7] He was an enigmatic individual. The following account, from John Sweeney, the detective at Scotland Yard who pursued him, gives a glimpse of von Weissenfeld's character and the extent to which he managed to deceive those with whom he came into contact:

[4] Odin Dekkers, 'Walter Matthew Gallichan: fiction and freethought in the 1890s', *English Studies* 83/5 (2002): 407–22.

[5] Vincent Broome, *Havelock Ellis: Philosopher of Sex: A Biography* (London: Routledge & Kegan Paul, 1979): 96.

[6] In his biography of Ellis, Arthur Calder-Marshall writes that Ellis chose WUP over Wilson & Macmillan, suggesting Calder-Marshall (or Ellis) was unaware that both company names belonged to the same enterprise. Calder-Marshall asserts that *Sexual Inversion* was published by WUP, but it was, in fact, published under the imprint Wilson & Macmillan. However, the 1900 edition was published under the WUP imprint. See Arthur Calder-Marshall, *Havelock Ellis* (London: Rupert Hart-Davis, 1959).

[7] See Dekkers, 'Walter Matthew Gallichan', 419.

Weissenfeld … was born in Germany. His father was an eminent judge, and he was brought up in luxury. He matriculated at Giessen, where he passed all his examinations with highest attainable honours, obtaining degrees in science, medicine and literature. He married a German lady of good family, who lived with him till his death. He became estranged from his father through sundry peccadilloes, and finally fled the country after forging and uttering cheques and a number of negotiable securities. He settled in England in 1880, under his own name, and made a living by swindling until he was hauled up at the police court, and sentenced to twelve months' hard labour for perjury, amongst other indictments. On his exit from prison he and his wife disappeared, to emerge as Mr and Mrs Wild, who made a fairly good living by various questionable industries. In 1885 he became bankrupt, and subsequently a warrant was issued for his arrest for fraud. This warrant was never executed. Later, he registered the Concentrated Produce Company, Limited, inventing various names under which he appeared as shareholders, managers and directors, all in one … In 1891 he promoted a company called the Branders Distillers Company, Limited. By the issuing of a glowing prospectus, giving photographs of various vineyards, none of which belonged to the company, he managed to get thousands of pounds subscribed … His aliases were now innumerable, and to avoid confusing the identity of the various characters he had invented, he kept a register in which he entered every alias he used, together with its own specific signature.[8]

In addition to de Villiers and von Weissenfeld, other names he assumed included Winter, Willing, Macmillan, M'Corquodale, von Jarchow, Perrier, Grant, Wilson and Davies.[9] By the time he set up University Press Limited, von Weissenfeld had accumulated plenty of experience as a trickster. The law finally caught up with him in 1902: he was arrested in Cambridge, whereupon he committed suicide by piercing his skin with poison discharged from a bracelet on his wrist.[10]

When Newman finished writing his biography of Gluck in 1895 (which is discussed in the next chapter), he contacted his publisher Bertram Dobell to

---

[8] Francis Richards (ed.), John Sweeney, *At Scotland Yard: Being the Experiences during Twenty-Seven Years' Service of John Sweeney* (London: Grant Richards, 1904): 191–2.

[9] John Sweeney, *At Scotland Yard*, 194.

[10] John Sweeney, *At Scotland Yard*, 195–6. Sweeney's account of von Weissenfeld is one of few accounts of von Weissenfeld and Watford University Press. See also Dekkers, 'Walter Matthew Gallichan', 417–19; Arthur Calder-Marshall, *Havelock Ellis*, 157–72; and Vincent Broome, *Havelock Ellis*, 96–108. A variant of the method of suicide is given in Phyllis Grosskurth, *Havelock Ellis: A Biography* (New York, Alfred Knopf, 1980): 203: 'When handcuffed, he called for a glass of water, took a few drops, and dropped dead'.

ask if he knew anyone in London who would be interested in offering him further work.[11] Newman was keen to write full-time and was desperate to clear an unspecified financial debt that was causing him considerable stress. Dobell replied to Newman, indicating that Matthew Gallichan (a fellow free-thinker and critic) had mentioned Newman's plight to a sympathetic Dr de Villiers.[12] After contacting de Villiers, Newman was commissioned to 'do a book on Drummond, Kidd & Balfour', payment for which would be a very respectable £50, payable on receipt of the completed typescript.[13] By the end of September 1896, that is, in just over seven months, Newman had fulfilled his commission.[14]

In the meantime, however, Gallichan had published an article in the July issue of the *Free Review* that was deeply critical of Kidd, Drummond and Balfour (amongst others).[15] It is possible that Gallichan's essay was published as a teaser for *Pseudo-Philosophy*. It is also possible that Gallichan had wanted to write a book along the lines of *Pseudo-Philosophy* but, for whatever reason, passed this task to Newman who was just as well qualified to write it. In 1895 and 1896, as president of the Liverpool Branch of the National Secular Society, Newman delivered a series of lectures, some of which covered the same topics that appeared in *Pseudo-Philosophy*: 'Mr Balfour's *Foundations of Belief*' (7 and 8 April, and 8 September, 1895); 'Social evolution' (15 March 1896); and 'The evolution of humanity' (22 March 1896).[16] Even though Newman had material to work with (assuming he re-used copy from his lectures), writing a book in such a short period while working full-time was no mean feat. Newman had mentioned Kidd, Drummond and Balfour in an article on Nietzsche in the *Free Review* on 1 May 1896, so by that time, some parts of the book would have been formed in his mind.[17]

Pseudo-Philosophy at the end of the Nineteenth Century contained the long sub-title, 'Volume I: An irrational trio: Kidd—Drummond—Balfour'. Multiple

---

[11] Correspondence from Newman to Dobell, 5 February and 9 February 1896, MSS Dobell 38484–5.

[12] Correspondence from Newman to Dobell, 11 February 1896, MSS Dobell 38484–5.

[13] MSS Dobell, 21 February 1896.

[14] Correspondence from Newman to Dobell, 24 September 1897, MSS Dobell 38484–5.

[15] Democritus (pseud. Matthew Gallichan), 'Biology with a snuffle', *FR*, 1 July 1896, 337–53. Newman has been erroneously attributed as the author of this article in an unsigned piece, 'Mr Ernest Newman', *MH*, 1 May 1912, 131. Odin Dekkers has confirmed that the attribution to Newman is wrong: personal communication, 30 November 2005.

[16] See Appendix for a complete list of lectures and the dates and places of their presentation.

[17] Ernest Newman, 'Friedrich Nietzsche', *FR*, May 1896, 113–22.

volumes (on other irrationalists) were intended but were never published. As Matthew Gallichan explained to Bertram Dobell in a letter on 19 April 1896, 'Mr G.A. Singer has offered me a very fair sum for a book on the social question, to be signed with the pseudonym as Newman's volume of Balfour, Drummond and Kidd. It's his intention to issue four books under one pen-name.'[18]

The book was written to discredit three recently published books that offended freethought sensibilities and Newman's own intellectual proclivities: Benjamin Kidd's *Social Evolution* (1894), Henry Drummond's *Ascent of Man* (1894) and A.J. Balfour's *The Foundations of Belief* (1895).[19] These books repulsed Newman because they railed against everything he stood for: rationalism, evolution, scientific method and the high value placed on social progress. The ideologies operating in these three books were a far cry from the utopian and secular future as promised decades earlier by such writers as Herbert Spencer. His work, *Social Statics: The Conditions Essential to Human Happiness* (1850), Newman had most likely read, and made the work of these so-called irrationalists seem especially retrograde. Yet the books had made a significant impact and Newman rightly claimed that each of them had 'at the time of their publication caused a literary sensation in England and the United States'.[20]

Kidd's book was first published in February 1894 and reprinted nine times by November 1895.[21] Drummond's book was destined to be a success as his previous work, *Natural Law in the Spiritual World* (1883), had sold 70,000 copies in five years, reaching a sales total of 120,000 copies by 1897.[22] Balfour's book had reached its sixth edition by 1896 and was later translated into 'at least ten languages' including Arabic and Chinese.[23] The late nineteenth-century public devoured books that counter-argued Darwin and theories of evolution

---

[18] Correspondence from Gallichan to Dobell, 19 April 1896, MSS Dobell 38463.

[19] Benjamin Kidd, *Social Evolution* (London and New York: Macmillan and Co., 1894); Henry Drummond, *The Lowell Lectures on the Ascent of Man* (London: Hodder and Stoughton, 1894) and A. J. Balfour, *The Foundations of Belief, Being Notes Introductory to the Study of Theology* (London, New York, Bombay: Longmans, Green, and Co., 1895).

[20] Hugh Mortimer Cecil (pseud. Ernest Newman), *Pseudo-Philosophy at the end of the Nineteenth Century* (Watford: University Press, 1897): 1.

[21] Kidd, *Social Evolution*, 1895 edition, vi.

[22] Henry Drummond, *Natural Law in the Spiritual World* (London: Hodder and Stoughton, 1883). These figures are cited in Peter Morton, *The Vital Science: Biology and the Literary Imagination, 1860–1900* (London, Boston: Allen & Unwin, 1984). This figure of 120,000 is given in chapter 4, note 17, 114–15.

[23] Balfour, *Foundations of Belief*, sixth edition, iii; D.P. Crook, *Benjamin Kidd: Portrait of a Social Darwinist* (Cambridge: Cambridge University Press, 1984): 1.

and heredity; cynicism about the promise of science was rife and these books provided fodder for such doubters, most of whom were Christians.[24] Newman was appalled by the content, as, undoubtedly, were many of his freethought confreres.

In his book, *Social Evolution*, Kidd attacked the writings of three of Newman's heroes: Comte, Mill and Spencer. He described Comte's positivism as a 'failure', Mill's utilitarianism as 'unduly narrowed and egotistical', and Spencer's synthetic philosophy as 'unsatisfactory'.[25] Moreover, Kidd ridiculed doctrines of unbelief, especially 'like those of Mr Charles Bradlaugh' and argued that widespread interest in atheism was now waning in favour of 'respect for religion'.[26] Kidd's main argument, however, was that despite all the advances made in scientific thought, 'science now stands dumb before the problems presented by society as it exists around us'.[27] As he wrote:

> Science has obviously herself no clear perception of the nature of the social evolution we are undergoing. She has made no serious attempt to explain the phenomena of our western civilization. We are without any real knowledge of the laws of its life and development or of the principles which underlie the process of social evolution which is proceeding around us.[28]

Kidd promoted an altruistic view of society, where members worked with each other to promote a common good, rather than striving, individually, for their own well-being. This was clearly at odds with the ideals of utilitarianism and Spencer's theory of the survival of the fittest. Indeed, Kidd denounced such egoism as immoral and unethical. He believed that Christian churches alone should define and mould an ethical and social sensibility. According to Robert Macintosh, the author of *From Comte to Benjamin Kidd* (1899), Kidd had appropriated Weismann's germ-plasm theory to argue for the hegemony of religion. As Macintosh argued, germ-plasm theory was analogous to the 'high church doctrine of apostolic succession' for, just as the germ-plasm cell was absolute and universal, so too was the structure of the Church.[29]

---

[24] This reaction is discussed at length in John Hedley Brooke, 'Darwin and Victorian Christianity' in Jonathan Hodge and Gregory Radick (eds), *The Cambridge Companion to Darwin* (Cambridge: Cambridge University Press, 2003): 192–213; see especially 202–7.

[25] Kidd, *Social Evolution*, 80, 23, 97 respectively.

[26] Kidd, *Social Evolution*, 16.

[27] Kidd, *Social Evolution*, 2.

[28] Kidd, *Social Evolution*, 3.

[29] Robert Macintosh, *From Comte to Benjamin Kidd: The Appeal to Biology of Evolution for Human Guidance* (London: Macmillan and Co., Limited, 1899): 222.

Kidd was critical of the rationalists and devoted a large part of chapter 9, 'Human evolution is not primarily intellectual' to the topic:

It is to be feared that the rationalistic school which has been in the ascendant during the greater part of the nineteenth century, and which has raised such unstinted paens in honour of the intellect, regarding it as the triumphant factor of progress in the splendid ages to come, is destined to undergo disillusionment in many respects … Since man became a social creature the development of his intellectual character has become subordinate to the development of his religious character. It would appear that the process at work in society is evolving religious character as a first product, and intellectual capacity only so far as it can be associated with this quality. In other words, the most distinctive feature of human evolution as a whole is, that through the operation of the law of natural selection, the race must grow ever more and more religious.[30]

It is no wonder the freethinkers loathed this book.

Drummond was to refute Darwin outright, as the title of his book suggests: *The Ascent of Man* was in direct contrast to Darwin's *The Descent of Man* (1871). As far as Drummond was concerned, 'evolution was given to the modern world out of focus, and has remained out of focus to the present hour', further claiming that 'evolutionary philosophy had gone astray'.[31] Drummond had obviously read Kidd as he also argued that altruism was the key to progress: 'but now that there is Altruism enough in the world to begin the new era, there must be wisdom enough to direct it'.[32] Yet Drummond was a staunch defender of natural selection and argued, like Kidd, that Christianity was still—and should always be—the bedrock of civilization.

A.J. Balfour's book annoyed Newman by supposing that 'we have at the present time neither a satisfactory system of metaphysics nor a satisfactory theory of science'.[33] In Balfour's view, rationalism held no promise for the future, whereas religious belief did. In discussing the seventeenth-century rationalists, Balfour concluded that 'rationalists as such are not philosophers'.[34] Like Kidd, Balfour argued that Christianity was still relevant and was a glue by which society could be held together: 'a Church is something more than a body of more or less qualified persons engaged more or less successfully in the study of theology. It requires a very different equipment from that which is sufficient for a learned society. Something more is asked of it than independent

[30] Kidd, *Social Evolution*, 244.
[31] Drummond, *The Ascent of Man*, vi, 15.
[32] Drummond, *The Ascent of Man*, 51.
[33] Balfour, *Foundations of Belief*, 163.
[34] Balfour, *Foundations of Belief*, 170.

research. It is an organisation charged with a great practical work'.[35] Balfour's unguarded empiricism would never wash with the freethinkers, a group that valued scientific method.

There was plenty of material in the books by Kidd, Drummond and Balfour that Newman would have found offensive to his rationalist ideology, but the insistence that the church was still an important, ethical and useful institution was perhaps most perplexing of all to Newman, second only to the appropriation of Darwin's evolutionary theory.

In defiance of the three writers, Newman dedicated his book 'To the memory of Charles Darwin'.[36] But the book clearly had a broader focus, for its aim was:

> the refutation of the fallacies and errors contained in three books ... The ephemeral nature of these productions is so self-evident that most persons of culture and intelligence will assert that similar works do not call for a volume especially devoted to their errors, and that in a few years they will die a natural death and go the way of all fallacy and deception ... no one could be more convinced that the vogue of these books, great as it was at first, is destined to grow smaller and smaller, until the particular form of pseudo-philosophy which they represent has passed into deserved oblivion.[37]

This book was clearly not written with the sole purpose of defending Darwin; it might equally have been dedicated to Spencer or even Mill, or a miscellany of positivists or scientists, so sweeping was Newman's attack on all forms of late nineteenth-century religious thought.

Newman's critique of his foes was harsh, and reminiscent of the truculent tone that he employed in his *National Reformer* essays when he was most perturbed by pseudo-science. Newman analysed each of the writers' arguments in excruciating detail: his argument—for modern readers at least—is often complex and difficult to follow. Newman's position was that the truth of evolutionary theory is resolute and undeniable. He lampooned his opponents' works, writing that 'no one now disputes the main facts of the evolutionary theory'.[38] Newman's book devoted three sections to each writer, following a similar pattern of analysis in each section; first of all he summarised their arguments, sometimes in great detail, and secondly embarked on a page-by-page attack on each of their points. His approach was sarcastic and posed many rhetorical questions. While at his combative best, this style is also common in the more

[35] Balfour, *Foundations of Belief*, 282–3.

[36] Cecil (pseud. Ernest Newman), *Pseudo-Philosophy*, v.

[37] Cecil (pseud. Ernest Newman), *Pseudo-Philosophy*, 1.

[38] Cecil (pseud. Ernest Newman), *Pseudo-Philosophy*, 9.

aggressive writings of Newman's mentor, Robertson, and of other social and political writers in the *National Reformer* whose tone was often belligerent in proselytising for freethought causes.

❧ Critical Reception of Pseudo-Philosophy

Pseudo-Philosophy was reviewed very favourably by two major journals. *The Academy* described Newman as 'a clear thinker, a cogent reasoner, a lucid and accomplished writer'.[39] But the most praiseworthy review came from the *Literary Guide*:

> Seldom has the rationalist position been more clearly or more forcibly stated than by Mr Hugh Mortimer Cecil in this book. We confess to having opened the volume with a suspicion that there was 'not much in it'; but we were not long in discovering that it was one of such sterling worth as to entitle it to rank with the very best works in the Rationalist library, and that in its author we have a scholar and a thinker of whom any intellectual movement ought to feel proud. We look forward with hope and confidence to further productions from the same brilliant and trenchant pen.[40]

Robertson reviewed *Pseudo-Philosophy* with much enthusiasm.[41] He described the book as a 'perfectly competent and perfectly vigorous attack' on what he termed 'religious unreason'.[42] He admired Newman's 'breezy outspokenness' and closed his review in glowing praise for his protégé and his publisher:

> In fine, Mr Cecil is a most valuable recruit to the cause of rationalistic propaganda. His literary gift is no less marked than his faculty for dialectic; and all along the line he shows himself abundantly well read on the topics he handles ... In publishing a book so likely to be boycotted by orthodoxy, the new University Press has established a claim on the gratitude of all Freethinkers.[43]

But Robertson also used his review to further peddle freethought propaganda. He argued that even though the three irrationalist books had sold in vast quantities, it did not equate to a swing against freethought. He also tried

---

[39] Cited in an advertisement for *Pseudo-Philosophy*, in *UMFR* 11 (1899): 405.

[40] Cited in an advertisement for *Pseudo-Philosophy*, in *UMFR* 11 (1899): 405. Extracted from Unsigned, 'An indictment of latter-day irrationalism' [Review of *Pseudo-Philosophy at the end of the Nineteenth Century*], *Literary Guide*, 1 April 1897, 147–8.

[41] John M. Robertson, 'Current pseudo-philosophy', *UMFR*, May 1897, 190–6.

[42] Robertson, 'Current pseudo-philosophy', 190.

[43] Robertson, 'Current pseudo-philosophy', 193; 196.

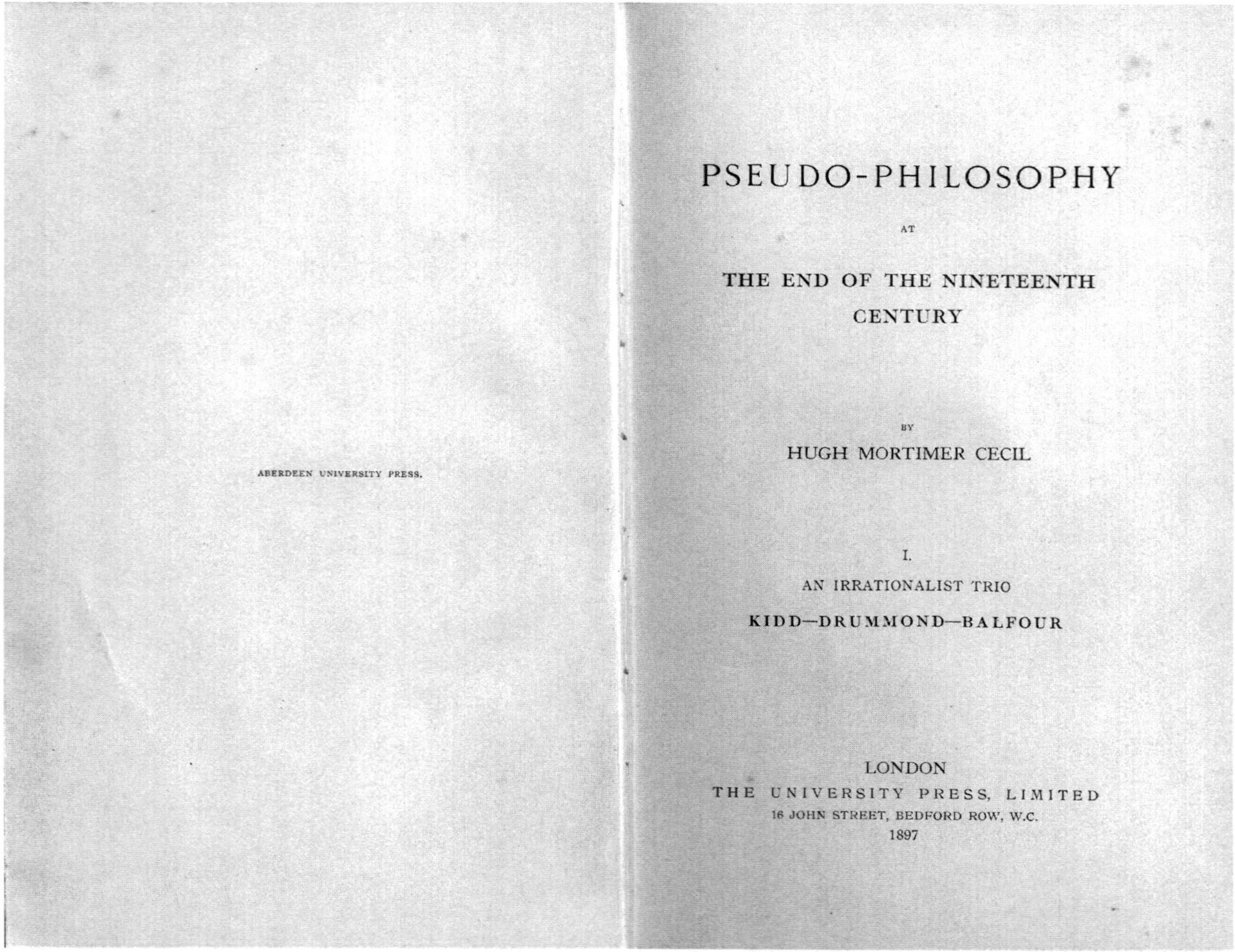

Figure 3
Title page
and verso
of *Pseudo-
Philosophy*
(1897)

PSEUDO-PHILOSOPHY

AT

THE END OF THE NINETEENTH
CENTURY

BY

HUGH MORTIMER CECIL

I.

AN IRRATIONALIST TRIO

KIDD—DRUMMOND—BALFOUR

LONDON

THE UNIVERSITY PRESS, LIMITED

16 JOHN STREET, BEDFORD ROW, W.C.

1897

ABERDEEN UNIVERSITY PRESS.

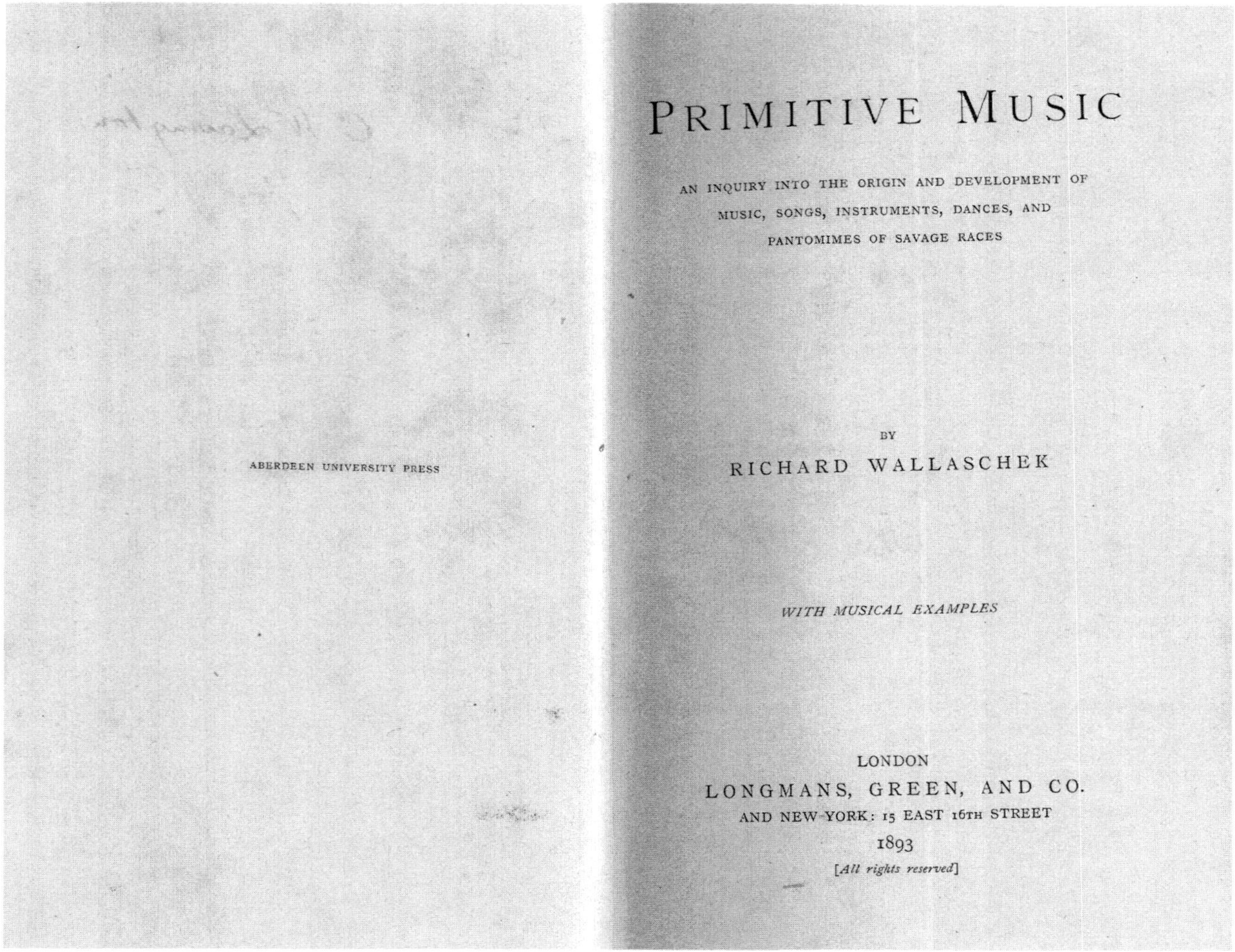

ABERDEEN UNIVERSITY PRESS

PRIMITIVE MUSIC

AN INQUIRY INTO THE ORIGIN AND DEVELOPMENT OF MUSIC, SONGS, INSTRUMENTS, DANCES, AND PANTOMIMES OF SAVAGE RACES

BY

RICHARD WALLASCHEK

WITH MUSICAL EXAMPLES

LONDON

LONGMANS, GREEN, AND CO.

AND NEW-YORK: 15 EAST 16TH STREET

1893

[*All rights reserved*]

Figure 4
Title page and verso of Wallaschek's *Primitive Music* (1893)

to explain away the overwhelming commercial success of the books, claiming 'the truth is such books [as these three] prove the decline and not the revival of real belief. Converts they cannot and do not make' and he hoped that 'there are fewer believers to-day than ten years ago; and there will be still fewer ten years hence'.[44] *Pseudo-Philosophy*'s impact continued into the later twentieth century: in D.P. Crook's biography of Kidd (1984), *Pseudo-Philosophy* is singled out as being the 'crescendo' of all the criticism levelled at Kidd's *Social Evolution*.[45]

🞂 A Brush with the Law

Given the criminal record of the founder of University Press Limited, it is not surprising that breaches of the law are easy to find in *Pseudo-Philosophy*. Opposite the book's title page are printed the words 'Aberdeen University Press', suggesting it is an imprint of University Press Limited (see Figure 3). However, de Villiers had stolen this imprint, which belonged to the very respectable house of Longmans, Green, and Company, as Figure 4 shows. Moreover, the typography and arrangement of the text on the title pages and the versos of both books is strikingly similar. It can only be wondered whether Robertson and Newman were aware of, and condoned, this imprint theft or whether they became aware of the situation only after the book was published. Galley sheets for proofreading and indexing may have been issued to Newman with the rogue page left blank. De Villiers or his staff could easily have inserted the imprint at the very last moment, shortly before the book was printed, and without the author noticing.

Newman's relations with University Press Limited did not end happily because de Villiers avoided paying Newman his commission. By 6 August 1897 Newman had written to Dobell explaining he had 'broken altogether with Dr de V. and have refused to write any more for him, he still owes me three guineas, which I can only get out of him by a summons'.[46] By February 1898, de Villiers wrote to Newman with an apology (apparently, Newman did not pursue the summons) and asked him to write again for *UMFR*; Newman obliged (subject to being paid) and wrote his final essay for this journal, 'An eighteenth-century view of opera'.[47] But this reconciliation was short-lived. By

[44] Robertson, 'Current pseudo-philosophy', 190.

[45] D.P. Crook, *Benjamin Kidd*, 75.

[46] Correspondence from Newman to Dobell, 6 August 1896. MSS Dobell 38484–5.

[47] Correspondence from Newman to Dobell, 19 February 1896. Newman had obviously never met de Villiers or Singer for he would have realised they were the same person. Newman's plans to stay a week with de Villiers from 23 March 1896 seems therefore not to have taken place. See MSS Dobell 38484–5, 21 February 1896.

January 1899 Newman had wiped his hands completely of de Villiers, at last becoming aware of the villain's double-life. He wrote to Dobell that 'de Villiers seems to have returned to England under the alias of Singer—as far as I have any proof the warrant still stands against him … de Villiers is a liar of no mean capacity'.[48]

🐚 *Impact of* Pseudo-Philosophy

Pseudo-Philosophy enjoyed a modest afterlife. Robertson's criticisms of the works of Kidd, Drummond and Balfour were meted out in books in 1902 and 1912, and it seems likely (given his positive appraisal of Newman's book) that his attacks on these writers were directly inspired by *Pseudo-Philosophy*. In Robertson's *Letters of Reasoning* (1902), for example, Kidd is castigated for his 'absurd species of argument' and in *Rationalism* (1912), Robertson further criticised the irrationalist trio along much the same lines as Newman had done.[49]

Newman was not alone in his severe criticisms of the work of these three writers. Robert Macintosh interpreted Kidd's book as a type of social Darwinism (or hyper-Darwinism) based on what he called the 'fairy tale' behind the theory of the germ-plasm theory. Macintosh also criticised Drummond's work for its unoriginality (more specifically its dependence upon Spencer's work), but fell short of actually accusing Drummond of plagiarism.[50] This had already been done in 1894, when E. Lynn Linton undertook a parallel text analysis of Drummond's book, writing—and quoting—in the *Contemporary Review* that Drummond had, in fact, plagiarised Spencer.[51]

Did Newman write under this pseudonym again? The answer is possibly. There are two articles published under Hugh Mortimer Cecil for *University Magazine & Free Review* in June 1897 that could have been written by him.[52] The first article, 'On atheism', was an attempt to define more clearly the scope and role of atheism; in it he accused Thomas Huxley of propagating 'a grave misconception' about the subject.[53] The second article, 'An ethical excursion',

---

[48] Correspondence from Newman to Dobell, 14 January 1899. MSS Dobell 38484–5.

[49] John M. Robertson, *Letters on Reasoning* (London: Watts & Co., 1902): 4; John M. Robertson, *Rationalism* (London: Constable and Company Ltd., 1912): 27–47; 62–8.

[50] Chapter 18 of *From Comte to Benjamin Kidd* is entitled 'A fairy-tale of science?' and is a detailed critique of the influence of Weismann on Kidd. Part IV of the book is called 'Hyper-Darwinism—Weismann and Kidd'.

[51] E. Lynn Linton, 'Professor Henry Drummond's Discovery', *CR*, September 1894, 448–57.

[52] Hugh Mortimer Cecil (pseud. Ernest Newman), 'On atheism', *UMFR*, June 1897, 347–52 and 'An ethical excursion', *UMFR*, June 1897, 238–52.

[53] Cecil (pseud. Ernest Newman), 'On atheism', 347.

was a book review of Goldwin Smith's *Guesses at the Riddle of Existence* (1897).[54] Either Newman or Walter Matthew Gallichan could have written these articles since they shared similar intellectual interests and writing style.[55]

Sydney Grew has noted that Newman 'never acknowledged the authorship' of works written by Hugh Mortimer Cecil.[56] Neither had Newman confided this use of his pen-name to his good friend, Henry George Farmer. We can only suppose that this is an episode in Newman's life he would rather forget. He may have wanted to put his dubious association with de Villiers behind him for, at a time when he was desperate to make his living as a mainstream writer, such a colourful association may not have been looked upon favourably by a less liberally inclined employer.

The publication of *Pseudo-Philosophy at the end of the Nineteenth Century* was an important milestone in Newman's career because, in freethought circles, it cemented for him a reputation as an intellectually militant and dextrous writer. It might be said to have little relevance to his work in literary or music criticism, yet we see in this book an aggressive and forensic streak in Newman that would appear later and often in many of his works. Newman's capacity to attack and belittle his opponents in print became legendary. It was played out in later books such as *Fact and Fiction about Wagner* (1931) (in which a similar forensic critique of argument is made in extremely close detail) and in *The Man Liszt* (1934), in which Newman's loathing of his subject—as in *Pseudo-Philosophy*—was unapologetic and palpable. Robertson's description of Newman's tone as representing 'youth's spontaneous pugnacity' was not the last we would see of this trait in Newman's writing.

---

[54] The book under review is Goldwin Smith, *Guesses at the Riddle of Existence, and Other Essays in Kindred Subjects* (London and New York: Macmillan, 1897).

[55] 'Hugh Mortimer Cecil' is the author of 'The illusion of progress', *Agnostic Annual*, 1898, 29–32.

[56] Grew, 'Mr Ernest Newman', 127; Henry George Farmer, 'Ernest Newman as I saw Him', MS Farmer 44, 7.

CHAPTER 5

Music History and the Comparative Method: *Gluck and the Opera*, 1895

G LUCK *and the Opera*, published in 1895, was Newman's first book and the first biography of the composer to be published in English. By employing the comparative method, Newman wrote what he considered to be a pioneering work of music history. Even though the book's methodology suggests the influence of many writers, Newman seems to have drawn mostly on the work of Hippolyte Taine. Taine's *History of English Literature* was published in 1864, translated into English in 1871, and was regarded for more than a generation afterwards as a model use of the comparative method. The critical reception of *Gluck and the Opera* reveals much about Newman's grasp of the comparative method and his familiarity of its application across a range of European literature. The book's critical reception shows that Newman was highly regarded by his peers as a promising music historian and biographer.

❧ *Genesis of* Gluck and the Opera

Newman began the research for *Gluck and the Opera* some time in the late 1880s.[1] He later wrote about the difficulties he encountered while writing it:

> There is one person … for whom I always feel the greatest sympathy—the young student who, anxious to do original music research, finds himself checked at every turn by the difficulty of getting the necessary material. This was my own case when I was writing *Gluck and the Opera*. Gluck affected me as powerfully in those days as Wagner and Brahms, Elgar and Wolf … Had I been free I would gladly have devoted my whole time to research in the Continental libraries. But not much research of that kind is possible to a young man who is cooped up in business all day for eleven and a half months of the year: it was impossible even for me to visit the British Museum … I did the best I could under the circumstances. I had a fair amount of material at my disposal in the Picton Library, Liverpool, and I bought all the books and music I could.[2]

[1] Newman, 'Confessions', 1–41; 33.

[2] Newman, 'Confessions', 23. Newman felt keenly his isolation in Liverpool. He bought and borrowed many books from Bertram Dobell for the writing of this

Newman did not explain why he chose to write on Gluck in favour of other composers whose works he admired. Henry George Farmer suggested that the motivation for the book came after Newman attended a performance of *Iphigenia* in 1888, which fits neatly into the timeframe when the research was undertaken.[3] However, Newman probably wrote the book out of a broader interest in the history of operatic reform, a topic he encountered through his early research on Wagner.

Whatever the circumstances surrounding the idea for the book, the decision to write it could not have been made with the view to making money. Gluck was barely known in late nineteenth-century England and consequently the readership for this book would have been small. But Gluck and his music were not entirely unknown. A Gluck Society had been formed in London in the late 1870s and *Orfeo* had been revived in Cambridge in 1890.[4] George Bernard Shaw, however, doubted this initial interest would last. When he heard of the plans for a Gluck revival in the 1890s, Shaw wrote that it 'was not a hopeful one' because 'Gluck ... has bored many generations of Frenchmen, just as Handel has bored many generations of Englishmen.'[5] Yet, in the 1890s, *Orfeo* had been staged at Covent Garden for six seasons.[6] If Shaw was right, however, Newman's biography was not going to attract a huge market, and this turned out to be one reason why the book took so long to interest a publisher.[7]

John M. Robertson outlined other reasons why *Gluck and the Opera* was an unattractive proposition for publishers in an article entitled 'The problem of publishing' in the *Free Review* in May 1895. Robertson painted a gloomy

---

book and other projects, including *A Study of Wagner* (London: Bertram Dobell, 1899).

[3] Henry George Farmer, 'Ernest Newman as I saw Him', MS Farmer 42.

[4] George Bernard Shaw, 'Italian opera and the French Dickens', *The World*, 20 August 1890, in Dan H. Lawrence (ed.), *Shaw's Music: The Complete Musical Criticism of Bernard Shaw*, 2nd rev. edn (London: The Bodley Head, 1981): vol. II, 151–7, 152–3, 523. Shaw noted, 'Anyhow, there was a Gluck society in London some dozen years ago' (155). Performances were staged from Tuesday 13 to Saturday 17 May 1890, directed by Charles Stanford. See John F. Runciman, 'Gluck's *Orpheus* at Cambridge', *SR*, 17 May 1890, 606–7.

[5] George Bernard Shaw, 'Italian opera and the French Dickens', 152–3. The revival of which Shaw wrote was the 1891 staging of *Orfeo* at Covent Garden.

[6] 1892, the 1892–3 Autumn–Winter season, 1893, 1894, 1895 and 1898. See Harold Rosenthal, *Two Centuries of Opera at Covent Garden* (London: Putnam, 1958).

[7] An earlier champion of Gluck in Britain was music critic H.F. Chorley, who complained of that composer's music 'coming scantily to English performance'. Quoted in Ernest Newman (ed.), *H.F. Chorley, Thirty Years' Musical Recollections* (New York: Knopf, 1926): 395.

picture of the economics of the London book trade.[8] He criticised the Society of Authors for making authors greedy by demanding large advances and royalties.[9] He also explained that the cost of typesetting and the substantial discounting of books meant that 'it is the author without money and without a popular product or a sure market who has need to cast about for some other way of getting into print'.[10] This was Newman's position. 'Besides', Robertson wrote, 'times are bad—very bad. Between one thing and another, publishers, I am told, refuse now-a-days to take any risk on many books which ten or fifteen years ago they would have risked without hesitation'.[11]

In turning his attention to *Gluck and the Opera*, Robertson wrote: 'a leading firm of publishers have declared that they would be "glad to be associated with it", but it is the old story: they cannot undertake the pecuniary task of publishing. They have more reason to hesitate because there is still so little demand in England for musical literature, despite the growing study of music'.[12]

Robertson was sympathetic to Newman's plight because he was having trouble finding a publisher for his own book, *Buckle and his Critics*. Undeterred, Robertson took matters into his own hands. In 'The problem of publishing', he announced that three books—*Gluck and the Opera*, *Buckle and his Critics* and *Human Documents* (by Arthur Lynch)—would be published by subscription.[13] Thanks to Robertson's advocacy the three books secured sufficient support and Swann Sonnenschein published *Buckle and his Critics* in 1895, while Bertram Dobell published *Gluck and the Opera* in 1895 and *Human Documents* in 1896.[14]

In pitching *Gluck and the Opera* to subscribers, Robertson heaped praise on Newman's typescript:

---

[8] John M. Robertson, 'The problem of publishing', *FR*, May 1895, 97–112.

[9] Robertson, 'The problem of publishing', 97.

[10] Robertson, 'The problem of publishing', 100.

[11] Robertson, 'The problem of publishing', 101.

[12] Robertson, 'The problem of publishing', 103.

[13] Robertson, 'The problem of publishing', 102–3.

[14] John M. Robertson, *Buckle and his Critics: A Study in Sociology* (London: Swan Sonnenschein & Co., 1895). In the preface Robertson notes 'It remains to express here my earnest thanks to the subscribers—about a hundred and fifty—who by undertaking in advance to purchase this book, after seeing a conspectus of its contents in the *Free Review* of May last, have made possible its printing and publication' (vii). Arthur Lynch's book *Human Documents: Character-Sketches of Representative Men and Women of the Time* (London: Bertram Dobell, 1896) was a series of biographical sketches of notable contemporaries, some of which had been previously published in the *National Reformer*.

It will make about 320 pages of a medium octavo size; and if it were issued in ordinary course by a publisher would probably be priced at 7s. 6d. or more. Those who send me notice before the end of June … may have it post free, for 5s. They are not asked to remit now … When the book is printed it will be sold to booksellers at 5s. 6d., and to direct purchases, at 7s. Whether before or after publication, any one, bookseller or not, who gets six subscribers, or buys six copies, will receive one *gratis* in addition.[15]

Robertson further talked up Newman's writing style and his freethought connections—and interest in method—to garner interest in the book:

One contributor, Ernest Newman (whose article on 'Women and Music' in the last number has attracted some notice, and whose former articles, no less note-worthy, include one on 'Mascagni and the Opera'), has completed a work on 'Gluck and the Opera', which embodies much special study of music, musical history, and the influence of Gluck in particular … Are there readers enough of the *Free Review* interested in music and the scientific criticism of it to undertake to buy some two hundred copies of this book if printed?[16]

The pitch continued with Robertson putting himself on the line for Newman: 'I can give my personal assurance, on my credit as a critic with readers who give me any, that the book will be well worth buying and reading, to all you who are interested in the application of scientific method to criticism. The author is young, and therefore all the better worth encouraging.'[17] Despite such strong recommendation, *Gluck and the Opera* secured only eighty-three subscriptions, yet the London bookseller, Bertram Dobell, agreed to publish it.[18]

ɬ Bertram Dobell to publish Gluck and the Opera

At the time of publishing *Gluck and the Opera*, Dobell owned two bookshops in Charing Cross Road.[19] But Dobell was much more than a bookseller: he was

[15] Robertson, 'The problem of publishing', 103.

[16] Robertson, 'The problem of publishing', 103.

[17] Robertson, 'The problem of publishing', 106.

[18] This figure is noted by Robertson in a letter to Dobell on 23 October 1895 (MSS Dobell 38490.) There were a small number of later subscribers.

[19] Dobell had previously run book businesses in other parts of London but his move to the famous Charing Cross Road is a reflection of his success and ambition. I have based my description of Dobell on the following sources, the first of which is the most comprehensive: Frans Korsten, '"An heretical bookworm": Bertram Dobell's life and career', *English Studies* 81/4 (2000): 305–27; Anthony Rota, 'Dobell, Bertram

also a poet, editor, freethinker, publisher and author.[20] His literary fame was made on his attribution of some anonymous manuscripts to Thomas Traherne that scholars had misattributed to Henry Vaughan. He also held an abiding interest in contested authorship, especially in relation to Shakespeare, which was a topic of much interest to his customer and friend, John M. Robertson. Dobell's poems were published in the *National Reformer* and *Freethinker*; he openly associated with many of the leading freethinkers, including Bradlaugh and Robertson, and was a member of some of the Ethical Societies in London.[21] Dobell joined the National Secular Society in the 1860s but he wore his membership cautiously, fearing some of his more conservative customers would take their business elsewhere if they discovered his radical leanings.

Apart from literary and freethought pursuits, Dobell's leisure activities included opera, concerts and the theatre. As Dobell's son, Percy Dobell, wrote, 'his interest in music and the stage never deserted him, and he had a large fund of information relative to the leading actors, actresses and operatic performers of the nineteenth century'.[22] Dobell's love of opera, freethought connections, interest in helping emerging authors, and his long-standing desire to produce books in addition to selling them, all undoubtedly contributed to his decision to publish *Gluck and the Opera*.[23]

(1842–1914)', in *ODNB* (accessed 13 December, 2005); J.M and F.J.M Blom, 'Bertram Dobell and Samuel Bradbury: the literary friendship between a bookseller and an industrial chemist', *English Studies* 79/5 (1998): 447–61; Robert J. Dobell, 'Bertram Dobell and T.J. Wise', *The Book Collector* 19/3 (1970): 348–55; Percy J. Dobell, *In memoriam, Bertram Dobell, 1842–1914* (London: Dobell, 1915); and 'Mr Dobell's collection: sale of privately printed books and pamphlets', the *Times*, 29 November 1913, 7. See also S. Bradbury, *Bertram Dobell: Bookseller and Man of Letters* (London: Bertram Dobell, 1909).

[20] For example a volume of his own verse, *Rosemary and Pansies*, was published under the Dobell imprint in 1904. He also published works on or by James Thomson (*The Laureate of Pessimism: A Sketch of the Life and Character of James Thomson ('B.V.') author of 'The City of Dreadful Night'*, London: Dobell, 1910); Shelley (*Alastor: Or, The Spirit of Solitude: And Other Poems* [The Shelley Society's Publications: Second Series, Number 3], London: Reeves and Turner, with Dobell, 1885); and *Goldsmith: A Prospect of Society by Oliver Goldsmith Being the Earliest Form of his Poem from the Traveller* (London: Dobell, 1902).

[21] For more on these societies see Ian MacKillop, *The British Ethical Societies* (Cambridge: Cambridge University Press, 1986).

[22] Percy J. Dobell, *In Memoriam*, 5.

[23] One of Dobell's many projects included the cataloguing of books printed for private circulation, defined as 'the class of books of which the circulation is restricted to the friends of their authors, or to a limited circle of subscribers', hence his keen interest in participating in the publication of *Gluck and the Opera*. This quote is from page

Newman recalls his association with Dobell in his 'Confessions': 'He [Dobell] had, it seems, read several of my essays and had liked them. The summary of *Gluck and the Opera* [in the *Free Review*] had taken his fancy, and he declared his willingness to publish the book'.[24] In facilitating publication of *Gluck and the Opera*, Robertson wrote to Dobell: 'I trust you will find the Gluck book satisfactory: it struck me as a very able performance indeed. The author tells me that he means to revise it carefully, all the same'.[25]

Newman's long association with Dobell began on 20 May 1895 when he wrote to thank him for his offer of publication.[26] In this and subsequent letters, Newman outlined how he envisaged the complete typescript would be revised. He claimed the book was 'finished a year or two ago' but said the introduction 'was written three or four years ago, and intended as a magazine article'.[27] Newman undertook to revise the typescript substantially, writing to Dobell that there was 'little to be altered' but the 'style was abominable'.[28] Newman promised that his Gluck 'will be practically re-written throughout. If we cannot make it a financial success we can make it a literary one'.[29]

On a receipt of 14 November 1895 in the Newman–Dobell correspondence, the fully revised *Gluck and the Opera* is thus described:

> This work comprises a Memoir of Gluck, concerning whom there is no work in English which deals at all adequately with the subject: and a critical account of the Rise and Progress of Operatic Performances. Mr. Newman's work embodies much special study of music, musical history, and of Gluck's influence on the evolution of the opera. It will be found to contain much matter which will be new to English readers on the subject with which it deals.[30]

The book was dedicated to John M. Robertson—after all, it was he who facilitated its publication.

Gluck and the Opera begins with an introduction in which Newman sets the methodological scene, and this is followed by Part 1, 'Life', which comprises six

---

2 of Bertram Dobell, *Catalogue of Books Printed for Private Circulation* (London: Bertram Dobell, 1906).

[24] Newman, 'Confessions', 32.

[25] Correspondence from John M. Robertson to Bertram Dobell, 17 May 1895, MSS Dobell 38490.

[26] Correspondence from Newman to Dobell, 20 May 1895, MSS Dobell 38484–5.

[27] Newman, 'Confessions', 22–23.

[28] Correspondence from Newman to Dobell, 20 May 1895, MSS Dobell 38484–5.

[29] Correspondence from Newman to Dobell, 20 May 1895, MSS Dobell 38484–5.

[30] It is difficult to tell if this receipt is a sales receipt or a receipt from the lodgement of copyright in the book.

chapters (183 pages) and charts Gluck's life and times in chronological order. The second part of the book (96 pages), is called 'Gluck's relations to the intellectual life of his epoch' and contains four numbered, but untitled, chapters (however, the content of each chapter is given in the running heads). The first chapter deals with the opera in Germany, Italy and France; the second chapter is 'The opera and its critics'. The third chapter covers 'Gluck's manifesto', 'Art and nature' and 'Music and the other arts', while chapter 4 discusses 'Gluck's theory and practice', 'Music and poetry' and 'Gluck's place in art'. The book was not merely a biography on Gluck but, as its subtitle suggested, 'A study in musical history'.

℘ Gluck and the Opera *Outlined*

In the preface, Newman described the 'method and purport of the present volume':

> So far as the biographical portions of it are concerned, I have, of course, been entirely dependent upon the recognised authorities, whose united labours have covered the whole field exhaustively. In the critical portions I have attempted to sum up the measure of Gluck's achievements in relation to the intellectual life of his day. As the book is meant rather as a tentative contribution to the culture-history from a side hitherto painfully neglected, than as a mere narration of a thrice-told tale, I have thought it well to dispense with the history, in detail, of the technical side of the opera. This can be had in many excellent works, and it were superfluous to devote another volume to the task. I have rather endeavoured to view the subject philosophically, and to bring the opera of the eighteenth century in general, and Gluck's work in particular, into line with the whole intellectual tendencies of the time. Thus in the sketches in Part II of the rise and development of the opera in Italy, France, and Germany, I have dealt only with such phases of it as fall within the province of culture-history.[31]

Newman disclosed that the biographical sections of his book were not entirely original, since much of Part 1 was derived from A.B. Marx's *Gluck und die Oper* (1863) and the second edition of Gustave Desnoiresterres' *Gluck et Piccini, 1774–1800* (1875). Indeed, the preface to *Gluck and the Opera* details the wide range of Newman's sources and the research he undertook to write the book. He drew on a large body of secondary literature in English, German and French. In the musical literature in English he found Gustave Chouquet's article on Gluck in *Grove's Dictionary of Music and Musicians* to be 'grossly

---

[31] Newman, *Gluck and the Opera*, xii–xiii.

inadequate' and that 'little more can be said of the late Dr Hueffer's article for the "Encyclopaedia Britannica" (9th ed.)'.[32]

Further afield, Newman sourced material he thought particularly helpful in his research including Anton Schmid's *C. W. Ritter von Gluck, dessen Leben und tonkünstlerisches Wirken* (1854) and August Reissmann's *Christoph Willibald von Gluck, sein Leben und seine Werke* (1882). French literature on which Newman drew included the second edition of *Gluck et Piccinni, 1774–1800: La musique française au 18me siècle* (1882) by Gustave Desnoiresterres and a range of secondary sources including Planelli's *Dell' Opera in Muisca* (Naples, 1772) and unnamed works by Diderot, Rousseau, Grimm, Suard, La Harpe, Goldsmith, Harris and Du Bos. Newman also drew on related sources such as Berlioz's *A travers chants* (1862) and numerous articles on Gluck from *Revue des deux mondes*, *Revue contemporaine* and *Revue Germanique*. Other texts Newman read in research for the book were Ludwig Nohl's *Gluck und Wagner, ueber die Entwicklung des Musikdramas* (1870) and C.H. Bitter's *Die Reform der Oper durch Gluck und Richard Wagner's Kunstwerk der Zukunft* (1884).

Despite drawing on material from secondary literature, Newman argued that the originality and value of the book lay in the synthesis of the relation of Gluck's musical works to the composer's life, times and works. This synthesis or method he thought not only original but was unconventional for its use of the comparative method:

> To make a plea in these days for the use of the comparative method in criticism would seem to be a work of supererogation. That method, so distinctive of our century in its purposes and results, has, through the labour of a number of men, raised the historical criticism of literature almost to the rank of science. Apart from the question as to whether the comparative method covers the whole field of criticism; apart, indeed, from the main question as to what the purpose and function really are; it is indisputable that certain forms of literary criticism have, in our own day, attained to something like the certainty and the comprehensiveness of physical science; and even in the minds of those who disclaim the method and deny its validity, there is an underlying conviction of its truth, and an unconscious application of its principles. While, however, the use of the historical method is thus at the present time practically universal in the criticism of literature and of art in general, there is one department which is as yet almost innocent of scientific treatment; we look in vain for any attempt to bring the criticism of music within the scope of method.[33]

[32] Newman, *Gluck and the Opera*, ix.
[33] Newman, *Gluck and the Opera*, 1–2.

Newman took the opportunity to criticise English music critics to advance the cause of his *Gluck*: 'until now, music has known no other criticism than that of personal taste, unaided by reflection and lacking in basic principles' and complained that the literature on music was most in need of development:

> Even yet we are, for all practical purposes, in the lowest stages of musical culture … in the criticism of literature and art we have attained to some measure of civilisation; in our judgments on music we are for the most part still untutored barbarians. While in other departments we have progressed beyond the static conditions of previous ages to the dynamic criticism of art and letters, in the musical world we are yet centuries behind the time; we are still with the scholiast, the commentator, the expositor, the pedagogue. Nothing is more disappointing to the general student of culture than the dead stop that is given him as soon as he reaches music.[34]

He further complained that 'among liberal-minded men there is no rational criticism of music' and 'out of the whole library of English writings on music it would be impossible to name ten works … that could bear comparison for one moment with good contemporary literary criticism'.[35] Newman blamed Wagner for setting a bad example in his pedestrian and self-referential prose works: 'it is perfectly futile to go on discussing the aesthetic of music *in abstracto*, without reference to the historical conditions under which the art has lived and by which it has been moulded from century to century'.[36] Wagner's historical method, Newman claimed, was:

> used to discover the causes of certain historical changes in the 'national character' of this or that people, and endow abstract terms with the qualities of concrete forces, and generally explain everything most learnedly in terms of itself. In the Wagnerian dialectic we still have the metaphysical method in all its pristine glory and all its primitive irresponsibility.[37]

For Newman, the real meaning of Gluck's music 'can only be estimated by a study of the culture-conditions in which he lived'.[38] He ended the introduction hoping for this approach of musical scholarship in the future:

> Some day a real history of music will have to be written; not an anatomical history, merely marking out the lines these forms have taken, but a physiological history, having reference to structure and to function. Here, as in every other

[34] Newman, *Gluck and the Opera*, 2.

[35] Newman, *Gluck and the Opera*, 3.

[36] Newman, *Gluck and the Opera*, 6.

[37] Newman, *Gluck and the Opera*, 7–8.

[38] Newman, *Gluck and the Opera*, 13–14.

department of knowledge, it is synthesis that illuminates; it is the spectacle of one mental phenomenon bound up causally with another that widens knowledge and gives it certainty and coherence. And when this physiological method of musical criticism comes, it will be found that no intellectual matter can surpass it in interest or value. Music is just as important a factor in the history of civilisation as poetry or philosophy; and to elucidate it by scientific criticism will be a service to culture as valuable as any other that can be rendered.[39]

These extracts from Newman's preface and introduction illustrate the intensity of his views on the weaknesses of music criticism. They also show the promise of the comparative or scientific methodology as an antidote to studies of musical works, disconnected from historical context, as he argued was the case with Wagner's prose works. Though Newman failed to cite from where exactly his use of the comparative method was derived, it was a mix of many approaches to literature and history from a number of writers, including Robertson, H.M. Posnett and Hippolyte Taine.

❧ The Comparative Method: A Brief History and Context

Newman would have come across the comparative method in a range of historical, scientific and literary scholarship in German, English and French. Despite its ubiquity (or, indeed, because of it) the origin of the 'comparative method' has an uncertain pedigree and multiple roots. Commonly, the term is attributed to Goethe or Matthew Arnold.[40] Scholars have referred to Goethe's

---

[39] Newman, *Gluck and the Opera*, 14. In 1921 Newman expressed plans for such a history to be written: 'I have been thinking over the matter of the History, and I have decided to begin with Beethoven. If I start with Berlioz, or some other volume, I shall have to make it an independent volume or else say that it is the second or third or fourth volume of a History: whereas if I begin with Beethoven I begin at the natural starting-point, and I can say in the preface that this is intended to be the first of a series of volumes covering all the developments of the nineteenth century, and I can bring out the later volumes in almost any order'. Letter from Ernest Newman to Vera Newman, cited in Vera Newman, *Ernest Newman: A Memoir* (London: Putnam, 1963), 25. The date of the letter is not given. Newman was later to define in more detail his notion of a physiological history in terms of journalistic criticism in three instalments in the *Sunday Times*: 'A "physiology" of criticism', 16 December 1928, 27 January 1929 and 3 February 1929, reproduced in Felix Aprahamian (ed.), *Essays from the World of Music: Essays from 'The Sunday Times'* (London: John Calder, 1956): 13–27.

[40] For the background and histories of the comparative method see Henry H. Remak, 'Comparative Literature, its Definition and Function', in Newton P. Stallknecht and Horst Frenz (eds), *Comparative Literature: Method and Perspective* (Carbondale: Southern Illinois Press, 1961): 3–37; and Susan Bassnett, *Comparative Literature: A*

term *Weltliteratur* to denote the comparative method, because of its implica-
tion of studying 'literature of the world', although Goethe's purpose for coining
this term is debated.[41] In English, an extract from Matthew Arnold's inaugural speech at Oxford signals the birth of comparative literature: 'Everywhere
there is connection, everywhere there is illustration. No single event, no single
literature is adequately comprehended except in relation to other events, to
other literatures'.[42] In French, Ulrich Weisstein attributed the birth of the comparative method to the works of Abel-François Villemain and Jean-Jacques
Ampère in the 1830s and 1840s.[43] However, as the literary historian Susan
Bassnett points out, comparative literature (and thus the comparative method)
had become widely diffused in the nineteenth and twentieth centuries and
came to represent a number of different approaches (historical and sociological) to comparative literature.[44]

One of the most highly regarded and complex uses of the comparative method in English in the late nineteenth century was H.M. Posnett's
Comparative Literature, published in 1886.[45] In this book, with which Newman
was probably familiar, Posnett 'showed how clan, tribe, city, nation has left,
or is leaving, its marks in a literature peculiarly its own, and how this social
evolution has wrought new kinds of literature, distinguished literature from
science, and rendered the very definition of literature a different thing at different periods'.[46] Posnett's study of world literature was unmistakably couched
in terms of evolutionary theory—an emphasis that will be apparent on its

Critical Introduction (Oxford: Blackwell, 1993). For a discussion of the comparative
method in political discourse see, for example, Stefan Collini, Donald Winch and
John Burrow (eds), *That Noble Science of Politics: A Study in Nineteenth-Century
Intellectual History* (Cambridge: Cambridge University Press, 1983): 207–75.

[41] See, for example, René Wellek and Austin Warren, *Theory of Literature: A Seminal
Study of the Nature and Function of Literature in all its Contexts* (Harmondsworth,
Mddx: Penguin, 1986 [1949]): 48.

[42] Matthew Arnold, 'On the Modern Element in Literature', inaugural lecture delivered at the University of Oxford, 14 November, 1857, cited in Bassnett, *Comparative
Literature*, 1.

[43] Abel-François Villemain, *Cours de littérature française: Tableau de la littérature au
moyen âge en France, en Italie, en Espagne et en Angleterre*, 2 vols (Paris: Pichon
et Didier, 1830) and Jean-Jacques Ampère, *Histoire de la littérature française au
moyen âge comparée aux littératures étrangères* (Paris: Tessier, 1841). See Bassnett,
Comparative Literature, 21–2 and Ulrich Weisstein, *Comparative Literature and
Literary Theory* (Bloomington: Indiana University Press, 1973): 170–1.

[44] Bassnett, *Comparative Literature*, 22–3.

[45] H.M. Posnett, *Comparative Literature* (London: Kegan Paul, Trench & Co., 1886).

[46] Posnett, 'The science of comparative literature', *CR*, June 1901, 855–72; 859.

further use, as we will see below.[47] Posnett observed that, with the comparative method now widespread, the European mind was 'more ready to compare
and contrast than it was before'.[48] By 'comparative thinking' Posnett believed
that both individuals and groups could be understood only if they 'project
themselves beyond the circle of their own associations'.[49]

Posnett wrote again on the comparative method in 1901. In an article in
the *Contemporary Review* he made explicit the connection between the comparative method and historical method.[50] He argued that the terms were synonyms, though ultimately he preferred the word 'comparative' over 'history'
because he argued it lent itself more to the study of the present than to the past.
The term 'comparative method' was also problematic, but not just for Posnett.

For Wellek and Warren, writing in *Theory of Literature* (1949), the comparative method was 'troublesome'.[51] Its origins were difficult to locate, they
claimed, and the term was not, in their words, 'illuminating ... since comparison is a method used by all criticism and sciences, and does not, in any way,
adequately describe the specific procedures of literary study'.[52] This problem
of the comparative method's pedigree has persisted. For example, Kenneth
Bock attributed the use of the comparative method to early writers such as
Thucydides and Aristotle, and argued that over the centuries the method of
comparison was used widely by many theorists eventually becoming a *modus
operandi* for writers such as Comte and Mill, though Bock's article lacked
examples.[53] Despite these generalisations, Bock asserted that the comparative method has been central to the entire Western intellectual tradition.[54]
By the nineteenth century, he wrote, 'the comparative method was, therefore,
presented full-blown to nineteenth century sociologists, anthropologists,
folklorists, and other students of comparative religion, art, music, myth, law,
technology, and economic and political institutions'.[55]

The comparative method was also full-blown, to use Bock's terminology, in
the disciplines of anatomy (by Georges Cuvier, 1769–1832) and anthropology

[47] Posnett's work is scrutinised in more depth in Odin Dekkers, *J.M. Robertson:
Rationalist and Literary Critic* (Aldershot: Ashgate, 1998): 119–22.

[48] Posnett, *Comparative Literature*, 76.

[49] Posnett, *Comparative Literature*, 75, 74.

[50] H.M. Posnett, 'The science of comparative literature'.

[51] Wellek and Warren, *Theory of Literature*, 46.

[52] Wellek and Warren, *Theory of Literature*, 46.

[53] Kenneth E. Bock, 'The comparative method of anthropology', *Comparative Studies
in Society and History* 8/3 (1966): 269–80.

[54] Bock, 'The comparative method of anthropology', 277.

[55] Bock, 'The comparative method of anthropology', 272.

(by Edward Tylor (1832–1917). Newman would likely have encountered the comparative method in these areas in his research on evolution for articles in freethought journals. Cuvier was an early evolutionist.[56] His research concentrated on fossils and his 'reconstructions of giant extinct mammals and reptiles'.[57] The comparative elements of Cuvier's work involved juxtaposing skeletons of contemporary specimens against ancient fossils. However, it is disputed whether comparative anatomy originated with Cuvier. N. von Hofsten, for example, claims that the term was coined in the middle of the sixteenth century.[58] It might also be argued that J.B. Lamarck's *Philosophie zoologique* (1809) was the precursor to Cuvier's work.[59]

In addition to studies of comparative anatomy, the comparative method migrated to anthropology, especially in the work of Edward B. Tylor (1832–1917), with which Newman may have been familiar.[60] Tylor's comparative method was outlined in his 1881 book, *Anthropology*, in which 'by comparing such a set of races [Chinese and Europeans] with our own countrymen, we are able to make out the utmost differences of complexion and feature among mankind.'[61] Tylor was interested in the comparative study of foreign communities, which he believed would affirm the superiority of modern civilisation.

Newman may have found greater inspiration in the comparative method in studies of history, especially those with a broadly anthropological or sociological hue. But this inspiration is difficult to untangle without reference to George H. Johnson and Hippolyte Taine. In George H. Johnson's 'The comparative method of study', published in the journal *Science* in 1893, he argued that the comparative method was crucial to the construction of a historical narrative:

---

[56] D.R. Oldroyd, *Darwinian Impacts: An Introduction to the Darwinian Revolution* (Sydney: University of New South Wales Press, 1980): 37–8.

[57] Oldroyd, *Darwinian Impacts*, 37.

[58] N. von Hofsten, 'From Cuvier to Darwin', *Isis* 24/2 (1936): 361–6; 361.

[59] See the introduction by Richard W. Burkhardt in his edition of J.B. Lamarck's *Zoological Philosophy: An Exposition with Regard to the Natural History of Animals* (Chicago: University of Chicago Press, 1984): xv–xxxix.

[60] Edward B. Tylor, *Researches into the Early History of Mankind and the Development of Civilization* (London: John Murray, 1865). For a modern edition see Paul Bohannan (ed. and abr.), *Researches into the Early History of Mankind* (Chicago: University of Chicago Press, 1964). *Primitive Culture: Researches into the Development of Mythology, Philosophy, Religion, Art, and Customs*, 2 vols (London: John Murray, 1871). An in-depth study of Tylor and the use of comparative method by other anthropologists can be found in George W. Stocking, *Victorian Anthropology* (New York and London: The Free Press, 1987), chapter 4.

[61] Edward B. Tylor, *Anthropology: An Introduction to the Study of Man and Civilization*, ed. A.C. Haddon (London: Watts and Co., 1930 [1881]).

The great advantage of the philosophical study of history is that by this method the constituent elements of events and the movements to which they belong are made apparent, and for this purpose we must be provided with the data for expressing the trend and phase of all the political, philosophical, and religious movements to which they are related ... More than this, is it not possible that a new psychology will be able to weigh and measure the volitions, tastes and emotions of the mind, so that this science as well as history and political economy may become partly quantitative?[62]

Johnson's ideas were by no means new; they are particularly reminiscent of Taine's historical method. Indeed, Johnson's essay provides a useful link to the synthesis of the comparative method, history and psychology in Taine's work, which is evident in Newman's *Gluck*, though not articulated by its author.

Taine's most important and influential works were his *Histoire de la littérature anglaise* (*History of English Literature*), first published in 1864, and *D'Intelligence* (*On Intelligence*), published in 1871.[63] His *History of English Literature* began with something of a manifesto on historiography. First, Taine noted that 'history has been revolutionised, within a hundred years in Germany, within sixty years in France, and that by the study of their literatures'.[64] Without giving any further details he went on to write that 'a work of literature is not a mere play of imagination, a solitary caprice of a heated brain, but a transcript of contemporary manners, a type of a certain kind of mind'.[65]

Taine then set out his philosophy of history by posing some preliminary questions imbued with scientific, especially anatomical, analogies:

What is your first remark on turning over the great, stiff leaves of a folio, the yellow sheets of a manuscript—a poem, a code of laws, a declaration of faith? This, you say, was not created alone. It is but a mould, like a fossil shell, an imprint, like one of those shapes embossed in stone by an animal which lived and perished. Under the shell there was an animal, and behind the document there was a man. Why do you study the shell, except to represent to yourself the animal? So do you study the document in order to know the man. The shell and the document are lifeless wrecks, valuable only as a clue to the entire and living

---

[62] George H. Johnson, 'The comparative method of study', *Science* 21/529 (March 1893): 155–6; 155.

[63] Hippolyte Taine, *History of English Literature*, trans. H. Van Laun, 2nd edn (Edinburgh: Edmonston and Douglas, 1972 [1864]); *On Intelligence*, trans. T.D. Haye (London: L. Reeve, 1871 [1870]).

[64] Taine, *History of English Literature*, 1.

[65] Taine, *History of English Literature*, 1.

existence. We must reach back to this existence, endeavour to re-create it. It is a mistake to study the document, as if it were isolated.[66]

This is what Taine saw as a 'first step' in history: to know the subject intimately, not simply the description of what one 'sees' or perceives.[67] Taine then suggested a further step—to 'unveil a psychology'—and he wrote at length of the importance of C.A. Sainte-Beuve's biography of a religious community, *Port Royal* (published 1840–59), as the finest example of such work.[68] In order to discern a historical-psychological interpretation, Taine proposed three contexts in which a historical subject should be studied: its race ('innate and hereditary dispositions)', surroundings ('physical or social circumstances') and epoch ('acquired momentum').[69] Taine concluded his preamble by declaring that 'I am about to write a history of a literature, and to seek in it the psychology of a people'.[70]

Taine's *On Intelligence* yields additional insight into his vision of history as psychology and elucidates the nomenclature he used in his work, which Newman possibly drew on in *Gluck and the Opera*. In the preface to *On Intelligence*, Taine writes that 'history is applied psychology'.[71] He elaborates the point:

> Every perspicacious and philosophical historian labours at [the psychology] of a man, an epoch, a people, or a race; the researches of linguistics, mythologists, and ethnographers have no other aim; the task is invariably the description of the human mind, or of the characteristics common to a group of human minds; and, what historians do with respect to the past, the great novelists and dramatists do with the present.[72]

In chapter 3 we saw Newman's desire for novelists and playwrights to evoke some semblance of realism in their works. This literary-historical analogy by Taine would undoubtedly have further stirred Newman's imagination. Yet Taine would have aroused Newman's interests because in the preface—and at points throughout this book—he wrote enthusiastically about Spencer and Mill. Of particular interest in *On Intelligence*, however, was his use of the term 'physiological analysis'. This is a vital link to Newman's methodology in *Gluck and the Opera*, for Newman described his desire for a 'physiological history'

[66] Taine, *History of English Literature*, 1.
[67] Taine, *History of English Literature*, 4.
[68] Taine, *History of English Literature*, 5.
[69] Taine, *History of English Literature*, 10, 11, 12.
[70] Taine, *History of English Literature*, 20.
[71] Taine, *On Intelligence*, xi.
[72] Taine, *On Intelligence*, xii.

using a 'physiological method'. Although the word 'physiology' was used extensively in the nineteenth century in works proclaiming to be in the fields of psychology and aesthetics, I propose it is most likely that Newman adopted the use and meaning of this term from Taine.[73]

Taine discussed the physiological method in *On Intelligence* in a section titled 'Of the function of the nervous centres'. This is not an essay on historiography or psychology per se, but a long exposition on the functioning of nerves. Taine argued that each nerve possessed a particular action, that every kind of action is different and that external events trigger many different sensations. After twenty pages of analysis and explanation, Taine connects this particular discussion of nerves to 'mental events'; that is, he sees an individual's mind like a nerve. Just like each nerve, Taine argues, each brain, hence each human being, has unique reactions to external stimuli or events. The process of charting these stimuli and events produces history.

We know that Newman read Taine, as Taine is cited briefly in *Gluck and the Opera*. More to the point, Newman's specific reference to literary criticism, the historical method and the criticism of literature in the preface to *Gluck* is highly suggestive of Taine. It is also possible that Newman's opening manifesto in *Gluck* was an idea borrowed from Taine's *History*.

❧ *Newman's Use of the Comparative Method*

Nowhere in *Gluck and the Opera* did Newman specifically identify his sources for the comparative method and he referred to it by other names. The comparative method was so well known and widely used in the late nineteenth century that a number of synonyms for it had emerged, such as 'culture-history', 'historical method', 'physiological method' and 'scientific method'. These synonyms developed out of the many ways in which the so-called comparative method was framed in particular fields of thought, and Newman also used these terms interchangeably. His use of the term 'culture-history' might well have been derived from Tylor, and his use of the terms 'historical method' and 'physiological method' may both be derived from the works of Taine. Clearly all terms were coined to suggest an approach to history grounded in method, or 'scientific' method as described by Robertson and Taine, especially in Taine's analogy to nerve cells.

---

[73] Two examples are William Carpenter's *Principles of Mental Physiology* (London: Henry S. King, 1874) and Grant Allen's *Physiological Aesthetics* (New York: Appleton and Co., 1877); a third example is Nietzsche's physiological aesthetics as described in Gregory Moore in 'Art and evolution: Nietzsche's physiological aesthetics', *British Journal for the History of Philosophy* 10, no. 1 (2002): 109–26.

In his process of comparison, Newman aired the same concerns that Wellek and Warren would later define as one of the key problems of the comparative method: it was not the process of *simple* comparison. In fact, Newman explained that such an elementary and literal working-out of the method would be foolish:

> The climax of metaphysical absurdity comes in the making of analogies between Gluck and Wagner on the basis of a supposed similarity between their method of reform, unmindful of the fact that while Gluck and the eighteenth-century thinkers in general held that music should be wholly subordinate to poetry, and should strive to express not musical but poetical ideas, the practice of the nineteenth century, whatever its theories may occasionally be, is to subordinate poetry to music in any combination between them, and to use the poetry merely to supply the definiteness that is lacking in music.[74]

Essentially, Newman suggested that a comparative study of two composers across different centuries ran the risk of not comparing 'like with like' and that such an investigation was ultimately ahistorical. In what sense, then, is *Gluck and the Opera* representative of the comparative method?

The answer to this question lies in the contexts which Newman positions the composer, most evident in the second part of the book. Here Gluck is studied in relation to the 'intellectual life of his epoch' and in the context of the operatic life, traditions and customs in Italy, Germany and France.[75] Gluck's esteem and success is then measured by a study of the critical reception of some of his works. Newman goes on to discuss at considerable length the aesthetics of Gluck as outlined in his 'great manifesto', the preface to *Alceste*, and an examination of Gluck's compositional theory and practice in relation to nature, the other arts and poetry.[76] The book concludes with a short section entitled 'Gluck's place in art' in which Newman waxes lyrical over Gluck's achievements, making him into a hero. This is, ironically, the chief criticism he had of A.B. Marx's biography of Gluck.[77] Newman's use of the comparative method is achieved simply by placing the composer in various contrasting historical and contemporary contexts. Indeed, this is the sole purpose of the arrangement of the second part of the book. Setting Gluck against the backgrounds of operatic reform and musical developments in Italy, Germany and France, Newman compared Gluck to other aspects of musical culture.

---

[74] Newman, *Gluck and the Opera*, 10–11.

[75] Newman, *Gluck and the Opera*, 200.

[76] Newman, *Gluck and the Opera*, 238.

[77] Newman, *Gluck and the Opera*, vi.

Gluck's psychology or 'mind' comes under scrutiny in two sections of Newman's volume. The first occurs in the biographical section of the book, where Newman argues that Gluck was oppressed by court patronage, and that the censoring of music had damaged the composer's creativity and sense of well-being. For Newman, court patronage was 'dignity-destroying' but Gluck 'by virtue of his strong physical and mental organisation and genuine humanism of feeling' was able to overcome times of adversity.[78] Moreover:

> without his [Gluck's] dogged self-sufficiency of character he would never, in the age in which he had the misfortune to live, have been at all equal to the reformation of the opera. During all these years of servitude and imitation he must have frequently realised with shame and self-contempt that he was pandering to meanness of spirit and unintelligence of soul.[79]

Newman continued with a 'physiological' description of Gluck emphasising Gluck's character, intelligence, fearlessness and strength:

> Gluck's personal character shows itself both in his music and in his physical structure. To the last he was the hardy, virile peasant, trained to rough and sturdy habits of life. In his face can be clearly seen those qualities that appear again in his music and in correspondence; the head is thrown back proudly and confidently; the large and mobile mouth has an air of quick intelligence; and the eyes look out straight and fearless on the beholder. He was a man whose native strength often showed itself unpleasantly, as in his frequently harsh relations with other men; but this native uncompromising strength was absolutely necessary to the man who should effect the reform of the opera. Different from Wagner, less nervously constituted, less self-conscious, he yet did a work which, though it cannot be compared to Wagner's in real depth of importance, yet marks him out far above any musical figure of his time.[80]

Although there are clear parallels in *Gluck and the Opera* with the nomenclature of other writers—especially Taine—it is most useful to regard Newman as a 'self-styled comparitist'.[81] The term is Bassnett's, and is coined as part of her explanation that in the nineteenth century the use of the term 'comparative method' was flexible. Indeed, this is how we should interpret Newman's approach to the comparative method in this study of Gluck.

---

[78] Newman, *Gluck and the Opera*, 50, 51.

[79] Newman, *Gluck and the Opera*, 52.

[80] Newman, *Gluck and the Opera*, 198–9

[81] Bassnett, *Comparative Literature*, 22

🍂 *Reception of* Gluck and the Opera

Gluck and the Opera was reviewed widely in freethought and mainstream publications including the *Freethinker, Speaker, Scotsman,* the *Times, Realm, Notes and Queries, National Observer* and *Manchester Guardian.*[82] Particularly searching reviews were published in the *Free Review, New Quarterly Musical Review* and the *Saturday Review.* Not surprisingly, the book was reviewed favourably in the *Free Review.* As Robertson wrote to Dobell in February 1896 'I have read it with great pleasure & feel that it will do you credit as a publisher, as it does the author. I am going to try today if I can arrange to get it competently reviewed here [in the *Free Review*].'[83] The task of reviewing the book fell to 'W.M.G.' (presumably Walter Matthew Gallichan who was, at the time, assistant editor of the *Free Review,* edited by G.A. Singer: see chapter 4). Gallichan described the book as a 'sound and conscientious work of musical criticism' that 'reveals careful and extensive research, and considerable power of literary collocation'.[84] He concluded his review with glowing praise:

> Mr Newman's work cannot fail to find students of music who will be grateful to the author for the excellent biography and useful treatise on the development of the opera. The construction of the volume is admirable, and the style is by no means heavy and uninviting, but abounding in graceful phrases, and written with evident enthusiasm for the subject.[85]

J.A. Fuller Maitland reviewed *Gluck and the Opera* in *New Quarterly Musical Review.* Newman was particularly keen for his book to be reviewed in this journal, as he thought it 'the best of all the music journals'.[86] Written by someone outside his close-knit circle of freethinkers, the review is more critical, but Fuller Maitland was generally receptive to the project and its method:

> Mr Ernest Newman has given us not only an excellent biography of the composer, the first that has appeared in English, but a thoughtful and well-written monograph on the early opera in general. Gluck's own operas are analysed and described in a way that makes one's mouth water to see some more of them on the stage … The writer has a fresh, if not always a very elegant, way of putting things, although he is rather overpowered occasionally by the conviction that he must

---

[82] Cited in correspondence from Newman to Dobell, 13 November 1895, 19 November, 6 December, 7 December, 27 December, 27 December, 11 February 1896, 21 February 1896 and 6 March 1896 respectively. MSS Dobell 38484–5.

[83] Correspondence from Robertson to Dobell, 9 February 1896. MSS Dobell 38490.

[84] W.M.G., 'Gluck and the opera', 432, 433.

[85] W.M.G., 'Gluck and the opera', 435.

[86] Correspondence from Newman to Dobell, 13 November, 1895. MSS Dobell 38484–5.

be continually philosophising at all hazards. On the relations between words and music Mr Newman is always worth listening to ... One is duly impressed by the writer's fastidious taste in his introductory chapter, part of which is devoted to some reflections on the poverty of current musical literature in England; but it is disappointing to find him quoting with approbation from two works on music, which, though they have met with the sanction of philosophical readers, cannot be accepted as among the best contributions to the musical side of their subjects.[87]

Despite the criticism for failing to consult primary sources, another positive review of the book was printed in the *Times*, though Newman failed to mention it in his correspondence with Dobell. For its reviewer, *Gluck and the Opera* was a landmark in music literature; and the reviewer was not concerned, as Fuller Maitland was, at the paucity of sources:

An admirable work, not only of the great reformer's career and artistic world, but of the philosophy of musical drama, with more especial reference to its earlier manifestations ... the book is one of those rare achievements in musical literature that is likely to gain a certain amount of recognition from literary people as well as from musicians. It will deserve it, for a more thorough, temperate and right-minded piece of work has not lately been seen in England.[88]

The leading London music critic, John F. Runciman, wrote the most probing review of *Gluck and the Opera* in the *Saturday Review* in January 1896.[89] Like Newman, Runciman had complained occasionally about old critical ways and the need for a fresh style of music criticism.[90] Although both men were committed to the reform of music criticism, they did not always sympathise with each other's work, which Runciman's review demonstrates. And he found some serious faults with the book:

The design is laudable as well as daring, and I sincerely wish I could add that the execution is equal to the design, for any effort to bring music within the range of ordinary human interests should be welcomed and encouraged. Unfortunately

[87] J.A. Fuller Maitland, 'Musical literature', *NQMR*, February 1896, 192–3. The two items Maitland disparaged may have been Edmund Gurney's *The Power of Sound* (London: Smith, Elder and Co., 1880) and Newman's article 'Women and music' from the *Free Review* (April 1895), both of which seem to be the only two sources that Newman praises that deal with philosophy. Fuller Maitland makes no mention at all of Newman's biographical method.

[88] Cited in Farmer, 'Ernest Newman as I saw Him', 103. Farmer does not provide the date of publication or the name of the critic.

[89] John F. Runciman [signed J.F.R.] 'Gluck', *SR*, 11 January 1896, 36–8.

[90] See, for example, 'Concerning musical criticism', *SR*, 28 January 1899, 108–9.

at times the execution falls a good deal beneath the design, and for obvious reasons. Three qualifications were indispensable. First, a knowledge of Gluck's music; second a highly developed critical faculty … last, a power of entering into the inner essential life of the eighteenth century. That last Mr Newman has to a considerable degree; but in the first and second he is more than a little weak.[91]

Runciman complained that Newman drew too heavily from Marx's biography of Gluck to the extent he 'felt suspicious as to the amount of original Gluck study he [Newman] may have done'.[92] He further admonished Newman for the 'scantiness and wrongness' of his account of Gluck's predecessors and for his 'cold intellectual analysis'.[93] And Runciman agreed to disagree with Newman on minor points of detail, but conceded that:

> I am glad to acknowledge that he [Newman] has brought brains and a good deal of knowledge to a difficult task, and has produced a book which will certainly rank as the best Gluck study extant until some one—let us hope it will be Mr Newman himself—writes one which is more complete, and free from errors which undoubtedly exist in this.[94]

Newman took exception to parts of Runciman's review, writing to Dobell within a few days of its publication, that his neglect in studying earlier opera was a criticism 'really beside the question'.[95] As Newman explained, the operas were not printed 'but simply exist in score at Vienna & elsewhere, and I couldn't go all over the world to examine them, even if I had wished to do so. Runciman is an impressionist critic, not a scientific one, & what he wants is a dramatic biography in the Carlyle style. That sort of thing doesn't interest me however. When I want to write fiction I will do a novel'.[96]

Later in his life, Newman's views on the success and limitations of *Gluck and the Opera* concur with Runciman's criticism made almost thirty years earlier. As Newman wrote in 'Confessions':

[91] Runciman, 'Gluck', 37.
[92] Runicman, 'Gluck', 37. Adolph Bernhard Marx, *Gluck und die Oper*, 2 vols (Berlin: O. Janke, 1863). There is no evidence or suggestion that Newman drew on Marx's writings on his own interpretative method, the *Idee*; perhaps its metaphysical slant was too objectionable for Newman's rationalism. On Marx's *Idee* see Scott Burnham, 'Criticism, faith and the "Idee": A.B. Marx's early reception of Beethoven', *19th-century Music* 13/3 (1990): 183–92.
[93] Runciman, 'Gluck', 37.
[94] Runciman, 'Gluck', 37.
[95] Correspondence from Newman to Dobell, MSS Dobel 14 January 1896. MSS Dobell 38484–5.
[96] Correspondence from Newman to Dobell, MSS Dobel 14 January 1896. MSS Dobell 38484–5.

I have not glanced at the book for twenty years or more, and shall probably never do until I happen to write on Gluck again. But I chanced a little while ago upon a critique of it, which I am sure sums it up pretty accurately, by a German expert, Dr Stephan Wortsmann ... [who] points out, quite rightly, my indebtedness to Marx and others in the matter of biographical detail, but—this amuses me—he says that 'the imagination of the author has painted some episodes ... in such lively colours that the uninitiated reader ... will come to the conclusion that he is dealing with an extraordinarily well-equipped Gluck expert. For none of his conjectures, however, has Newman brought forward the least new evidence ...'. Dr Wortsmann thinks the second part of the book ... the better of the two. I am sure if I were to re-read the book I should agree with him. I was so fired by my subject that I have not the least doubt I wrote about the incidents of Gluck's career as if I had personally been a witness of them. I was very young, very ardent, and Gluck-drunk. Gluck was more real to me than most of the people I rubbed shoulders with every day'.[97]

It is easy to dismiss *Gluck and the Opera* as a derivative work, as a book too closely reliant on secondary sources, and one that offers very little new information on an old subject. It also might be considered an experimental work, in which the author, for the first time, laid the foundation for a new brand of musical scholarship. That the book was on Gluck is, in a sense, inconsequential: its subtitle, a 'study in musical history' is much more telling. *Gluck and the Opera* may not only be celebrated for being Newman's first book or the first biography of the composer in English, but it represented for Newman the culmination of many years' work, in which he synthesised his theoretical learning in history, psychology and scientific method. His proselytising for the historical or comparative method, though, and his interest in music biography, had just begun.

[97] Newman, 'Confessions', 34–5.

PART II

The Mainstream Years

CHAPTER 6

From Manchester to Moscow:
Essays on Music, 1900–1920

NEITHER fame nor fortune would come Newman's way if he published solely in the freethought press. The demise, reinvention and ultimate failure of the *National Reformer*, followed in quick succession by the short-lived *Free Review*, indicated a limited readership for freethought journals, and Dobell's loss-making ventures on books such as *Gluck and the Opera* were not sustainable. To survive as a writer, Newman had to find a more stable and mainstream avenue of publication.

Newman's foray into the mainstream press occurred in 1895 (the same year in which *Gluck and the Opera* was published) with an essay on Flaubert in the December issue of the *Fortnightly Review*, a liberal periodical of arts and letters.[1] Although Newman wrote for multiple publications throughout his career, 1900 to 1920 was a particularly gruelling period because he juggled an extremely heavy workload. In 1905, for example, he issued a collection of his previously published essays, *Musical Studies*, and between 1904 and 1920 wrote seven books and issued a further collection of his own essays.[2] Journals and newspapers for which he wrote included, but were not limited to, the *Speaker* (1901–1906), *Weekly Critical Review* (1903–1904), *Manchester Guardian* (1905–1906), *Birmingham Daily Post* (1906–1919), *Musical Times* (1910–1923), *New Witness* (1915–1918) and the London *Observer* (1918–1920).[3] By anyone's

---

[1] Ernest Newman, 'Gustave Flaubert', *FoR*, December 1895, 813–28.

[2] Ernest Newman, *Musical Studies* (London and New York: John Lane, The Bodley Head, 1905); *Wagner* (London and New York: John Lane, The Bodley Head, 1904); *Elgar* (London and New York: John Lane, The Bodley Head, 1906); *Hugo Wolf* (London: Methuen & Co., 1907); *Richard Strauss* (London and New York: John Lane, The Bodley Head, 1908); *Wagner as Man and Artist* (London: J.M. Dent, 1914); and *The Piano-Player and its Music* (London: Grant Richards, 1920). The second volume of collected essays was *A Musical Motley* (London: John Lane, The Bodley Head, 1919).

[3] The lesser-known periodical, *New Witness*, was published between 1912 and 1924 and was a precursor to G.K's Weekly. *The New Witness* published articles on social, political and artistic issues. Newman wrote occasionally for other periodicals in the period: *Atlantic Monthly*; *Chesterian*; *Eclectic Magazine of Foreign Literature*; *English Review*; *Etude*; *Glasgow Herald*; *Harvard Musical Review*; *Living Age*; *Monthly Musical Record*; *Musical Standard*; *Musical World*; *Musician*; *National News*; *New*

standard, Newman was extremely busy. A consequence of all this industry, however, is that Newman covered the same material in many articles in order to buy time, though he rarely recycled an article in full.

The topics on which Newman wrote varied, as did his tone and style of writing, depending upon the publication and audience for which his work was pitched. For example, in the *Speaker*, a liberal weekly founded in London in 1890 (changing its name to the *Nation* in 1907), Newman wrote in a formal tone unaffected by the belligerence and wit evident in some of his work in the provincial press. The same is true for Newman's articles in the *Weekly Critical Review*, a French–English arts journal published in Paris in 1903–4 as a literary expression of the entente cordiale that sought scholarly essays from leading French and English critics.[4] His reviews of concerts in the regional papers, but especially the *Manchester Guardian*, were succinct, encouraging and some-times amusing, in support of local musical talent. This was in opposition to his later work in the *Musical Times*, which was sometimes confrontational and provocative. The seriousness of the subject matter also affected Newman's style. In his essays in the *New Witness* and *Observer* that dealt with the effects of war on music—and negative attitudes towards German politics and cul-ture—Newman's prose was more reflective and guarded, most likely due to the sensitiveness of the subject matter. However, Newman was no shrinking violet. He was an assured and confident writer: forthright, even bossy.

Newman's musical criticism from 1900 to 1920 was a mix of concert reviews and essays. He reviewed concerts in his hometowns of Manchester, Birmingham and Liverpool but he also wrote on general-interest topics in music and literature. Newman occasionally wrote about musical and cultural life in London before moving there in 1918 to take a job at the *Observer*, and then continued to write a column for the *Manchester Guardian* on music in the nation's capital. Between 1895 and 1903 Newman wrote seven articles for the *Fortnightly Review* and the *Contemporary Review* and this put his name before a readership beyond the freethought and musical circles. The topics included Flaubert, Wagner, Berlioz, Tchaikovsky and Strauss.[5]

Music Review and Church Music Review; New Quarterly Musical Review; and *Werner's Magazine.*

[4] Paul Watt, 'Musical and literary networks in the *Weekly Critical Review*, Paris, 1903–1904', *Nineteenth-Century Music Review*, 14/1 (2017), 33–50.

[5] Ernest Newman, 'Gustave Flaubert'; 'Wagner's "Ring" and its Philosophy', *FoR*, June 1898, 867–84; '"The old music and the new"', *CR*, September 1900, 415–29; 'Berlioz', *CR*, February 1901, 212–20; 'The essential Tchaikovsky', *CR*, June 1901, 867–98; 'English music and musical criticism', *CR*, November 1901, 734–48; 'Richard Strauss and the music of the future', *FoR*, January 1903, 30–45.

This chapter considers some of the subjects that occupied Newman's mind from 1900 to 1920, before he moved to the *Sunday Times*. Of particular interest in this twenty-year period is Newman's advocacy of English music, audience behaviour—especially in relation to Elgar's reception in London and Manchester—the state of music-making in the post-World War I period, his enthusiasm for certain Russian composers and repertory, and his continued analysis of contemporary musical criticism.

❧ *Waving Flags for British Music*

In the 1890s, Newman became friends with Granville Bantock, Joseph Holbrooke and Edward Elgar. Newman contributed two articles to Bantock's short-lived periodical, the *New Quarterly Musical Review,* in 1893 and a friendship developed.[6] When Bantock became musical director at the New Brighton resort in 1897—a post he held until 1900—he called on Newman to write many of the programme notes for the concerts, and through this work Newman's friendship with Elgar and Holbrooke was formed.[7] Newman developed an interest in their music and was deeply sympathetic to a host of other British composers, most of whom had difficulty in getting their works performed.

Buoyed by Bantock's enterprise, Newman saw a rosy future for British music led, in part, by his newly found friends, and wrote about these prospects in a series of articles from November 1901 to April 1902. In the first article, 'English music and musical criticism'—published in the *Contemporary Review* in November 1901—Newman observed two factors that affected the appreciation and patronage of locally produced music: a change in public taste and the diminished reliance on foreign musicians. With his first observation, Newman wrote:

> Only the outcasts of musical society—at each end of the social scale—now hanker after the worst products of Italian opera. Mendelssohn's influence and

---

[6] Ernest Newman, 'The culture of the emotions', *NQMR*, August 1893, 57–62, and 'The difficulties of musical criticism', *NQMR*, November 1894, 105–12.

[7] Correspondence between the men are held at Special Collections, Cadbury Research Library, University of Birmingham: XGB Granville Bantock Collection and MS79 Joseph Holbrooke Collection. Newman's relationship with Bantock is discussed in Paul Watt 'A "gigantic and popular place of entertainment": Granville Bantock and music-making at the New Brighton Tower in the late 1890s', *Royal Musical Association Research Chronicle* 42 (2009): 109–64. Newman's relationship with Holbrooke is discussed in Paul Watt, 'A "Nationalist in art": Holbrooke's *Contemporary British Composers*' in *Joseph Holbrooke: Composer, Critic, and Musical Patriot* eds Paul Watt and Anne-Marie Forbes (Lanham, MD: Rowman and Littlefield, 2015): 153–74.

following are becoming smaller year after year. The passion for oratorio is dying—whether of repletion or a lack of nourishment, whether of too great a satisfaction of the appetite by the few good oratorios, or the too little satisfaction afforded by the many bad ones, is comparatively unimportant.[8]

Newman described these 'worst products'—a love of Italian opera, works by Mendelssohn and performances of oratorio—as 'the evil, the absurdity and the vulgarity ... that have till now retarded the development of English music'.[9] In trying to overcome public attachment to this seemingly old-fashioned repertory, Newman suggested a three-pronged approach. He proposed that English music should be brought to the public through 'one or two courageous publishers' just as English poetry had been supported in the recent past, though he provided no examples of such undertakings.[10] The second part of the plan was to decentralize music outside London:

> At present, London is almost the only city where the higher kinds of symphonic and operatic music can be persistently cultivated on a large scale. The result is, that nine out of ten of our younger composers have only London to look to for performance. There is painful overcrowding, and the infantile death-rate is very high in consequence. 'Back to the country' should be our motto here, as in social and economic matters generally.[11]

The third part of Newman's rescue mission for British music involved casting doubt on plans to subsidise composers: 'no one who advances £50 towards the publishing of a young man's score is likely to find it come back to him, in later years, bringing a smiling five hundred per cent along with it.'[12]

Newman argued this three-point plan would provide 'simple and practical' measures by which English music could be improved, though I doubt that many publishers, town-planners or arts patrons would have agreed. But Newman proposed these ideas as starting points, explaining that other initiatives could play a part in supporting British music, such as changes to musical education, including amended examination processes, as well as:

> a restriction of the output of worthless degrees to mere pianists and organists, the burning of a few academies, the assassination of a few semi-moribund professors—along all these paths much good work might be done; and the man

[8] Ernest Newman, 'English music and musical criticism', CR, November 1901, 734–738; 735.

[9] Newman, 'English music and musical criticism', 735.

[10] Newman, 'English music and musical criticism', 735.

[11] Newman, 'English music and musical criticism', 738.

[12] Newman, 'English music and musical criticism', 739.

who will devote his life disinterestedly to any one of them may find himself immortalised in English musical history.[13]

Newman continued to talk positively about the future of a new school of British music in the article, hoping he would live to see the long awaited English musical renaissance. He described Elgar's *Enigma Variations* as 'the most important piece of music till then produced by an Englishman'.[14] He placed high hopes on Bantock's 'H.F.B. Variations' as a second vital contribution to local composition 'which, it is hoped, is the basis for a career of sustained organic energy'.[15] Joseph Holbrooke's *The Skeleton in Armour* Newman regarded as 'a work that will bring joy into the heart of every musical patriot. Nothing so rich and strong has ever been before written by an English musician of twenty'.[16]

His campaign to cultivate an interest in British composers gathered pace. In December 1901 Newman published the first of ten articles in the *Speaker* called 'The New School of British Music'.[17] The first article published on 7 December, outlined Newman's aims for the series: he confined his discussions to composers no older than Elgar and then gave his overall reason for writing on the subject:

> In the nature of the case, no man can hear much new English music. In the first place, comparatively little of it is performed; in the second place, one work is given here, another there, and no critic can possibly hear them all. The only course for any man to adopt who wishes to know what musical England is now doing is to have recourse to the scores themselves.[18]

Newman explained how he had been lucky enough to study a significant number of works in manuscript and he was enthused by some of it:

> I know there is music in England; I know what fiery energy is being put into the work; I know how intelligently our young musicians think about their art, and how seriously they apply themselves to the practice of it; and I believe most firmly that the majority of work I have seen is very good and unhackneyed, and that some of it is excellent.[19]

---

[13] Newman, 'English music and musical criticism', 741.

[14] Newman, 'English music and musical criticism', 742

[15] Newman, 'English music and musical criticism', 742

[16] Newman, 'English music and musical criticism', 742

[17] Newman, 'The New School of British Music I', *Sp.* 7 December 1901, 271–3; 271.

[18] Ernest Newman, 'The New School of British Music I', 272.

[19] Ernest Newman, 'The New School of British Music I', 272.

'The New School of British Music' series did not only contain appraisals of musical works: Newman remarked upon wider aspects of musical culture and was often critical of institutions, musical infrastructure, and the causes of the sometimes poor reception of newly composed English music. In the article on Elgar, for example, Newman argued that the composer's works written for festivals were not his best achievements (*The Dream of Gerontius* was identified as an exception) and put forward the argument that festival culture produced mediocre music:

> What is 'a Festival work'? It is an attempt to breathe the breath of life into the stalest, most pedantic, most unhappy form that was ever known in music. In its worst mode, the English Festival cantata or oratorio is bad verse set to bad music; in its immediate mode it is good music hampered by passable words; in its best form it is good music and good poetry each doing its utmost to cut each other's throat—we get neither the poet at his best nor the musician at his best.[20]

Newman believed a festival work stifled a composer's creativity and the bulk of music written for these events were inferior. According to Newman, the problem was not with the works' tonal language, rather their consistent lack of a balanced or well-proportioned structure.

Newman also wrote about genre in this series of articles. For example, in the article on Granville Bantock, in which Newman discussed the composer's gift for opera, he supposed Bantock's operas 'came to an end when he realised how hopeless is the present outlook in England for operatic music'.[21] He also addressed the subject of the musically neglected, especially Frederick C. Nichols, whose *Love Songs of Lord Tennyson* was a case in point: Newman called its composer 'the finest song writer England has yet produced'.[22] Newman praised Wallace for his ability to set good poetry to good music (e.g. in *The Freebooter Songs*) and admired his versatility to compose in numerous genres, but was slightly critical of his uniformity of style.[23]

Newman's best hope for contemporary British music came in the sixth instalment, an article on his good friend Joseph Holbrooke. Newman recounted the happy occasion of their meeting and was bold enough to claim that Holbrooke's music was 'something without parallel in English music,

---

[20] Ernest Newman, 'The New School of British Music II: Edward Elgar', *Sp.* 21 December 1901, 331–2; 331.

[21] Ernest Newman, 'The New School of British Music III: Granville Bantock', *Sp.* 4 January 1902, 385–6; 386.

[22] Ernest Newman, 'The New School of British Music IV: Mr Frederick C. Nicholls', *Sp.* 18 January 1902, 442–3; 442.

[23] Ernest Newman, 'The New School of British Music V: William Wallace, *Sp.* 1 February 1902, 499–501.

something that instinctively set me thinking of the big names that come to us from over sea.[24] Newman enthused: '[I] have studied carefully almost everything Mr Holbrooke has written; and each successive experience has deepened in me the conviction that if this young man does not leave his mark upon the history of modern music there is no other Englishman who will. Anyone who can write music like Mr Holbrooke when he is scarcely out of his teens will certainly be heard of in later days'.[25] Newman's hyperbole continued to the end of the article: 'Wagner, Tchaikovsky, Richard Strauss! These are great names to mention in connection with a young Englishman of twenty-two or twenty-three; but I do not repent of my temerity. Nor do I fear that I shall ever have cause to'.[26] Years later, Neville Cardus would cite Newman's youthful zeal for Holbrooke as one of his greatest critical misjudgements.[27]

Newman also had high hopes for Samuel Coleridge-Taylor, the subject of the seventh article in the series.[28] Acknowledging that Coleridge-Taylor had produced a hit with *Hiawatha's Wedding-Feast*, Newman imagined the best was yet to come from this composer. In the eighth article, on Percy Pitt, Newman tried hard to convince the reader that Pitt's French training fostered an individuality of style and that his compositions were not 'mere imitators of things French'.[29] Newman held Pitt in very high regard though did not position him as equal to Elgar or Bantock. The penultimate article in the series discussed a number of composers, including Arthur Hinton (whom Newman believed to be a skilled song-writer) and Rutland Boughton (whom Newman admired, despite his 'too vigorous, too turbulent spirit').[30] The tenth and final article continued the discussion of minor composers from the ninth instalment and the series concluded with a list of works by some of the composers mentioned, along with their publishers, to encourage readers to purchase their scores.[31]

---

[24] Ernest Newman, 'The New School of British Music VI: Mr Josef Holbrooke', *Sp*. 15 February 1902, 557–8; 557.

[25] Newman, 'The New School of British Music VI: Mr Josef Holbrooke', 557.

[26] Newman, 'The New School of British Music VI: Mr Josef Holbrooke', 557–8.

[27] Newman, 'The New School of British Music VI: Mr Josef Holbrooke', 558. For Cardus's view on Newman and Holbrooke see Robin Daniels (ed.), *Conversations with Cardus* (London: Victor Gollancz Ltd., 1976): 41.

[28] Ernest Newman, 'The New School of British Music VII: Mr S. Coleridge Taylor', *Sp*. 1 March 1902, 608–10.

[29] Ernest Newman, 'The New School of British Music VIII: Mr Percy Pitt', *Sp*. 15 March 1902, 669–70; 669.

[30] Ernest Newman, 'The New School of British Music IX', *Sp*. 29 March 1902, 725–6; 726.

[31] Ernest Newman, 'The New School of British Music X', *Sp*. 12 April 1902, 40–1.

After writing these articles on British music in the *Speaker* in late 1901 and early 1902, Newman took up the subject again in the *Manchester Guardian*— he was a regular contributor in 1905 and 1906, and in 1919 to 1923. In 1905–6 Newman wrote approximately fifty articles but had little to say about British music. However, he reviewed concerts of works by Henry Walford Davies, York Bowen and Hubert Parry. On 8 November 1905, Newman reviewed a performance of Davies' *Everyman* and found few faults with it.[32] The following March, Newman reviewed York Bowen's *Symphonic Fantasia* and described it as derivative and 'dull'.[33] Two months later, while reviewing English works from the Morecambe Festival, Newman failed to like many works, including Parry's *Pied Piper of Hamlin*, though he conceded it was a widely popular work and commented favourably on the style of Parry's *The Twelve Days of Christmas*.[34] However, these reviews of works produced in, or near, Manchester reveal little of Newman's thoughts on the plight of English music. He mentioned in an article in mid-April 1906 that 'the making of music in England still goes on apace, but comparatively little of it is worth attention', but he was to write much more emphatically and regularly on English music in his stint on the *Manchester Guardian* from 1919–23, and in the early years of his appointment to the *Sunday Times*.[35]

When Newman wrote for the *Speaker* in 1901 he was most enthusiastic about Elgar, Bantock and Holbrooke. He was also hugely taken with Holst:

> Mr Gustav Holst had a great success on Monday, at the London Symphony Orchestra's concert, with his 'Planets'. To hold an audience always interested in an orchestral work lasting about an hour is a great test of a composer. Mr Holst came through it triumphantly. The work not only definitely marks him out, as regards both imagination and technique as the most significant figure among the British composers of the post-Elgar-Delius-Bantock period, it gives him a high place among the contemporary European composers who really matter.[36]

Apart from writing on his musical preferences and favourite composers, Newman commented occasionally on infrastructure and moral support for English music. For example, upon the foundation of the British Music Society by Dr Arthur Eaglefield Hull in late April to early May 1920, Newman urged musicians to join it, but he did not believe that the formation of a society alone would much alter the course of locally produced music:

---

[32] Ernest Newman, 'Everyman in Liverpool', *MG*, 8 November 1905, 7.

[33] Ernest Newman, 'The Hallé concert', *MG*, 9 March 1906, 7.

[34] Ernest Newman, 'Morecambe Festival', *MG*, 12 May 1906, 8.

[35] Ernest Newman, 'Some recent music', *MG*, 17 April 1906, 5.

[36] Ernest Newman, 'The week in music', *MG*, 17 November 1920, 5.

I am not one of those who believe very much can be done for English music by any society. We need only two things for complete success—great composers and a public to listen to them; and I am afraid the making of these two principal links in the chain is a little beyond the power of any society. But something can be done for music in England by a united effort; and as the British Music Society is the most enlightened thing of the kind that we have, one cordially wishes it all good luck.[37]

Newman continued to be cynical about the effectiveness of the British Music Society. A little over a year later, in 1921, he criticized the Society for its poorly executed concert series. Newman wrote that it would be better not to give any concerts at all than to give poorly performed ones, and he noted that the quality of its concert of Elizabethan madrigals was especially bad.[38]

By the 1920s, Newman's outlook on British music was rarely optimistic, but he tried hard to promote those who fought for the local product. In 1920 he was enthusiastic about the establishment of the 'Patron's Fund' set up by Sir Ernest Palmer at the Royal College of Music, and he wrote enthusiastically about the repertoire given at a student concert, including a 'Bergomask' by Jane Joseph as well as works (that Newman did not name) by Gerrard Williams, Frederic Lawrence and L.A. Collingwood. Newman occasionally used his essays to proffer advice to students, suggesting they write smaller works so they could easily be accommodated into programmes.[39] These were small, but important steps in helping to publicize British music and musicians.

❧ Audiences and Programming

Articles about audience taste and behaviour are ubiquitous in any critic's writings and Newman's articles in the *Manchester Guardian* in 1919 and 1920 were no exception. Although Newman had moved from Manchester to London in 1918 to work on the *Observer*, from 17 September 1919 to 7 July 1920 he continued to write a weekly column for the *Manchester Guardian* called 'Music from London'.[40] He was shocked by the lack of musical activity in the capital and thought most performances hardly worth writing about.[41] He was also

---

[37] Ernest Newman, 'Music in London', *MG*, 28 April 1920, 7.

[38] Ernest Newman, 'The week in music', *MG*, 23 June 1921, 5.

[39] Ernest Newman, 'The week in music', *MG*, 17 November 1920, 5.

[40] From 14 July 1920 his column title was changed to 'The week in music' until 15 November 1922, whereupon Newman wrote (more or less) exclusively for the *Sunday Times*.

[41] Ernest Newman, 'Music in London', *MG*, 31 December 1919, 5; 'Music in London', *MG*, 4 February 1920, 5.

puzzled and irritated by the tastes and behaviour of London's audiences, especially their lukewarm embrace of works by Elgar.

In early October 1919 Newman wrote about a Promenade Concert of Elgar's First Symphony, conducted by Henry Wood, and was confounded by the audience's reception, even taking into account a rail strike: 'The house was almost empty. Was this because of the strike, or because the London public still remains curiously inappreciative of our leading composer? The public is really beyond comprehension'.[42] Three months later, Newman revisited the subject of Elgar's London reception. In a review of the first performance of Elgar's Cello Concerto on 3 December 1919, Newman was dismayed by its poor performance, suggesting that it had been under-rehearsed.[43]

By the end of March 1919, however, Newman could write that Queen's Hall 'was virtually full' for a performance of Elgar's Second Symphony, and he seemed relieved that 'it cannot be said that Elgar keeps people away'.[44] Newman acknowledged that the enthusiasm for this concert was due to the calibre and popularity of the conductor, Adrian Boult. This full house was a one-off. However, the next month another Elgar concert was given in London, and Newman was at the end of his tether over the low audience numbers:

> On Monday evening Mr. Landon Ronald and the Albert Hall Orchestra, with Mr Gervase Elwes as the soloist, gave an all-Elgar concert at the Queen's Hall to the usual miserably small audience. The neglect of Elgar by the London public is a mystery that I have given up tying to solve. No one in England can compare with Mr [Landon] Ronald as interpreter of the larger works of Elgar: there is perhaps no music that calls out so surely as this does everything that is best in him. The 'Polonia', which was written during the war in aid of a Polish relief fund, is now recognized only as a clever *pièce d'occasion*. But the Enigma Variations have mellowed into a classic—the earliest classic that English orchestral music can show; while the second symphony, which will be a classic some day, is as yet, one suspects, too severe a strain on the imagination of the average Englishman, who finds fifty minutes' continuous hard thinking in modern music a little beyond him.[45]

Newman's criticisms of audiences, as well as those responsible for programming and directing music, are a mainstay of Newman's columns no matter where he wrote. In his work on the *Manchester Guardian*, opera, promenade concerts and competition festivals were subjects on which he offered

[42] Ernest Newman, 'Music in London', *MG*, 8 October 1919, 5.

[43] Ernest Newman, 'Music in London', *MG*, 3 December 1919, 7.

[44] Ernest Newman, 'Music in London, *MG*, 24 March 1920, 7.

[45] Ernest Newman, 'Music in London', *MG*, 14 April 1920, 7.

advice on artistic direction. In late 1920 through to the middle of 1921, for example, Newman articulated his concerns over the winding-up of Thomas Beecham's opera company and wrote in two articles that Beecham was the only person with the talent and practical expertise required to bring decent opera to London audiences.[46] Turning his attention to promenade concerts, Newman wrote in an article in August 1922 that the repertory was too safe and not nearly adventurous enough. He strongly supported the scheduling of such concerts on Saturday evenings when they would attract larger audiences, but there appeared to be little interest in this idea.[47] He also endorsed the various competition festivals throughout Britain—for example, in Blackpool and Glasgow, where he had been a judge—as good avenues for music education and the advancement of English music. Newman suggested that locally produced, and more demanding, music could be written for choirs, and that the publication of modern editions of foreign songs would expand choristers' horizons. He urged festival and committee councils to back such enterprises.[48] Later, Newman called for 'some rich man' to put forward funds to help improve the standard of choirs he judged at festivals, concerned that standards had slipped during wartime.[49]

In addition to providing musical advice, Newman also gave financial guidance. In late February 1906, for example, he put forward a budget for staging the *Ring* in Manchester.[50] His article on the topic was published on the morning of the organizing committee's meeting, and he seized the opportunity to tell them how to go about their business. He directed the committee to allocate £2000 to the event and strongly advised that further guarantees should be pursued, writing that one man had already offered £50. He also argued against a matter raised by a recent correspondent that a performance of the *Ring* should not go ahead unless a better English translation could be secured, until a 'perfect' production could be reached. But Newman was pragmatic: 'I am afraid that if we are to wait for the "Ring" when we can be quite sure that everything in it will be faultless we shall have to wait a very long time; indeed if the same rule were applied to all our musical performances there would not be occasion for us to leave our homes too often.'[51]

[46] Ernest Newman, 'The week in music', *MG*, 3 November 1920, 5; 'The week in music', *MG*, 10 November 1920, 7.

[47] Ernest Newman, 'The week in music', *MG*, 8 November 1923, 5, 6.

[48] Ernest Newman, 'The week in music', *MG*, 27 October 1920, 5.

[49] Ernest Newman, 'The week in music', *MG*, 3 May 1923, 16; 'The week in music', *MG*, 9 March 1922, 5.

[50] Ernest Newman, 'The "Ring" in Manchester', *MG*, 23 February 1906, 6.

[51] Newman, 'The "Ring" in Manchester', *MG*, 23 February 1906, 6.

Newman also offered advice on musical infrastructure, such as fixing the poor acoustics in the Royal Albert Hall and Mortimer Hall. His solution was drastic: to build two or three new concert halls. He argued that London needed a concert hall 'larger than Queen's Hall [but] one much smaller than the Aeolian or the Wigmore [Hall].[52] On many occasions, Newman suggested the publication of a London concert diary so that clashes in programming could be avoided; he also recommended that the performing rights' fee should be the responsibility of managers, not soloists.[53] He further proposed that music-making in London should consider the needs and desires of people living in the less fashionable East End.[54]

Newman was very critical of the concentration of musical activity in the West End and wrote about it in an article in 1923: 'concerts are confined too exclusively to the three or four well-known halls. But the population that can reach these halls is, after all, a limited one. There must be tens of thousands of music-lovers a little distance away who would be glad to hear a West End concert but simply cannot spare the time to make the double journey'.[55] Newman came to this view after attending a sports event at White Hart Lane, when he noticed that he 'could find no trace' of the suburb in various directories.

A topic on which Newman did not give advice as much as offer reflective thoughts for the future, was music-making after the First World War.[56] He wrote about it in two newspapers, the *Manchester Guardian* and *New Witness*. In a reply to an article in the *Musical Times* by M. Jaques Dalcroze in 1915 outlining musical culture in Switzerland after the war, Newman took the opportunity to reflect on the situation in London, and it was not a particularly encouraging one:

> Everywhere works have been given without adequate rehearsal; wretched music has been dug up, and foisted upon long-suffering audiences in the name of patriotism; orchestras have been reduced in size; singers and players have been allowed to appear who, purely on their merits, had no right to expect a hearing. Criticism has kept a silent tongue in its head, in part because it did not wish to say anything that might discourage the co-operation of willing amateurs and semi-amateurs in the sacred work of charity, or shill the enthusiasm and diminish the size of the audiences; in part because it was evident that economic

---

[52] Ernest Newman, 'The week in music', *MG*, 6 January 1921, 5.

[53] Both of these suggestions are made in 'The week in music', *MG*, 20 January 1921, 5

[54] Ernest Newman', 'The week in music', *MG*, 16 February 1922, 5.

[55] Ernest Newman, 'The week in music', *MG*, 18 January 1932, 5.

[56] For a study of the broader milieu in which Newman wrote on music and war, see Kate Kennedy and Trudi Tate, 'Literature and music of the First World War', *First World War Studies* 2/1 (2011): 1–6.

stringency and enlistment combined have made it impossible to maintain the old standard of performance.[57]

Newman went on to discuss the emotional effects of war. He had met a soldier who argued that the war would not affect music but Newman could not agree. Newman wrote that there should be no under-estimating—or senti-mentalizing—the potential adverse impact of war on the psychological health of the nation and its music. At the same time, Newman saw the significant potential of music—opera and light music, in particular—as a means to lift the gloomy public mood.

Newspaper editors were still publishing inane concert reports, according to Newman, and he returned to the topic of criticism, once more despairing that it had fallen on bad times. Newman surveyed some examples of this sec-ond-rate journalism—which invariably consisted of a mere listing of reper-tory and the manner in which it was performed—describing it as 'generally unreadable; they are rarely read; they bore the critic; they displease or disap-point the persons criticized; and they are of no commercial value to the paper in which they appear'.[58] Newman's remedy was to encourage newspapers to run musical criticism a few times a week instead of every day 'and let him [the critic] deal critically, carefully, imaginatively, with such episodes of the week as are of interest to him and may be presumed to be of interest to his readers'.[59]

Newman explored the topic of war and its effect on musicians, again, in 1918, asking 'How will they [musicians] look at music after two or three years' deprivation of it, and after the intensity of their experiences in France or Mesopotamia'?[60] Responding to comments made by the critic Gerald Cumberland, writing of his heightened sensibility to music upon returning to England and the instant effect it had on his sense of well-being, Newman hoped that music would be the panacea for other soldiers' trauma over the terror of war. But Newman was not ready to make a definite pronouncement on the matter:

> No one can prophesy the result of it all [the war] upon the composers of the new day. Will it leave some permanent sensitivity in them that would not have been there for their experiences in war, or will it all pass away in a very little while like a bad dream that shakes us only for a minute or two after waking? The musicians

[57] Ernest Newman, 'Music after the war', NW, 25 November 1915, 100, 102; 100.

[58] Ernest Newman, 'Musical criticisms after the war: a hint to editor', NW, 23 December 1915, 222, 224; 222.

[59] Ernest Newman, 'Musical criticisms after the war: a hint to editor', NW, 23 December 1915, 222, 224; 222.

[60] Ernest Newman, 'When the music-men come back', NW, 21 June 1918, 152–3; 152.

now or recently at the front have not yet begun to express themselves … Will the experiences of war add very much to the sensitivity of the predestined artistic creator? I am not answering these questions either in the affirmative or the negative. I am only posing them.[61]

Newman could comment without hesitation, though, on the effect of war on audience numbers and their sometime anti-German sentiment. Reporting on an all-Wagner concert in September 1919, he was convinced that the packed audience at Queen's Hall was not the slightest bit troubled by hearing the work of a German composer:

I think I understand why the audience was still so engrossed with this Wagner music, even after all its varied musical experiences of the last five years. It is not simply that Wagner deals in emotions that German music has made especially familiar to us, and perhaps made us excessively susceptible to; it is rather that the least instructed music-lover feels instinctively not only the intensity but the range of the man; and it is just in the matter of range that the majority of our late allies fail us in music.[62]

In the same article, Newman noted the proliferation of concerts of English music and was critical of patriotic sentiment guiding the programming of lesser, local music.

One of Newman's most substantial and reflective articles on music and war was published in the *Manchester Guardian* in January 1920.[63] He reported a growing acceptance of German music in various concert programmes and was pleased to see that a recent performance of Schoenberg's Sextet had attracted a large enough audience to fill the Aeolian Hall and that it 'was listened to in silence and received with the greatest enthusiasm'.[64] He went on to say that 'after an experience of this kind it is no longer possible to doubt that the time has come for the forgetting of the war, so far as music is concerned'.[65] But Newman was wary of importing second-rate foreign music, as he accused impresarios of doing during wartime. Newman recounted his recent attendance at concerts and was unimpressed with the quality of Italian, French and Russian works on the programme. However, he confessed he was unsure if this was the result of his heightened critical awareness of music formed during the war years, or

---

[61] Newman, 'When the music-men come back', 152–3.

[62] Ernest Newman, 'Music in London, *MG*, 24 September 1919, 5.

[63] Ernest Newman, 'Music in London', *MG*, 7 January 1920, 5.

[64] Newman, 'Music in London', *MG*, 7 January 1920, 5.

[65] Newman, 'Music in London', *MG*, 7 January 1920, 5.

an indication of changes in his personal taste. He further admitted that many works by Debussy and later works by Ravel left him 'cold'.[66]

Newman was often irked by the politics of concert programming and concerned about the reaction of audiences to German music. He was irritated to learn that a concert by the tenor Mischa Léon, scheduled for performance in late February or March 1920, had songs in German pulled from the programme at the eleventh hour for fear of a hostile critical reception.[67] Newman was also worried about how the audience would react to a concert of Strauss's *Don Juan* ('the first English performance since the outbreak of hostilities of any large work by a living German composer') but reported on 10 March that the performance went off without a hitch; that Queen's Hall was full, and 'those who expected a disturbance of some sort were disappointed'.[68] A week later, in another concert by Mischa Léon at Aeolian Hall, the soloist was met with hisses and cries: Newman reported there was a 'half-hour of pandemonium' after which the disaffected audience members left.[69]

🎵 *Russian Music*

Russian music was a relatively safe topic on which to write, given the alliance between Russia and England, and Newman had plenty of provocative things to say about it. Newman had first written in detail on Russian music in an article on Tchaikovsky in the *Contemporary Review* in 1901, but took up the topic again in the *Musical Times*, *Manchester Guardian* and *New Witness* in the late 1910s. Although Rosa Newmarch emerged as the British expert on Russian music in this period, Newman nevertheless felt he had something to add, especially on the subject of nationalism in music.[70]

As early as June 1901, when his article on Tchaikovsky was published in the *Contemporary Review*, Newman argued that Tchaikovsky's music in general, and Russian music in particular, 'ha[d] not been quite fairly treated by the

---

[66] Newman, 'Music in London', *MG*, 7 January 1920, 5.

[67] Ernest Newman, 'Music in London', *MG*, 3 March 1920, 7.

[68] Ernest Newman, 'Music in London', *MG*, 10 March 1920, 5.

[69] Ernest Newman, 'Music in London', *MG*, 17 May 1920, 7.

[70] See Philip Ross Bullock, *Rosa Newmarch and Russian Music in late Nineteenth and Early Twentieth-Century England* (Aldershot: Ashgate, 2009) and Charlotte Purkis, "'Leader of fashion in musical thought:" The importance of Rosa Newmarch in the context of turn-of-the-century British music appreciation', in *Nineteenth-Century British Music Studies* vol. 3, eds Peter Horton and Bennett Zon (Aldershot: Ashgate, 2003): 4–19.

British public or the British critic?[71] Yet in the opening pages of the article Newman was more concerned with writing about nationalism than about Tchaikovsky per se. He was quick to point out the difficulties of pigeonholing Tchaikovsky as a typically Russian composer because he was half French, and because 'Russia is a very large country, containing more than one type of physical and mental structure'.[72] In many later articles, Newman was to label as folly the approach to slotting composers into particular national traditions and warned against the use of an 'all-embracing racial type' when intellectualizing about nationalities.[73] As he explained: 'just as all Chinamen are unprogressive, all Boers hypocritical, all Frenchman hysterical, and all Englishmen brave and honest, so all Russians are alternately simple barbarians and morbid, lachrymose decadents'.[74] Newman then criticized Edward Dannreuther's article on Tchaikovsky in the *Grove Dictionary of Music and Musicians* for characterizing the composer as possessing a so-called 'Slavonic temperament' and for offering a barely descriptive account of the composer's music using ineffective adjectives such as 'exuberant' and 'gorgeous'.[75] Newman explained that 'there is really no excuse for a critic who writes in this way. If he does not know a composer's work thoroughly he should say so frankly, and not mislead the public, who look to him for guidance'.[76] Newman continued the article with an appraisal of some of the Russian composer's works, including the *Pathetic Symphony*, concluding that, despite the lack of knowledge of Tchaikovsky's life and music in England, the Russian composer was 'one of the biggest of the moderns, and one of the most original and independent musicians of any time'.[77]

Newman wrote again on Russian music between 1916 and 1920. He appears to have taken up the topic following a circular he received from the Russian Musical Committee asking him to publicize their activities. The patrons of the committee comprised the Russian ambassador, the consul-general, Grand Duke Michael, a selection of Russian composers (whom Newman did not name) and a Russian conductor and publisher (also not named) as well as 'Sir Thomas Beecham, Mrs Rosa Newmarch, and Sir Henry Wood—to whom

---

[71] Ernest Newman, 'The essential Tchaikovsky', *CR*, June 1901, 887–98; 887. For background to the reception of Russian composers in England see Stephen Muir, '"About as wild and barbaric as well could be imagined …": The critical reception of Rimsky-Korsakov in nineteenth-century England', *ML*, 93/4 (2012): 513–42.

[72] Ernest Newman, 'The essential Tchaikovsky', 888.

[73] Newman, 'The essential Tchaikovsky', 888.

[74] Newman, 'The essential Tchaikovsky', 888.

[75] Newman, 'The essential Tchaikovsky', 889.

[76] Newman, 'The essential Tchaikovsky', 889.

[77] Newman, 'The essential Tchaikovsky', 898.

we in England are very deeply indebted for what we already know of Russian music, and a number of names more or less ornamental'.[78] In the same way he had argued in his 1901 article on Tchaikovsky that the British public was not well acquainted with Russian music, Newman made the point again in this 1916 article: 'for Russian music in particular the English public has for many years showed a decided partiality. The twenty-year-old Tchaikovsky boom has even yet not exhausted itself: and the other Russians, big and little, are slowly coming into their own'.[79] Yet Newman believed there was an appetite for the performances of works by many Russian composers, especially 'Mussorgsky, Rimsky-Korsakov, Borodin, Balakirev, Scriabin, Medtner, Stravinsky, and half a dozen others'.[80] But Newman doubted that a committee would be able to arouse sufficient musical interest in the public.

Just as Newman had been sceptical about various ventures set up to support English music, he felt the Russian Committee was also doomed to fail:

> The Committee's object is 'to encourage the introduction of Russian music into the United Kingdom'. It 'proposes to present to exercise the following functions': (a) 'to maintain a watchful observation'; (b) 'to tender advice as called for'; (c) 'to patronise suitable literature and suitable undertakings'; (d) 'to act generally as a referee'; (e) 'it will be in contact here with musical societies, concert-givers, opera-directors, conductors, lecturers, teachers, students and amateurs'.[81]

Newman was not convinced: 'I am afraid all this is too nebulous to have the slightest efficacy'.[82] He wrote that aims a, c and d 'mean nothing'. He felt the overall tone of the committee's aim was patronizing and the many musicians and lecturers would not want, or need, the committee's advice because they already knew, 'without the assistance of any Committee, which is the good Russian music … Amateurs and students also know perfectly well which music they are longing to hear or buy. No Committee is necessary to tell the music-lover of Manchester or Birmingham that they ought to hear Chaliapan in "Boris Godunov", or see the Russian ballets'.[83] Newman concluded the article in a cynical vein, suggesting the Committee was really a ploy by businessmen exploiting the British and Russian alliance to make money, and he reproached publishers for the exorbitant prices of scores of Russian music.

---

[78] Ernest Newman, 'The Russian Music Committee', *NW*, 10 February 1916, 446, 448; 446.

[79] Newman, 'The Russian Music Committee', 446.

[80] Newman, 'The Russian Music Committee', 446.

[81] Newman, 'The Russian Music Committee', 446.

[82] Newman, 'The Russian Music Committee', 446.

[83] Newman, 'The Russian Music Committee', 446

Newman suggested that one of the surest ways for Russian music to make its mark in England was for Russian musicians to lower their fees: 'If *they* [Russian musicians] will not make these sacrifices [of remuneration] in order to make their national music better known and loved in England—and I myself cannot quite see them doing it!—what good does this Committee think it can do by vague appeals to *us* to do something or other?'[84]

More articles by Newman on Russian music in the *New Witness* continued to champion the works of particular composers and to question the nationalist labels attached to their works. In an article on 18 May 1916, for example, Newman wrote enthusiastically about an upcoming production of *Boris Godunov* in Manchester, under the direction of Sir Thomas Beecham.[85] Newman was unperturbed by the singing of the opera in French because he felt the existing English translation of it was so poor. Although he believed a performance in English would be necessary for the opera to be truly appreciated in England, Newman argued it could only be properly and fully understood when sung in Russian. In the rest of the article Newman wrote about the fallacy of nationalism in music, believing that 'tradition, sympathy, environment count for more than mere race in art' and 'travel and the easy access to scores and performances of the music of every nation will make each composer not a mere German or Frenchman or Englishman, but a citizen of the world'.[86] In Newman's view of the future, music would be 'cosmopolitan' rather than 'national'.[87]

These historiographical debates over nationalism propelled Newman in another direction: criticisms of books on topics relating to Russian music. Two articles in *New Witness* in late March and early April 1917 constituted a negative review of the recently published *Contemporary Russian Composers* by M. Montagu-Nathan.[88] While at first praising this author's previous work on Russian music, Newman disliked the section on Glinka. He found this chapter dated, bloated and inaccurate, writing that Glinka 'was never a great composer, and he is of scarcely any significance in the history of any music but

---

[84] Newman, 'The Russian Music Committee', 448. Newman continued his criticism of the Committee in a follow-up article in the *New Witness* a week later: 'That Russian Musical Committee again', 17 February, 478, 480, in which he criticised Robin Legge of the *Daily Telegraph* for exhorting English musicians to support the committee.

[85] Ernest Newman, '"Boris Godounov" and nationalism in music', *NW*, 18 May 1916, 82–3; 82. 'Godounov' is Newman's spelling.

[86] Newman, '"Boris Godounov" and nationalism in music', 82.

[87] Newman, '"Boris Godounov" and nationalism in music', 82.

[88] Ernest Newman, 'Glinka—I', *NW*, 29 March 1917, 600–601 and 'Glinka—II', *NW*, 5 April 1917, 623, 624.

Russian music'.[89] Moreover, the second article disputed the claim that Glinka wrote in a typically Russian style arising from the use of folk-songs. Newman supposed Michael Calvocoressi's book on Glinka to be 'rather more critical' on the topic because Calvocoressi at least saw that 'a life for the Tsar' was banal and vulgar.[90] In a later article, published in June 1917, Newman was to write a similar review of Montagu Nathan's book on Mussorgsky, again regarding it as 'adequate' yet compromised due to its reliance on dated sources.[91]

༄ Music Criticism

In addition to criticizing writers of books, Newman also commented on contemporary critics, thereby continuing another preoccupation from his free-thought years. In 1916, for example, he wrote an article on his rival John F. Runciman.[92] Despite expressing his admiration for Runciman, Newman was critical of him: 'Head and shoulders as he was above the ruck of his colleagues both as musician and as writer, he was still sadly lacking in some of the qualities of a great critic'.[93] Although Newman regarded Runciman to be 'the most readable critic in England', he argued his work was compromised by inconsistency and moodiness. According to Newman, Runciman's writing style, rather than critical acumen, was his best attribute: 'He had the musician's feeling for music—a very different thing from the literary man's feeling for it. His tongue savoured all sorts of excellences in a great work that only a musician can feel …'.[94] At the end of the article, Newman suggested that further volumes of Runciman's essays from the *Saturday Review* should be published.

Newman wrote again in the *New Witness* on the style and language of criticism after reading an article on 'fine writing' by Leonard Liebling, editor of New York's *Musical Courier*.[95] Newman wrote of Liebling's disdain for 'verbal impressionism that tries to translate music into literature'.[96] Newman was not interested in impressionist criticism, which he argued was 'valueless' because of its reliance on description.[97]

---

[89] Newman, 'Glinka—I', 601.

[90] Newman, 'Glinka—I', 601, quoting Calvocoressi, *Glinka: Biographie Critique* (Paris: H. Laurens, 1911).

[91] Ernest Newman, 'Moussorgsky', *NW*, 7 June 1917, 134–3; 134.

[92] Ernest Newman, 'J.F.R.', *NW*, 27 April 1916, 798–99; 800.

[93] Newman, 'J.F.R.', 798.

[94] Newman, 'J.F.R.', 799.

[95] Ernest Newman, 'Concerning musical criticism', *NW*, 3 May 1917, 14–15.

[96] Newman, 'Concerning musical criticism', 14.

[97] Newman, 'Concerning musical criticism', 14.

In the *New Witness* in October 1916, Newman took up other problems he encountered with contemporary music criticism.[98] First, the number of critics was insufficient: according to Newman, there were 'hardly five decent music critics in Europe' because they were a product of the narrow frames of reference, given their self-education. Second, the lack of a history of musical criticism meant that it was difficult for critics to judge contemporary works in the context of past intellectual trends. To illustrate this point, Newman referred to Matthew Arnold's essay on the function of criticism, which established that its main purpose was, in Newman's words, 'to distinguish the vital current among the many currents of the time', though Newman felt that musical criticism in this regard had 'always failed most lamentably'.[99]

Newman addressed the failure of music criticism in a further two articles entitled 'The Critic in the confessional' in November 1916.[100] In the first article, he wrote that too many London critics were pressed to write notices for 'trivial concerts' whereas a provincial critic, not bound by the need for so much reporting, could 'feel himself freer' to write on a greater variety of topics.[101] This freedom to write on music-related subjects was, according to Newman, representative of a 'true criticism', not merely reporting. In the second article, Newman suggested that concert reporting should be abolished to make room for this 'true' or scholastic criticism.[102]

By 1918 Newman had returned to the same ideas about music criticism that he had fashioned in the 1890s: that it should be based on method, and that the critic needed absolute detachment. As he wrote in an article in the *New Witness* at the beginning of January 1918:

> The question, it will be seen, thus becomes one of finding a genuine critical method, equally reliable in its application to the old art and the new. So far from any critic of music in any country having ever attained such a method, no one has yet realised the necessity of it and begun to try to dig out the first principles of it.[103]

[98] Ernest Newman, 'A school for critics?', *NW*, 12 October 1916, 754–55.

[99] Newman, 'A school for critics?', 754. Matthew Arnold, 'The function of criticism at the present time' *National Review* 2, no. 1 (1864): 280–307. Reproduced in Stefan Collini (ed.), *Arnold: Culture and Anarchy and other Writings* (Cambridge: Cambridge University Press, 1993): 26–52.

[100] Ernest Newman, 'The critic in the confessional', *NW*, 9 November 1916, 50–1 and 7 December 1916, 178–9.

[101] Newman, 'The critic in the confessional', 50.

[102] Newman, 'The critic in the confessional', 178–9.

[103] Ernest Newman, 'Putting the classics in their place II', *NW*, 24 January 1918, 294–5; 294.

Newman had not written extensively on the need for principles in criticism in the first two decades of the twentieth century, but this situation was to change when he began writing for the *Sunday Times* in 1920, in which he advanced principles, not just for criticism, but also for the writing of music history and biography. He would continue to write on music from many countries especially Germany—and the changing fortunes of Bayreuth—and he would comment widely on concert and operatic culture and audiences. However, he would write much less on British music, with the exception of the artistic direction of the Royal Opera House, Covent Garden.

CHAPTER 7

'The World of Music':
Essays in the *Sunday Times*, 1920–1958

I N 1918, Newman was plunged into grief after his first wife, Kate, died from kidney disease. When he emerged from despair some months later, Newman married his second wife, Vera, and decided on a career change: he left the *Birmingham Daily Post* and moved to London.[1] According to Vera, Newman 'spoke of his determination to leave Birmingham as soon as possible. His years there had seemed an endless time of frustration and misery'.[2] In Newman's letter of resignation to the *Post*'s editor, he wrote:

> I am sorry to have to give you notice of my intention to leave the *Post* on the expiration of the present agreement. I feel that this town will never do anything in music, and I am very tired of struggling to rouse it. I feel, too, that I must settle somewhere where I shall have more opportunities of hearing new things and keeping my knowledge up to date.[3]

Feeling trapped and intellectually stale Newman wanted a change, and an opportunity soon presented itself.[4] J.L. Garvin, editor of London's *Observer*

---

[1] This period in Newman's life is chronicled in Vera Newman, *Ernest Newman: A Memoir by his Wife* (London: Putnam, 1963): 8–12.

[2] Vera Newman, *Ernest Newman*, 12.

[3] Newman, *Ernest Newman*, 12.

[4] Newman was criticised for his overly heavy-handed criticism on the *Birmingham Post*, which facilitated complaints about him that could have contributed to his decision to leave. For details of Newman's contentious work on the *Birmingham Daily Post* see an unsigned article, 'Mr Ernest Newman', *MH*, May 1912, 131–4; Eva Mary Grew, '"E.N.": a recollection of his Birmingham days', *MOMTR*, October 1925, 46–8 and, in a more stinging vein than her previous article, Eva Mary Grew, 'Ernest Newman: English music critic', *S*, November 1928, 113–28. A third article offered a more balanced appraisal of his Birmingham career: W. Beeson, 'Ernest Newman's departure from Birmingham', *MT*, 60/195 (1 May 1919): 215. In 1906 Newman had involuntarily left the *Manchester Guardian* for allegedly attacking the reputation of Hans Richter's shortcomings as a conductor. See Neville Cardus, *Autobiography* (London: Collins, 1947): 51. The episode is given context in an unsigned article, 'Mr Ernest Newman', *MH*, 1 May 1912, 131–4; Eva Mary Grew, 'Ernest Newman: His life and opinions', *British Musician*, June 1934, 126–8, Christopher Brookes, *His Own Man: The Life of Neville Cardus* (London: Methuen, 1985): 110–13; and Christopher Fifield, *True Artist and Friend: A Biography of Hans Richter* (Oxford: Clarendon,

Figure 5 Newman c. 1900 and his first wife, Kate Woolett
and their pet dog, Boodle. Photographer unknown.
Reproduced by kind permission of the Estate of Ernest Newman.

and creator of 'serious Sunday journalism', wrote to Newman offering him a job.[5] Newman 'felt he could take the plunge and move to London', even though he was not given a contract.[6] Newman first wrote for the *Observer* in late March 1918, contributing articles on an ad hoc basis, until he began a weekly column entitled 'Music and musicians' on 15 September 1918, which ran until 15 February 1920.[7] However, Newman's term on the *Observer* was short-lived.

1993): 438, 459. For a retrospective on this episode from Newman himself see 'Music and Musicians: Hans Richter', *NW*, 14 December 1916, 210–11.

[5] Francis Williams, *Dangerous Estate: The Anatomy of Newspapers* (London: Longmans, Green and Co., 1957): 258.

[6] Vera Newman, *Ernest Newman*, 12. It is speculated that Garvin failed to offer Newman a contract because he was 'too old at 51 to begin a new full-scale career'. Cited in Harold Hobson, Phillip Knightley and Leonard Russell, *The Pearl of Days: An Intimate Memoir of the Sunday Times, 1822–1972* (London: Hamish Hamilton, 1972): 139.

[7] Ernest Newman, 'Debussy: an appreciation and a criticism', *Observer*, 31 March 1918, 5.

In January 1920, he was invited to join the *Sunday Times* for five years with an annual salary of £850. The contract prohibited Newman from writing on music for other London papers but he could contribute on other subjects for publications, regardless of their location.[8] He continued to write a weekly column for the *Manchester Guardian* until late 1923.

Newman joined the *Sunday Times* during a period in which the newspaper experienced spectacular growth.[9] In 1915, four years before Newman started to work on the *Sunday Times* it had a modest circulation of 50,000. By 1932 it had risen to 187,000, and it had soared to 270,000 by 1937. At the time of Newman's retirement in November 1958, the *Sunday Times*' readership numbered 900,000 in a market where there were 30 million readers of Sunday papers, up from 15 million in 1937.[10] Each week, 300 to 400 letters were received for the 'letters to the editor' column and between 100 and 300 books were sent in for review.[11] According to a history of the *Sunday Times*, the paper was 'for everyone, not a highbrow paper, not a lowbrow paper, not a middle brow paper' because 'it does not believe in type-labelling intelligent people'.[12] The *Sunday Times* also saw itself as holding a 'very special responsibility in dealing with books, music, the theatre, the cinema, painting'.[13] This account of the paper's history also claimed that in the *Sunday Times* 'criticism is the news'; a view reflected in another study published in 1957, which claimed that both the *Sunday Times* and the *Observer* met a significant demand for 'serious newspaper reading'.[14]

Apparently, Newman came to the *Sunday Times* job through his association with its owner and fellow boxing enthusiast, Lord Kemsley, though the authors of a history of the *Sunday Times* have defended any accusation that cronyism played a part in Newman's appointment because he was, in their

---

[8] Vera Newman, *Ernest Newman*, 16.

[9] A history of the *Sunday Times* is given in Harold Hobson, Phillip Knightley and Leonard Russell, *The Pearl of Days*.

[10] Figures for the 1910s to 1930s are cited in Franklin Reid Gannon, *The British Press and Germany 1836–1939* (Oxford: Clarendon, 1971): 53. Figures from the 1950s are from *The Sunday Times: A Pictorial Biography of One of the World's Great Newspapers* (London: Thomson House, 1961): 39. The figures of 30 million and 15 million are cited in Francis Williams, *Dangerous Estate*, 207.

[11] *The Sunday Times: A Pictorial Biography*, 15, 23. Dates indicating any fluctuation or concentrations to particular years for these figures are not provided.

[12] *The Sunday Times: A Pictorial Biography*, 1.

[13] *The Sunday Times: A Pictorial Biography*, 1.

[14] *The Sunday Times: A Pictorial Biography*, 22 and Francis Williams, *Dangerous Estate*, 233.

words, 'already famous.'[15] But Newman was to become 'immensely feared and respected' after decades of service.[16] At any rate, his appointment was announced in the *Sunday Times* on 29 February 1920:

> Mr Ernest Newman, the leading musical critic of the day, has joined the staff of 'The Sunday Times', and will contribute his first articles to the paper next Sunday.
>
> Mr Newman's critical contribution to the 'Manchester Guardian' and other papers have aroused the interest of the musical world by their fine literary quality. He has also made valuable contributions to musical literature, notably by his 'Study of Wagner' and 'Wagner as Man and Artist', and he is at present engaged on a 'History of Modern Music'.

Newman was contracted to write two columns a week. The first column, 'The World of Music', was an essay on a musical topic, usually ranging from around 1500 to 2000 words, and carried his full name in the by-line. The second column—usually comprising half a dozen lines or a short paragraph placed immediately under or beside the first column—constituted a notice of a recent concert or opera performance in which Newman briefly passed judgment. This column was signed with his initials, 'E.N.'

Although Newman's column provides a window to London concert life, his essays in the 'The World of Music' section illustrate the scope of his intellectual range. 'The World of Music' covered a variety of formats: a book review; the occasional extended concert, recital or opera review; the formal analysis of a musical work (sometimes with hand-worked musical examples); a synopsis of an opera; and essays in which he advocated—and complained about—a wide range of issues. Topics on which Newman wrote fairly consistently were the so-called 'opera problem' in England; the theory and practice of musical criticism; biographical method; and modern music. Early in his *Sunday Times* career Newman wrote on British music, but this topic languished in his column between 1927 and 1945. After the extremely negative reception following the publication of *The Man Liszt* in 1934 (in which Newman's credibility was called into question, and which is the subject of the next chapter), Newman turned to writing about current trends in German-language musicology and the deficiencies of British musical scholarship.

The composers on whom Newman wrote most favourably and frequently in the *Sunday Times* were Berlioz and Wagner. He was a great admirer of Berlioz as a composer and critic, and wrote more than sixty articles on the subject during his *Sunday Times* career. Likewise, Wagner's presence is ubiquitous

[15] Hobson, Knightley and Russell, *The Pearl of Days*, 138.
[16] *The Sunday Times: A Pictorial Biography*, 22.

in 'The World of Music'. The extent of Newman's love of Wagner was only over-shadowed by his ambivalence towards most French music and his dislike of most modern music. Newman reviewed dozens of Wagner books and performances, and surveyed and scrutinized new primary sources and scholarly arguments as they came to light. He also occasionally commented on the political and musical fortunes of the Bayreuth Festival. Material that eventually found its way into his *Life of Wagner* is first aired in 'The World of Music', as is material used in *The Man Liszt* and other books Newman wrote in the period, including *A Musical Critic's Holiday* (1925) and *The Unconscious Beethoven* (1927). In the *Sunday Times* Newman was an advocate for various causes, including the type of musical, operatic and intellectual country he wished Britain to become. He also commented on war, politics and German–British diplomatic relations.

❧ Battle Fatigue for British Music

Newman's writings on British musical culture for the *Sunday Times* were concentrated within the first four years of his employment, 1920 to 1924. By the 1920s Newman had become cynical about the prospects of local composers and their music. After 1924, he wrote only occasionally about British composers, concentrating on praising the very few works he admired. His friendships with Bantock and Holbrooke had petered out and he grew increasingly intolerant towards the patriotic rhetoric and ideology that accompanied the rationale for new works by local composers.

Newman's first article on British music in the *Sunday Times*, 'British music and the public', published on 18 April 1920, was indicative of his waning enthusiasm on the subject. He began the article defending this ambivalence: 'some people often wonder why it is so difficult for critics to write about English music and its prospects except in a tone of melancholy irony'.[17] Against this gloomy introduction Newman went on to explain why he declined to endorse the provision of subsidies for local composers: he believed that financial support would not guarantee quality work. He further worried about the inability of those in charge of awarding subsidies to identify quality. Moreover, Newman saw no reason why the British public should feel it their national duty to patronize British music: 'I still maintain that to a large extent the public is right in not going to British music. It cannot reasonably be expected to go to any music merely because it is British! We can only expect it to go to British music because it is good'.[18] Newman argued that too much local music was

[17] Ernest Newman, 'British music and the public', *ST*, 18 April 1920, 6.
[18] Newman, 'British music and the public', 6.

second-rate music and doubted that 10 per cent of it written in the last five years would be 'really worth hearing'. He opined that the public had taken a dislike to British music 'from hearing too many of the feebler specimens of it'.[19]

Newman followed this April 1920 piece with two articles on the fortunes of composers of English song.[20] In the first article, Newman criticized the provision of financial and material support for emerging local talent: 'you cannot turn a poor composer into a good one by encouraging him'. He apportioned part of the blame for this misguided altruism to the British Music Society, of which he was a member: 'I am unrepentant in the matter of my strictures on the British Music Society for having wasted so many pages of its annual report on the lists of complete works of so many utterly unimportant composers'.[21] Although Newman admitted there were some good song composers in England, he failed to name them, though he singled out Joseph Holbrooke's *Tennyson Songs* in the second article for their inferiority. In Newman's opinion, England had not yet produced a truly outstanding song-composer, but he was forever hopeful that one would eventually emerge and emulate the skilled German songwriters such as Hugo Wolf. So glum was Newman about the prospects of local music that even rumours circulating in October 1921 of a new British ballet could not pique his interest: 'The danger I think I can foresee ... is not so much that the British ballet will try to be pretty, as that it will try to be British'.[22]

By 1924, Newman had grown weary in his support of British music. In an article in March that year—the last extensive piece on British music Newman was to write in the *Sunday Times*—he despaired about a recent meeting with a young entrepreneur to discuss plans for establishing a 'national opera devoted exclusively to British works'. As Newman told his readers:

> The young man left me with [his] enthusiasm still undamped, whereas I spent the rest of the day musing sadly over our conversation. For I have seen so many attempts to make England musical! I and a hundred others have written so many articles on the subject; we have read so many; we have joined so many societies; we have sat on so many committees! And at the end of it all, music in England is, to all intents and purposes, just where it was half a century or so ago.[23]

---

[19] Newman, 'British music and the public', 6.

[20] Ernest Newman, 'The modern English song', *ST*, 2 May 1920, 6 and 'The modern English song II', *ST*, 9 May 1920, 6.

[21] Newman, 'The modern English song', 2 May, 6.

[22] Ernest Newman, 'A British ballet?', *ST*, 23 October 1921, 5.

[23] Ernest Newman, 'The more it changes', *ST*, 24 February 1924, 3.

Notwithstanding his despair for British music, Newman occasionally wrote about local works he liked including Walton's *Violin Concerto*, which he described as 'one of the finest of modern works in its own genre' and praised *Troilus and Cressida* as 'a significant new chapter in the development of not only William Walton but of English opera'.[24] He also wrote glowingly of Holst's opera *At the Boar's Head* after its premiere in Manchester in April 1925 describing it as 'successful' mainly because of its 'clever libretto' to which he thought the music was a good fit.[25] Six years later he remarked enthusiastically of Holst's *Choral Symphony* and the composer's novel use of form. He described Holst as 'the most restlessly inquiring and adventurous mind in the English music of today'.[26] Towards the end of his life, Holst's work had become a solace to Newman: 'In some ways Holst is the more interesting mind in the English musical scene of about 1910 to 1930: I find myself often going to my shelves for his scores and making fresh discoveries in them as I read them'.[27]

Newman devoted few articles to Delius but defended a common criticism of the composer's works for their apparent formulaic structure and sameness of sound. Newman could appreciate this criticism but argued that Delius's 'mannerisms' were subtle: 'But with Delius, as with Brahms, though the music remains superficially the same throughout the years, its inner tissues and timbre and clang are subtly modified in one work after another'.[28] On the other hand, Newman did not warm to Delius's opera *Koanga*, the score of which was published posthumously, describing the composer's 'lack of sense of theatre' and for not having 'quite grasped a new form'.[29]

🥀 *Fighting for Opera*

The *Sunday Times* was no stranger to the world of opera. Augustus Harris, an opera impresario who had a lease on Covent Garden in the late 1880s, bought the paper in 1896.[30] According to the music critic Herman Klein, who worked on the *Sunday Times* during this period, Harris was desperate to buy

---

[24] Ernest Newman, 'Walton today', *ST*, 5 April 1942, 2 and 'Troilus and Cressida', *ST*, 5 December 1954, 11.

[25] Newman, 'Shakespeare set to music', *ST*, 5 April 1925, 5.

[26] Ernest Newman, 'Holst's Choral Symphony', *ST*, 11 October 1925, 9.

[27] Ernest Newman, 'Holst today', *ST*, 11 March 1951, 2.

[28] Ernest Newman, 'Delius', *ST*, 17 June 1934, 7.

[29] Ernest Newman, 'Delius and the opera', *ST*, 29 September 1935, 5.

[30] Harold Rosenthal, *Two Centuries of Opera at Covent Garden* (London: Putnam, 1958): 222–5; Desmond Shawe-Taylor, *Covent Garden* (London: Max Parish and Co. and New York: Chanticleer Press, 1948): 48.

the paper to provide 'a shield to protect himself from his unfair adversaries'.[31] Harris's productions had been severely criticized in the *Sunday Times* and by purchasing the paper he attempted to quell the critics. Klein admitted his part in convincing Harris to purchase the paper, but was insistent this intervention did not constitute a conflict of interest.[32] Meanwhile, another *Sunday Times* connection to opera in general, and to Covent Garden in particular, was the critic Desmond Shawe-Taylor. He succeeded Newman on the *Sunday Times* in 1958, and had written a frank and critical account of Covent Garden's history in 1948.[33] Newman was therefore a link in a chain of *Sunday Times* critics who were interested in opera. Newman wrote regularly on opera throughout his career with the *Sunday Times* and largely concerned himself with operatic reform on all fronts, including its infrastructure and artistic direction.

Years before his appointment to the *Sunday Times* Newman had shown a particular affinity for vocal music, especially opera. In the early 1900s he worked as a singing teacher at the Midland Institute in Birmingham under the direction of Granville Bantock, although there is no evidence that Newman took singing lessons or worked as a singer. In 1912, he began work on English translations to the librettos of some Wagner operas, beginning with *The Flying Dutchman*. In addition to these works he also published an edition of songs by Wolf (1909) and, at the time of his appointment to the *Sunday Times*, was working on *Modern Russian Songs* (2 vols 1921). When he joined the *Sunday Times* in 1920, Newman had established himself as something of an authority on vocal music.

Much of Newman's opera criticism dealt with his belief that opera had failed in Britain.[34] First, he blamed the singers. On 3 December 1922, in an article on Grand Opera, Newman argued that opera could not succeed in Britain because local singers lacked technique.[35] He was concerned that British singers

[31] Hermann Klein, *The Golden Age of Opera* (London: George Routledge & Sons, 1933): 137.

[32] Klein, *The Golden Age of Opera*, 137, footnote 1.

[33] Shawe-Taylor, *Covent Garden*.

[34] Other music critics besides Newman had devoted considerable energies in the past to addressing the poor state of opera in England. An example was W.J. Galloway, who wrote opera criticism for the *Speaker* in the 1890s and was particularly outspoken on artistic standards in direction at Covent Garden, just as Newman was in the *Sunday Times*. Galloway wrote two short books on the subject and related matters: *The Operatic Problem* (London: John Long, 1902) and *Musical England* (London: New York, John Lane, 1910). Galloway and Newman are discussed also in Paul Watt, 'Critics', in Helen Greenwald (ed.), *The Oxford Handbook of Opera* (New York: Oxford University Press, 2014): 881–98.

[35] Ernest Newman, 'English opera and English singers', *ST*, 3 December 1922, 7.

were insufficiently trained and, in an article on 28 March 1926, called for more attention to be given to vocal production and direction.[36] A few years later, in 1931, Newman revisited the topic of pedagogy for opera singers, asserting that additional training was required to teach British opera singers how to act.[37]

On the topic of acting in opera, Newman considered women to be inferior to men. In his column for 7 May 1933, Newman proposed that women were 'unable to move fully into character' because they were 'too feminine'. In tragic and pathetic roles, as Newman termed them, women were 'outside the realism of their everyday experience'.[38] This stance was at odds with Newman's first article for the *Sunday Times*, in which he claimed women had an easier time of acting in opera because their parts 'are purely convention'.[39] By 1935 Newman continued to assert that female singers had it easier than men because they found gesture a more natural activity, and he raised again the issue of pedagogy of British singers, arguing that proper training would rescue singers from acting to formula.[40]

In Newman's view, the biggest issue confronting opera in England was its lack of economic support.[41] But the opera problem also apparently extended to philistine audiences. Writing in June 1933, Newman complained that 'the very worst of all is the audience: I make bold to say that we shall never have a real opera in London until there is a drastic improvement in this department. It is an audience largely without traditions of taste, and with little musical culture of its own'. However, Newman conceded that 'the devotees of the German season are not so bad'.[42] The lack of taste, according to Newman, was best exemplified by the public's attraction to Italian opera, particularly the support given to this repertory by Covent Garden. As Newman continued, in the June 1933 article:

> [T]he bulk of the audience is made up of people who are not used to music as musicians understand the term, and who therefore can hardly be expected to be particularly discriminating in their tastes. I am not insulting them, in arrogant high-brow fashion: I am merely stating the most obvious of facts ... they have no standards whatsoever ... A present-day season at Covent Garden, and especially

[36] Ernest Newman, 'Science, sensation and singing', *ST*, 28 March 1926, 7.

[37] Ernest Newman, 'Acting in opera', *ST*, 10 May 1931, 7 and 'Miming in opera', *ST*, 17 May 1931, 5.

[38] Ernest Newman, 'Acting in opera: the eternal feminine', *ST*, 7 May 1933, 7.

[39] Ernest Newman, 'Actors and actresses in opera', *ST*, 7 March 1920, 8.

[40] Ernest Newman, 'Acting in opera: how might it be improved', *ST*, 23 June 1935, 7.

[41] For more on the 'opera problem' see Paul Rodmell, *Opera in the British Isles, 1875–1918* (Aldershot: Ashgate, 2013).

[42] Ernest Newman, 'Ecrasons L'infâme!', *ST*, 11 June 1933, 7.

the Italian part of it, is in large part not a service but a menace to the cause of music in England, for so long as the listeners' mentality that makes these things not merely possible but rapturously admired persists, no progress is possible. But what is the remedy? This I shall try to outline in a following article.[43]

And Newman did attempt a remedy—an overhaul of artistic direction— and expressed it in an extremely forthright tone:

> Covent Garden is a deadweight on the shoulders of opera. It has almost ceased to be an artistic institution and become a mere routine, and a routine of a dangerous kind. The repertoire has sunk into a Byzantine stagnation ... let us get this Covent Garden poison out of our British operatic system once and for all ... Covent Garden has long been an anachronism and is now a menace.[44]

In his hope to fix British opera, Newman found an ally in Thomas Beecham, describing him as 'the only person in Britain who is fit to have the destinies of British opera in his hands' and who would 'before long create a standard of taste that would make Covent Garden seem, in retrospect, merely the bad dream of bad indigestion'.[45] In 1929 Beecham had established the Imperial League of Opera which, Newman reported, boasted 40,000 subscribers, though he noted cynically that not even the safety of numbers could deliver British opera from what he described as its state of 'inertia'.[46] At the root of that inertia, according to Newman, was a familiar condition: the public's insatiable demand for Italian opera, which he himself disliked: '[I]n many respects Covent Garden is still living in the eighteen-nineties or the first decade of the nineteenth century. It labours under the pathetic delusion that there are enough great Italian singers in the world to keep an Italian season going in London for several weeks. There are not'.[47] Four years on, nothing had changed in Newman's view: 'our public has no real interest in opera in the larger sense of the term, and perhaps never will have: opera simply isn't in its blood'.[48]

Newman's tirade against the artistic direction of Covent Garden continued into the 1940s and 1950s. In late November 1949, for example, he claimed that

---

[43] Newman, 'Ecrasons L'infâme!', 7.

[44] Newman, 'Ecrasons L'infâme!', 7.

[45] Ernest Newman, 'The sins of Covent Garden: repentance and salvation', *ST*, 18 June 1933, 7. For more on Beecham's mission to improve opera in Britain see John Lucas, *Thomas Beecham: An Obsession with Music* (Woodbridge: Boydell Press, 2008).

[46] Ernest Newman, 'The last laps', *ST*, 5 May 1929, 7.

[47] Ernest Newman, 'Some Covent Garden errors', *ST*, 6 July 1930, 5.

[48] Ernest Newman, 'Covent Garden's problems: English opera audiences', *ST*, 4 July 1937, 7.

Covent Garden was 'the laughing stock of the operatic world'.[49] Two months later, Newman's assault on Covent Garden was unrelenting: 'What is Covent Garden going to bring us in 1950 in the way first of all of new or unhackneyed works, and secondly of methods of opera production'?[50]

Newman also had much to say about public subsidies for London opera. In the early 1920s the British National Opera Company was formed to promote local opera, and subsidies formed part of its financial plan. But Newman argued that using London as a base for a national opera project deprived the provinces of their right to musical facilities in their own cities. In his 'World of Music' article of 29 November 1925, Newman suggested that if the trustees of the National Opera Trust successfully argued for a London base then Londoners alone should fund that project. Newman argued that ten cities around the UK could be home to their own opera house but asked, 'Who will live to see it realized?[51]

❧ Radio and Television Broadcasts

In the 1920s opinion was divided amongst critics and composers about the quality and benefit of radio broadcasting. In April 1921 the *Bookman* ran an article entitled 'Musical taste in England, and the influence of the gramophone' to garner opinion on the topic.[52] The respondents were J.A. Fuller Maitland, Ernest Newman, Joseph Holbrooke, Norman O'Neill, Edward German, Eugène Goosens, Arnold Bax, Julius Harrison, Landon Ronald and Cyril Scott. The critics and composers were asked to respond to a statement in the recently published *Rhythm, Music and Education* by Emile Jaques Dalcroze: 'As to the musical feeling of the English, it is by no means of so low a standard as generally asserted on the Continent. The people undoubtedly love music, and their hearing and vocal capacities are normal'. The introductory paragraph continued: 'The following distinguished musicians and musical critics have been kind enough to favour us with their opinions on this and on the statement made elsewhere that the gramophone has been largely responsible for the revival of musical taste in this country'.[53] None of the respondents were united on the matter. Fuller Maitland, for example, argued that 'mechanical inventions' such as the gramophone and pianola had not had 'any appreciable effect

---

[49] Ernest Newman, 'Covent Garden', *ST*, 27 November 1949, 2.

[50] Ernest Newman, 'The "garden" again', *ST*, 22 January 1950, 2.

[51] Ernest Newman, 'The opera problem', *ST*, 29 November 1925, 7.

[52] 'Musical taste in England, and the influence of the gramophone', *Bookman*, April 1921, 38–41.

[53] 'Musical taste in England', 38.

in improving the nature of the English'. O'Neill put any such improvement down primarily to music education.[54] German wrote that it depended upon what records were chosen while Bax felt he lacked the expertise to comment.[55] Ronald and Scott believed that the gramophone and pianola together were important advances in music education.[56] All writers agreed that the gramophone was of some benefit but they all took exception to Dalcroze's patronizing comments. Newman was the most succinct and arguably pithy respondent writing simply: 'It is exceedingly good of M. Jaques-Dalcroze. I am reminded of Lowell's [1869] essay 'On a Certain Condescension in Foreigners'".[57]

Other critics were clearer on the subject. In the *Musical Times* in June 1924, M.D. Calvocoressi wrote of his severe disdain for the gramophone in disseminating new music: 'To me, mechanical reproductions of music are both excruciating and meaningless'.[58] By contrast, Aldous Huxley embraced the gramophone (and player-piano) and argued that people should move with the times:

> There are still some people—they happily become fewer and fewer every year—who disapprove on some strangely ill-founded William-Morrisish principle, of all mechanical devices for the making or reproduction of music. The gramophone disgusts them, the pianola makes them feel quite faint. Or rather, it is generally the mere idea of these machines that offends them; for, as often as not, you will find that these good people have never taken the trouble to listen to the devices which they condemn. It is enough for them that they are machines; machinery is *a priori* incompatible with music, which is an Art, capital lettered and high'.[59]

Newman was slowly converted to the benefits of gramophone recording during his time at the *Sunday Times,* though it got off to an unpromising start. As early as January 1924, Newman informed his readers he was 'not an enemy of the new science', but his reservations about broadcasting were obvious.[60] He admitted to not owning a wireless set, but had been told (by whom, he did not

---

[54] 'Musical taste in England', 40.

[55] 'Musical taste in England', 40.

[56] 'Musical taste in England', 41.

[57] 'Musical taste in England', 39. See Tucker Brooke (ed.), *Two Essays of James Russell Lowell, On a Certain Condescension in Foreigners and Democracy* (New York: H. Holt & Co., 1927).

[58] M.D. Calvocoressi, 'On broadcasting new music', *MT*, 65/976 (1 June 1924): 500–2.

[59] Aldous Huxley, 'Music and machinery', *Weekly Westminster Gazette*, 29 April 1922. In Michael Allis (ed.), *Temporaries and Eternals: The Music Criticism of Aldous Huxley, 1922–1923* (Newcastle: Cambridge Scholars Publishing, 2013): 71–3; 71.

[60] Ernest Newman, 'Broadcasting music: some reflections and a suggestion', *ST*, 13 January 1924, 5.

say) that opera broadcasts were 'good' insofar as the voices sounded satisfactory, but not the orchestras. In March 1924, Newman reported the BBC had offered wireless sets to all its London critics but he had declined the gift. He was, at this time, lukewarm about radio broadcasts, claiming 'transmission is a travesty of the original'.[61] This view stayed with Newman for four more years; he resisted reviewing radio broadcasts—and this must have been annoying to his editor and readers—for on 18 March 1926 the following announcement was printed in the body of Newman's 'World of Music column':

> The 'Sunday Times' having provided Mr Ernest Newman with the most complete and up-to-date system of wireless installation, he will, from time to time, deal with the musical programmes both at home and abroad, presented through this medium.[62]

Within a couple of months Newman had followed his editor's orders: he reviewed *Oedipus Rex* on 20 May 1928, claiming the broadcast quality was 'generally good' and by June appeared to be coming round to the benefits that the wireless could provide, suggesting that someone with sufficient capital should devise a course in music theory to be taught over the radio with the aid of books.[63] By 1933 Newman had been fully converted to the benefits of radio broadcasts, relishing the fact he could enjoy opera in the comfort of his own home in Surrey without the trouble of travelling to concerts in London only to be inconvenienced by late starts, long intervals, never-ending encores, and time wasted by soloists taking prolonged rest breaks.[64]

Newman was equally reticent about television broadcasting, which had commenced in the 1950s. In his first article on the topic in 1953, he claimed that some music broadcasters engaged in 'some appalling crimes of television against St Cecelia' and, when dealing with opera a couple of months later, he complained about the problems posed by television cameras.[65] One of his complaints was that close-ups on singers' faces prohibited views of their costumes, the sets and other singers, thereby compromising the dramatic effect. Despite the medium in which opera was performed, Newman was always concerned with its dramaturgy.

[61] Ernest Newman, 'Music and radio', *ST*, 16 March 1924, 7.

[62] Ernest Newman, 'A problem of musical criticism: The composer and his period', *ST*, 18 March 1928, 7.

[63] Ernest Newman, 'Oedipus Rex', *ST*, 20 May 1928, 7; 'A chance for a millionaire', *ST*, 10 June 1928, 7.

[64] Ernest Newman, 'Wireless and the time factor', *ST*, 26 February 1933, 7.

[65] Ernest Newman, 'Thoughts on television', *ST*, 21 June 1953, 9; 'Television opera', *ST*, 16 August 1953, 4.

❧ Music Criticism in Need of Improvement

Newman's articles in the *Sunday Times* frequently drew attention to the inadequacies of British music criticism and stressed the need for scientific principles
to guide it. These were common tropes from his earlier writings on the subject,
as we have seen in previous chapters. One of his most concerted efforts to agi-
tate for method in criticism was a series of three articles entitled 'A physiology
of criticism' published in January and February 1929.[66] In the first instalment,
Newman acknowledged that personal biases got in the way of objective criticism and any appeal for a scientific method would be ridiculed. Undeterred,
Newman proposed a 'system of musical physiology'. In this initial article,
Newman discussed Paul Bekker's 1911 biography of Beethoven, in which he
felt its author had 'read things into Beethoven's music that are not to be found
in the music'.[67] Newman insisted that his physiological approach could arrive
at a more tangible interpretation of a composer's psychology, but many of his
readers were not entirely convinced.

Newman turned to his book *The Unconscious Beethoven*, published two
years before, in 1927, as an example of how a physiological study of a composer
might be realized. In this book, Newman argued that Beethoven had employed
three ascending notes (arranged and re-arranged in about six different config-
urations) as the basis for all his compositions, and that Beethoven was:

> the only composer in whom you will find such a sequence of three notes used
> with such frequency, always at the same equivalent point in the melody, and
> always as the obvious expression of a certain state of mind. The three-note
> sequence, I contend, is a veritable Beethoven fingerprint, because it is not found
> in any other composer.[68]

Although *The Unconscious Beethoven* was not widely reviewed, some critics
disagreed with Newman's fingerprint thesis on the grounds it was overly spec-
ulative. One reviewer, however, argued Newman's formal-analytical treatment
did not go far enough.[69] Newman admitted in his first article on physiology that

---

[66] Ernest Newman, 'A physiology of criticism', 20 January 1929, 7; 10 February 1929, 7;
and 17 February 1929, 7. Reprinted in Felix Aprahamian (ed.), *Essays from the World
of Music* (London: John Calder, 1956): 13–27.

[67] Newman, 'A physiology of criticism 1'. Bekker's biography of Beethoven was first
published in 1911 in Berlin by Schuster and Loeffler; it was translated into English
by J.M. Dent in 1925. For background on Bekker's career see Christopher Hailey,
'The Paul Bekker collection in the Yale University Library', *Notes*, second series, 51
(1994): 13–21.

[68] Newman, 'A physiology of criticism 1', 7.

[69] A particularly trenchant and hostile review of *The Unconscious Beethoven* was written by Carl Engel in 'Views and reviews', *MQ*, 13/4 (October 1927): 646–62. Engel

the Beethoven book had met with 'small success', but he remained convinced of its argument. Newman asserted that his type of musical analysis, which was concerned, in part, with discerning compositional processes, could go one step further: to 'see a certain mood' when particular formulae were used, as in the case of Beethoven.[70] If undertaking a study of Schubert, for example, Newman argued it would not be difficult to find a set of devices that would be 'always unconsciously employed when Schubert wished to express a certain mood', just as his study of Beethoven had concluded. This establishment of a mood, argued Newman, was the benefit that a physiological study would bring and should be approached in a particularly scholarly way:

> I would argue that on the practical aesthetic side [of this physiological method] alone a good deal would be achieved if for a few years writers upon music would abandon their too easy psychological methods—which mean, in the last resort, only saying the first thing that comes into your head—and devote themselves to establishing a preliminary physiology of each of the great composer's styles.[71]

Newman's readers were puzzled. He spent the next two instalments (27 January and 3 February 1929) answering readers' letters in a convoluted fashion, going over old ground about the difficulties of impartial criticism and the perils of the so-called 'personal equation'. Newman was at pains to point out that a physiology of criticism did not mean 'a study of the composer in the light of his nerves and arteries, or even of his liver'.[72] Readers were still confused, and the letters continued to pour in. In the last instalment of the article, on 17 February, Newman called a truce:

> The sooner I end this series of articles the better, for it is evident from the letters I receive on the subject that no one has the slightest idea what it is I am driving at. I must wait and see if I have better luck in a treatment of the subject on a larger scale elsewhere. The term 'physiology' is plainly a stumbling-block for most people; they read into it a meaning I never intended, and then write me long letters that are most interesting in themselves, but hopelessly irrelevant to the theme.[73]

lambasted Newman for throwing 'mud' (646) at Beethoven's reputation and found the formal analysis section of the book unconvincing. On the other hand, writing in 1929, Paul Miles was disappointed that 'Newman's book received too little attention, I think, and its suggestiveness was not fully realised'. In 'Beethoven sketches', *Gramophone*, 29 October 1929, 12.

[70] Newman, 'A physiology of criticism 1', 7.
[71] Newman, 'A physiology of criticism 1' 7.
[72] Newman, 'A physiology of criticism 3', 7.
[73] Newman, 'A physiology of criticism 4', 7.

Newman ventured a longer work on musical criticism in 1925, just five years into his tenure at the *Sunday Times*: a book entitled *A Musical Critic's Holiday*. It was a reflective—if sometimes ponderous—treatise on criticism, but it stopped short of articulating a theory or method of criticism, which was implied in the opening pages. Consequently, the book confounded many readers, as Newman readily admitted.[74] *A Musical Critic's Holiday* considered the need to separate objectivity from subjectivity in criticism, and for a critic to be able to stand apart from 'the clichés of his day'.[75] Newman saw detachment and perspective as characteristics of a process he termed 'back thought' and argued strongly that 'genuine criticism must always function in the past, not the present'.[76] The book tells us nothing significantly new about Newman's view on the value of impartiality in criticism or about his own prejudices, for example his ambivalence towards the aesthetics of Walter Pater (for over-interpretation) and towards modern music (for its lack of melodic invention).[77] For these and other biases, Edwin Evans, a fellow critic, heavily criticized Newman's book in the August 1925 issue of the *Musical Times*.[78]

Evans appears to have misunderstood *A Musical Critic's Holiday*. He claimed that Newman's purpose was to 'envisage a work of art in complete detachment from all considerations arising from its, and from the critics' period, environment, and personal idiosyncrasies'—but this was not so.[79] Newman had long advocated that musical works should be judged free of a critic's bias and appraised outside its immediate historical environment. For example, Newman argued that a study of the historical circumstances and later reception surrounding Wagner's 'unsavoury reputation' was needed 'as regards general public recognition of his work'.[80] This process is an example of Newman's

---

[74] Ernest Newman, *A Musical Critic's Holiday* (New York: Alfred A. Knopf, 1925). Following its publication, Newman wrote three articles on his purpose for the book, admitting people had been confused by it: 'A postscript to "A Musical Critic's Holiday"', *MT*, 66/992 (1 October 1925): 881–4; 66/993 (1 November 1925): 977–81; 66/994 (1 December): 1076–9.

[75] Newman, *A Musical Critic's Holiday*, vii–viii.

[76] Newman, *A Musical Critic's Holiday*, xi.

[77] Newman, *A Musical Critic's Holiday*, 23, 186.

[78] Edwin Evans, 'Objectivity in contemporary criticism', *MT*, 66/990 (1 August 1925): 692–5. Newman provided a long-winded reply to Evans in a series of articles, 'A postscript to "A Musical Critic's Holiday"' in the *Musical Times* in October 1925, 881–4; November, 977–81 and December 1925, 1076–79. Evans and Newman were locked in an ideological battle for years and the battle is briefly discussed in Nigel Scaife, 'British music criticism in a new era: studies in critical thought, 1894–1945', DPhil thesis, University of Oxford, 1994, 158–61.

[79] Evans, 'Objectivity in contemporary criticism', 692.

[80] Newman, *A Musical Critic's Holiday*, 124.

'back thought' in operation: the use of history and historical method, a process Newman long advocated and is most self-consciously evident in *Gluck and the Opera* (1895).

Curiously, Newman made little or no mention of two related books on critical method published in the two years prior to *A Musical Critic's Holiday*: *The Principles and Methods of Musical Criticism* (1923) by M.D. Calvocoressi and *Principles of Literary Criticism* (1925) by I.A. Richards. Newman gave a brief and positive review of Calvocoressi's book in his 'World of Music' column on 9 December 1923 and referred to it only in passing in *A Musical Critics' Holiday*. However, Richards' book appeared to have escaped Newman's attention entirely.[81] In the case of Calvocoressi's volume, Newman need not have engaged long on it, for both authors were in strong agreement with their central arguments about the need for objectivity and method; indeed, Calvocoressi invoked John M. Robertson's work on rationalism and method in his argument. Potentially, Richards' book—with its emphasis on the psychological interpretation of texts, especially poetry—would surely have interested Newman, but the opportunity for Newman to connect with this book appears to have been lost.

In *A Musical Critic's Holiday* Newman had stressed his long-held view that judgements about music should be made through an appeal to history, context and comparison. Such appeals to method in music were certainly not new by the time *A Musical Critic's Holiday* was published; Austrian and German musicologists had been advocating them from the 1880s, but Newman was not to engage fully with this literature until the mid-1930s.

﴾﴿ Music History and Musicology

The announcement of Newman's appointment to the *Sunday Times* in February 1920 mentioned he was writing a history of modern music. He was still working it in 1927, though it was now called *History of Music*, and he was desperate to finish it.[82] But this project, like many others, including a biography of Berlioz and a book on *Parsifal*, never eventuated.[83] Still, Newman wrote frequently on

---

[81] Ernest Newman, 'The critic and his critics', *ST*, 9 December 1923, 7.

[82] Vera Newman, *Ernest Newman*, 69.

[83] Plans for the history of music, which appear to have been first raised in 1921, are recorded in Vera Newman's *Ernest Newman*, 25. Mention is made of Newman's planned *Parsifal* book on page 269 of the book. It is well known that Newman had planned to write a Berlioz biography; see, for example, Peter Heyworth (ed.), *Berlioz, Romantic and Classic: Writings by Ernest Newman* (London: Gollancz, 1972): 11: 'He [Newman] did in fact intend to write a full-length study of Berlioz's music. That even in the last years of his life he had not abandoned this project is clear from the fact that he allowed no articles on Berlioz to be included in the two

Figures 6–9
Official photographs of
Newman taken for the *Sunday
Times c.* 1920s. Photographer:
Reginald Haines. Reproduced
by kind permission of the
Estate of Ernest Newman.

music and historical method in some form or another in approximately fifty articles for the *Sunday Times*. Much of the material for these articles may have come from parts of his unfinished book. Newman's essays on music history and musicology appeared in a dozen articles published between 1922 and 1934 and concentrated largely on English and French literature. After 1934, however, Newman's attention turned to German-language musicology.

Time and again Newman wrote that the best vantage point for assessing musical works was twenty years after their creation. He also wrote about authority in history and the need for historians of music to know their subject thoroughly. But this point troubled him in relation to his own work. In an article from 6 January 1924 (which was, ostensibly, a review of Paul Landormy's *Histoire de la musique* from 1923), Newman wondered whether it was possible for one author to have sufficient grasp of the whole sweep of Western music history, given the great strides music scholarship had taken up to the early 1920s. He believed that with such proliferation of knowledge, it would become almost impossible for a single hand to write books on music history. This anxiety may be why Newman's history of music was never completed. But he found hope in the work of Paul Landormy.

Landormy's *Histoire de la musique* was a chronological account of Western music from antiquity to the present. It included biographical synopses of composers and was essentially a social and institutional history: it was not a survey of key works and musical style plotted along an evolutionary timeline. Landormy explained his inadequacy in writing a book in which so much would have to be left out: 'a work of the kind must necessarily be incomplete, owing to its very nature. In it we can do no more than underline a few salient facts, sketch the outlines of a few great figures, indicate a few important transitions'.[84] Despite criticizing the book for its cursory treatment of sixteenth-century music, and the music of Germany and France, Newman nevertheless considered it a 'gallant' effort and shared Landormy's concern regarding authority and comprehensiveness when working on a large-scale general history.

Newman devoted another article to the subject in September 1932:

> The twentieth century will probably see the end of many of our old illusions about music, among them the illusion that a general history of music is possible. Historical studies, yes; essays in historical generalisation, yes; but a real history of music, no. And that for three reasons. In the first place, detailed knowledge of all periods of music, all styles, the work of individual composers; the field is

anthologies of his writings in the *Sunday Times*, which appeared near the end of his life … '.

[84] Paul Landormy, *A History of Music* trans. Frederick H. Martens (New York: Charles Scribner's, 1927): vii.

far too vast for that. In the second place no human being who has ever lived, or will ever live, can have the same imaginative insight into all the varieties of the musical mind. In the third place, a history is no history without a science or philosophy of history; that is to say, the historian must at all events try to see the whole development as a chain of forces with an inexorable logic of causation between them all and between the successive readjustments of them. The dilemma is a hopeless one.[85]

In the course of this article Newman reviewed George Dyson's recently published book, *The Progress of Music* (1932). Like Landormy's book, Dyson's volume was an institutional history of music that considered the effect of the church, state, theatre, concert hall and technology on the consumption and politics of culture. Dyson's work was akin to Landormy's volume because it was not simply about composers' lives and works. In the chapter entitled 'The Stage', for example, Dyson proposed that the 'intimate relation between religion, ritual, and drama is one of the axioms of scholarship'.[86] It was, for want of a better term, an early sociology of music. For example, Dyson discussed dogmatism in the historiography of medieval music, the place of song in the formation of identity amongst slaves, and the effect of war and the rise of the middle class on concert-hall patronage in the classical and romantic periods.[87] Despite Newman's gloomy prognosis for musical history, he saw the possibility in Dyson's book for a writer to construct an objective and authoritative history. Even though Newman criticized Dyson for occasional over-generalization, he claimed the author was an example 'of the scientific historian wasting as little of his own time and his readers' time in the description of his personal reactions to this composer or that, but concentrating on the business of showing the rationale of the connection between one epoch and another, one hidden force and another'.[88]

Until he encountered the works of Paul Bekker in the late 1920s, Newman's engagement with German-language musicology and criticism was slight. There is little mention in any of his works to the founders of the discipline from the 1880s, such as Guido Adler and Eduard Hanslick.[89] It is often claimed

---

[85] Ernest Newman, 'Generalise in haste ...', *ST*, 25 September 1932, 7.

[86] George Dyson, *The Progress of Music* (London: Oxford University Press/Humphrey Milford, 1932): 96.

[87] Dyson, *The Progress of Music*, 15, 46–7 and 183–91 respectively.

[88] Newman, 'Generalise in haste ...', *ST*, 25 September 1932, 7.

[89] For a brief background to Adler's work, as well as a translation of his purpose and schema for the then new discipline of musicology, see Erica Mugglestone, 'Adler's "The scope, method, and aim of musicology" (1885): an English translation with an historico-analytical commentary', *Yearbook for Traditional Music* 13 (1981): 1–21.

that early twentieth-century British historians were influenced by late nine-teenth-century German scholarship in the careful marshalling of facts and evidence, the need for detachment on the side of the scholar, and for the guarded synthesis of fact with interpretation.[90] Newman advocated all of these attributes in scholarship but he rarely articulated specific sources: it is thus assumed that the ideals of science and method in scholarship, adopted in his freethought years, were his guiding light.

Newman wrote on Paul Bekker's work in an article early in 1928, entitled 'Musical history: towards a theory'.[91] Newman was curious about Bekker's idea that musical history can be situated, not in a strictly evolutionary line, but as 'the ebb and flow of waves'.[92] Yet Newman also found some chinks in Bekker's historiography, especially in his writings on Mozart. He disagreed with Bekker's view that Mozart was 'difficult to understand, too serious, too complex and artificial'. Though Newman was far from keen on Mozart's music, he disagreed with Bekker's negative appraisal of him, writing, 'I know of no evidence to that effect'. Newman also thought Bekker was clutching at straws when psychologizing on Mozart: 'but does not Bekker go too far when he asserts that Mozart is "the first composer whose works directly reflects his personality and his ideas"?'[93] Newman manifestly disagreed with Bekker that modern composers expressed their personalities more so than composers of past generations. Yet Bekker's work in general, and on Mozart in particular, excited Newman's mind, and he went on to discuss the difficulty of marrying particular personality traits to musical style.

In the late 1920s and the 1930s Newman's interest in German-langauge musicology gathered pace. In April and May 1936 he devoted three articles on the subject.[94] In the first article, 'Progress in musicology: law in musical history', Newman began by surveying the state of music criticism in Britain as a point of comparison to the situation in Germany:

> For a particularly rich and recent exploration of the work of Adler and Hanslick see Kevin C. Karnes, *Music, Criticism, and the Challenge of History: Shaping Modern Musical Thought in Late Nineteenth-Century Vienna* (Oxford University Press, 2008). Hanslick's criticism is discussed in Sandra McColl, *Music Criticism in Vienna, 1896–1897: Critically Moving Forms* (Oxford: Clarendon, 1996).

[90] See, for example, Richard J. Evans, *Cosmopolitan Islanders: British Historians and the European Continent* (Cambridge: Cambridge University Press, 2009): 1–58.

[91] Newman, 'Musical history: towards a theory', *ST*, 12 February 1928, 7.

[92] Newman, 'Musical history: towards a theory', 7.

[93] Newman, 'Musical history: towards a theory', 7.

[94] Ernest Newman, 'Progress in musicology: law in musical history', *ST*, 19 April 1936, 7; 'Some aspects of 18th-century music, Dr Balet's generalisations', *ST*, 26 April 1936, 7 and 'The Germans and the "Beggar's Opera"', *ST*, 3 May 1936, 7.

Writing about music still means, for the most part in this country, one or all of three rather antiquated things—'criticism' of composers past and present, i.e., graciously approving or disapproving of them according to whether their minds are like or unlike that of the critic; informing a public palpitating for the information how Miss Smith produced her voice in its upper register last night, or how Herr Geigmörder got on with the octaves in the Beethoven violin concerto; and the laboratory dissection of composition.[95]

According to Newman, the grass was greener in Germany: 'In Germany a scholar, for various reasons rooted in German history and German culture, can devote himself to scholarship … a Riemann or an Adler is not expected to spend his evenings listening to some young lady struggling through a performance of songs that are completely beyond her intellectual capacity'.[96] Newman's point was that Britain lacked a critical mass in musicology, reflected in the type of work that music critics undertook: 'scholars in Germany can devote themselves to musicology, not to reporting music-making by other people; to musicography, not to "musical criticism"'.[97] In 1944 Newman would claim that Britain 'has never yet produced an all-round musical scholar and thinker of the continental giants' though he singled out the two people he considered to be closest to this mark: Charles Sanford Terry for his work on Bach, and Frank Arnold for his extensively illustrated book on the thorough bass, the latter described by Newman as 'the finest piece of musicography ever produced in this country'.[98] Newman blamed the poor state of musicology in Britain on scholars' lack of engagement with primary sources. Curiously, Newman failed to comment on Edward Dent's interest in British and German musicology despite their friendship.[99] He also had virtually nothing to say about Donald Tovey's musicological work, except for some brief commentary on Tovey's analysis of Beethoven's Ninth Symphony.[100]

[95] Newman, 'Progress in musicology', 7.

[96] Newman, 'Progress in musicology', 7.

[97] Newman, 'Progress in musicology', 7.

[98] Ernest Newman, 'A job for a dictator', ST, 2 July 1944, 2. Frank Arnold, The Art of an Accompaniment from a Thorough Bass, 2 vols (London: Oxford University Press, 1931).

[99] Dent's engagement with British and German musicology is discussed in Annegret Fauser, 'The scholar behind the medal: Edward J. Dent (1876–1957) and the politics of music history', Journal of the Royal Musical Association 139/2 (2014): 235–60. See also Karen Arrandale, Edward J. Dent: A Life of Music and Words (Woodbridge: The Boydell Press, 2017). Newman's friendship with Dent is examined briefly in Paul Watt, 'The catalogue of Ernest Newman's library: Revelations about his intellectual life in the 1890s', Script and Print 31/2 (2007): 81–103.

[100] Newman, 'The case of the Ninth Symphony', ST, 1 April 1922, 7.

Newman also focused his attention on German musicology through various examinations of method. The first such study was Leo Balet's *Die Verbürgerlichung der deutschen Kunst, Literatur und Musik im 18 Jahrhundert* (1936), which Newman praised for its specialization in a single period.[101] He described it as 'the first attempt to a totalitarian history of art, literature and music' and was drawn to its emphasis on parallelism over causation, especially the links the book made to contemporary intellectual currents in politics, literature and philosophy.[102] He also highlighted two German books, written twenty years previously, that further favoured this 'parallelism' to history, including Adler's *Der Stil in der Musik* (1912) and *Methode der Musikgeschichte* (1919).[103]

British musicology continued to be belittled by Newman. In 'The Germans and the "Beggar's Opera"', Newman voiced his jealousy of the pianist Eberhard Rebling: 'happy the student, who like Dr Rebling, is brought up under half-a-dozen masters any one of whom makes even the totality of English musicology look rather small'.[104] But in Rebling's reading of *The Beggar's Opera* Newman was amused by the German scholar's over-thinking of it: 'the Teutonic passion for categorizing and generalizing, for seeing everything as a "symbol" of something or other can be distracting as that this particular work was not about a triumph over aristocracy—it was just "good fun"'.[105] And on this note Newman described what he considered the key markers of national historiographies:

> We have to keep a close eye on the German thinkers, then, when they start philosophizing: their inborn passion for neat schematisation is so compelling that they will indulge in it on any pretext, or on no pretext at all that is visible to the English, the French or the Italians.[106]

Given Newman's interest in music analysis, noted particularly in *The Unconscious Beethoven*, it comes as no surprise to find he was especially interested in the work of Heinrich Schenker. Newman's first article on Schenker was a review of his book on Beethoven's ninth symphony in which Newman commented broadly, and briefly, on what he thought of Schenker's thoroughgoing,

---

[101] Newman, 'Progress in musicology', *ST*, 19 April 1936, 7.

[102] Newman, 'Some aspects of 18th-century music, Dr Balet's generalisations', *ST*, 26 April 1936, 7.

[103] Newman, 'Some aspects of 18th-century music', 7.

[104] Newman, 'The Germans and the "Beggar's Opera"', *ST*, 3 May 1936, 7.

[105] Newman, 'The Germans and the "Beggar's Opera"', 7.

[106] Newman, 'The Germans and the "Beggar's Opera"', 7.

if dry, approach to analysis.[107] However, in an article published two years later, at the end of 1940, Newman devoted more time to a discussion of Schenker, who, according to Newman, was 'unknown in England'. Newman praised him for having 'a passion for unrelaxing thoroughness and scrupulous exactitude' and for 'providing an imaginative insight into the workings of a composer's mind that is too often lacking in the technical analysis of music'.[108] Yet Newman made no attempt to detail Schenker's analytical methods, only noting his good work in preparing editions of music and consulting historical documents, such as manuscripts. Newman would have been drawn to Schenker's analysis given that Newman's Unconscious Beethoven strove to marry analysis with psychology or criticism. It is a pity—and a lost opportunity—that Newman did not comment on Schenker in more detail.

Despite his interest in German-language musicology, Newman was critical of some of its endeavours during the Second World War. He accused German scholars, including musicologists, of re-writing history to reflect Nazi propaganda. As Newman wrote in September 1939, in an article entitled 'Regimentation of German Thought': 'only those of us who have kept in touch with the German intellectual world during the last few years know how thoroughly the ideological poison has infiltrated into every layer and every activity of German life'.[109] He went on to write how 'book after book appears in which the history of European culture is complacently treated as purely and simply a matter of the history of German culture'.[110] Newman omitted to provide a specific case on this occasion, but he offered one two years later, in 1941, in an article on Ernst Bücken's Die Musik der Nationen (1937), 'The nations and their music'.[111] Newman began the article with the claim 'for several years there has been a growing tendency among German musicologists to treat music as a specifically German art, and to claim credit for "the Germanic race" for every

---

[107] Ernest Newman, 'More about conducting: Schenker on notation', ST, 24 October 1937, 5. See Schenker's Beethovens Neunte Sinfonie (Vienna: Universal Edition, 1912). An English translation was made in 1992 by John Rothgeb and published by Yale University Press. Other studies on Schenker include Karnes, Music, Criticism, and the Challenge of History, 78–108; Nicholas Cook, The Schenker Project: Culture, Race, and Music Theory in fin de siècle Vienna (Oxford: Oxford University Press, 2007); and William Drabkin, 'Heinrich Schenker', in Thomas Christensen (ed.), The Cambridge History of Western Music Theory (Cambridge: Cambridge University Press, 2002): 812–43.

[108] Ernest Newman, 'Schenker and the composer', ST, 15 December 1940, 3. Newman claimed again in 1954 that Schenker was still barely known in England; 'Shenkerism', ST, 14 November 1954, 11.

[109] Ernest Newman, 'Regimentation of German thought', ST, 24 September 1939, 7.

[110] Newman, 'Regimentation of German thought', 7.

[111] Ernest Newman, 'The nations and their music', ST, 5 January 1941, 3.

vital element in its evolution'.[112] Newman was lukewarm about Bücken's scholarship generally and was deeply critical of the book's many gaps, claiming, with a now familiar refrain, 'Dr Bücken's volume should really be entitled … 'A History of German Music, with an Occasional Condescending Side-Glance at the Surface of the Music of Other Countries'.[113]

﹩ Wagner, the Nazis and Bayreuth

Inevitably, Newman wrote about Wagner in the context of war and the Nazi appropriation of the composer's writings and music. To a point, Newman had to protect his subject and his reputation: he had much to lose if seen to be defending Wagner's anti-Semitism, or if he was silent on the appropriation for political purposes of Wagner's music and ideology. In an article in March 1939, for example, Newman wrote of a recent essay that had appeared in the German musical press claiming the Boer War was an expression of Wagner's political ideology. Newman thought the evidence was extremely flimsy.[114] Newman described the alleged events of Wagner's suspect ideology as 'ludicrously trifling' and argued particular actions by Wagner had gained 'exaggerated significance' in the hands of some writers.[115] In Newman's view, the article said more about the hand of German colonization and its 'fanatical ideology' than about anything Wagner may have created.

On occasion, Newman was defensive of Wagner. In an article, 'Wagner and the Germans', in May 1940, he argued that Wagner was more of a Prussian than a German and that the composer did not share the German 'lust for

---

[112] Newman, 'The nations and their music', 3.

[113] Newman, 'The nations and their music', 3. For a more complete picture of the German musicology in the early twentieth century and of Büchen's ideological scholarship see Pamela M. Potter, 'Musicology under Hitler: New sources in context', *Journal of the American Musicological Society* 49/1 (Spring 1996): 70–113 and Pamela M. Potter, *Most German of the Arts: Musicology and Society from the Weimar Republic to the end of Hitler's Reich* (New Haven: Yale University Press, 1998).

[114] Ernest Newman, 'In the service of ideology: Wagner and the Boers', *ST*, 26 March 1939, 5. Wolzogen was a literary associate of Wagner's as well as his biographer and editor of volumes of poems and letters. The article in question, which Newman translated as 'Richard Wagner on the Boer Fight for Freedom', was predicated on the belief that Wagner supported the Boers, 'both by getting Hans von Wolzogen to write on the subject in the "Bayreuther Blätter" and by addressing a letter (hitherto unpublished, apparently, and now in the State Library, Berlin) to a certain Captain-Lieutenant Darmer who has appealed for his support in March, 1881' (all quotes, p. 5).

[115] Newman, 'In the service of ideology: Wagner and the Boers', 5

mastery' over other nations.[116] In fact, according to Newman, Wagner 'hated and scorned everything in the German character that has brought itself to the sorry state it is today'.[117] In a less defensive article written in 1945, Newman tackled the appropriation of Wagner's writings by the Nazis, fully admitting that Wagner 'would have approved today of the Nazi attitude towards Judaism in Germany. But never for a moment would he have countenanced the disgraceful Nazi ill-treatment and personal degradation of the Jews'.[118] A week later, Newman put his case more emphatically: 'It is time, for instance, to call a halt in the gross misunderstanding and misrepresentation of him [Wagner] as an artist that is now current in circles that have no connection with art'.[119]

While keeping an eye on Wagner scholarship and historiography in the *Sunday Times*, Newman was also focused on developments in Bayreuth. Newman appears to have commented little on his visit to Bayreuth in 1911, but had more to say in 1951 on the re-opening of Bayreuth after the war. In 'Bayreuth re-visited' on 3 August 1930, however, Newman reflected that not much had changed since his 1911 visit though he found the new buildings aesthetically disagreeable and its immediate vicinity noisy.[120] But he used the article to comment favourably—like many other devotees of Bayreuth had done before him—on the theatre's simple design, sunken orchestral pit and fine acoustic. Newman found the orchestra mellow and the theatre possessing an uncanny ability to project sound, especially voices. In comparing Friedrich Schorr's Bayreuth performance with his recent appearance at Covent Garden, Newman observed his voice carried better in the Bayreuth theatre given its superior design.

In addition to acoustics, Newman loved the stage design at Bayreuth and its dramaturgical effect:

> Particular use is made of the height of the stage. The characters frequently make their first appearance on some peak or lofty road or other. The device is not only effective in the more obvious way—in the sense that the character at once draw's the spectator's eye—but carried out as it is here in Bayreuth we get a curious feeling that most of these people are something more than merely human.[121]

[116] Ernest Newman, 'Wagner and the Germans', *ST*, 5 May 1940, 3.

[117] Newman, 'Wagner and the Germans', 3.

[118] Ernest Newman, 'The truth about Wagner', *ST*, 20 May 1945, 2.

[119] Ernest Newman, 'The truth about Wagner II', *ST*, 27 May 1945, 2.

[120] Ernest Newman, 'Bayreuth revisited', *ST*, 3 August 1930, 4. For Vera Newman's recollection of this visit see Vera Newman, *Ernest Newman*, 110–15. Vera's Newman's unclear chronology makes is difficult establishing the date of Newman's first visit to Bayreuth.

[121] Newman, 'Bayreuth revisited', *ST*, 3 August 1930, 4.

Figure 10 Newman at Bayreuth, probably 1951. People shown left to right are
probably Iris Wagner, Gertrud Wagner, Walter Legge and Wieland Wagner.
Photographer unknown.
Reproduced by kind permission of the Estate of Ernest Newman.

In a follow-up article the following week, Newman heaped praise on
Siegfried Wagner as a producer, describing him as a 'genius'.[122] Siegfried had
died on 4 August and Siegfried's wife, Winifred Wagner, succeeded him, but
Newman wrote cautiously about this succession: 'as a young Englishwoman
in her thirties [it] remains to be seen whether she has all the qualifications for
carrying on the Bayreuth work'.[123] He went on to write about talk of establishing a committee to manage Bayreuth though he felt 'few of us have any
faith in committees where art is concerned'.[124] By 1933, however, a Richard
Wagner Foundation was proposed by the Mayor of Bayreuth, and Newman,
Alfred Einstein, Arnold Schönberg, Paul Hindemith and Arthur Honneger
were proposed as advisers, with Thomas Mann as honorary president. This
nascent project did not come to pass. However, in 1973 such a foundation was

[122] Ernest Newman, 'Bayreuth revisited II', *ST*, 10 August 1930, 5.
[123] Newman, 'Bayreuth revisited II', *ST*, 10 August 1930, 5.
[124] Newman, 'Bayreuth revisited II', *ST*, 10 August 1930, 5.

established and the Wagner family gifted the Wagner archive, Festspielhaus and villa to Bayreuth.[125]

Writing about his visit to Bayreuth in 1951, Newman did something extraordinary and quite out of character. He reflected on how music had profoundly moved him and had changed his life. Rarely, if ever, had he written with such warmth and emotion:

> About the musical part of the performance I can hardly bring myself to speak, so ravishingly, heart-breakingly beautiful was it. This was not only the best *Parsifal* I have ever seen and heard but one of the three or four most moving spiritual experiences of my life. The exquisiteness of the orchestral playing was beyond the power of words to describe.[126]

⁊ *Musical Biography*

Musical biography was a subject on which Newman wrote extensively, despite its sometime neglect at the hands of German-language musicology.[127] During his time on the *Sunday Times,* he wrote in excess of seventy-five articles on the subject and showed a strong interest in methodology, the role of psychology in life writing, and the aims of contemporary biography. Like all topics on which Newman wrote, he identified many 'problems' with the genre.

The need for biographers to work with primary-source documents to help stop the perpetuation of myths and errors was a common thread in Newman's writing on biography. In an article published on 13 May 1924, he outlined the need for a biographer to portray a subject 'as he really was', which was an adaptation of Matthew Arnold's famous pronouncement that the role of the critic was to see 'the object as in itself it really is'.[128] Newman explained how this

---

[125] For more on the musical and political life of Bayreuth see Penelope Turing, *New Bayreuth* (London: St Ann's Press, 1969); Frederic Spotts, *Bayreuth: A History of the Wagner Festival* (New Haven and London: Yale University Press, 1994); and Jonathan Carr, *The Wagner Clan* (London: Faber and Faber, 2007).

[126] Ernest Newman, 'Bayreuth revisited', *ST,* 5 August 1951, 2.

[127] For example, Adler rated biography of composers (*Tondichter*) low on his list of auxiliary of sciences in his scheme for musicology; see Mugglestone, 'Adler's "The scope, method, and aim of musicology" (1885)': 9, 14. For background on the place of biography in musicology generally, see Jolanta T. Pekacz, 'Memory, history and meaning: musical biography and its discontents', *Journal of Musicological Research* 23/1 (2004): 39–80 and Pekacz, 'Introduction' in Jolanta Pekacz (ed.), *Musical Biography: Towards New Paradigms* (Aldershot: Ashgate, 2006): 1–16.

[128] Matthew Arnold, 'The function of criticism at the present time' in *Essays in Criticism* (London and Cambridge: Macmillan, 1865): 1–47; 1. The essay was first published in *National Review,* 1864.

line of inquiry—or what he described as the only ethical path of biography—
landed him in trouble upon completion of his *Wagner as Man and Artist* in
1914. He claimed that 'when I made a close detective study of the composer's
autobiography and letters and reminiscences of his friends, and showed ...
how unscrupulously untruthful he was, the true Wagnerians were down on me
to a man'.[129] In Newman's mind, he had written a complete and accurate biography, even if an unpopular one. It also proved that attempting a biography
that sees a subject 'as he really was' is fraught with differences of emphasis and
interpretation. No biography could be entirely impartial, no matter how hard
an author tried or what documents they used to portray their subject.

Newman took up the subject of authority in biography in articles in 1926
that dealt with Mozart and Beethoven.[130] Apart from asserting that an English
edition of Mozart's letters was welcome and long overdue, Newman claimed
'neither Beethoven nor Mozart can even be said to be quite clear to us. The
objective study of Mozart has been hampered for nearly three generations by
the romantic and in some ways false portrait of him painted by Otto Jahn'.[131]
Yet, Newman was optimistic that a 'new redaction' of the Jahn book by
Hermann Abert 'is only one sign of a new attitude towards Mozart that has
been developing during the last twenty years in Germany'.[132] Reiterating his
concern for the use of documents in biography, Newman wrote in the second
article that 'we cannot afford to neglect any documents however seemingly
trivial, that they may throw light on a composer's mentality'.[133] Writing on
Beethoven biography again in 1926, Newman went so far as to claim that
'There comes a time when most biographies should be scrapped, and for a real
picture of the man we should go straight back to the original documents'.[134]

In addition to using documents, Newman frequently articulated the
requirement for distance in biographical writing. In a review of C.L. Graves'
biography of Hubert Parry, Newman supposed the biographer was 'too near
his subject in point of time to see him in proper perspective, and was too fond
of the man to see him quite objectively as an artist. His biography, again, is not

---

[129] Ernest Newman, 'Musical biography: a division of labour', *ST*, 13 April 1924, 7.

[130] Ernest Newman, 'Letters, the man, and the musicians', *ST*, 28 February 1926, 7 and
'Letters, the man and the musician II', *ST*, 7 March 1926, 7.

[131] Newman, 'Letters, the man, and the musicians', 7.

[132] Newman, 'Letters, the man, and the musicians', 7. See Otto Jahn, *The Life of Mozart*,
trans. Pauline D. Townsend, 3 vols (London: Novello, 1992; [Leipzig, 1856–59]).
Hermann Abert, *W.A. Mozart,* trans. Stewart Spencer, ed. Cliff Eisen (New Haven:
Yale University Press, 2007 [Leipzig, 1919–21]).

[133] Newman, 'Letters, the man and the musician II', 7.

[134] Ernest Newman, 'Beethoven material', *ST*, 19 September 1926, 7.

only over-long, but lacks proportion and design'.[135] Newman further criticized Graves' biography for covering too many inconsequential details, and complained that the section on music was 'too much of a patchwork'.

A couple of months later, in June 1926, in an article entitled 'Legend and reality', Newman similarly argued that 'every composer needs a fundamental re-studying a century or so after his own day, with the object of disentangling him from the legend that has become woven around him in the interval. Broadly speaking, a great musician's contemporaries see him as he really is'.[136] Years later, in 1955, Newman declared that 'most nineteenth century biographies call for rewriting now'.[137]

Although Newman devoted considerable time to reflecting on the ills of musical biography, he was enthusiastic about some of its successes, and he wrote on more than one occasion about his admiration for Sanford Terry's *Bach: A Biography*, published in 1928. We have already seen Newman's admiration for books by Landormy and Dyson, which were not concerned so much with great men and works but with positioning music history in social and cultural contexts. The same characteristics held true of Terry's biography of Bach. Like Landormy and Dyson, Terry took a chronological approach to his subject but steered well clear of formal analyses of musical works. Although a small number of musical examples were dotted throughout the book, they did not dominate and distract from the narrative. In his preface, Terry described this biography as 'a record of Bach's career, not a critical appreciation of his music' and went on to write that '[Bach's] personality has been so buried under the towering pyramid of his manuscript that, for the most of us, he is but faintly visible on a background of the Bachgesellschaft folios'.[138] Terry criticized previous Bach biographers for ignoring source materials in favour of anecdote, especially Forkel's often celebrated biography of Bach from 1802, for its focus on 'critical appreciation, based on incomplete materials, of his hero as teacher, player, and composer'.[139] By contrast, Terry gave a five-page list of 'Authorities and abbreviations' at the front of the book (in lieu of a bibliography at the back of it), which listed the documents he consulted, a practice not uncommon in book publishing at the time. Newman regarded Terry as

[135] Ernest Newman, 'Hubert Parry', *ST*, 4 April 1926, 5. The book under review was Charles L. Graves, *Hubert Parry: His Life and Works,* 2 vols (London: Macmillan and Co., 1926).

[136] Ernest Newman, 'Legend and reality', *ST*, 20 June 1926, 7.

[137] Ernest Newman, 'Two Beethovens', *ST*, 23 January 1955, 11.

[138] See Charles Sanford Terry, *Bach: A Biography,* 2nd rev. edn (Oxford: Oxford University Press, 1933), v.

[139] Johann Nicolas Forkel, *Ueber Johann Sebastian Bachs Leben, Kunst und Kunstwerke* (Leipzig: Hoffmeister und Kühnel, 1802); English translation by Terry in 1920.

'almost alone among the writers of music in this country [because] he has approached his many tasks not only in the spirit of the genuine historian but with a genuine historical method.'[140] Terry's method, of course, was to rely on source materials and to position Bach in historical context, considering matters such as Bach's concerns for the education of his children, his financial state of affairs, and the politics and connections of his various employment as outlined, for example, in the chapter of his time in Cöthen and Leipzig. Later, Newman would note that Terry was 'now recognized everywhere as the leading living authority in matters connected with Bach research'.[141] The emphasis on studying a composer's life in context of time and place was, for Newman, a much more meaningful history than one that studied only the works.

♪ 'Music as Hard as Nails': The Moderns

There were a number of composers whose music Newman simply could not tolerate. First among these was Debussy, who Newman considered to be the father of atonalism.[142] Indeed, Newman's life-long lack of interest in French music, with the exception of Berlioz, is an unexplainable blind-spot. Then there were the moderns. His dislike of their music was articulated early in his *Sunday Times* career in an article on 13 November 1921 entitled 'Schönberg, Stravinksy and others' arguing that:

> The journalists who make a particular pose of 'modernism' always think that those of us who rank this sort of music lower than they do, do so because we are incapable of understanding anything so new. With all respect they are mistaken. We see quite clearly what it is composers like Schönberg and Stravinsky (in some of his later works) are aiming at, and we watch their experiments, which are often interesting, with every sympathy. All that we contend is that generally they do not succeed in doing all they set out to do.[143]

When, in 1923, Newman heard *Pierrot Lunaire*, probably for the first time, he wrote that it was the 'cruelest of all musical torture' and that he did not want to hear the work again. He wrote that Schoenberg's music was 'not of a genius but of a brain that has lost every vestige of the musical faculty it once had except for the power to put notes together without the smallest concern for whether they mean anything or not'.[144] This contradicted Newman's appraisals

---

[140] Ernest Newman, 'Dr Terry's Bach', *ST*, 2 September 1928, 5.

[141] Ernest Newman, 'Bach and his orchestra', *ST*, 12 March 1933, 7.

[142] Ernest Newman, 'Thoughts on the present discontents VI', *ST*, 12 January 1930, 5.

[143] Ernest Newman, 'Schönberg, Strauss and others', *ST*, 13 November 1921, 5.

[144] Ernest Newman, 'The Schönberg case', *ST*, 25 November 1923, 5.

of Schoenberg's earlier works made nine years earlier. As Deborah Heckert has outlined, Newman was most enthusiastic about the composer's *Gurreleider*. He wrote favourably about its expressive and harmonic range in an article in the *Musical Times* in 1914, claiming that the work was 'the finest musical love poem since "Tristan".'[145]

In Stravinsky's case, Newman believed that critics had taken to the composer's works without enough scrutiny. In an article in March 1924, Newman declared that a 'full treatment' of Stravinsky's works was needed and that 'it is time we dropped the expository attitude towards Stravinsky and become purely critical'.[146] Newman could not even muster much enthusiasm for Stravinsky's conducting, asserting that it did 'more harm than good' to his reputation and that 'his psychological range is very limited'.[147] Curiously, Newman admitted in the midst of this article that he admired *Firebird* and *Petroushka* but only parts of the *Rite of Spring*. A few years later he admitted that he liked some of Schoenberg's early works—that demonstrated a Wagnerian hue: 'I find a good deal of it admirable music with a strong Wagnerian infusion, some of it an interesting foreshadowing of the later changes in Schönberg's conception of the art, and some it is ugly and almost incomprehensible'.[148]

Newman's attack on modern music did not abate, even by the mid 1940s:

> The music truly typical of our epoch is that of such composers as Hindemith, Krenek and Schönberg, a music as hard as nails, music as unemotionally efficient as a calculating machine, a music occupied solely with the pitilessly logical working out of certain dimly perceived new theoretic possibilities of melodic line, harmony and counterpoint, a music that makes no appeal whatever to nine hundred and ninety-nine out of a thousand listeners because their emotion-craving souls can find no nourishment in it (I am one of the nine hundred and ninety-nine myself, by the way).[149]

However, by 1947 Newman was starting to accept that modernist music was a mainstay, conceding that Schoenberg's music was for the future rather than the present.[150] Still, he harboured a strong dislike of other modern music,

[145] Deborah Heckert, 'Schoenberg, Roger Fry and the Emergence of a Critical Language for the Reception of Musical Modernism in Britain, 1912–1914', in Matthew Riley (ed.), *British Music and Modernism, 1895–1960* (Aldershot: Ashgate, 2010): 49–66; Ernest Newman, 'Arnold Schönberg's Gurre-Lieder', *MT*, 55/851 (1 January 1914): 11–13; 13.

[146] Ernest Newman, 'Stravinsky and criticism', *ST*, 9 March 1924, 7.

[147] Ernest Newman, 'Stravinsky today', *ST*, 25 January 1925, 7.

[148] Ernest Newman, 'This Schönberg case', *ST*, 19 February 1928, 7.

[149] Ernest Newman, 'Our music and our epoch', *ST*, 12 March 1944, 2.

[150] Ernest Newman, 'Schönberg once more', *ST*, 10 August 1947, 2.

including jazz. Aesthetically, Newman found it unsatisfying and a genre of 'extremely limited possibilities', which he considered an industry rather than an art.[151] Moreover, Newman insisted in 1932 that 'the day of jazz is over' and, in 1944, that there is 'nothing wonderful' about improvisation because 'any ordinarily good musician can turn it out by the yard'.[152]

Despite his grumpiness towards the moderns, Newman admired Berg's music, especially *Wozzek* and the *Violin Concerto*. Newman rarely spoke in glowing terms about any musical work, even ones he greatly admired, but he once described *Wozzek* in euphoric, but also possibly quite sarcastic terms: 'how much longer is the remarkable "Wozzeck" to wait for a stage production in London?' He continued: 'everything about 'Wozzeck' is amazing'.[153] No article by Newman in the *Sunday Times* engaged in any detail with Stockhausen, and Boulez was mentioned only in passing on one occasion when Newman wrote about the evolution of music, pointing out that the definition and form of music had varied enormously over the centuries.[154]

Newman was not the only British critic who eschewed modern music and nor was he always entirely negative on the subject. In an article by Charles Stuart published in *Tempo* in 1951, Newman was just one of many English critics, including M.D. Calvocoressi, whose ambivalence towards composers such as Stravinsky and Schoenberg was discussed.[155] When Newman worked as BBC adviser and broadcaster in the late 1920s and early 1930s, Newman's opposition to modern music was sometimes much more balanced and considered than his rants in the *Sunday Times*.[156] As Jennifer Doctor has noted, Newman 'played an important role in the BBC campaign to explain and defend contemporary music broadcasts'.[157]

[151] Ernest Newman, 'Jazz opera and national opera', *ST*, 28 December 1924, 4; Ernest Newman, 'Jazz and "The American composer"', *ST*, 1 February 1925, 7; 'Mr Whiteman goes on explaining', *ST*, 12 September 1926, 7; and '"So this is jazz"', *ST*, 26 December 1926, 4.

[152] Ernest Newman, 'Jazz and Dionysis', *ST*, 23 October 1932, 5; 'Audiences old and new', *ST*, 9 January 1944, 2.

[153] Ernest Newman, '"Wozzeck"', 27 March 1949, 2. Further articles praising this work were published in January 1952: 'Büchner and Berg', *ST*, 13 January 1952, 2; 'Berg and Wozzeck, *ST*, 20 January 1952, 2; and '"Wozzeck"', *ST*, 27 January 1952, 2.

[154] Ernest Newman, 'Music as language', *ST*, 26 May 1957, 22.

[155] Charles Stuart, 'Fifty years of music criticism', *Tempo* 19 (1951): 12–18.

[156] See Jennifer Doctor, *The BBC and Ultra Modern Music, 1922–36: Shaping a Nation's Tastes* (Cambridge: Cambridge University Press, 1999).

[157] Doctor, *The BBC and Ultra Modern Music*, 429.

🙖 *Retirement*

At the end of 1958, after more than thirty-eight years as chief music critic for the *Sunday Times*, Newman retired. His departure was announced—and his career appraised—in a column by the *Sunday Times'* editor, Harry Hodson:

> He [Newman] has achieved the highest distinction open to the journalist by winning the respect, and shaping the practice, of experts in his subject while engaging the attention and broadening the horizons of the general reader ... Eagerly read wherever music is heard, his contributions to the *Sunday Times* have prompted discussion in our columns with the greatest regularity. Equally unabashed by the arrogance of the expert and the massive non-comprehension of the common man, Ernest Newman has never hesitated to deflate the one and stimulate the other—to the benefit of all ... We of the *Sunday Times* salute this ageless veteran with gratitude and pride.[158]

To mark the end of Newman's career, the *Sunday Times* solicited appraisals about him from a range of musicians and writers. Arthur Bliss wrote of Newman as 'a unique and eminent figure in our musical history', and Sir Adrian Boult, while admitting that Newman had often criticized his work, felt the criticisms had 'always been kindly administered'.[159] J.A. Westrup claimed that 'for all of us he has been an oracle', and Boris Ord, organist and choir master of King's College Cambridge, wrote 'for so long have we rushed for our copy of the *Sunday Times* each week to see what Mr Newman had to say'. Other writers took their chance to praise Newman's other work; for example, Gerald Moore expressed his gratitude to Newman for his work on Hugo Wolf, while Ord praised Newman's *Life of Wagner* as 'a classic biography in any language'. Last, but by no means least, it was Sir Thomas Beecham, one of Newman's closest friends, who had the final say, describing Newman as a 'Great Englishman, Great Writer and Great Musician'.

While many people, such as the writers of these testimonies, regretted Newman's retirement, others were relieved he had finally chosen to leave, for they thought Newman had become cynical and out of touch.[160] In fact, in 1920, the year of his appointment, there had already been a feisty exchange between Newman, Cecil Gray and Philip Heseltine, in the then newly formed *Sackbut*, over Newman's supposed outdated views on the function of criticism. Although the *Sunday Times* had announced that it had employed a doyen of

---

[158] Unsigned, 'Ernest Newman's World of Music: Our critic retires after 38 years', *ST*, 9 November 1958.

[159] All quotations in this paragraph are from Unsigned, 'Ernest Newman's World of Music: our critic retires after 38 years', *ST*, 9 November 1958.

[160] Vera Newman, *Ernest Newman*, v.

Figure 11 Ernest Newman and Vera Newman, c. 1950s, with one of numerous
pet cats. Photographer unknown.
Reproduced by kind permission of the Estate of Ernest Newman.

music criticism, Gray and Heseltine believed Newman was a dodo. They saw him as a cold rationalist, ignorant of, and dismissive towards, modern music and modern criticism. Newman's preoccupation with situating composers and their works in a set time and place, with reference to evolving musical style, was at odds with their alternative view of history, which argued that genius and musical beauty were fixed attributes and universally recognisable across time.[161]

There were other moments during his *Sunday Times* career when Newman's supremacy was challenged. For example, in the lead-up to Newman's eightieth birthday in 1948, it was rumoured that he would announce his retirement, to be succeeded by his deputy, Neville Cardus, who was then based in Australia as the paper's cricket reporter. This arrangement seemed a done deal and was duly printed in the *Sydney Morning Herald*. However, when Newman got wind of this plan he wrote to William W. Hadley, the *Sunday Times'* editor, and called his bluff. Newman explained to Hadley that he had heard the rumour, at which point Hadley relayed this to Cardus, whereupon Cardus resigned from the *Sunday Times*.[162] (It is possible Hadley withdrew the appointment to appease Newman.) Some weeks later, however, Cardus joined the *Evening Standard* as its music critic. In announcing his appointment, the paper described Cardus as 'the foremost music critic in the country'.[163] There was clearly a ploy here on the part of the *Evening Standard* (and probably Cardus himself) to rival Newman on the *Sunday Times*.

Newman's work in the *Sunday Times* shows the critic as an agitator for musical change and improvement, in the case of opera at the Royal Opera House, Covent Garden, and of his advocacy of German-language musicology. Both of these pursuits illustrate a forward-looking writer, inspired by European musical and intellectual life. However, while Newman embraced musical change in the theatre and in musical literature, he was largely unable to adapt to developments in new music. While, on the one hand, Newman showed insight into discussions about the provision of opera subsidies that revealed a considered and egalitarian outlook, much of his work in the *Sunday Times*—especially his continuing harking back to the need for scientific criticism, that very outmoded late nineteenth-century paradigm—gradually put Newman out of touch with his own era. In other respects, Newman was very much in touch with his times, as his writings on the politics of German–British

---

[161] See further Sarah Collins, '"Never out of date and never modern": Aesthetic democracy, radical music criticism and *The Sackbut*', ML, 95/3 (2014): 404–28.

[162] Christopher Brookes, *His Own Man: The Life of Neville Cardus* (London: Methuen, 1985): 191.

[163] Brookes, *His Own Man*, 192.

political relations—especially on Wagner—clearly demonstrate. Through the 'World of Music' columns, Newman brought to British readers not only a raft of information about music, but insight into how criticism should work, especially in Britain.

CHAPTER 8

Biographical and Musicological Tensions:
The Man Liszt, 1934

IN 1934, Newman published a sensational biography of Franz Liszt. For all intents and purposes it was an exercise in character assassination, even though Newman refused to admit it.[1] During the 1910s and 1920s Newman had written favourably on Liszt, but by the 1930s his position had changed completely. The book's critical reception was devastating and caused Newman a crisis in confidence: he temporarily abandoned volume 2 of the *Life of Richard Wagner* and never wrote another musical biography. Although *The Man Liszt* remains a *bête noir* of Liszt literature, an overview of its genesis, intent and reception illustrates the ethics, scope and financial imperatives of musical biography in the 1930s. It also demonstrates the low esteem in which psychobiography was held by scholars, especially musicologists, in the 1930s and 1940s.

❦ *Genesis of* The Man Liszt

Newman's first article on Liszt, 'A Study of Liszt', published in 1900, gives no hint of the author's grievances with the composer. Newman wrote favourably of Liszt's 'thoroughly musical imagination', his 'stupendous charity and generosity' and 'unparalleled' musicianship.[2] Similarly, in an article in the *Nation* of 28 October 1911, Newman wrote appreciatively of Liszt as man and musician, arguing that ignorance and neglect of his music stood in the way of a sound knowledge of the composer in England, though Newman was not convinced of Liszt's dexterity with musical form.[3] However, in a separate series of articles published in the *Musical Times* in late 1911, Newman was mildly critical of Liszt.[4] Called simply 'Franz Liszt', the articles were written to mark the centenary of Liszt's birth and the fiftieth anniversary of the German Musical

---

[1] The term 'character assassination' is also used by Liszt's most authoritative biographer to describe Newman's *The Man Liszt*. See Alan Walker, *Franz Liszt vol. II: The Weimar Years, 1848–61* (London: Faber & Faber Ltd, 1989): 16.

[2] Ernest Newman, 'A study of Liszt', reprinted in *Liszt Society Journal* 8 (1983 [1900]): 32–3. The original place of publication is not known.

[3] Newman, 'The Liszt centenary', *Nation*, 28 October 1911, 162–3.

[4] Ernest Newman, 'Franz Liszt, October 22, 1811 – July 31, 1886', *MT*, 52/824 (1 October 1911): 52/825 (1 November 1911): 708–11; 52/826 (1 December 1911): 778–80.

Association.[5] The first article comprised a short biographical sketch of Liszt and an analysis of some of the composer's early songs. The second article dealt with Liszt's influence on later composers such as Wagner and Strauss, while the third article concentrated on issues concerning aesthetics and form. Although each article was severely critical of some of Liszt's works, Newman nevertheless gave high praise to some of Liszt's other compositions, which are discussed below. Newman's dislike of Liszt's personality is not immediately apparent in these articles: that would come later.

Newman's intention in these articles was to see Liszt 'in better focus and clearer definition.'[6] He was also keen to correct a stereotype: 'for most English people Liszt is still merely the greatest of pianists, the composer of a few showy pianoforte pieces, and the expert arranger of Hungarian melodies.'[7] Newman also wanted to correct some other stereotypes about Liszt: '[Liszt's] fine work—of which there is really a great deal more than the man in the street imagines—is sufficient to prove that he was a born composer, and not, as the foolish old taunt used to go, a mere pianist with a mania for composition.'[8]

In the 1911 articles, Newman considered the composer to be a pioneer, innovator and progressive whose impact on composers such as Wolf and Strauss surpassed any influence Wagner's music may have had.[9] Yet Newman qualified this praise with strident and, at times, inconsistent criticisms. He outlined Liszt's compositional weaknesses by focusing on a selection of songs, complaining they were un-lyrical and verbose. To illustrate this, Newman gave a brief account of the song 'Loreley' (composed 1843). Although he considered it 'undeniably beautiful in parts', he thought that 'the whole song unquestionably drags' and 'takes too long; it repeats itself too often.'[10] Newman then analysed two more songs 'Wer nie sein Brot mit Tränen aß' (composed 1845, revised 1849) and 'Kennst du das Land' (composed 1842 and revised in 1854 and 1860). In the first of these songs, Newman argued there was a 'too elaborate insistence on certain words', and that the 'magic seems squeezed out of the poem.'[11] In

[5] Newman, 'Franz Liszt', 633. A Proms concert on 20 September was also devoted to works by Liszt. See M.D. Calvocoressi, 'On Liszt and programme music', *Listener*, 12 September, 1934, 437.

[6] Newman, 'Franz Liszt', 633.

[7] Newman, 'Franz Liszt', 633. In 1934, M.D. Calvocoressi wrote an article concerning Liszt reception in England and attributed the rise in appreciation of the composer to Alexander Mackenzie, Constant Lambert, Ernest Newman, Cecil Gray and Sacheverell Sitwell. See Calvocoressi, 'On Liszt and programme music', 437.

[8] Newman, 'Franz Liszt', 780.

[9] Newman, 'Franz Liszt', 709, 780.

[10] Newman, 'Franz Liszt', 636, 637.

[11] Newman, 'Franz Liszt', 637.

respect to the second song, Newman criticised its weak final cadence.[12] With the aid of musical examples, Newman argued these early songs demonstrated 'Liszt's typical failings—excess of statement, a too anxious and too obvious search for drastic expression, inability to achieve a rapid and concentrated flight'.[13] Despite these harsh criticisms, Newman found plenty of praise for Liszt's 'Es war ein König in Thule' composed in 1843, considering it 'a masterpiece in many ways' because of its 'splendid coherence' and 'concision that Liszt too rarely attained'.[14]

By 1915, Newman's work on Liszt started to focus on his personality and the first signs of Newman's distaste for the composer and his music emerged. In the December issue of *New Witness,* entitled 'Concerning Liszt and Ravel', Newman's criticisms of Liszt were personal and vindictive.[15] The article got off to a reasonably fair start but quickly turned sour. At first, Newman wrote of Liszt's 'peculiar case' in the history of music: 'at least half the world of music still believes that he [Liszt] was a very poor and flashy composer, while in his own day hardly one per cent of musicians would admit that he was a composer at all'.[16] Newman then discussed the music: 'Liszt's weaknesses are obvious enough', he wrote, but he judged *A Faust Symphony* 'a really great work, though Liszt could not always live up to this standard'.[17] This last criticism was particularly harsh:

> But the great flaw in him ... was the tendency to what may be called gaseous inflation of idea. He is the supreme type of the musician that romanticism brought into being—the composer who was not content simply to compose, but must worry himself incessantly over questions of morals, sociology, and what not. Liszt is worse than Wagner, not only because the thin vapouring of the moralist got further into the tissue of his music. It is incredible today that any man should ever have taken seriously the goody-goody maunderings of the prefaces that Liszt wrote to his symphonic poems.[18]

This dislike of Liszt continued to gnaw at Newman well into the 1920s when he worked on the *Sunday Times.* The first of these articles, 'The Schumanns and Liszt', was printed on 31 January 1926. It consisted of a review of two recently published books, Herbert Bedford's *Robert Schumann: His Life and*

---

[12] Newman, 'Franz Liszt', 637.

[13] Newman, 'Franz Liszt', 637.

[14] Newman, 'Franz Liszt', 639.

[15] Ernest Newman, 'Concerning Liszt and Ravel', *NW,* 16 December 1915, 190–92; 190.

[16] Newman, 'Concerning Liszt and Ravel', 190.

[17] Newman, 'Concerning Liszt and Ravel', 190.

[18] Newman, 'Concerning Liszt and Ravel', 190.

Work (1926) and Guy de Pourtalès's *La vie de Franz Liszt* (1925). Newman commended Bedford's book for its modern approach to musical biography because it avoided hero worship and used 'now familiar material ... in a new and agreeable way'.[19] However, Newman also found fault with it for errors in some names and dates.[20] Newman then provided a brief outline of Pourtalès's book that covered 'The comical paradox of his [Liszt's] later life, with its mixture of religiosity and eroticism'.[21]

Newman used 'The Schumanns and Liszt' article to attack Liszt ferociously. Under the heading 'Half-priest, half circus-rider' Newman argued that 'much of Liszt's music arouses this repugnance [of personality] in the average man to-day. With all his finesse and nobility, there was a large dash of the vulgarian and charlatan in him'.[22] Newman elaborated:

> His [Liszt's] music, like his character, suffers from the absence of what I have called centrality, from the conflict of ill-blended elements in it, and from his ingrained virtuoso habit of covering a deficiency of matter with lavishness of gesture. No one doubts his sincerity, but too often there is something positively offensive—intellectually as well as emotionally shoddy—in the mentality of his music.[23]

In a follow-up article published the following week called 'The music and the man', Newman again pondered the role of the music biographer, which was clearly a veiled attempt to lampoon Liszt biography.[24] Newman considered the 'queer little ways' of the biographer, asking, 'Does a biographer depict his hero as a saint in a stained glass window?' He proposed that a musically

---

[19] Ernest Newman, 'The Schumanns and Liszt', *ST*, 31 January 1926, 7.

[20] Newman, 'The Schumanns and Liszt', 7.

[21] Guy de Pourtàles, *La vie de Franz Liszt: Un homme 'd'amour* (Paris: Gallimard, 1925).

[22] Newman, 'The Schumanns and Liszt', 7.

[23] Newman, 'The Schumanns and Liszt', 7.

[24] Ernest Newman, 'The music and the man', *ST*, 7 February 1926, 7. A.W. Thayer was the author of *Ludwig van Beethovens Leben,* 3 vols (Berlin: Schneider, 1866; Weber, 1872–79), which was the first scholarly biography of Beethoven to be published. Thayer published widely on music, as Robert Stevenson's article on Thayer in *Grove Music Online* demonstrates, so Newman was wrong to claim that Thayer was 'non-musical'. Newman may have taken this line given that Thayer had a degree in law and worked for a time as a librarian and foreign consul. On the other hand, William Ashton Ellis, translator of *The Life of Richard Wagner,* 6 vols (London: Kegan Paul, Trench, Trübner & Co., 1900–1908) was a medical officer; Romain Rolland, author of *Vie de Beethoven* (Paris: Hachette, 1903) was, amongst other things, a novelist and playwright.

trained biographer tends towards hagiography and that biography of composers would be better served by the non-musician:

> [S]ince we must have biographies of composers, we may as well have truthful ones, and I have suggested that we are more likely to get the sober truth from a non-musical biographer, such as Thayer, than from one who, like Ashton Ellis in the case of Wagner, or Romain Rolland in the case of Beethoven, cannot see the man clearly because he looks at him through the romantic heat-haze of the fine music that surrounds him.[25]

Over the next few years, Newman returned to the topic of Liszt biography in his *Sunday Times* essays. In a 1927 article entitled 'Poses et mensonges: women who ruined Liszt' Newman commented on the 'amiable bourgeois who keep on pathetically asking why we should concern ourselves with the lives of musicians when we have their music to enjoy', and went on to explain that 'biographers have to tell the truth, the whole truth and nothing but the truth'.[26] In November 1929, Newman wrote another pointed article on Liszt, entitled 'Another illusion shattered', in which he asserted that 'one of the most tiresome but most necessary jobs of criticism to-day is going about tidying up the mess left by the last couple of generations' and turned his attention, predictably, to Liszt: 'Liszt is supposed to have had a very special gift for discovering genius. I venture to maintain that this is a fallacy'.[27] On 23 April 1933, Newman was to write again in a similar vein suggesting that much of what passed for Liszt biography was '*fable convenue*' and, in an article on 10 December 1933, he asserted that there was 'no real life of Liszt' that had yet been published.[28] By the time Newman's *The Man Liszt* came out, readers who were following Newman's *Sunday Times* articles would have been predicting what kind of biography he was going to write. A perfect biographical storm was brewing.

﴾ *Outline*

In chapter 1, Newman undertook a survey of some previous Liszt biographies. He was scathing of Lina Ramann's biography, *Franz Liszt als Künstler und Mensch*, published between 1880 and 1894, which relied on Liszt's responses to questions she had sent him, but Newman considered Peter Raabe's *Franz*

---

[25] Newman, 'The music and the man', *ST*, 7 February 1926, 7.

[26] Ernest Newman, 'Poses et mensonges: women who ruined Liszt', *ST*, 24 April 1927, 7.

[27] Ernest Newman, 'Another illusion shattered', *ST*, 17 November 1929, 7.

[28] Ernest Newman, 'New light on Liszt', *ST*, 23 April 1933, 7 and 'Biographies of musicians', *ST*, 10 December 1933, 7. See Sacheverell Sitwell, *Liszt* (London: Faber, 1943).

Liszt (1931) the 'most reliable' biography to date; a view shared by recent scholars.[29] Newman regarded Julius Kapp's biography, first published in 1909 and reissued in 1924 in a nineteenth edition, as foolhardy for seeking to write a biography that gave 'the absolute truth' and, although impressed with Kapp's selective use of the primary sources, complained that Kapp was yet 'another illustration of the sad and sobering fact that no finality in biography is attainable'.[30] Newman's overview of Liszt biography, however, was incomplete. There was no mention of James Huneker's biography from 1924 that persuasively documented Liszt's unbecoming character and womanizing, and there was no mention of biographies by Calvocoressi (1906) or Jean Chantavoine (1901) that were solid biographical accounts in the 'life and works' fashion.[31] Moreover, Newman ignored completely William Wallace's book, *Liszt, Wagner and the Princess* (1927) that also covered Liszt's comedic and tragic life and his disgraceful treatment of his mistresses.[32] Even Frederick Corder's biography from 1925, which Newman referred to briefly in his review of Liszt biography, had already made an unflattering assessment of the composer.[33] In fact, La Mara's biography, *Liszt und die Frauen*, from 1911, had covered Liszt's relationships with some twenty-six women.[34]

[29] Lina Ramann, *Franz Liszt als Künstler und Mensch*, 3 vols (Lepizig, 1880–94); Peter Raabe, *Listzs Leben* (Stuttgart: Cotta, 1931). The historiography of Liszt biography is given in Alexander Rehding, 'Inventing Liszt's Life: Early Biography and Autobiography' in Kenneth Hamilton (ed.), *The Cambridge Companion to Liszt* (Cambridge: Cambridge University Press): 14–27 and James Deaville, 'Liszt and the Twentieth Century' in Kenneth Hamilton (ed.), *The Cambridge Companion to Liszt* (Cambridge: Cambridge University Press): 28–56. Raabe's work was both biography and source study, as Deaville explains (46–48), and Deaville positions it as the definitive Liszt biography for its 'stripping away of the Romantic accretions to Liszt' (47), ahead of Alan Walker's *Franz Liszt*, 3 vols (Vols I and II: New York: Macmillan, 1983–89; vol. III: New York: Random House, 1996). Rev. edn (Ithaca, NY: Cornell University Press).

[30] Julius Kapp, *Franz Liszt: Eine Biographie* (Berlin: Newman, Schuster & Loeffler, 1909); Newman, *The Man Liszt: A study of the tragi-comedy of a soul divided against itself* (London: Cassell, 1934, New York: Charles Scribner, 1935, London: Victor Gollancz Ltd., 1970): 6–7. All citations in this chapter are from the 1970 edition.

[31] M.D. Calvocoressi, *Liszt* (Paris: Laurens, 1906) and Jean Chantovoine, *Liszt* (Paris: Libraire Félix Alcan, 1910).

[32] William Wallace, *Liszt, Wagner and the Princess* (London: Kegan, Trench, Trubner and Co. Ltd, 1927).

[33] Frederick Corder, *Ferencz (François) Liszt* (London: Kegan Paul, Trench, Trubner and Co. Ltd., 1925).

[34] La Mara (peud. Ida Maria Lipsius), *Liszt und die Frauen* (Leipzig: Breitkopf und Härtel), 1911.

In 1934 it was a bumper year for Liszt biography in England with the publication of Sacheverell Sitwell's *Liszt*. Newman made no mention of it in the first chapter, possibly because galley proofs were well advanced and additions could not be made. However, he wrote a stinging attack on Sitwell's book in the *Sunday Times* in April of that year.[35] Newman dismissed the book, implying it contained no new knowledge about Liszt and ran along merely 'conventional lines'.[36] Newman strongly objected to Sitwell's claim that Liszt was the founder of conducting and deemed Sitwell's efforts to psychologise his subject as 'too facile and too sweeping … of the old romantic idealising kind'.[37]

Dissatisfied with previous attempts at Liszt biography, Newman stated his case for a psychological study: the reconciling of Liszt's supposed dual nature. In chapters 2, 3 and 4, Newman re-examined the circumstances surrounding Liszt's affair with Marie d'Agoult. Countess d'Agoult (1805–76) was a freethinker and writer, who used the pen name Daniel Stern. She was once married to Charles Louis Constant d'Agoult, but left him for Liszt, with whom she lived for approximately four years. Newman argued that previous Liszt biographers wrote of d'Agoult's manipulation of the composer but Newman argued she did not behave like this at all. These chapters, especially chapter 4, discussed Liszt's ferocious temper, his duplicity and other unsavoury aspects of his personality such as his 'arrogance' and 'philandering'.[38]

Chapter 5 discussed two works: *Béatrix*, written by Balzac between 1838–44; and *Nélida*, written by d'Agoult (under the pseudonym Daniel Stern) and published in 1846, which was a chronicle of her years with Liszt. Both books presented extremely unflattering reminiscences of Liszt, and Newman used them as examples to bolster his argument of the man as self-obsessed and cold-hearted. In chapter 6, Newman examined Liszt's relationship with Princess Carolyne Sayn-Wittgenstein, whom Liszt met in 1847, and the period in which Liszt worked in Weimar. Newman portrayed the Princess as a bluestocking who impeded Liszt's development as a composer and who was responsible for the couple being disliked in Weimar. Chapter 7 examined the demise of Liszt's relationship with Princess Sayn-Wittgenstein and is one of the few places in the book where Liszt is discussed in any detail as a composer—in this case, praising his early piano works. Chapter 8 contained the most probing character portrait of Liszt, describing all his unbecoming traits. Chapter 9 recounted

---

[35] Ernest Newman, 'Liszt and the biographers: Mr. Sitwell's contribution', *ST*, 29 April 1934, 7.

[36] Newman, 'Liszt and the biographers', 7.

[37] Newman, 'Liszt and the biographers', 7.

[38] Ernest Newman, *The Man Liszt*, 87, 102. All citations in this chapter are from the 1970 edition.

the association Liszt had with one of his students: a clearly troubled woman named Olga Janina, whom Newman believed had experienced first-hand the malicious temperament of her teacher. Newman used her damning, although unreliable, testimony to strengthen his case against the composer. In his summing-up, Newman concluded that Liszt was a troubled character who was unable to keep the extremities of his emotions and bad behaviour in check.

☙ *Motivations*

In the foreword to *The Man Liszt*, Newman explained why he wrote the book:

> As his [Liszt's] career touched that of Wagner at so many points, I felt myself under the necessity, in the course of my second Wagner volume, of defining Liszt himself more accurately than I could persuade myself had yet been done. I soon found, however, that to attempt this with even the smallest prospect of success meant devoting a disproportionate amount of space to Liszt in what is, after all, a Life not of Liszt but of Wagner. Then, finding myself with so much Liszt material on my hands, and becoming more and more fascinated with the contradictions of his complex nature, and more and more conscious that none of the existing biographies, not even the admirable recent one of Peter Raabe, takes stock of all we know about Liszt, I was suddenly assailed by the temptation to make him the subject of a full-length psychological study.[39]

Newman's plan was to write a biography that was fair and objective. 'Musical biography,' he wrote in the preface, 'has always tended to the diffusion of a romantic legend rather than an impartial record of the sober truth.'[40] But Newman's over-riding concern in *The Man Liszt*, as we have seen, was to study the duality of the composer's character. To force the point, Newman quoted Liszt's own description of himself as 'Half Zigeuner, half Franciscan'[41] then cited other writers who had noticed this same dual—even tripartite—compartmentalisation of the composer's troublesome character:

> Henry Thorbes describes him as 'one-third minstrel, one-third chevalier, one-third Franciscan'. Other descriptions of him have been 'half saint, half charlatan,'

---

[39] Newman, *The Man Liszt*, xi. Peter Raabe, *Listzs Leben*.

[40] Newman, *The Man Liszt*, 1

[41] This description was mentioned in a letter to the Princess from Liszt on 13 August 1856. See La Mara [Marie Lipsius] (ed.) *Franz Liszt's Briefe*, 316. Cited in Rehding, 'Inventing Liszt's Life', 14.

'half priest, half circus-rider'. Always, after studying him, there remains the impression of a soul hopelessly divided against itself.[42]

Here, Newman's subtitle for the book, 'The study of a soul divided against itself', was given a context. Furthermore, Newman saw *The Man Liszt* as both a historically corrective biography as well as a psychological study that would explain Liszt's personal failings. He saw Liszt as a flawed human being, unable to come to terms with his competing personas: 'the convivial man of the salons, the virtuoso, and the thoughtful creative artist' versus the unflattering descriptions listed earlier.[43] According to Newman, Liszt saw the need to reconcile these facets of his personality; he was aware of the need for 'self-correction'.[44] But Newman doubted whether Liszt ever managed this self-correction: 'we shall find, in the course of the present study, good reason for doubting whether Liszt ever succeeded'.[45]

Newman then discussed the theoretical framework for *The Man Liszt*, which he explained was derived from *Aspects de la biographie* by André Maurois published in 1930.[46] This book had its genesis in six lectures Maurois had read at Trinity College, Cambridge for the Clark Foundation in 1928. Maurois' biographical theory was developed around a set of questions:

> Is there such a thing as modern biography? Is there a literary form different from that of traditional biography? Are its methods legitimate or ought they to be abandoned? Ought biography to be an art or a science? Can it, like the novel, be a means of expression, a means of escape for the author as well as for the reader? Such are some of the questions which we shall be able to examine together; and that we may be loyal to the spirit of this foundation, our examples will be taken from English literature.[47]

---

[42] Newman, *The Man Liszt*, 8. Even as late as 1967 these conflicting personas of Liszt's personality were still not well understood by scholars, in the view of one writer at least: 'There is so general a conception of Liszt by now as a mixture of charlatan and virtuoso that, as time goes by, it becomes not easier but more difficult to arrive at the truth about him as a composer'. Sacheverell Sitwell, *Liszt*, xi.

[43] Newman, *The Man Liszt*, 8–9.

[44] Newman, *The Man Liszt*, 8–9.

[45] Newman, *The Man Liszt*, 9. Newman, unlike Thorbes, discusses Liszt's duality, not a tripartite persona.

[46] André Maurois, *Aspects de la biographie* (Paris: B. Grasset, 1928). English translation: *Aspects of Biography*, trans. S.C. Roberts (Cambridge University Press, 1929). All quotations are from the English edition. Newman made his own English translations.

[47] Maurois, *Aspects of Biography*, 5–6.

Maurois then elaborated on the virtues of modern biography by emphasizing the need for careful reflection:

> The modern biographer, if he is honest, will not allow himself to think: 'Here is a great king, a great statesman, a great writer; round his name a legend has been built; it is on the legend, and on the legend alone, that I wish to dwell'. No. He thinks rather: 'Here is a man. I possess a certain number of documents, a certain amount of evidence about him. I am going to attempt to draw a true portrait. What will the portrait be? I have no idea. I don't want to know before I have actually drawn it. I am prepared to accept whatever a prolonged contemplation of my subject may reveal to me, and to correct it in proportion to such new facts as I discover.[48]

In his foreword Newman scrutinised Maurois' question as to whether biography was an art or a science and decided that his Liszt biography lay somewhere between the two:

> If the present volume partakes to some extent of the character of each of these types [art and science], it has not been because, in writing it, I have consciously striven after a compromise of this kind. I have had before me, in the first place, the purely scientific ideal of accumulating all the relevant facts and setting them before the reader without prepossession and without prejudice. If a scientific word must be found for my method of procedure, perhaps I may be allowed to say that it has been inductive rather than deductive: I have not started, in the nineteenth century manner, from a definite point of view in my reading of Liszt's character and then used the arbitrarily selected material to drive this point home to the reader; I have marshalled the material and then tried to allow it to impose upon me the conclusions that seemed to me immanent in it.[49]

Despite the obvious evidence of thorough research, most of the critics who reviewed *The Man Liszt* did not accept Newman's claim that it was objective. Rather, they saw it as a deliberate, provocative and irresponsible attempt to sensationalize its topic.

ቈ *Incensed Critics*

The Man Liszt was savaged by most of the critics who reviewed it. Although recognized by some as 'painstaking and well documented' and as a product of 'tireless research', the majority of critics accused Newman of writing a

---

[48] Maurois, *Aspects of Biography*, 12.
[49] Newman, *The Man Liszt*, xiii–xiv.

debunking biography.[50] Constant Lambert could not even agree that the prevailing hero-worship, the 'Liszt Legend' as described by Newman, even existed: 'no one believes in the old Liszt Legend any more, and no one wants to'.[51]

Most of the reviewers regarded Newman's book a wholesale destruction of the legend, even though Newman protested that it was no such thing. In the foreword Newman had written:

> In collecting the relevant evidence as to the whole Liszt my intention has not been anything in the nature of that 'debunking'—an odious word for an odious thing—that is so much to the taste of certain modern biographers who, unable to see or to understand the complexity of human nature, take merely a malicious delight in exposing a great man's weaknesses or absurdities. It is because Liszt is so complex that his character becomes so fascinating a study to the modern biographer.[52]

Before the book was even published, Vera Newman had come to her own conclusion: '[*The Man Liszt*] was what one might call a debunking kind of book. When I ventured a remark to this effect one day, I was told to get on with the typing and never mind the criticism'.[53] Vera's description of the book was to be shared by many of the reviewers. Edward Sackville West commented that a 'more thoroughly debunking book is hard to imagine'.[54] Although Lambert appreciated Newman's effort to avoid the 'spirit' of this biographical genre, he claimed Newman had failed because of its clear bias against Liszt: the line between the marshalling of facts and the 'unconsciously subjective interpretation of them' was considerably blurred.[55] In his review of *The Man Liszt*, Richard Aldrich wrote sarcastically that '[Newman] abhors "debunking"—an odious name for an odious thing, as he calls it. Nothing like that for Mr Newman. Like Mimi, he doesn't want to kill Siegfried—he only wants to chop off his head. And quite thoroughly he does it'.[56]

---

[50] Constant Lambert, 'Heads I win, tails you lose', *New Statesman and Nation*, 12 January 1935, 46–47; 46; L.A. Sloper, [untitled] *The Christian Science Monitor Weekly Magazine*, 7 August 1935, 11.

[51] Lambert, 'Heads I win, tails you lose', 47. James Huneker had made this point years earlier, but with qualification: 'There is no longer a Liszt case; his music has fallen into critical perspective; but there is still a Liszt case, psychologically speaking'. See Huneker, *Franz Liszt* (New York: Charles Scribner's, 1924): 2.

[52] Newman, *The Man Liszt*, xvi.

[53] Vera Newman, *Ernest Newman*: 119.

[54] Edward Sackville West, 'The Task of Egeria', *Spectator*, 7 December 1934, 888.

[55] Lambert, 'Heads I win, tails you lose', 46.

[56] Richard Aldrich, 'Ernest Newman on Liszt's Loves', *New York Times Book Review*, 17 March 1935, 5.

Throughout his book Newman employed legal allegories to put his case, which led some reviewers to accuse Newman of putting Liszt on trial—in a kangaroo court. Newman described some earlier Liszt biographers as dealing with a 'prosecutor' and 'defendant' and arriving at a 'verdict'.[57] He accused Lina Ramann of sullying the Countess's character before she could 'be put into the witness box', and asserted that the 'court was prejudiced'.[58] If Newman's allegorical techniques were designed to entertain his readers, the reviewers were unimpressed. In an unsigned article in *Musical Opinion* of February 1935, the review's heading, 'Rex vs Liszt', played on Newman's legal discourse and was critical of the book: 'Mr Newman seems to hold a Treasury brief, and he has got up his case so well that the man Liszt will be lucky if he gets off with less than a hanging. It consists of an endless series of indictments, each supported by documents given more importance than a sworn affidavit'.[59]

Some reviewers explicitly commented on the success of Newman as Liszt's prosecutor, but with unmistakeable sarcasm. While commending Newman as a 'distinguished critic and biographer', L.A. Sloper suggested that Newman had missed his calling in life: 'Perhaps [Newman] would have been even more successful as a lawyer than as a critic and biographer'.[60] Edward Sackville West believed Newman, acting as a prosecutor, had 'overstated the case' against Liszt, and other writers, such as Paul Henry Lang and Constant Lambert, were far from satisfied that Newman gave Liszt a fair hearing. For Lambert it was 'clear which side [Newman] lies', but Lang was more irate, describing Newman's book as 'extraordinarily biased'.[61] Sloper described the book as entirely subjective and wondered whether the notion of objectivity was 'foreign' to Newman.[62]

Whatever their position, the critics agreed that Newman's portrayal of Liszt was unfair and evident especially in Newman's use of language, which irked some of the reviewers. In chapter 4, Newman described Liszt as 'drunk with vanity and reeking with vulgarity' and as a 'young careerist and social climber', living a life of 'outward waste'.[63] Such judgmental and colourful language was not considered by the critics to be from the pen of an impartial historian or biographer. Many times Newman wrote of Liszt's bad manners, lack of chivalry,

---

[57] Newman, *The Man Liszt*, 5, 6.

[58] Newman, *The Man Liszt*, 21, 23.

[59] Unsigned, 'Rex v. Liszt', *MOMTR*, February 1935, 409.

[60] Sloper, [untitled], *The Christian Science Monitor Weekly Magazine*, 11.

[61] Sackville West, 'The Task of Egeria', 890; Lambert, 'Heads I win, tails you lose', 46; Paul H. Lang, 'Mr Newman tries to Debunk Liszt', *SR*, 25 May 1935, 18.

[62] Sloper, [untitled], *The Christian Science Monitor Weekly Magazine*, 11.

[63] Newman, *The Man Liszt* 86, 105, 110.

his duplicity, vanity, womanising and arrogance; the book sneers at its subject and it was clearly deliberately skewed. In the words of Robert Anderson, 'Newman neither played fair nor had he the slightest intention of doing so'.[64]

The most devastating review of *The Man Liszt* was written by Carl Engel, editor of *Musical Quarterly* (and, like Lang, a founding member of the American Musicological Society), who wrote at considerable length of the book's failings in April 1935.[65] Engel's review was systematic and devastating because, more than any other review, it showed up Newman's bias and sloppy attention to detail.

Engel's review of *The Man Liszt* questioned Newman's credibility as a scholar. In the first article, Engel called Newman 'a crank' for pursuing 'the ends of the historian with the methods of a pamphleteer'.[66] Engel summarised the book's limitations, claiming it was full of 'inaccuracies, omissions, distortions, exaggerations'.[67] The most serious of Engel's criticisms were to do with Newman's errors in translation. Newman could read German and French, and had done so for decades, but tripped up in some of the texts he had translated in the Liszt book. Engel devoted considerable space in his review to pointing out the most glaring and obvious mistranslations, suggesting that Newman wrote the book too quickly.

To explain the debunking nature of Newman's *Liszt* it must be asked if financial gain was one of the author's motives. In the 1920s and the 1930s there was a 'biography boom' that 'became one of the chief literary phenomena in the English-speaking world.'[68] Figures cited by John A. Garraty show that 4,800 new biographies were published in North America between 1916 and 1930 and that in 1929 alone, there were 667 new biographies published, which was twice the annual average for the period.[69] These figures are relevant to Newman because his books were published in both London and New York. Garraty also details particularly successful examples of biography that reached sales in excess of 50,000 copies, the royalties from which would have been lucrative. In Britain, the demand for biography was insatiable and, by 1937,

[64] Robert Anderson, 'Liszt tragi-comedy', MT, 11/1524 (1 February 1970): 160. This comes from a review of the 1969 reissue of the *The Man Liszt*, published by Victor Gollancz in 1969.

[65] Carl Engel, 'Views and Reviews', MQ, 21/2 (April 1935): 230–40.

[66] Engel, 'Views and Reviews', MQ, April 1935, 231.

[67] Engel, 'Views and Reviews', MQ, April 1935, 239.

[68] Richard D. Altick, *Lives and Letters: A History of Literary Biography in England and America* (Westport, CT: Greenwood Press, 1965): 292. Another writer described biography in the late 1920s as 'now a very popular form of literary sport'. See H.M., 'A handbook to biography', *Listener*, 24 April 1929, 559.

[69] John A. Garraty, *The Nature of Biography* (London: Jonathan Cape, 1958): 110.

it was felt by at least one biographer that the market had become flooded.[70] Part of the enthusiasm for biography in general, and debunking biography in particular, was triggered in 1918 by the publication of Lytton Strachey's *Eminent Victorians: Cardinal Manning, Dr Arnold, Florence Nightingale and General Gordon*, which exposed 'the wordliness of Manning, the harsh muddle-headedness of Arnold, the ill-temper of Florence Nightingale, the eccentricity of Gordon'.[71] Strachey's book was so confronting to some that its impact on biography has been equated with the impact of Schoenberg on the history of Western music.[72] But it was also inspirational. According to Paul Murray Kendall, following the publication of Strachey's *Eminent Victorians*, 'a host of imitators sprang up. Debunking biographers laid low the heroic figures of the past, exuberantly proving that marble statues had feet of clay'.[73] It could be concluded that the tradition of this biographical model would probably have been an attractive medium for Newman, given its vogue in Britain. If Newman intended to write a biography in Strachey style, he had much to gain financially. We know that Newman was keen to make more money for his writing at this particular time because in November 1933 he withdrew the book from Knopf, furious with them for refusing a US$200 advance.[74]

Michael Saffle has pointed out that 'rather surprisingly, no sophisticated book-length examination of Liszt's "psychology" has ever appeared in print'.[75] It seems to me, though, that Newman intended his *The Man of Liszt* to fill this gap, but it was too iconoclastic, and insufficiently grounded in psychological theory, to even come close. But, to be fair, Newman's Liszt was published well ahead of later extended theorizing on music biography and psychoanalysis, especially Maynard Solomon's biography of Beethoven published in 1977.[76]

[70] Garraty, *The Nature of Biography*, 110. No source is provided for the remark about the insatiable demand; Harold Nicolson is quoted, without reference, regarding the saturated market.

[71] Harold Nicolson, *The Development of English Biography*, 3rd edn (London: The Hogarth Press, 1947): 150.

[72] Paul Murray Kendall, *The Art of Biography* (London: George Allen & Unwin Ltd, 1965): 113.

[73] Kendall, *The Art of Biography*, 113. See further A.E. Dyson, 'The technique of debunking', *Twentieth Century* 157 (1955): 244–56.

[74] Correspondence from Ernest Newman to Newman Flower, 11 November 1933. Knopf Papers, File 660.1.

[75] Saffle, 'Liszt research since 1936', 242.

[76] Maynard Solomon, *Beethoven* (New York: Schirmer, 1977). For a critical examination of this work and the influence of psychoanalytic thought on Solomon see Marie-Elisabeth Tellenbach, 'Psychoanalysis and the historiocritical method: On Maynard Solomon's image of Beethoven', *Beethoven Newsletter* vols 8 and 9 (1993–4): 84–92; 119–27.

In his review of *The Man Liszt* for the *Saturday Review*, Paul Henry Lang strongly criticised Newman's lack of focus on music and objected to its pre-occupation with psychology.[77] Lang saw the book as a 'psychoanalytic mixture of *chronique scandaleuse* in which "foul whisperings are abroad", but its lack of theoretical sophistication meant it fell short of a credible psychoanalytical study.[78] On the other hand, a review of *Liszt* by Elbert Lenrow in the *Journal of Nervous and Mental Disease* in 1935 praised Newman's 'psychological contribution' in relation to teasing out Liszt's dual personality, but even so, like all the other reviews, Lenrow believed Newman had ventured too far in 'over-emphasizing Liszt's flaws'.[79]

Attacks such as Lang's on biographies that were seen to be works of psychiatry or psychohistory were perhaps inevitable, given the hostility towards psychology on the part of American scholars in the first half of the twentieth century. Jacques Barzun referred to these kinds of works as 'New biography', which sought to blend elements of Freudian psychology with anthropology. Barzun argued that a biography of this sort 'established a new vocabulary and a new attitude. It was concerned with "depth" (that is, the hidden and unconscious) and with "science" as the instrument of disclosure'.[80] Barzun was extremely critical of this 'grafting' of the historical method.[81] But Barzun was not alone in his criticism of new biography or psychohistory. In the 1940s there was considerable tension expressed by historians in North America about the possibility of training historians in psychoanalysis. There was a widespread view that psychohistory was trivial and a sham, and replaced facts with speculation, thus compromising historical method.[82] This scepticism towards Freud may explain the negative reception of Newman's *Liszt*, especially in North

---

[77] Lang, 'Mr Newman tries to debunk Liszt', 18.

[78] Lang, 'Mr Newman tries to debunk Liszt', 18.

[79] Elbert Lenrow, Review of *The Man Liszt* in *Journal of Nervous & Mental Disease* 82/6 (1935): 693–5; 695. For a fuller discussion of Lenrow's work in context of Liszt reception, see Alan Davison, 'Liszt Among the Degenerates: On the Vagaries on Being a Musical Genius c. 1890–c. 1935', in James Deaville and Michael Saffle (eds), *Liszt Legacies* [Analecta Listziana IV, Franz Liszt Studies No. 15] (Hillside, NY: Pendragon Press, 2014): 236–58.

[80] Jacques Barzun, *Clio and the Doctors: Psycho-history, Quanto-history and History* (Chicago and London: University of Chicago Press, 1974): 7–8.

[81] Barzun, *Clio and the Doctors*, 10–11.

[82] David E. Stannard, *Shrinking History: On Freud and the Failure of Psychohistory* (New York and Oxford: Oxford University Press, 1980): xiii, 116. See also Peter Gay, *Freud for Historians* (Oxford: Oxford University Press, 1985). For a more recent account of the resistance to Freud in North America see George Makari, *Revolution in Mind: The Creation of Psychoanalysis* (Melbourne: Melbourne University Press, 2008): 405ff.

America, as Charles Seeger had provocatively described studies in psychology from as early as 1924 as an 'invasion' to the hallowed halls of musicology.[83]

Nigel Scaife has suggested that Newman's biography of Liszt failed because Newman refused to accept Liszt's religiosity—a worldview that was anathema to his freethought ideology.[84] But the book fails because it simply offered very little fresh knowledge about Liszt. Newman's preface promised a radical look at Liszt, but the book was hardly a new endeavour. To deride Liszt, Newman has used many expressions such as 'circus rider', but these terms had already been used by Huneker, and previous biographies, such as La Mara's, had already addressed the composer's womanising. Moreover, as early as 1878 George Bernard Shaw had described Liszt as a charlatan for writing the symphonic poem *Mazeppa*, which he described as a 'false art' for its lack of musical power.[85] Newman's Liszt book may have been debunking, but it also lacked new and original ideas.

Perhaps the last word on Newman's Liszt goes to Alan Walker from 1970:

> This is the place, I think, to comment briefly on Newman's book which enjoys a reputation in the Liszt literature out of all proportion to its true worth ... Newman's book is a dismal failure . . . The result is a piece of malevolent mischief-making, not an 'objective' biography at all ... *The Man Liszt* is, with respect, fascinating mainly for the light it throws on the author.[86]

Such mischief-making had always been a part of Newman's critical armoury: *A Study of Wager* (1899) was in some respects a biography in this mould, calling into question Wagner's philosophical outlook (as we will see in the following chapter); and the first part of *The Unconscious Beethoven* was also an act of character assassination, for it criticised aspects of Beethoven's personality. But, as we have seen, Newman's Liszt was neither ground-breaking nor objective. It drew on material already covered in previous biographies of the composer. Newman lost sight of his subject, blinded by his zeal to write a sensational and provocative book. Newman's *The Man Liszt* simply went too

---

[83] Charles Seeger, 'On the principles of musicology, *MQ*, 10/2 (April 1924): 244–50; 249.

[84] Nigel Scaife, 'British music criticism in a new era: studies in critical thought, 1894–1945', DPhil thesis, University of Oxford (1994): 169. For a modern study of Liszt's religious ideology see Paul Merrick, *Revolution and Religion in the Music of Liszt* (Cambridge: Cambridge University Press, 1987).

[85] George Bernard Shaw, 'Liszt the charlatan', *Hornet*, 20 December, 1876. Reproduced in Dan H. Lawrence (ed.), *Shaw's Music: The Complete Musical Criticism of Bernard Shaw* vol. 1, 2nd revised edn (London: Bodley Head, 1989): 72–3.

[86] Alan Walker (ed.), *Franz Liszt: The Man and his Music* (London: Barrie & Jenkins, 1970): 14.

far. In his review of Sitwell's *Liszt* in 1934, Newman predicted that his own Liszt undertaking would bring him 'dislike' and 'approbrium' from those who reviewed it, but these sentiments would only last 'for a time'. But they did not. Apart from eventually completing volumes 2 to 4 of his *Life of Richard Wagner*, Newman never wrote another biography.

CHAPTER 9

Sceptical and Transforming:
Books on Wagner, 1899–1959

*T*HE *Life of Richard Wagner*, published in four volumes between 1933 and 1946, was Newman's magnum opus. Most reviewers considered the book to be a monument not only to Wagner—but to Newman—demonstrating his mastery of musical biography. For the book's publisher, Alfred A. Knopf, Newman's *Wagner* was 'one of the great biographies of my period' even though the book did not sell as well as Knopf had hoped.[1] *The Life of Wagner* was a sympathetic and measured account of the composer's life and works, though this was not the case in some of Newman's earlier writings on Wagner. In *A Study of Wagner* (1899), *Wagner as Man and Artist* (1914) and *Fact and Fiction about Wagner* (1931), Newman was not the perfect Wagnerite. Although charmed by Wagner's music, Newman was at times extremely critical of Wagner's philosophical and political writings, anti-Semitism, and reputation for arrogant and manipulative behaviour. These books not only bring to light Newman's ambivalence about aspects of Wagner's career but demonstrate Newman's expertise on a wide range of concomitant issues in European thought, such as debates over the theories of the evolution of music.

John Deathridge has described Newman as 'Wagner's most outstanding biographer' and in the context of Wagner scholarship it is not difficult to see why.[2] In the nineteenth century, for example, readers of British newspapers and musical literature had contended with fierce opposition to Wagner by the leading critics of the day, including Henry Chorley (*Athenaeum*, 1830–1866) and J.W. Davison (*Times* 1846–1879).[3] Even though more judicious work on Wagner, by Francis Hueffer, for example, had been published in the 1870s, the largely anti-Wagnerian tide had begun to change, especially with such

---

[1] Correspondence from Alfred A. Knopf to Ernest Newman, 5 March 1941, Knopf Papers, File 660.3.

[2] John Deathridge, *Wagner Beyond Good and Evil* (Berkeley: University of California Press, 2008): 75.

[3] Charles Reid, *The Music Monster: A Biography of James William Davison* (London: Quartet Books, 1984); Robert Bledsoe, *Henry Fothergill Chorley: Victorian Journalist* (Aldershot: Ashgate, 1998). For a contextualisation of the critical reception of Wagner in late nineteenth century England, see Paul Cummings, 'The pivotal role of Hans Richter in the London Wagner Festival of 1877', *MQ*, 98/4 (2016): 395–447.

strong advocacy through George Bernard Shaw's *The Perfect Wagnerite* in 1898.[4] Moreover, Newman's Wagner scholarship was more concerned with questions of continental aesthetics and historiography, and were more intellectually wide-ranging than what Chorley, Davison, Hueffer and Shaw had accomplished in their work in the previous twenty years.[5] *The Life of Wagner* demonstrates Newman's close acquaintance with a vast European literature on Wagner—a familiarity unparalleled by many other British writers.

A Wagner Sceptic: A Study of Wagner *(1899)*

A Study of Wagner, written in the wake of *Gluck and the Opera* (1895), is a mixed bag. It consists of eleven chapters ranging from details of the genesis of some of Wagner's operas to explanations of the composer's anti-Semitism. It was not a conventional biography. Readers who had followed Newman's previous essays on Wagner in the freethought press in 1892—where Newman had described the composer to be the 'deepest and clearest thinker ... that ever expressed himself in music'—were in for a surprise.[6] By 1899 Newman had changed his mind and regarded Wagner as an intellectual bankrupt.[7] In later biographies, Newman would moderate this view but, in *A Study of Wagner*, his criticism of Wagner was fierce and his inclination for debunking biography was first demonstrated.

The idea for *A Study of Wagner* came from Bertram Dobell. After commissioning the biography of Gluck, Dobell asked Newman to produce two more books: an anthology of his essays from the *Free Review* and a biography of Wagner.[8] Despite correspondence between the pair over the scope of the anthology, it was never published although a chapter for it, described by Newman vaguely as 'something on Wagner', materialized into *A Study of*

---

[4] Francis Hueffer, *Richard Wagner and the Music of the Future* (London: Chapman and Hall, 1874) and *George Bernard Shaw, The Perfect Wagnerite* (London: Grant Richards, 1898).

[5] Anne Dzamba Sessa, *Richard Wagner and the English* (London: Associated University Presses, 1979) provides an overview of English responses to Wagner in the nineteenth and early twentieth centuries. See also Anne Dzamba Sessa, 'At Wagner's Shrine: British and American Wagnerians', in David C. Large and William Weber (eds), *Wagnerism in European Culture and Politics* (Ithaca and London: Cornell University Press, 1984): 246–77.

[6] Ernest Newman, 'Poetry and music', *NR*, 30 October 1892, 277.

[7] Newman, 'Poetry and music', 277.

[8] Dobell's letter has not survived, but Newman's reply to it was made on 20 May 1895. MSS Dobell 38484–5.

Wagner.[9] It was to be Newman's third book, his second music biography, and the first of his five Wagner biographies.[10]

Parts of *A Study of Wagner* were reproduced from articles Newman had written for the short-lived *Musician*.[11] Another article that Newman recycled was from the *Fortnightly Review* with the essay 'Wagner's "Ring" and its philosophy', which formed the basis of chapter 6.[12] These articles put Newman's name before a different audience and may have helped to pique the interest of potential buyers.

❧ *Aims of* A Study of Wagner

In a letter to Dobell in February 1896, Newman naively declared that 'I am going to make the Wagner volume the best piece of musical criticism ever published in any language'.[13] His enthusiasm was still fervent in September that year: 'I shall certainly spare no effort to make it the best book of its kind; and I look forward to a winter of delightful work'.[14] For three years Newman faced many delays on the book, but he finally submitted the typescript to Dobell in July 1898. By the time he had finished writing the book, however, Newman's aims, articulated in the preface, were considerably more modest:

[9] Correspondence, Newman–Dobell, 20 May 1895. MSS Dobell 38484–5.

[10] See the Bibliography for details of Newman's other four biographies.

[11] *Musician* was a weekly paper commenced by Robin Gray. It ran for 28 issues from 12 May until 17 November, 1897. Newman's articles were to be recycled for *A Study of Wagner*, but were subject to some editing: Newman sometimes provided new introductions and conclusions, re-arranged text, and edited out or paraphrased extracts from others' works (thus avoiding the necessity of seeking permission to reproduce third-party material). He also left out huge chunks of detail. 'One view of Wagner' (*Mus*, June 1897, 75–6) appears on pp. 148–55 of *A Study of Wagner*; 'Wagner's theory of music, poetry, and music-drama', published in four instalments (*Mus*, 21 July 1897, 214–16; 28 July, 233–4; 4 August, 253–4; 11 August, 273–6), appears on pp. 100–6, 110–13, 117–20, 126–30, 130–3, 143–9, 157–61, 164–71, 171–4, 177–9, 200–1, 179–86, 201. 'Wagner on Beethoven' (*Mus*, 1 September 1897, 331–3) appears on pp. 327–38. 'Music and race' (*Mus*, 16 January 1897, 116–17) is, in part, a review of Hubert Parry's *The Evolution of the Art of Music* (London: Kegan Paul, Trench, Trübner, 1896) and engages with what Newman labels as 'pseudo-scientific explanations' (302) and 'the problems of national psychology' (310), which he aired at length in his *Wagner*. 'Wagner in excelsis' (*Mus*, 27 October 1897, 450–3) is a review of Houston Stewart Chamberlain's *Richard Wagner*, trans. G. Ainslie Hight (London: J.M. Dent, Philadelphia: J.P. Lippincott, 1897), a book he quoted, and complained about, at length in *A Study of Wagner*.

[12] Ernest Newman, 'Wagner's "Ring" and its philosophy', *FoR*, June 1898, 867–84.

[13] Correspondence, Newman to Dobell, 9 February 1896. MSS Dobell 38484–5.

[14] Correspondence, Newman to Dobell, 24 September 1896. MSS Dobell 38484–5.

The present volume is not intended to add another to the many 'Lives' of Wagner, but to make an attempt at estimating the work of his practical achievements on the one hand and of his theoretical speculations on the other ... It may be necessary to forewarn readers that no account is taken here of sundry writings that do not bear closely on a general study of Wagner's genius ... My object has been to study Wagner as a psychological and aesthetic phenomenon; to try to answer the questions 'in virtue of what constitution of brain was he so great a musician?' and 'How did his peculiarities of mental structure affect his views of the other arts and of life in general?'[15]

If readers were expecting an objective and sympathetic account of Wagner's life, they would be mistaken. Although Newman explained that the book was a work of scientific criticism, it was a debunking biography. Because Newman framed *Gluck and the Opera* in the comparative method (see chapter 5), it might be expected that this would be replicated in *A Study of Wagner*, but it was not to be. The first chapter, 'A psychological preliminary', suggested an introductory profiling of Wagner's personality, but it was no such thing. Rather, the chapter argued that the many contemporary writers on Wagner and Wagnerism, preoccupied by the lack of form in Wagner's music, had misunderstood the composer.[16] Newman urged these anti-Wagnerians to change their minds, to get beyond their criticisms of the music's formlessness. Although the book discussed Wagner's music in considerable detail, Newman's objective was to argue that, despite being a great composer, Wagner was no thinker.

The first chapter also took account of other views on Wagner and dealt briefly with the issue of Wagner's psychology. Newman claimed that other critics had overlooked the relevance of studying Wagner's mind, claiming it was ripe for examination because the composer had 'one of the most highly organised brains in modern Europe'.[17] Chapters 2 and 3 were a musical analysis of the genesis and compositional style of *Rienzi*, *Flying Dutchman*, *Tannhäuser* and *Lohengrin*. Chapter 4, 'Art and Life', described and analysed some of Wagner's prose writings, including *Art and Revolution* and *The Art-Work of the Future*. Chapter 5 dealt with the evolution of music (which I detail below); while chapter 6 was a study of the *Ring*. Chapter 7, 'Wagner as a German', dwelt largely on accounting for Wagner's anti-Semitism. Chapter 8 discussed *Tristan and Isolde* and *Die Meistersinger*, while chapter 9 explored some of Wagner's later writings. The final chapter focused on Wagner's psychology.

[15] Ernest Newman, *A Study of Wagner* (London: Bertram Dobell, New York: G.P. Putnam's, 1899): vii–viii.

[16] Newman, *A Study of Wagner*, 8.

[17] Newman, *A Study of Wagner*, 15.

There is a great deal of material throughout the book on the relationship between music and poetry, and detailed discussions of opera aesthetics and Wagner historiography. It was also a fairly long and sometimes rambling book. Occasionally, Newman interrupted the narrative to summarise his argument, probably aware that the reader might be disorientated. Unlike all his other work at this time, however, *A Study of Wagner* was heavily referenced. Among the many footnotes are citations of other studies on Wagner, philosophy and history published in English, French and German.

Newman was well aware of the vastness of the contemporary Wagner literature and probably knew his book would have to have a different emphasis to distinguish it from other work. In fact, he had allowed himself a self-depreciating joke about the voluminous Wagner literature in *Musician* in October 1897:

> Truly of the making of books on Wagner there is no end. One shudders as one thinks of the mass of literature that is being piled up for the man who, some time in the next century, shall write the history of the music of this composer; and one prays for some kind of cataclysm that shall sweep away the bulk of this Wagner-literature into unending oblivion. As one who has been compelled by malignant fate to read many scores of books on Wagner—mostly, I am sorry to say, in the German tongue—I can testify to the horror with which a good many people regard a new book on him at the outset ... I shall, from mere reaction, become a pronounced anti-Wagnerian.[18]

In the preface to *A Study of Wagner*, Newman drew up the battle-lines. On one side sat Newman, determined to write a corrective work on Wagner; and on the opposing side were writers including Erna Schlüter, François-Joseph Fétis, Eduard Hanslick, John Hullah, George Alexander Macfarren, Henry Chorley, Moritz Hauptmann, Otto Gumprecht, Carl Kossmaly, Paul Scudo, Gustav Engel, Otto Jahn and Joseph Bennett who, according to Newman, had merely served to 'enrich the humorous literature of music by their criticisms of Wagner'.[19] Indeed, as far as Newman was concerned, these writers were 'the recognised musical critics of Europe [who] denied Wagner's possession of either melodic, harmonic, orchestral, or dramatic gift, and prophesied his speedy extinction.'[20] But Newman's defence of Wagner's musical greatness was not the principal direction that *A Study of Wagner* took. Essentially, it was a damning critique of Wagner's prose works.

Newman's hostility towards Wagner undermined any claim to scholarly method and his sarcastic tone only made this less convincing. He argued

[18] Newman, 'Wagner in excelsis', 477.

[19] Newman, *A Study of Wagner*, 2.

[20] Newman, *A Study of Wagner*, 2.

that Wagner was an unsystematic and haphazard thinker, and an unlikeable person. He described Wagner's writings as 'illogical' and 'shoddy'.[21] In relation to Wagner's personality, Newman wrote of the composer's 'abnormality of constitution' and inability for 'sane thinking', and being the product of 'arrested development'.[22] These descriptions relied on invective reminiscent of the old school of criticism (and a far cry from the demands of scientific criticism that Newman championed). It is not the work of a historian but the musings of an armchair psychologist.

Another example of Newman's homespun analysis is evident early in *A Study of Wagner* book when he vaguely pondered that:

> Here, for the first time, we get something like the key to the real Wagner. It will be argued, in the course of the subsequent chapters, that he was of an intensely impressionable artistic temperament, but only of minor intellectual powers. His own mental and emotional life was so opulent and so vivid that he saw nothing clearly beyond its borders; his own personal desires, his own personal struggles, became in his mind epitomes of the desires and the struggles of the whole modern world.[23]

This is hardly a convincing psychological or historical premise; however, this is not to say the book lacked merit. It provides an important insight into Newman's intellectual life, revealing his dramatic change of view on Wagner in his scrutiny of Herbert Spencer's theory on the evolution of music. Newman's discussion of Spencer occupies a significant part of the book and is the most scholarly and provocative portion of the entire work.

In *A Study of Wagner* Newman's sympathy with Herbert Spencer's work was tested along with continuing antagonism towards Wagner's philosophizing. In chapter 5, 'Wagner's theory of music, poetry, and music-drama', Newman undertook a detailed critique of Spencer's theory on the evolution of music. In the fifth section of this chapter (after summarizing Wagner's theories on music, poetry and music-drama) Newman concluded that 'it has been insisted throughout that he [Wagner] made a fundamental error in asserting the "drama" to be the end in a combination of poetry and music, and that he constantly loses sight of the peculiar significance of poetry apart from music, as of music apart from poetry'.[24]

Newman disagreed with Wagner that absolute music 'was a degenerate branch of that primal art of sound whose origin was the human cry'. The origin

---

[21] Newman, *A Study of Wagner*, 72, 158, 171 and 214 respectively.

[22] Newman, *A Study of Wagner*, 36.

[23] Newman, *A Study of Wagner*, 32.

[24] Newman, *A Study of Wagner*, 161.

of music as a human cry was argued by Spencer in his essay, 'The Origin and Function of Music', published in 1857, but Newman proposed this was a 'fallacy'.[25] In brief, Spencer claimed that music evolved from speech.[26] Newman disagreed:

> While non-musicians have been impressed by his theory, aestheticians of really musical constitution have disagreed with it absolutely. It errs in supposing that because song exhibits some of the characteristics of speech, the one has necessarily taken its rise in the other ... the main objection to the speech-theory is, briefly, that it leaves unexplained precisely those elements in music that *make* it music.[27]

Newman based his argument on the work of Jules Combarieu who hypothesized that the singer operates in 'une pensée musical' (translated by Newman as 'a musical manner of thinking')—a quite separate process to speech.[28] Newman was interested in Combarieu's argument but interpreted it a little more broadly, recognizing that it points to a different 'atmosphere' at play in speech and song, or when playing a musical instrument.[29] These activities, according to Newman, operated 'upon quite a different plane of psychology'.[30]

By the end of the nineteenth century, the writings of Herbert Spencer had lost much of their appeal; in fact, they had become the subject of ridicule.[31] It is likely that Newman was motivated by this trend to look at Spencer far more critically than he had before and, in doing so, came to the conclusion that Spencer's argument was flawed.

In his search for evidence to disprove Spencer's theory, Newman found allies and ammunition in works by Salomon Stricker and Richard Wallaschek. In reference to Stricker's book, *Du langage et de le musique* (1885) Newman

---

[25] Herbert Spencer, 'The Origin and Function of Music', *Fraser's Magazine* 56, October 1857, 396–408; Newman, *A Study of Wagner*, 162.

[26] For detail on the nuances of Spencer's theory see John Offer, 'An examination of Spencer's sociology of music and its impact on music historiography in Britain', *International Review of the Aesthetics and Sociology of Music* 14/1 (June 1983): 33–52; Bennet Zon, *Music and Metaphor in Nineteenth Century British Musicology* (Aldershot: Ashgate, 2000): 120–5; and Delia da Sousa Correa, *George Eliot, Music and Victorian Culture* (London: Palgrave Macmillan, 2003): 11–58.

[27] Newman, *A Study of Wagner*, 162–3.

[28] Newman, *A Study of Wagner*, 164. This term is from Jules Combarieu, 'Les rapports de la musique et de la poésie, considérées au point de vue de l'expression', dissertation, University of Paris (1893), cited on 164.

[29] Newman, *A Study of Wagner*, 163.

[30] Newman, *A Study of Wagner*, 163.

[31] See da Sousa Correa, *George Eliot*, 12.

outlined how the scientist had proven that speech and song were activated by separate organs controlled by discrete parts of the brain.[32] In Wallaschek's study on aphasia—which Newman described as 'brilliant'—he asserted that different parts of the brain controlled speech and music function, and argued that some people afflicted by aphasia retain the ability to sing.[33] The study also found that one part of the brain, the third left frontal convolution, while 'small in idiots and lower races' was also 'highly susceptible to music'.[34] Armed with this scientific data, Newman could quite plainly refute Spencer. And he wasted no time at all in using this evidence to discredit Wagner:

> Now all this throws a light on the psychology of Wagner and on his theories. It shows in the first place how wrong he was in basing music upon 'the primal cry' of early man, and in regarding song 'as just speech aroused to highest passion'; and in the second place it shows how abnormal his own mental constitution must have been for him to wish to limit the enjoyment of music to only that music which was suffused with 'poetical contents'.[35]

A Study of Wagner was not merely a study of a composer: it was a wide-ranging attack on related issues of history, criticism and biography. It also exhibited a debunking spirit: a modus operandi Newman would take up again in *Wagner as Man and Artist* (1914) as well another Wagner book, albeit it a relatively short one, that he wrote in the meantime for the 'Music of the Masters' series in 1904.

❧ *Still Sceptical:* Wagner *(1904)*

Newman's antipathy towards Wagner's intellectual life continued and found expression in his second book on Wagner published five years later, in 1904, in the 'Music of the Masters' series. In just over two hundred pages, *Wagner*—like all the short books in this series—was a general guide to the composer's main works. In this volume, Newman provided biographical background to Wagner

---

[32] Salomon Stricker, *Du langage et de la musique* [On Language and Music] (Paris: Félix Alcan, 1885).

[33] Newman, *A Study of Wagner*, 165. He was referring to Wallaschek's 1891 article, 'Über die Bedeutung der Aphasie für den musikalischen Ausdruck' [On the significance of aphasia in musical expression], *Vierteljahrsschrift für Musikwissenschaft* 7 (1891): 53–73. For a critical discussion of this and Wallaschek's other work on music psychology see Amy B. Graziano and Julene K. Johnson, 'Richard Wallaschek's nineteenth-century contribution to the psychology of music', *Music Perception* 23/4 (2006): 293–304.

[34] Newman, *A Study of Wagner*, 165–6.

[35] Newman, *A Study of Wagner*, 166.

followed by discussions of the music dramas, with eighty-nine musical examples illustrating particular leitmotifs and other points of musical interest.

While the Wagner of 1904 dealt much more explicitly with music than *A Study of Wagner* (because the series in which the 1904 volume was published required musical analysis), Newman's contempt for Wagner as a thinker prevailed. In the introduction Newman pointed out that although Wagner presented 'an interesting psychological problem' it was not his purpose to write about it, for his book was pitched to 'the plain man whose interest is primarily in Wagner as a music dramatist'.[36] Nevertheless, Newman wrote that 'A few enthusiasts still go on proclaiming that Wagner was a great thinker' and that, despite the growing popularity of Wagner's music, 'Wagner as a thinker, in short, is receding more and more from the public eye'.[37] Newman's introduction concluded by explaining his focus on the music-dramas: 'we shall confine ourselves to the consideration of them as music and dramas, dabbling no more in metaphysics than is absolutely necessary to show why Wagner makes a certain character do this or say that'.[38]

❧ *No Longer Sceptical:* Wagner as Man and Artist *(1914)*

Newman's research on Wagner continued, resulting in the publication of *Wagner as Man and Artist* in 1914. In the book's introduction Newman wrote that 'I have made all translations from the prose works, the letters, the autobiography, etc., direct from the originals', though he stated later he had referred to German editions, such as the fifth edition of the prose works, *Gesammelte Schriften und Dichtungen* (c. 1883), rather than manuscripts.[39]

To paraphrase Thomas Grey from 1995, it has long been a custom for authors on Wagner to preface their books with apologies for adding to the existing stockpile of literature.[40] Newman outlined why he did so in *Wagner as Man and Artist*:

> Some apology is perhaps needed from an author for writing three books on the same subject. I can only plead in extenuation that the subject of Wagner is inexhaustible; and I am defiant enough to refuse to pledge myself not to repeat the offence in another ten years or so. It is possible that readers who have done

---

[36] Ernest Newman, *Wagner* (London and New York: John Lane, The Bodley Head, 1904): xv.

[37] Newman, *Wagner* (1904): xvi, xvii.

[38] Newman, *Wagner* (1904): xx.

[39] Newman, *Wagner as Man and Artist*, x.

[40] Thomas S. Grey, *Wagner's Musical Prose: Texts and Contexts* (Cambridge: Cambridge University Press, 1995): xi.

me the honour to make themselves familiar with my *Study of Wagner* (1899) may discover that in my present book I express myself differently upon one or two points. My defence is that even a musical critic may be allowed to learn something in the course of fifteen years; and I can only hope that if here and there I have changed sides since then, the side I am now on is that of the angels.[41]

Newman's claim that *Wagner as Man and Artist* may have differed on 'one or two points' to *A Study of Wagner* was an understatement: the 1914 publication was an entirely different undertaking and a much better book. Unlike *A Study of Wagner*—which was largely polemical—*Wagner as Man and Artist* was less rambunctious. And although parts of it were derived from previously published articles (just as *A Study of Wagner* had been), it was a more cohesive book. Divided into three very long chapters (with sections and subsections in each) they cover 'The Man', 'The Artist in Theory' and 'The Artist in Practice'. By design, the book contained less formal musical and plot analysis, as Newman observed: 'his operas are so universally known that I could afford to dispense with detailed accounts of them'.[42]

Wagner as Man and Artist began with an explanation of the light it shed on the composer's autobiography and on the possibilities of a psychological analysis:

> While there is at present no really adequate Life of Wagner on a scale commensurate with the subject, there is probably more biographical material available in connection with him than with any other artist who has ever lived; and on the basis of this material it seems justifiable now to attempt—what was impossible until the publication of *Mein Leben* in 1911—a complete and impartial psychological estimate of him. There has probably never been a more complex artist, and certainly never anything like so complex a musician. A soul and a character so multiform are an unending joy to the student of human nature. It has been Wagner's peculiar misfortune to have been taken, willy-nilly, under the protection of a number of worthy people who combine the maximum of good intentions with the minimum of critical insight.[43]

With many more primary-source documents at his disposal, including Wagner's autobiography, Newman was probably much better placed than others to write Wagner's biography. However, this surfeit of material presented Newman with the difficulty of trying to 'disentangle' his subject 'from the complications and contradictions presented by his life, his letters, his prose works,

[41] Newman, *Wagner as Man and Artist*, ix.
[42] Newman, *Wagner as Man and Artist*, ix.
[43] Newman, *Wagner as Man and Artist*, 3.

his music, his autobiography, and the testimonies of his friends and ene-
mies'.[44] Newman's starting point was immediately to cast doubt on Wagner's
credibility in *Mein Leben*, and he devoted a significant part of the introduction to *Wagner as Man and Artist* to scrutinising its veracity. For example,
in going over the circumstances that facilitated the breakdown of Wagner's
friendship with Eduard Hanslick in the early 1860s, Newman was convinced
that Wagner's memory was not 'strictly accurate'.[45] Of course Newman had
no other evidence, no eyewitness, to corroborate Wagner's version of events,
but argued that Wagner exaggerated his version to belittle Hanslick. (Wagner
claimed to have snubbed Hanslick at a dinner party and that, later, Hanslick
begged Wagner to like him; Newman thought this was an unlikely situation.)
Newman went on to claim that Wagner plagiarised this account from an article by Wilhelm Tappert in the *Musikalisches Wochenblatt* of 1877 (in which
Tappert recorded what Wagner had told him). For this and other alleged fal-
sifications by Wagner, Newman warned his readers that 'where, then, written
words involve the interpretation of his own or other men's acts and motives,
they are to be accepted with caution'.[46]

   In chapter 1 of *Wagner as Man and Artist*, Newman returned to type with
a demolition of Wagner's character. The chapter began ordinarily enough
with accounts of Wagner's family background and environment in which he
grew up. But, before long, Newman explored the more unsavoury aspects of
Wagner's personality and behaviour. On the first page of the chapter, Newman
wrote of Wagner's 'superficial intellect', describing him as 'hopelessly incapable of managing his financial affairs with prudence'.[47] A little later in the
chapter, Newman wrote of Wagner's visit to London in 1855 to conduct the
Philharmonic Concerts, at which the composer was alleged to have behaved
improperly towards the press. As Newman explained (in reference to correspondence from Wagner to Otto Wesendock in early April of that year),
Wagner reported that two London critics, J.W. Davison and Henry Chorley,
were corrupt because they were paid to criticise him. Newman described
Wagner's allegations as 'reckless' because there was no proof of the matter.[48]

   The rest of chapter 1 unfolded as a list of Wagner's sins. Having scoured a
number of primary sources, including Wagner's *Mein Leben* and letters from
Minna Planer, Wagner's first wife, Newman described Wagner's appalling
treatment of her. Although Newman conceded that Wagner was 'often kind

[44] Newman, *Wagner as Man and Artist*, 3.
[45] Newman, *Wagner as Man and Artist*, 21–2.
[46] Newman, *Wagner as Man and Artist*, 26.
[47] Newman, *Wagner as Man and Artist*, 27, 28.
[48] Newman, *Wagner as Man and Artist*, 34–5.

enough to Minna at times', he wrote, nonetheless, that 'an unprejudiced reader of the records can hardly doubt that he [Wagner] was often cruel unconsciously and unintentionally'.[49] Newman continued the chapter with accounts of Wagner's many peccadilloes with Mathilde Wesendock, Friederike Meyer, Mathilde Maier and Henriette von Bissing. The chapter concluded with Newman ridiculing Wagner's impoverished intellectual outlook and outlining his maltreatment of Franz Liszt.

The second chapter, 'The artist in theory', positions Wagner against his musical heritage, especially in relation to Bach and Beethoven. The chapter begins with Newman's unflattering view of Wagner's personality traits, this time canvassing Wagner's 'mental malleability' and egocentricity, just as he had done in A Study of Wagner. Newman goes on to consider the influence of Beethoven and Weber in Wagner's music and the influence of Italian opera on the composer (which was not meant as a compliment).[50] A large portion of the chapter is taken up by an enthusiastic analysis of Wagner's use of words and music. For Newman it was a very particular relationship: 'Wagner did not set words to music; the words were merely the projection of an already conceived musical emotion into the sphere of speech'.[51] But Newman could not help but ridicule this talent: 'This explains why he [Wagner] was so unapt [sic] at setting anyone's poetry but his own'.[52] Newman argued that Wagner's ability to think about music in this personalized, blended manner, was what set him apart from other composers, but at the same time asserted that Wagner 'was by nature an instrumental composer of the line of Bach and Beethoven' in his ability to 'interpret great musical works in terms of poetry or life'.[53]

Some 140 pages later, Newman wrote on the relationship between Wagner, Bach and Beethoven in more concrete terms. He argued that Wagner was only the third composer in history to be able to think about music on such a massive and expressive scale:

> There is nothing in all other men's music comparable to Wagner's feat of keeping the vast scheme of The Ring in his head for more than a quarter of a century, and actually laying it aside completely for eleven years during that time, without his grip upon the smallest limb of the great drama relaxing for a moment. It is in virtue of the fiery and unceasing play of the imagination and this stupendous synthetic power that he takes his place among the half-dozen most

[49] Newman, Wagner as Man and Artist, 44.

[50] Newman, Wagner as Man and Artist, 157.

[51] Newman, Wagner as Man and Artist, 166.

[52] Newman, Wagner as Man and Artist, 166.

[53] Newman, Wagner as Man and Artist, 167.

comprehensive minds that have ever worked in art. In music there are only two brains—those of Bach and Beethoven—to compare with in breadth of span.[54]

This second chapter also analysed some of Wagner's prose writings in a more considered light, for example, *Art and Revolution* (1849). Here Newman outlined what he considered to be Wagner's main concern—'that art should be the pure expression of a free community's joy in itself'—and provided some background context to similar philosophizing in ancient Greek tragedies of Aeschylus and Sophocles on which Wagner had drawn his conception of *Gesamtkunstwerk*. Newman also discussed Wagner's 'The Art-Work of the Future' (1949), explaining that its 'theory is again the belief that we shall not have a real art until we have a new and free humanity'.[55] Newman wrote briefly on Wagner's theory on the relationship between dance, music and poetry (that 'dance' and 'tone' should be reunited into a singular art form), pointing out that it was a theory without much historical consciousness, a product of Wagner's 'own aesthetic bias'.[56]

The further into the book the reader goes, the further Newman shifts from ridiculing Wagner to admiring him. At times, Newman's praise of Wagner is effusive: 'Wagner was one of those dynamically charged personalities after whose passing the world can never be the same as it was before he came—one of the tiny group of men to whom it is given to bestride an old world and a new … Wagner is probably the only figure in the whole history of music of whom this can be said'.[57] At the end of this lengthy chapter, Newman was much less preoccupied by Wagner's shortcomings: he glossed over the composer's contradictions of personality and concentrated instead on positioning Wagner as a worthy successor to Beethoven.

The final chapter, 'The artist in practice', was a study of Wagner's style. Newman surveyed some of Wagner's earliest compositions, such as *Seven Compositions of Goethe's Faust* (1831–2). He praised them for their 'individuality', though he found some of the songs wanting due to 'one or two crudities in the vocal part-writing'.[58] On the other hand, Newman considered Wagner's vaudeville chorus, *La Descente de la Courtille* (1840) 'a frank prostitution of his genius to the most superficial French taste of his time'.[59] With the aid of musical examples, Newman charted the influence of Italian opera on some of Wagner's works, such as *Das Liebesverbot* (1834). Inevitably, Newman devoted

[54] Newman, *Wagner as Man and Artist*, 307–8.

[55] Newman, *Wagner as Man and Artist*, 186.

[56] Newman, *Wagner as Man and Artist*, 188–9.

[57] Newman, *Wagner as Man and Artist*, 218.

[58] Newman, *Wagner as Man and Artist*, 245.

[59] Newman, *Wagner as Man and Artist*, 246.

a section of the chapter to Wagner's use of the leitmotif in the *Ring*. The penultimate section of this chapter provided an overview of *Parsifal*, which Newman admired most of all for its ingenious use of symbol and symphonic treatment to plumb 'the obscurest depths of human psychology'.[60] The chapter ended by Newman writing about Wagner's 'towering greatness' and forecasting that Wagner 'may be no more to mankind than Monteverdi is to us; but music will still be something different from what it would have been had he never been born'.[61]

&. *Telling Some Home Truths:* Fact and Fiction about Wagner *(1931)*

Newman's next Wagner project was a book called *Fact and Fiction about Wagner*, published in 1931. In this book, Newman defended Wagner from what he thought to be misguided views from two sources: the *New Statesman's* music critic W.J. Turner, and Philip Dutton Hurn and Waverley Lewis Root, authors of *The Truth about Wagner*, published in 1930. Newman dedicated the book to Charles Sanford Terry, 'in admiration for his work in musical biography'.[62] As we saw in chapter 7, Newman was a great admirer of Terry's biography of Bach, considering it one of the best English-language biographies of any composer. The same rigour could not be said of *Fact and Fiction about Wagner*, and the dedication was a cheeky criticism at Hurn's and Root's project.

The Truth about Wagner was a deliberately provocative book whose authors had gained limited access to the Burrell Collection, the catalogue of which was published on 19 May 1929. This vast collection of Wagner-related correspondence, manuscripts, portraits and sketches had been amassed by Mary Burrell, a Wagner enthusiast and biographer, with most of the material sourced from Natalie Bilz-Planer, the illegitimate daughter of Wagner's first wife, Minna Planer. One of the most valuable items in the Burrell Collection was a unique copy of Wagner's *Mein Leben*, which had been made by Wagner's printer and which named Ludwig Geyer as Wagner's father. The other eighteen copies had been printed without this reference, and speculation was rife over the reasons for its omission.

Hurn and Root began the book in a deliberately sensational way, asking 'Who knows him [Wagner] as he really was'?, and answered the question themselves, in part, by exclaiming 'the whole truth about his inner life has

---

[60] Newman, *Wagner as Man and Artist*, 317.

[61] Newman, *Wagner as Man and Artist*, 323, 326.

[62] Ernest Newman, *Fact and Fiction about Wagner* (London: Cassell and Company, 1931): vii.

never come out. It is coming out now'.[63] They also asked 'How, then, can we discover anything new about Wagner? That is what the layman asks'.[64] In the first chapter, Root and Hurn gave a melodramatic account of Wagner's biography from 'new documents' in the Burrell Collection, some of which they believed 'would suffice to tumble the Bayreuth tradition ignominiously to the ground'.[65] One such new document was a letter from Wagner to his lover Mathilde Wesensdonk that was intercepted by Minna Planer, which Hurn and Root argued was evidence of the cause of the breakdown of Wagner's marriage. The appeal of this 'lost letter' appears to be the most sensational pitch of the book, along with at least one chapter that made Cosima Wagner out to be conniving, obsessed and paranoid. The authors also made much of Wagner's inability to manage money and his affair with Jessie Laussot, both topics that had already been addressed by Newman in *Wagner as Man and Artist*. The book was clearly written to cause a sensation: couched in a racy style and written with a particularly broad brush, sources were sometimes cited, but often not. Very little material in the book was a revelation; according to an article about the book in the *Musical Times* in 1950, the Burrell Collection 'contains no sensational new revelations'.[66]

Newman first responded to *The Truth about Wagner* in an article in the *Sunday Times* on 26 May 1929 where he speculated on what the newly discovered material might contain.[67] He was cautious and cynical—not to mention a trifle defensive—but the article sparked letters to the editor from Hurn (published in June), in which Hurn raised differences of opinion as to the number of extant copies of Wagner's *Mein Leben*.[68] In November and December 1929, excerpts from *The Truth about Wagner* were published in the *Sunday Times* in seven instalments.[69] In February and March 1931, ahead of publication of Newman's *Fact and Fiction*, three of Newman's articles in the *Sunday Times* pre-empted his own book.[70]

---

[63] Philip Dutton Hurn and Waverley Lewis Root, *The Truth About Wagner* (London: Cassell and Company Ltd., 1930): 1.

[64] All quotations are from Hurn and Root, *The Truth About Wagner*, 2.

[65] Hurn and Root, *The Truth About Wagner*, 213. Hurn and Root were referring to the letters between Wagner and Minna.

[66] Newman, *Fact and Fiction about Wagner*, 155.

[67] Ernest Newman, 'New light on Wagner?', *ST*, 26 May, 1929, 7.

[68] Philip Dutton Hurn, 'Wagner's "Mein Leben"' [Letter to the editor], *ST*, 2 June 1929, 7 and 'Mein Leben', *ST*, 16 June 1929, 7.

[69] The excerpts appeared on 3, 10, 17 and 24 November and 15 and 22 December.

[70] Ernest Newman, 'A new work about Wagner', *ST*, 16 February, 1930, 7; 'Fiction about Wagner II', *ST*, 23 February, 1930, 7; and 'Fiction about Wagner III', *ST*, 2 March, 1930, 7.

Fact and Fiction about Wagner was divided into roughly two sections: 'Fact about Wagner' (comprising 19 chapters) and 'Fiction about Wagner' (25 chapters). The book was a collection of short essays on aspects of Wagner historiography. It sought to provide corrective accounts of work by many writers, but especially W.J. Turner (music critic of the *New Statesman* and an affirmed anti-Wagnerian) in the first part of the book, and Hurn and Root in the second half.

Initially, Newman covered familiar territory: an apology for writing another book on Wagner; the need for history and biography to be informed by primary sources; and the need for 'constructive criticism'.[71] Newman explained that he wanted to investigate the 'sundry other complicated questions that are for ever cropping up in connection with Wagner biography'.[72] His book also had a further didactic mission to it: he proposed it would 'give the reader some indication of the immense amount of painful research work that is often necessary before a single disputable fact can be established'.[73] Newman argued that if it were not possible to establish facts, music biography would remain a 'facile farce' and that a definitive biography of Wagner was unachievable in any language, though he singled out books by Julius Kapp and William Wallace as good examples of the genre—for the time being.[74]

Some of the first few chapters in section I (e.g., chapter 5, 'Some specimens of contemporary criticism'; chapter 6, 'Hanslick'; and chapter 7, 'The reception of *Rienzi*) dealt with mis-readings of Wagner's successes by various critics. Newman believed there was a large gap between the views of the critics and that of the 'plain man'; that, despite extreme criticisms of Wagner's music, the composer remained popular with audiences.[75]

Newman took many critics to task for their doom-saying. One was an unnamed contributor to an unidentified Vienna paper that supposed Wagner 'a demon who is poisoning all the sources of the new musical life'.[76] Newman also denounced an unnamed critic in the *Neues Berliner Tageblatt* for writing that the only reason Wagner's music was constantly in the repertory was because of 'the "future-mania" that has ensnarled the higher circles of society'.[77]

[71] Newman, *Fact and Fiction about Wagner*, xi, xiv, 4.

[72] Newman, *Fact and Fiction about Wagner*, xi, xii.

[73] Newman, *Fact and Fiction about Wagner*, xii.

[74] Newman, *Fact and Fiction about Wagner*, xv. Julius Kapp, *Richard Wagner: Eine Biographie* (Berlin, Schuster & Loeffler, 1910) and William Wallace, *Wagner, As he Lived* (London: Kegan Paul, Trench, Trubner and Co.): 1925.

[75] Newman, *Fact and Fiction about Wagner*, 18.

[76] Newman, *Fact and Fiction about Wagner*, 18.

[77] Newman, *Fact and Fiction about Wagner*, 20, 21.

In chapter 6, Newman poured scorn on Hanslick's well-known antipathy towards Wagner, describing the Viennese writer as 'the most colossal ignoramus and charlatan that has ever succeeded in imposing himself on an editor as a musical critic'.[78]

Chapter 8 is a spirited, though less vitriolic, dispute with W.J. Turner over some historical facts and the premiere of *Rienzi* in Dresden in 1842. Turner supposed the work to be 'musically very poor stuff', but Newman could not agree: it 'was not poor stuff for its time; on the contrary, it was regarded as an advanced and rather difficult work, and its success was a tribute to the willingness of the Dresden public to adopt a new point of view'. However, Newman admitted he based this information on accounts of the premiere from Wagner's *Mein Leben*, which he had earlier regarded as a largely suspect source.[79] In these chapters, Newman argued that, despite a hammering from the press during much of his lifetime (especially in London), Wagner 'had no reason to complain of the public's attitude towards him' even if 'the Press there [in London] were hostile to him'.[80] Newman also felt redress was required on the re-examination of documents in relation to Wagner's publishers, for example, in chapter 15, 'Wagner and Breitkopf & Härtel', covering the failed negotiations over the publication of the *Ring*, and chapter 16, 'Wagner and Schotts', in which Wagner was criticised for demanding huge advances from the publishers while completing the *Meistersinger*. In these chapters, Newman's careful reconstruction of events from correspondence paints a picture, not of Wagner unable to manage his finances, but of a composer existing hand-to-mouth, desperate for advances in royalties to keep afloat financially. Newman concluded the first section of the book reiterating his initial view that 'no composer has ever had the critics so preponderatingly against him as Wagner: and no great composer has ever won such a public for himself during his lifetime'.[81]

The second part of the book dealt directly with an overview of sources available to modern Wagner scholars. These sources were so voluminous that Newman believed them to be an 'unmanageable mass'.[82] Some sources were frustratingly contradictory, for example, different accounts of events in letters versus those in *Mein Leben*. Newman then proceeded to name and shame some of the worst offenders among books on Wagner, including Ferdinand

[78] Newman, *Fact and Fiction about Wagner*, 31–2.

[79] Newman, *Fact and Fiction about Wagner*, 34, 35, quoting W.J. Turner's *Musical Meanderings* (London: Methuen & Co., Ltd., 1928): 37.

[80] Newman, *Fact and Fiction about Wagner*, 56. On Wagner critical reception in London in the late 1870s, see Cummings, 'The pivotal role of Hans Richter'.

[81] Newman, *Fact and Fiction about Wagner*, 159.

[82] Newman, *Fact and Fiction about Wagner*, 163.

Praeger's *Wagner as I Knew Him* (1892), which he regarded as 'not worth the paper it is printed on'.[83] Newman claimed that the only reason it was written was to make 'easy money'.[84] Furthermore, Houston Stewart Chamberlain's 1895 biography was discredited, according to Newman, because it relied heavily on copies of letters provided to the author by Praeger that 'had been manipulated wholesale'.[85] Finally turning his attention to the Hurn and Root book, Newman claimed it to be 'more reckless' than Praeger's volume due to its many inaccuracies.[86] Newman went so far as to allege that Hurn and Root were not acquainted with much of the Wagner literature, apart from what was available in English, and accused them of not consulting original documents.[87]

Having briefly discarded *The Truth about Wagner*, Newman turned his attention to wider matters of Wagner historiography, just as he had in the first part of the book. For example, he wrote of the inadequacies of Frederick Corder's *Life of Liszt*, which contained much on Wagner. Newman accused Corder of 'not doing any original research' and bemoaned the fact that biographers in general, and Wagner biographers in particular, were prone to repeating the same errors.

Fact and Fiction about Wagner ended with an appendix in which Newman claimed that *The Truth about Wagner* was written on the strength of the authors having only read the collections' catalogue. In Newman's view, Hurn and Root had worked with a mere fifteen photostats along with 'careful translations of a considerable number of letters ... and carefully prepared abstracts of the material'.[88] Newman's severe criticism of this book was echoed in a review of *Fact and Fiction About Wagner* by Edwin Evans who described the Hurn and Root volume as 'an egregious production which so blatantly proclaimed its character that it scarcely needed exposure in more than a few contemptuous lines'.[89]

In the preface to the first English edition of *Wagner as Man and Artist* in 1914, Newman wrote of his temptation to write another biography of Wagner at some future point.[90] In outlining the scope of the 1914 undertaking, he

[83] Newman, *Fact and Fiction about Wagner*, 164–5.

[84] Newman, *Fact and Fiction about Wagner*, 164–5.

[85] Newman, *Fact and Fiction about Wagner*, 166. Houston Stewart Chamberlain, *Richard Wagner* (Munich: Bruckmann, 1895) trans. G. Ainslie Hight (London: J.M. Dent, Philadelphia: J.P. Lippincott, 1897).

[86] Newman, *Fact and Fiction about Wagner*, 173–4.

[87] Newman, *Fact and Fiction about Wagner*, 182–4.

[88] Newman, *Fact and Fiction about Wagner*, 298.

[89] Edwin Evans, 'The plain man and Wagner', *Musical Mirror and Fanfare*, September 1931, 253–5; 253.

[90] Newman, *Fact and Fiction about Wagner*, ix.

wrote that, to see Wagner 'in every one of his many-sided activities—in all his political, ethical, economic, sociological and other speculations—would have necessitated not one book but four'.[91] This was to prove a prophetic statement.

&. Magnum Opus: The Life of Richard Wagner, 1933–46

Newman began work on Volume 1 of his *Life of Richard Wagner* around 1928. Three volumes were initially planned, according to Vera Newman, 'but as the material kept coming in, he [Newman] decided that it would need four volumes to contain all he wanted to write. This, he said, would be his very last book on Wagner and it had to be as complete and up to date as he could make it'.[92] It was not to be his last book on Wagner, of course: *Fact and Fiction about Wagner* was published in 1931, and in 1940 Novello published a thirty-page biography in its 'Short Biographies' series. Until *The Truth about Wagner* was published, however, Newman had made little progress on volume 1. But, as Vera Newman recounted, the Hurn and Root book so 'incensed' Newman it spurred him to get on with the first volume 'that had now been simmering inside him for some little time'.[93] The contract for the *Life of Richard Wagner* was agreed with Cassell's in 1931 or 1932 (they had also published *A Musical Critic's Holiday* in 1924 and *Fact and Fiction about Wagner*). The book was to comprise three volumes (up to 2000 pages in total) for which Newman would be paid £2000.[94]

In 1934, work on the *Life of Richard Wagner* came to a halt following the terrible critical reception of *The Man Liszt* (see chapter 8). According to Vera, Newman regretted ever starting his *Life of Richard Wagner* and did not intend to finish it; he had 'downed pen, so to say, so far as the Wagner Life was concerned. Every time I brought up the subject he asked me to please leave it alone. I couldn't believe it. This was the first thing I wanted very much that he had denied me'.[95] Within a year or so, however, Newman was coerced to keep on with the remainder of the *Life*, as Vera remembers from 1935:

> When we were there [on holiday in Folkestone, probably in July] I again brought up the subject of the Wagner book. I told him how it distressed me that he should be content to leave it unfinished. Not only was it a breach of faith with the publishers, but I was sure that he himself would regret it if he did not finish it. I

[91] Newman, *Fact and Fiction about Wagner*, ix.

[92] Vera Newman, *Ernest Newman: A Memoir by his Wife* (London: Putnam, 1963): 73.

[93] Newman, *Fact and Fiction about Wagner*, 83.

[94] Correspondence, Newman to Alfred A. Knopf, 28 January 1930. Knopf Papers, File 659.8.

[95] Vera Newman, *Ernest Newman*, 126.

pointed out that if the book was not a financial success, it would be an important one in Wagner literature. In the end he promised me that he would go on with it, and I was overjoyed. He said he would begin the work as soon as we were home again and I promised I would do everything I could to help him. He kept his promise and although there were many difficulties, and he got very tired of it before the end, he never again said he would not finish it.[96]

Like most of the other biographies Newman wrote, *The Life of Richard Wagner* was not concerned with an analysis of the composer's works. Instead Newman concentrated on Wagner's personality and milieu, as he explained in the Foreword to volume 1: 'in the vast majority of cases [of music biography] we know far too little of the personalities, the outer and inner lives, and the environment of musicians to be within a measurable distance of compiling authentic biographies of them'.[97] An authentic biography, in Newman's view, would be 'based on the whole of the evidence available at the time of writing'.[98] In relation to Wagner, Newman believed this had rarely been achieved: 'the present Wagner biographies are mostly hindrances rather than helps'.[99] In terms of method, Newman explained that 'I have accordingly devoted a fair amount of space to an attempt to reconstruct for the reader the musical, economic, and social conditions in Europe during the first part of Wagner's life, and the more significant of the personalities with which he was brought into contact'.[100]

The four volumes were divided into the years 1813–1848, 1848–1860, 1859–1866 and 1866–1883. The *Life of Richard Wagner* was not strung together solely by a focus on the works—though there are chapters on many of the operas—but by looking at specific events, people and places that were significant to Wagner. In volume 1, for example, chapters 1 and 4 deal with Wagner's time in Paris, while chapter 7 is a character portrait of Cosima Wagner. Other volumes have a similar emphasis on people and places, such as volume 4, on Wagner's time in Munich, the establishment of the Bayreuth theatre and writings by Nietzsche.

Newman's tone in the *Life of Richard Wagner* was less bellicose than in his previous Wagner books, and he felt the need to explain this change of register, especially in relation to *Wagner as Man and Artist*:

---

[96] Vera Newman, *Ernest Newman*, 148.

[97] Ernest Newman, *The Life of Richard Wagner vol. I, 1813–1848* (New York: Alfred A. Knopf, 1933): viii.

[98] Newman, *Life of Richard Wagner*, vol. I, viii.

[99] Newman, *Life of Richard Wagner*, vol. I, xi.

[100] Newman, *Life of Richard Wagner*, vol. I, xii.

If it be found that the tone and the conclusions of the present volume are not always those of my *Wagner as Man and Artist* of some twenty years ago, I may perhaps be allowed to plead that the deeper one goes into the Wagner story, the more one tries to understand the man, the less one is inclined to err on the side of harshness of judgment.[101]

Thus, unlike *A Study of Wagner* and *Wagner as Man and Artist*, the *Life of Richard Wagner* is a sympathetic and sober account of the composer's achievements. It steered well clear of sneering and undermining its subject as his previous books on Wagner had. When Newman first outlined his proposed multi-volume book to Alfred A. Knopf, Newman wrote that 'What the world wants now is a full and trustworthy Life of Wagner without any musical patter'.[102] And that is what he delivered. He did not need to resort to sarcasm or sensationalism to pique the readers' interest. The attention Newman paid to the listing of sources at the front of the book, and the many footnotes used throughout to carefully and thoroughly marshal evidence, befitted the scientific or scholarly style of biography that he had long championed.

ᨓ *The Critics*

Newman's books on Wagner were widely reviewed and received a generally positive critical reception. He was often praised for the thoroughness of his research, his attention to detail and style of writing (though some reviewers noted that the *Life of Richard Wagner* was especially hard-going). Some reviewers commented favourably on Newman's approach to biography, greatly appreciating his attempt at exploring Wagner's so-called psychology, while other critics, such as Carl Engel, deplored this approach, not least because it was often debunking in spirit, and failed to address or analyse the music in much detail. The critical reception of Newman's Wagner books illustrates their impact on other writers, and the conflicts they raised with Newman, such as on the role of method, as well as debates on Wagner-implicated issues such as the origins of music. The reviews also cast light on the kind of musicology Newman was writing and why it was not respected in some quarters.

A STUDY OF WAGNER

By March 1899, reviews of *A Study of Wagner* had been published and Newman wrote to his publisher, Bertram Dobell, about them. In one case, Newman was the victim of a malicious and biased review and was furious about it. He

---

[101] Newman, *Life of Richard Wagner*, vol. I, xii–xiii.

[102] Correspondence, Newman to Alfred A. Knopf, 28 January 1930. Knopf Papers, File 659.8.

omitted to identify the review, but told Dobell: 'what a farce reviewing is', and described the reviewer as 'an animal', believing the critic had not even bothered to read the book.[103] Newman complained about the 'safe shelter of anonymity', which so many of his literary counterparts had been complaining about for decades, remarking to Dobell that 'one doesn't mind adverse criticism, so long as it is really criticism ... What one objects to is the power of these ignorant hacks to give a reader a wrong impression of a book'.[104] This was, of course, old-school criticism in play, to which Newman had fallen foul.

On the other hand, a leader of the new age of criticism, John F. Runciman, reviewed *A Study of Wagner* in the *Saturday Review*. He praised Newman as 'a writer of altogether different calibre' and one that ought to be considered seriously, for 'whether one agrees or disagrees with him, it is obvious that he is capable of thinking about his subject and has thought about it'.[105] Although Runciman liked this book, he thought it was excessively long, and suggested it be shortened in the event of a second edition. He also believed Newman's treatment of Wagner was harsh, especially his criticisms of the prose works. Despite these shortcomings, Runciman urged the book to 'be carefully read and weighed by everyone who wishes to see Wagner put in his proper place'.[106]

Another review set Newman on a collision course with George Bernard Shaw, who wrote on a *Study of Wagner* in the *Daily Chronicle* on 8 June 1899.[107] This review illustrates the ideological differences between the pair over the rationalist's interest in scientific method. Shaw's contempt for rationalism is well documented, but it has a history that involves not just Newman, but also John M. Robertson.[108]

---

[103] Correspondence, Newman to Dobell, 15 March 1899. MSS Dobell 38484–5.

[104] Correspondence, Newman to Dobell, 15 March 1899. MSS Dobell 38484–5.

[105] John F. Runciman, 'After Wagner, books about Wagner', *SR*, 29 July 1899, 132–3; 132.

[106] Runciman, 'After Wagner, books about Wagner', 133.

[107] George Bernard Shaw, 'Recent Wagner books', *Daily Chronicle*, 8 June 1899, in Dan H. Laurence (ed.), *Shaw's Music: The Complete Musical Criticism of Bernard Shaw, vol. III, 1893–1950* London: The Bodley Head, 1981): 560–9. The review was unsigned and, in addition to *A Study of Wagner*, Shaw also reviewed books by David Irvine, *'Parsifal' and Wagner's Christianity* (London: H. Grevel and Co., 1899); Alfred Forman, *Wagner's 'Parsifal' in English Verse* (London: private subscription, 1899); and volume 7 of William Ashton Ellis's English translation of *Richard Wagner's Prose Works* (London: Kegan Paul, Trench, Trübner, 1899).

[108] On Shaw's association with, and rejection of, rationalism, see John von Rodenbeck, 'Bernard Shaw's revolt against rationalism', *Victorian Studies* 15/4 (June 1972): 409–37 and Odin Dekkers, 'Robertson and Shaw: "an unreasonable friendship"', *English Literature in Transition* 39/4 (1996): 431–49. Shaw himself articulated his distaste for rationalism in a number of letters in 1891, 1900 and 1923. See Dan H. Laurence (ed.), George Bernard Shaw, *Collected Letters* 4 vols (London: M.

In the late 1880s, Shaw and Robertson had become close friends and were committed socialists. Robertson was particularly interested in some of Shaw's early novels and facilitated their publication. Over time, however, Robertson found he no longer sympathised with the Fabian socialists: he thought they were anti-intellectual.[109] According to Dekkers, the split in their friendship was evident in 1891 from an entry in Shaw's diary, 'I went into their [freethinkers' lectures on] Darwinism and Haeckelism, and physical science, and the rest of it, and showed that it did not account even for bare consciousness. I warned them that if any of them fell into the hands of a moderately intelligent Jesuit—not that I ever met one—he would turn them inside out'.[110]

In the same year, 1891, in a review of Shaw's *Quintessence of Ibsenism*, Robertson argued that the book revealed Shaw to be 'a lightweight thinker, incapable of deep philosophical analysis':[111]

> But it is a pity, after all, to subject Mr Shaw's 'Quintessence' to analysis, or, at least, to do nothing else with it. He must needs work in his own way, and say just what he feels for the time being. He can never see more than part of a philosophic problem at a time, and he seldom goes far beyond the threshold of a truth; but his faculty of walking where others fear to tread, is at times of the greatest service to his public.[112]

Clearly, Robertson and Shaw were at odds, intellectually. And Newman was soon to be at odds with Shaw.

One of Shaw's complaints about rationalism was its misguided obsession with scientific method. He argued that rationalism denied the role of feelings as barometers of aesthetic judgement. Rationalism, in Shaw's view, was cold and clinical, and he jeered at Newman's interest in it in his review of *A Study of Wagner*:

> Mr Newman's position is no doubt to some extent still a representative English one. In the third quarter of this century, when rationalism and the most prosaic

Reinhardt, 1965–88). See vol. II (300–1), vol. III (215, 836–9) and vol. IV (668–70; 759–762). See also Dekkers, 'Robertson and Shaw'.

[109] Cited in a letter from Shaw to Augustin Hamon, 9 January 1907, published in *Collected Letters*. What Shaw means by this vague generalisation is that the rationalists over-intellectualise and are dogmatic, which he argues inhibits the true appreciation of works of art.

[110] Dan H. Laurence (ed.), George Bernard Shaw, *Collected Letters vol. I 1874–1897* (London: Max Reinhardt, 1965), 699, cited in Dekkers, 'Robertson and Shaw', 444.

[111] Dekkers, 'Robertson and Shaw', 446.

[112] John M. Robertson, 'Critical chat: the Quintessence of Ibsenism', *NR*, 6 December 1891, 359, cited in Dekkers, 'Robertson and Shaw', 446.

'scientific' materialism dominated culture, it would have been *the* representative one on every point concerning Wagner, except the beauty of his music.[113]

In the preceding paragraph, Shaw had described Newman as an anti-Wagnerian, typical of so many English critics. In Shaw's retrospective to his *Perfect Wagnerite* in January 1899, he claimed 'Wagner's position is now established: failure to appreciate it convicts the delinquent either of hopeless fogeyism or provincial crudity'.[114] Shaw wrote very little about Newman's praise of Wagner's music in the book but was critical of Newman's 'amazement at Wagner's stupidity', presumably because Wagner's prose works were well known to be philosophically slip-shod.[115] However, what upset Shaw most of all was Newman's jibe at Shaw's *Perfect Wagnerite*, which interpreted the *Ring* as a socialist manifesto. In a bad-tempered tone Shaw retorted:

> On one page he [Newman] demands 'Who cares for all this vaporing about "the individual" and "constituted authority" and "the immorality of convention"? Who wants the characters of an opera to be a procession of dull abstractions, drawn alternately from anarchistic and socialist handbooks?[116]

To which Shaw replied: '*I do*. Such questions depend for all their force on the certainty of the reply being "Nobody", as it would be if Mr Newman were to ask in a ring at Newmarket, Who wants to offer up a prayer?'[117]

Shaw saw some good in *A Study of Wagner*, even if his praise was delivered tongue in cheek: he described Newman as a 'progressive anti-Wagnerite' especially when he 'exposes the errors of his predecessors'.[118] But overall Shaw was dissatisfied with the book: 'Mr Newman is not "constructed somewhat upon Wagner's pattern"; and that it is precisely why it takes him four hundred pages to "reiterate that Wagner had no more capacity for philosophical speculation than an average curate".[119] Newman tried to see Shaw's review in a positive light, writing to Dobell that 'Shaw's article ought to be a good thing for the book, as most people take him contrariwise. He drivels like a Christian Evidence lecturer. I have written a short letter to the *Chronicle*, in a style of

[113] Shaw, 'Recent Wagner books', 561.

[114] George Bernard Shaw, 'Some imperfect Wagnerites', *The Critic*, supplement, 28 January 1899, in Dan H. Laurence (ed.), *Shaw's Music*, 546–53, 546. Shaw's *The Perfect Wagnerite* was first published in London by Grant Richards in 1898.

[115] George Bernard Shaw, 'Recent Wagner books', 562.

[116] George Bernard Shaw, 'Some imperfect Wagnerites', 546. Shaw is citing from 225 of *A Study of Wagner*.

[117] George Bernard Shaw, 'Some imperfect Wagnerites', 546.

[118] Shaw, 'Recent Wagner books', 565.

[119] Shaw, 'Recent Wagner books', 562.

sub-acid banter, inviting Shaw to *prove* … that Wagner was a thinker in any department. I don't think they will insert it, however'.[120] This was not the last of the battles *A Study of Wagner* would incite.

A STUDY OF WAGNER BEYOND 1899

A Study of Wagner thrust Newman's name into the spotlight when Herbert Spencer published a rejoinder to it in a book called *Facts and Comments*.[121] One of the essays in this collection, 'The origin of music', was a reply to Newman's criticisms of his work in *A Study of Wagner*, but it was also a defence of Spencer's theory against the arguments brought by Jules Combarieu and Richard Wallaschek.[122] However, it is Spencer's reply to Newman that is of interest.

Spencer described Newman's book as 'a clever, and in most respects, rational work' but accused Newman of making 'adverse arguments' in the same way that Combarieu and Wallaschek had.[123] He began by arguing that Newman, like Combarieu, had misunderstood 'what a musical composition is' and described Combarieu's criticism as confusing the 'origin of a thing and the thing which originates from it'.[124] Although Spencer argued that Combarieu expected him to have fleshed out an idea of 'a conception of music as fully developed', Spencer thought this unnecessary because it is impossible to know the complete development of music in retrospect, since the process of evolution is 'the gradual assumption of traits which were not originally possessed'.[125]

Spencer challenged Newman's criticism that his theory neglected an 'explanation of the place of harmony in modern music'.[126] He claimed that harmony was a recent musical development and had no place in the discussion of the origins of music, for music originated with melody. He also found Newman's work inconsistent in its theorizing, pointing out that, should Newman deny that there is 'no natural transition from excited speech to recitative', then it would be illogical for Newman to claim there can be a transition from recitative to song.[127]

---

[120] Correspondence, Newman to Dobell, 11 June 1899. MSS Dobell 38484–5.
[121] Herbert Spencer, *Facts and Comments* (London: Williams & Norgate, 1902).
[122] Herbert Spencer, 'The origin of music', in *Facts and Comments*, 38–44.
[123] Spencer, 'The origin of music', *Facts and Comments*, 40.
[124] Quoted from Newman, *A Study of Wagner*, 164; Spencer, 'The origin of music', *Facts and Comments*, 40.
[125] Spencer, 'The origin of music', *Facts and Comments*, 40.
[126] Quoted from Newman, *A Study of Wagner*, 163.
[127] Herbert Spencer, 'The origin of music', 41–2.

Newman wrote a long and detailed reply to Spencer, which was published three years later, in 1905, after Spencer's death.[128] Newman argued that Spencer's theory failed to take account of the 'musical sense' or psychology at play that gives rise to music, a separately evolving species to song:

> Everywhere, in truth, we come down to the really fundamental fact, that there is even in primitive man a real *musical sense*, independent of speech in origin, and, as far as we can see, much earlier than speech in the order of time, for man certainly expressed his feelings in pure indefinite sound long before he had learned to agree with his fellows to attach certain meanings to certain stereotypical sounds.[129]

By 1905, Newman's contempt for the prevailing theories of the evolution of music—especially those by Darwin and Spencer—was complete. This 1905 article debunked Darwin's theory of music and evolution as 'humorous and unprofitable' and dismissed Spencer's theories as '"pseudo-ideas" upon which he himself has emptied the vials of his scorn in *First Principles*'.[130]

A second example of the impact of *A Study of Wagner* was to come in 1913. In his own biography of Wagner published in that year, John F. Runciman, who had reviewed *Gluck and the Opera* ambivalently, recognised the value of the Newman's 1899 *Study of Wagner*:

> In the Introduction I announced my intention of dealing with Wagner's prose-writings only in so far as they reveal anything of value concerning the artist. His theories have been explained and elucidated to death; hundreds of books have been written about them; never was a man so much explained; never did a man suffer more from the explanations. The day when Wagner began, not to theorise, but to publish his theorisings, was an unlucky one for him ... I will dismiss, therefore, much of the prose with very brief notice, and some of it without any notice at all. It may be remarked that of all the commentaries I have waded through (and been well-nigh choked with), on the prose, there is, to my mind, only one worth reading, Mr Ernest Newman's valuable *Study of Wagner*.[131]

---

[128] Ernest Newman, 'Herbert Spencer and the origin of music', in *Musical Studies* (London and New York: John Lane, The Bodley Head, 1905): 189–220. An earlier and shorter version of this article appeared, by the same title, in *MMR*, 1 November 1902, 205–6; 1 December 1902, 224–5.

[129] Newman, 'Herbert Spencer and the origin of music', 210–11.

[130] Newman, 'Herbert Spencer and the origin of music', 189, 218.

[131] John F. Runciman, *Richard Wagner: Composer of Operas* (London: G. Bell and Sons, Ltd., 1913): 210–11; 212.

Runciman was cynical about the reason Wagner wrote so much prose and why so many people bought his books:

> But he [Wagner] needed money, and in the 'forties and 'fifties there were, strangely enough, numbers of people who would pay money for such stuff. Anything dull, 'philosophic' in tone, anything full of long words, longer sentences, and meanings too profound to be understood by mortals—anything of this sort was sure of a paying audience, if small, in 'philosophic' Germany, no matter how fallacious were the premises, how wrong the history, how perverse the inferences. Hundreds of people must have arisen from reading Wagner's essays feeling themselves very deeply intellectual.[132]

WAGNER AS MAN AND ARTIST (1914)

Although *Wagner as Man and Artist* was a fairly hard-hitting work, an unnamed critic on the *Saturday Review* thought it an entirely reasonable book. This critic praised Newman for a 'valiant, brilliant and successful attempt' to write 'a true and final biography of Wagner' even though the reviewer acknowledged that Newman's aim was not to be exhaustive.[133] Although admitting that Newman's book contained some 'fads and prejudices' (though these are not detailed), it was a book 'worth reading'.[134] The unnamed critic also suggested the book would prompt the rewriting of some previous Wagner biographies whose authors, like John F. Runciman (at least according to this critic), had praised Wagner too much.[135] Another unnamed critic, in the *English Review*, wrote that Newman had provided music history with a great service by writing a book on Wagner that was neither 'ludicrously sentimental nor romantic'.[136] George Sampson, writing in the *Bookman*, claimed that *Wagner as Man and Artist* was the 'sanest' book on Wagner yet published, though he was critical of Newman for dwelling too much on Wagner's insobrieties and, in this respect, doubted that Newman had successfully represented Wagner 'the man', as suggested by the book's title.[137]

[132] Runciman, *Richard Wagner*, 211.

[133] Unsigned, 'Wagner the man', *SR*, 30 May 1914, 706–7.

[134] Unsigned, 'Wagner the man', 707

[135] Unsigned, 'Wagner the man', 706.

[136] Unsigned, 'Wagner as man and artist', *English Review*, July 1914, 566–67; 566.

[137] George Sampson, 'Wagner with a difference', *Bookman*, July 1914, 172–3; 172. 'W.M.' referred to *Wagner as Man and Artist* as 'the soundest, sanest, and liveliest on its subject before us' in context of reviews of Newman's work, George Ainslie Hight's *Richard Wagner*, 2 vols (London, Arrowsmith, 1925) and L. Archier Leroy's *Wagner's Music Drama of the Ring* (London: Noel Douglas, 1924) in W.M., 'Reviews of books', *ML*, 6/4 (1925): 371–3.

Limelight editions in New York bought out a revised edition of *Wagner as Man and Artist* in 1924. In the ten years since the first edition, new material had come to light, including letters from Wagner to his patron Julie Ritter. Newman took the opportunity to write more extensively about Wagner's paternity. On publication, the music critic William Mann wrote that the book remained 'soundest, sanest, and liveliest on its subject in English' since its first publication.[138]

LIFE OF RICHARD WAGNER, 1933–46

Like his other Wagner books, the *Life of Richard Wagner* was generally well received, especially when the last volume was published in 1946. A writer signed E.B. wrote a particularly rapturous review in *Music & Letters*, describing the four-volume project as a masterpiece, and claimed that it would be neither possible, nor desirable, for another biography of Wagner to be published on such a scale, not even by Newman himself.[139]

Although other critics wrote enthusiastically as each volume was published, some of them were troubled by Newman's attempt at psychologizing his subject, and by his inability to reconcile Wagner the man with Wagner the artist. Although sympathetic to the demands of biography to employ 'psychological understanding', in a review of the second volume, a writer signed G.A. (possibly Gerald Abraham) asserted that Newman had taken things too far, pointing out that on occasion Newman put words into Wagner's mouth.[140] While admitting that Liszt fared better in the volume than he had by Newman's hand in *The Man Liszt* (1934), G.A. was also not sold on Newman's psychological method: 'Mr Newman is at his best when he gets away from personalities he dislikes and settles down to the business of real critical scholarship.'[141] By contrast, Theodor Adorno thought Newman a historian *par excellence* and described the book as 'an effective antidote against current popular biographies'.[142] While careful not to label him a psychologist, Adorno praised Newman for

---

[138] Mann, 'Review of books', 371.

[139] E.B., 'The Life of Richard Wagner. Vol. IV: 1866–1883', *ML*, 29/2 (1948): 185–7.

[140] G.A., 'The Life of Richard Wagner. Vol. II: 1848–1860', *ML* 18/2 (1937): 194–6. G.A. referred specifically to Newman's account of Wagner's experiences in Dresden and Weimar.

[141] G.A., 'The Life of Richard Wagner, 196.

[142] Theodor W. Adorno, 'Wagner, Nietzsche and Hitler', *Kenyon Review* 9/1 (1947): 155–62; 155. For an analysis of this review in relation to Adorno and Wagner historiography, see Karin Bauer, 'Adorno's Wagner: History and the potential of the artwork', *Cultural Critique* 60 (2005): 68–91, especially pages 82–3, and John Deathridge, 'Waiting for Wagner: Reluctant musicology, radical philosophy, and the resue of a fraught legacy', *Opera Quarterly* 30/2–3 (2014): 267–85.

his ability to untangle and interpret complex personalities and for 'destroying' the '*convenus*' assumed by lesser scholars and carried down the subsequent literature.[143]

Opinions over Newman's attempt to write about Wagner the man and Wagner the artist in his four-volume *Life of Richard Wagner* were aired in two reviews upon the publication of the fourth volume. Carl T. Arlt, in *Notes*, wrote of Newman's skill in successfully managing the man versus artist dichotomy:

> Mr Newman's thorough and sympathetic understanding of his subject has quali-fied him for the enormous task of gathering the relevant material and fashioning it into a rich colourful tapestry, always keeping the greatness of Wagner's musical achievements as a beautiful pattern, a glorious structure, against the background of his tempestuous and complicated existence.[144]

On the other hand, Robert L. Jacobs was less sure that Newman had the man versus artist balance right. Jacobs claimed that, despite Newman's best efforts with these facts, the artist and man in the *Life of Richard Wagner* were not reconciled.[145] For Jacobs, however, Newman's *Life of Richard Wagner* was 'history with a capital "H"' and 'a tremendous tour de force of research and scholarship, but also a tale, told with relish, inviting pity, indignation and amusement'.[146] Jacobs wanted to know more about the artist in the book rather than the man. This was also the opinion of Carl Engel.

Engel was Newman's long-time nemesis. Over the years he had written hostile reviews of *The Unconscious Beethoven* (1927) and *The Man Liszt* (1934), in which Newman was severely criticised for debunking his subjects and for taking a psychological approach over an historical one. As far as Engel was concerned, Newman's recourse to psychology was 'merely another name for fiction masquerading as "historical criticism"'.[147]

Engel's most comprehensive criticism of Newman's *Life of Richard Wagner* came in 1941 in the *Musical Quarterly*.[148] He accused Newman of bringing the office of critic and biographer into disrepute by developing and promoting a 'Wagnerian inferiority complex'.[149] Newman was cast as opinionated and

---

[143] Adorno, 'Wagner, Nietzsche and Hitler', 155.

[144] Carl T. Arlt, 'The Life of Richard Wagner: Volume Four, 1866–1883', *Notes*, September 1946, 359–61; 361.

[145] Robert L. Jacobs, 'The Life of Richard Wagner, Vol. 4', *MT*, 89/1259 (1 January 1948): 16, 19; 16.

[146] Jacobs, 'The Life of Richard Wagner, Vol. 4', 19.

[147] Carl Engel, 'Views and reviews', *MQ*, 13/4 (October 1927): 646–62; 662.

[148] Carl Engel, 'View and reviews', *MQ*, 27/2 (April 1941): 243–8; 243.

[149] Carl Engel, 'View and reviews', *MQ*, (April 1941), 243.

arrogant, but worse was in store: Engel implied that Newman and his publisher were insensitive in issuing a book on Wagner during wartime and quipped that, in order to deal with the Nazis:

> we should ban and burn every scrap of Wagner's music and writings, and every book written about the amazing wizard, beginning with the books of the Anglo-Wagnerian Ernest Newman. What a small price it would be to pay, if it could help to fight and finally extinguish the Wagner-fanned fire of Nazism.[150]

This was nasty criticism, indeed.

Engel completed this review of the third volume of the *Life of Richard Wagner* by making fun of the final three appendices. The first appendix, in which Newman elaborated on the theory of Wagner's paternity, Engel described as 'silly and quite immaterial'. The second appendix, on Newman's reasons for doubting the madness of King Ludwig, was 'peculiar', according to Engel. In the third appendix, Newman described a set of letters exchanged between Wagner and Berta Goldwag, a Viennese milliner, to be of little interest to Wagner scholars, yet Engel disagreed, for they throw 'light upon some of the composer's idiosyncrasies and eccentricities'.[151]

Such hostile comments did not stand in the way of the book's success or continued positive criticism. In fact *The Life of Wagner* enjoyed a long afterlife and continues to do so. Theodor Adorno escalated his initial praise of it in 1963, writing: 'I mention Newman deliberately; the relevance of Wagner calls for the translation of his truly authentic work, the outstanding achievement of the entire panoply of Wagner biographies'.[152] Adorno even went so far as to exhort the book's worth to the audience of the 1966 Bayreuth Festival in the hope that someone would facilitate its translation into German, which is still wanting.[153] Correspondence between Alfred A. Knopf and Vera Newman in the 1960s, in which Knopf clarified their rights to secure the translation of volume 4 of the *Life*, strongly suggests a translation, presumably into German, was at least under consideration.[154] Earlier, an abridged version was also mooted but

---

[150] Carl Engel, 'View and reviews', *MQ*, (April 1941), 248.

[151] Carl Engel, 'View and reviews', *MQ*, (April 1941), 246–7

[152] Theodor W. Adorno, 'Wagner's relevance for today', is reproduced in Theodor W. Adorno, *Can One Live after Auschwitz?: A Philosophical Reader* ed. Rolf Tiedemann (Stanford, CA: Stanford University Press, 2003): 314–32; 316. The article is also published in Adorno's *Gesammelte Schriften* (Frankfurt am Main: Suhrkamp, 1978): vol. 16, 543–64.

[153] Hans Rudolph Vaget, 'The importance of Ernest Newman', *Wagner Journal* 1/3 (2007): 19–34, 19.

[154] Correspondence from Alfred A. Knopf to Vera Newman, 11 June 1963. Knopf Papers, File 392.4.

such an edition, like the translation, never materialized.[155] However, the *Life* was reprinted in 1948, 1960 and 1969. Cambridge University Press published a paperback edition of the *Life* in 1972 (as the inaugural title in the Press's music list) and again in 2014.

🐾 A Versatile Biographer

Newman's books on Wagner demonstrate his versatility as a biographer, given the variety of approaches he took in writing them. Ranging from a collection of essays in *A Study of Wagner* in 1899 to the final volume of the *Life* published almost fifty years later, they differed greatly in function: *Fact and Fiction about Wagner* was a defensive book that sought to rescue Wagner from the clutches of amateur historians and sensationalist journalists, while *Wagner as Man and Artist* (1914) was a debunking biography that was very much in the mould of books for which Newman was to become famous—or infamous—*The Unconscious Beethoven* (1927) and *The Man Liszt* (1934). In all of his Wagner books, Newman's aim was to write accurately about Wagner's life even if, at times, some of the reviewers thought that Newman's opinions got in the way of the facts, or that there was not enough synthesis between Wagner the man and Wagner the artist. But each of the books was pitched at readers of a different era and on topics that were apposite for their time.

Although they are quite dissimilar to each other, Newman's Wagner books were largely typical of biographies of their time: they were concerned with positioning the composer's life and works in historical context rather offering a highly structured and detailed appraisal of his music. Formal musical analysis was rarely attempted; on the contrary, it was arguably undeveloped in Britain until after the 1950s, when it became a branch of musicology.[156] But Newman was not writing only for the benefit of the musicologist. His readership was much wider.

The critical reception of Newman's Wagner books facilitated discussions on culture, criticism and, indeed, history and biography in hundreds of articles and books. And they continue to do so. Hardly a new book on Wagner is published without reference to Newman's *Life*. Of all Newman's Wagner books, *Wagner as Man and Artist* and *The Life of Richard Wagner* were heralded by most of the reviewers as great leaps forward in music biography, shaking themselves free of nineteenth-century panegyric models. This is the reason why the *Life* especially is remains a mainstay in Wagner literature.

[155] Correspondence from Vera Newman to Alfred A. Knopf, 27 August 1960. Knopf Papers, File 294.7.

[156] Joseph Kerman, *Musicology* (London: Fontana, 1985): 60–112.

❧ *End of an Era*

On 9 April 1946 Vera Newman recounts in her memoir:

> The Wagner *Life* was finished. For so many years it had been a burden to him.
> So many times he had nearly given up in despair. Now he seemed like a man
> released from prison. We opened a bottle of champagne at dinner and drank
> it all. E.N. said he never wanted to write another line about Wagner as long as
> he lived. I reminded him that he had the book on the Wagner operas to do, but
> he said that didn't count and anyway it was child's play compared to the other
> one.[157]

Newman died in 1959 resenting the years he had spent on his Wagner *Life*;
it had prevented him from working on at least three other books that he had
desperately wanted to write: a general history of Western music, a book on
Parsifal and a biography of Berlioz.[158] For posterity it was best that Newman
concentrated on his *Life of Richard Wagner* for it, along with his other books
on the composer, made a formidable contribution to Wagner literature.

---

[157] Vera Newman, *Ernest Newman*, 211.

[158] Plans for the history of music, which appear to have been first raised in 1921, are
recorded in Vera Newman's *Ernest Newman*, 25. Mention is made of Newman's
planned *Parsifal* book on page 269 of the book. It is well known that Newman
had planned to write a Berlioz biography; see, for example, Peter Heyworth (ed.),
Berlioz, Romantic and Classic: Writings by Ernest Newman (London, 1972): 11.

CHAPTER 10

Conclusion:
Ernest Newman Remembered

How should Ernest Newman be remembered? Had he become a 'sour old cynic' in his old age, as Vera Newman feared? Or was he a forward thinker, a progressive biographer? Was he mean-spirited for his sometime confrontational arguments with his readers and rivals? Is he remembered as a naïve and cantankerous old-school positivist, harbouring utopian dreams for an unrealizable system of principles in history, criticism and biography?

In the course of writing this book, I have pondered these questions many times. If Newman was a sour old cynic, he was merely being consistent. His cynicism is evident early in his career in *A Study of Wagner* (1899), where he cast doubt on the quality of Wagner's prose works. His damning biography of Franz Liszt was certainly a low point in his career. But should one careless book tarnish the reputation and legacy of a scholar whose other works were generally successful and highly regarded?

One of Newman's greatest legacies is 'The Word of Music' column for the *Sunday Times* that, by all accounts, was a highlight of that paper. Newman often wrote affectionately of his audience—'the plain man', as he termed it—but he sometimes railed against his readers, thinking them stupid and ignorant. He stopped writing articles on the physiology of criticism from the early 1920s, on the grounds that his readers could not get to grips with his argument. Newman's confrontations with his rivals make for amusing reading, and his stubbornness (some might say arrogance) was often on display. He rarely backed down from a tussle and he always had the last say. He never admitted he was wrong, and certainly never apologized. His fiery exchange with Robertson in the late 1890s is a case in point. But Newman made something of a blood sport of these heady confrontations. He loved a literary spectacle, a good fight.

It is not surprising that Newman lacked sympathy for much of the music composed in his own lifetime. His first love was the romantics and the neo-romantics. It *is* surprising, though, that he kept his job on the *Sunday Times* for so long, considering his blind spot for most French music, new music and his resistance to technology. But Newman had become an institution, and institutions are sometimes difficult to refurbish. But before we cast Newman as an old-fashioned grump, we should remember he lived in an age that placed little value on Berlioz and it is largely thanks to Newman—and his North American counterpart, Jacques Barzun—that Berlioz became better known.[1] The lavish coverage of the premier of *Les Troyens* at Covent Garden in 1957, printed in the *Sunday Times*, was surely a consequence of Newman's influence.[2] He had long thought Berlioz a missing presence in contemporary music-making: he felt the same for many other composers in whom he tried to spark interest, including Hugo Wolf.

Newman's engagement with musicology—or 'musicography' as he sometimes referred to it—was fairly peripheral until he wrote about German-language musicology in the 1930s. He was well acquainted with some of Britain's leading musicologists of the day—Edward Dent, Henry George Farmer, J.A. Westrup, Gerald Abraham and Winton Dean were amongst his friends and admirers—but I am yet to come across writings in which Newman extensively details the development of the local discipline.[3]

Newman sits uncomfortably with the label of musicologist or theorist, probably because he never held a university position in which those professions were institutionalized. Most of the time he described himself as a critic; less often he labelled himself a biographer and historian. But what kind of critic, biographer and historian was he?

Newman styled himself as a critic of the new and scientific school of the late nineteenth century. His wide knowledge of national literatures, science and social theory would never constrain him to the mere reporting of musical news, which was the mainstay for much of the periodical press in the first half of the nineteenth century. Neither was Newman an impressionist critic, a type of writer he perceived to be reflective, meandering, self-referential and blind to the cultural and social environments in which the musical work was made. Yet Newman was not always the noble new critic he made himself out to be. He was, at times, as cantankerous and bad-tempered as Davison, the old-school critic, and much of his work in *A Musical Critics' Holiday* could be described as impressionistic musings.

Newman was a versatile biographer, so much so that some of the biographies (such as *Gluck and the Opera* and *The Unconscious Beethoven*) were not

---

[1] Jacques Barzun, *Berlioz and the Romantic Century* (Boston: Little Brown, 1950).

[2] See Ernest Newman, 'The Trojans', *ST*, 9 June 1957, 21; 'On the Trojans', *ST*, 16 June 1957, 22; and 'The Trojans: A final word', *ST*, 29 June 1957, 8.

[3] Newman's association with Dent is discussed in Paul Watt, 'The catalogue of Ernest Newman's library: revelations about his early intellectual life', *Script and Print*, 31/2 (2007): 81–103. The recognition Newman received from Edward Dent, J.A. Westrup, Gerald Abraham and Winton Dean is implied by their essays in a tribute volume to Newman, *Fanfare for Ernest Newman* ed. Herbert van Thal (London: Arthur Baker, 1955). For background to Newman's friendship with Henry George Farmer, see chapter 1.

so much life and times, but studies of the composers' relationships with either time period (in the case of Gluck) or musical process (in the case of Beethoven). The books are characterized by attention to detail and wide-ranging research. Newman was especially interested in the psychology of his subject, even if the books were not couched as psychobiographies (*The Man Liszt* is arguably a borderline case), but Newman never fully articulated a sound psychological theory. His psychologizing, mostly without any recourse to detailed musical analysis, especially in the Wagner biographies, was largely of the armchair variety.

Newman described himself as a historian less often, though his appeal to history—or 'back thought' as he termed it in *A Musical Critic's Holiday*—was his guiding principle. At many points in his career he was writing an account of music from pre-history to the present, but at middle-age he became increasingly nervous of this undertaking believing that he had insufficient grasp on the vast contemporary scholarship to do this satisfactorily. He worried that a book by a single hand, which would take many years to write, would become outdated quickly and wondered whether such a project would be better achieved by a group of writers. Newman never articulated the shape or scope his book would take, or how an edited volume might be constructed. When he came across the work of other historians in the 1940s, his interest was piqued by their approaches to what we today would call social or cultural history.

Underpinning all of Newman's work, whether as a critic, historian or biographer, was the rationalist principle that logical thought, reasoned argument, careful exposition of ideas, the balancing of one's views against the views of others, and the judicious marshalling of evidence, was necessary to engage the reader's interest and trust. These were the hallmarks of John M. Robertson's brand of rationalism. Its purpose was to counter the self-styled and unmediated copy of the journalist and belletrist. This was the stuff of the so-called new criticism. Yet, if applying all of these criteria to criticism, history and biography, there is not much room left for the marking out of a personal style of writing and it could lead, in the case of Robertson's two books on the topic, to extremely dull reading. It was surely naïve of Newman to take the high moral ground on rationalism as often as he did, for there are too many glimpses in his career of a bellicose, truculent, combative writer. Newman is often at his best when he abandons the strictures of the rationalist agenda.

The extent to which rationalism should feature in biographies of Newman has been a point of conjecture since his death, as we saw in chapter 2 with the biographies by Henry George Farmer and Vera Newman. Farmer's account gave a narrative of Newman's freethinking activities, while Vera Newman argued that Newman's early intellectual life had no bearing on his later work. It is true that Newman's works after 1900 were less indignant over religion and society as his pre-1900 work. However, the freethought years gave him an extremely solid footing in method, apparent in his composer-studies and in many articles in which he expressed the desire for biography, criticism and history to be impartial, informed and considered. These more modest principles were an integral part of his rationalist agenda, their subtleties missed by Farmer and by Vera Newman.

As we will recall from the epigraphs by Eva Mary Grew, Ralph Hill and Neville Cardus printed at the front of this book, Newman was considered a legend in his own lifetime. In 1928, Grew mused that anyone unfamiliar with his work—his 'good books on musical subjects'—was an 'ignoramus'. Hill, writing in the early 1940s, credited Newman with exercising a 'dominating influence over musical taste' in Britain. And Cardus, reflecting on Newman's career just a few years before Newman's death, proposed that 'Ernest Newman was perhaps the first writer to truly Europeanize our music and our humane response to music'. Certainly, Newman shamed his readers for their parochial view of Liszt and Wagner and for their sometime poor musical taste, for example, in the case of Italian opera.

Like Cardus, I can see that Newman was extensively engaged with European intellectual thought, probably unlike many other critics of his stature and time. Though some of his early contemporaries, such as Francis Hueffer, George Bernard Shaw and John F. Runciman, were well read and were highly influential and effective writers, their intellectual horizons were arguably not so wide. The breadth of topics on which Newman wrote—and his close attachment to the latest research emanating from France and Germany in particular—set Newman apart from many of his peers. Even a seemingly unimportant booklet Newman wrote for the Leeds Public Library—*What to Read on the Evolution of Music*—introduces and lists approximately 190 books and articles on the subject in English, French and German. Few other music critics of his generation would have been this well read.[4]

There will be those readers who believe that Newman was old-fashioned, perhaps, at times, something of a fossil, just as Heseltine and Gray did in the 1920s (see chapter 7). To be sure, Newman's admiration of music was of a late nineteenth-century hue, just as his view of criticism was shaped and nurtured by the some of the greatest writers to have lived in that century. However, this book has sought to show the influences on Newman's intellect and how the ideas and values informed by these influences played out in his books and criticism. I have also sought to highlight Newman's gift for writing. Ralph Hill was right when he once commented that Newman could 'write about

---

[4] Ernest Newman, *What to Read on the Evolution of Music* (Leeds: Leeds Public Library, 1928).

barbed wire and still be interesting'.[5] But I would go one step further and say that everything Newman wrote, whether on music, science, history or social questions, was direct, compelling and easy to read. Most of the time, Newman wore his erudition lightly, yet operating in the background were an array of influences that shaped and nurtured his thinking and which have given insight into the forces that shaped, and sometimes skewed, his work.

---

[5] Ralph Hill, *Reflected Music and Other Essays* (London: Methuen, 1930): 10.

Newman's Freethought Lectures, 1894–1896[1]

DATE	LOCATION	TITLE
1894		
7 January	Liverpool	Optimism and pessimism
29 April	Liverpool	Modern Christianity
20 May	Liverpool	Modern Christianity
3 June	Manchester	Modern Christianity
8 July	Liverpool	Ibsen[2]
29 July	Manchester	The social philosophy of Ibsen
7 October	Liverpool	Inaugural address on moral philosophers[3]
14 October	Liverpool	Moral philosophers: Descartes
28 October	Liverpool	Moral philosophers: Spinoza
28 October	Liverpool	Progress and compromise
4 November	Liverpool	Moral philosophers
11 November	Liverpool	Moral philosophers
18 November	Manchester	Progress, compromise and the religious spirit
25 November	Liverpool	Moral philosophers: Berkeley
2 December	Chester	Modern Christianity
9 December	Liverpool	Moral philosophers: David Hume
9 December	Liverpool	Theism, atheism and pantheism
30 December	Liverpool	Christianity and modern life
1895		
6 January	Liverpool	Modern philosophers: Kant
13 January	Liverpool	Modern philosophers: Kant

[1] Source: 'Additions to Ernest Newman biography', MS Farmer 43/7. This list appeared in the penultimate draft of Farmer's biography but was not included in the final typescript, 'Ernest Newman as I saw Him', MS Farmer 44. At the end of the appendix title, Farmer inserts his first footnote: 'Newman's friend Laurence Small, B. Sc. (London), and a protégé of Sir Oliver Lodge, had been giving similar lectures in 1892–3'.

[2] Newman had published an article on Ibsen nine months earlier: 'The Real Ibsen', *FR*, October 1893, 20–37.

[3] Farmer's second and final footnote reads 'These lectures on Moral Philosophy were given to a public class in the mornings. All the remaining were evening lectures'.

3 February	Liverpool	Modern philosophers: Kant
10 February	Liverpool	The logic of the faithful
17 February	Liverpool	Modern philosophers: Kant
24 February	Liverpool	Modern philosophers: Kant
3 March	Liverpool	Modern philosophers: Kant
31 March	Liverpool	The culture of the emotions[4]
7 April	Liverpool	Mr Balfour's *Foundations of Belief*[5]
28 April	Liverpool	Mr Balfour's *Foundations of Belief*
8 September	Liverpool	Mr Balfour's *Foundations of Belief*
6 October	Liverpool	The Reunion of Christendom[6]
3 November	Liverpool	The origin and development of legends
17 November	Liverpool	The common-sense of atheism
22 December	Liverpool	The common-sense of atheism

1896

26 January	Liverpool	Life in Ancient Greece
1 March	Liverpool	Oscar Wilde[7]
15 March	Manchester	Social evolution
22 March	Leicester	The evolution of humanity
10 May	Liverpool	The life of Frederick Douglass

---

[4] Newman had published an article bearing the same name as this lecture approximately two years earlier in *NQMR*, August 1893, 57–62.

[5] Balfour's work was later attacked by Newman in his *Pseudo-Philosophy*.

[6] Newman published an article by the same name as this lecture the following month: *FR*, November 1895, 127–38, but signed it 'Wm Roberts'.

[7] Newman had published an article bearing the same name as this lecture approximately nine months earlier in *FR*, June 1895, 194–206. The article's sub-title is 'A literary appreciation'.

Bibliography

PRIMARY SOURCES

NATIONAL LIBRARY, SCOTLAND

MS 25513, D.C. Parker Papers. Correspondence between Vera Newman and D.C Parker.

UNIVERSITY OF GLASGOW, SPECIAL COLLECTIONS

MS Farmer 42. Typescript [early draft, undated] of 'Ernest Newman as I saw Him'.

MS Farmer 43/7–8. Additions to Ernest Newman biography. Appendices of freethought lectures and articles by Newman, 1889–98.

MS Farmer 43/9. Additions to Ernest Newman biography. Miscellaneous revised, corrected and discarded pages.

MS Farmer 44. Typescript copy [final, 1962] of 'Ernest Newman as I saw Him'.

MS Farmer 45/2–29. Correspondence during research for 'Ernest Newman as I saw Him'. Correspondence about Newman with the National Secular Society, various Freethinkers, Rationalist Press Association, and numerous museums and libraries, 1927, 1943–4, 1959–60.

MS Farmer 45/30. Correspondence during research for 'Ernest Newman as I saw Him'.

MS Farmer 46/1–44. Correspondence regarding Farmer's attempt to find a publisher.

MS Farmer 47/1–83. Autographed letters from Ernest Newman and Vera Newman.

MS Farmer 589. Scrapbook containing press cuttings relating to Ernest Newman, 1954–1961.

UNIVERSITY OF OXFORD, BODLEIAN LIBRARY

MSS Dobell. Papers of Bertram Dobell. Correspondence from Ernest Newman to Bertram Dobell, 38463, 38484–5 (c. 32–8) and 38490.

UNIVERSITY OF TEXAS, AUSTIN, HARRY RANSOM CENTER

The Alfred A. and Blanche W. Knopf Papers. Correspondence between Alfred A. Knopf and Blanche W. Knopf to Vera and Ernest Newman and editorial files relating to Newman's books. Boxes 103.9, 127.7, 136.1, 184.15, 266.6, 294.7, 326.10, 336.8, 360.8, 392.4, 421.3, 432.6, 441.3, 470.2, 509.12, 525.9, 533.3, 553.9,

554.3, 561.7, 659.7, 659.8, 659.9, 660.1–660.7, 660.9, 694.2, 700.4, 870.9, 878.4, 884.10, 889.2, 890.7, 895.4, 896.3

ARTICLES AND BOOKS BY NEWMAN CITED IN THE TEXT (CHRONOLOGICAL ORDER)

'Morality and belief', *NR*, 15 September 1889, 170; 22 September, 1888–9.
'The doctrine of evolution in modern poetry', *NR*, 27 October 1889, 260–2.
'The meaning of science', *NR*, 24 July 1892, 52–3.
'The coming menace', *NR*, 14 August 1892, 99–100.
'Crucifixion: To the Editor of the "NR" ' [Letter to the editor signed 'W. Roberts' attrib. Newman], *NR*, 28 August 1892, 139.
'A note on death', *NR*, 4 September 1892, 146–8.
'Mr Harrison and Mr Huxley', *NR*, 23 October 1892, 259–60.
'Poetry and music', *NR*, 30 October 1892, 277.
'Marriage as a science', *NR*, 13 November 1892, 309–11.
'Poetry and music: a reply', *NR*, 4 December 1892, 355–7; 11 December, 373–5.
'Wagner and the music-drama', *NR*, 1 January 1893, 11–12.
'A note on Amiel', *NR*, 26 February 1893, 136; 5 March 1894, 147–8; 12 March, 163–4; 19 March, 180–1; 26 March, 200.
'Our morality', *NR*, 4 June 1893, 355–7.
'Mr Meredith and the eternal-feminine', *NR*, 23 July 1893, 54–5.
'The culture of the emotions', *NQMR*, August 1893, 57–62.
'Some thoughts on Weismann', *NR*, 6 August 1893, 84–5; 13 August, 102–3; 20 August, 116–17.
'The Real Ibsen', *FR*, October 1893, 20–37.
'Mr Kipling's stories', *FR*, December 1893, 236–48.
'Mascagni and the opera', *FR*, June 1894, 210–23.
'George Meredith', *FR*, August 1894, 398–418.
'The difficulties of musical criticism', *NQMR*, November 1894, 105–12.
'Concerning Weismann', *FR*, December 1894, 210–38.
'Women and music', *FR*, April 1895, 48–62.
'Oscar Wilde: a literary appreciation', *FR*, June 1895, 193–206.
'Amiel', *FR*, October 1895, 44–57; November, 197–205.
'Gustave Flaubert', *FoR*, December 1895, 813–28.
'Buckle and his critics', *FR*, March 1896, 600–15.
'Friedrich Nietzsche', *FR*, May 1896, 113–22.
'The philosopher at the music hall', *FR*, September 1896, 653–8.
'Nietzsche and Wagner', *FR*, December 1896, 268–75.
Pseudo-Philosophy at the end of the Nineteenth Century. (London: University Press), 1897.
'Music and race', *Mus*, 16 January 1897, 116–17.
'Tourgenieff', *UMFR*, April 1897, 56–64; May, 144–55.
'An ethical excursion', *UMFR*, June 1897, 238–52 [signed Hugh Mortimer Cecil].
'On atheism', *UMFR*, June 1897, 347–52 [signed Hugh Mortimer Cecil].

'Nancy', *UMFR*, June 1897, 299–322.

'One view of Wagner', *Mus*, June 1897, 75–6.

'Wagner's theory of music, poetry, and music-drama', *Mus*, 21 July 1897, 214–16; 28 July, 233–4; 4 August, 253–4; 11 August, 273–6.

'Wagner on Beethoven', *Mus*, 1 September 1897, 331–3.

'On music and musical criticism', *Mus*, 20 October 1897, 450–3.

'An open letter' [to John M. Robertson], *UMFR*, December 1897, 397–409.

'The substance and the shadow, or, the ethics of controversy: being a brief epistolary sermon suggested by a recent American blizzard', *UMFR*, April 1898, 82–90.

'The eighteenth century view of opera', *UMFR*, June 1898, 262–74.

'Wagner's "Ring" and its Philosophy', *FoR*, June 1898, 867–84.

A Study of Wagner (London: Bertram Dobell, New York: G.P. Putnam's), 1899.

'A study of Liszt', reprinted in *Liszt Society Journal* 8 (1983 [1900]), 32–3. The original place of publication is not known.

'"The old music and the new"', *CR*, September 1900, 415–29.

'Berlioz', *CR*, February 1901, 212–20.

'The need for banking reform', *Sp.* 9 February 1901, 508–11 [attrib. Newman].

'The essential Tchaikovsky', *CR*, June 1901, 867–98.

'English music and musical criticism', *CR*, November 1901, 734–48.

'The New School of British Music I', *Sp.* 7 December 1901, 271–3.

'The New School of British Music II: Edward Elgar', *Sp.* 21 December 1901, 331–2.

'The New School of British Music III: Granville Bantock', *Sp.* 4 January 1902, 385–6.

'The New School of British Music IV: Mr Frederick C. Nicholls', *Sp.* 18 January 1902, 442–3.

'The New School of British Music V: William Wallace', *Sp.* 1 February 1902, 499–501.

'The New School of British Music VI: Mr Josef Holbrooke', *Sp.* 15 February 1902, 557–8.

'The New School of British Music VII: Mr S Coleridge Taylor', *Sp.* 1 March 1902, 608–10.

'The New School of British Music VIII: Mr Percy Pitt', *Sp.* 15 March 1902, 669–70.

'The New School of British Music IX', *Sp.* 29 March 1902, 725–6.

'The New School of British Music X', *Sp.* 12 April 1902, 40–1.

'Mr Herbert Spencer and the origin of music', *MMR*, November 1902, 205–6; 1 December, 224–6.

'Richard Strauss and the music of the future', *FoR*, January 1903, 30–45.

Wagner (London and New York: John Lane, The Bodley Head), 1904.

'Hugo Wolf', *CR*, 1 January 1904, 707–20.

Musical Studies (London and New York: John Lane, The Bodley Head), 1905.

'Everyman in Liverpool', *MG*, 8 November 1905, 7.

Elgar (London and New York: John Lane, The Bodley Head), 1906.

'The "Ring" in Manchester', *MG*, 23 February 1906, 6.

'The Hallé concert', *MG*, 9 March 1906, 7.

'Some recent music', *MG*, 17 April 1906, 5.

'Morecambe Festival', *MG*, 12 May 1906, 8.

Hugo Wolf (London: Methuen & Co. Limited), 1907.

'Hugo Wolf as a song-writer', *New Music Review and Church Music Review* 6/64 (1907): 234–7; and 6/65 (1907): 307–10.

Richard Strauss (London and New York: John Lane, The Bodley Head), 1908.

Fifty Songs by Hugo Wolf, ed. Newman. (Boston: Oliver Ditson Company), 1909.

'Franz Liszt, October 22, 1911 – July 31, 1886', *MT*, 52/824 (1 October 1911): 52/825 (1 November 1911): 708–11; 52/826 (1 December 1911): 778–80.

'The Liszt centenary', *Nation*, 28 October 1911, 162–3.

'Arnold Schönberg's Gurre-Lieder', *MT*, 55/851 (1 January 1914): 11–13.

'Music after the war', *NW*, 25 November 1915, 100, 102.

'Concerning Liszt and Ravel', *NW*, 16 December 1915, 190–2.

'Musical criticisms after the war: a hint to editor', *NW*, 23 December 1915, 222, 224.

'The Russian Music Committee', *NW*, 10 February 1916, 446, 448.

'That Russian Musical Committee again', *NW*, 17 February 1916, 478, 480.

'J.F.R.', *NW*, 27 April 1916, 798–9.

'"Boris Godounov" and nationalism in music', *NW*, 18 May 1916, 82–3.

'A school for critics?', *NW*, 12 October 1916, 754–5.

'The critic in the confessional', *NW*, 9 November 1916, 50–1; 7 December, 178–9.

'Music and Musicians: Hans Richter', *NW*, 14 December 1916, 210–11.

'Glinka – I', *NW*, 29 March 1917, 600–1.

'Glinka – II', *NW*, 5 April 1917, 623, 624.

'Concerning musical criticism', *NW*, 3 May 1917, 14–15.

'Moussorgsky', *NW*, 7 June 1917, 134–3.

'Putting the classics in their place II', *NW*, 24 January 1918, 294–5.

'Debussy: an appreciation and a criticism', *Observer*, 31 March 1918, 5.

'When the music-men come back', *NW*, 21 June 1918, 152–3.

A Musical Motley (London: John Lane, The Bodley Head), 1919.

'Music in London', *MG*, 24 September 1919, 5.

'Music in London', *MG*, 8 October 1919, 5.

'Music in London', *MG*, 3 December 1919, 7.

'Music in London', *MG*, 31 December 1919, 5.

The Piano-Player and its Music (London: Grant Richards), 1920.

'Music in London', *MG*, 7 January 1920, 5.

'Music in London', *MG*, 4 February 1920, 5.

'Music in London', *MG*, 3 March 1920, 7.

'Actors and actresses in opera', *ST*, 7 March 1920, 8.

'Music in London', *MG*, 10 March 1920, 5.

'Music in London', *MG*, 24 March 1920, 7.

'Music in London', *MG*, 14 April 1920, 7.

'British music and the public', *ST*, 18 April 1920, 6.

'Music in London', *MG*, 28 April 1920, 7.
'The modern English song', *ST*, 2 May 1920, 6.
'The modern English song II', *ST*, 9 May 1920, 6.
'Music in London', *MG*, 17 May 1920, 7.
'A note on musical criticism', *ST*, 30 May 1920, 6.
'The week in music', *MG*, 27 October 1920, 5.
'The week in music', *MG*, 3 November 1920, 5.
'The week in music', *MG*, 10 November 1920, 7.
'The week in music', *MG*, 17 November 1920, 5.
'The week in music', *MG*, 6 January 1921, 5.
'The week in music', *MG*, 20 January 1921, 5.
'Music in London', *MG*, 23 June 1921, 5.
'A British ballet?', *ST*, 23 October 1921, 5.
'Schönberg, Strauss and others', *ST*, 13 November 1921, 5.
'The week in music', *MG*, 16 February 1922, 5.
'The week in music', *MG*, 9 March 1922, 5.
'The case of the Ninth Symphony', *ST*, 1 April 1922, 7.
'The week in music', *MG*, 31 August 1922, 5.
'English opera and English singers', *ST* 3 December 1922, 7.
'The week in music', *MG*, 3 May 1923, 16.
'The week in music', *MG*, 8 November 1923, 6.
'The Schönberg case', *ST*, 25 November 1923, 5.
'The critic and his critics', *ST*, 9 December 1923, 7.
'Broadcasting music: some reflections and a suggestion', *ST*, 13 January 1924, 5.
'The more it changes', *ST*, 2 March 1924, 3.
'Stravinksy and criticism', *ST*, 9 March 1924, 7.
'Music and radio', *ST*, 16 March 1924, 7.
'Musical biography: a division of labour', *ST*, 13 April 1924, 7.
'Jazz opera and national opera', *ST*, 28 December 1924, 4.
A Musical Critic's Holiday (New York: Alfred A. Knopf), 1925.
'Stravinsky today', *ST*, 25 January 1925, 7.
'Jazz and "The American composer"', *ST*, 1 February 1925, 7.
'Shakespeare set to music', *ST*, 5 April 1925, 5.
'A postscript to "A Musical Critic's Holiday"', *MT*, 66/992 (1 October 1925): 881–4; 66/993 (1 November 1925): 977–81; 66/994 (1 December): 1076–9.
'Holst's Choral Symphony', *ST*, 11 October 1925, 9.
'The opera problem', *ST,* 29 November 1925, 7.
'The Schumanns and Liszt', *ST*, 31 January 1926, 7.
'The music and the man', *ST*, 7 February 1926, 7.
'Letters, the man, and the musicians', *ST*, 28 February 1926, 7.
'Letters, the man and the musician II', *ST*, 7 March 1926, 7.
'Science, sensation and singing', *ST*, 28 March 1926, 7.
'Hubert Parry', *ST*, 4 April 1926, 5.
'Legend and reality', *ST*, 20 June 1926, 7.

'Mr Whiteman goes on explaining', *ST*, 12 September 1926, 7.

'Beethoven material', *ST*, 19 September 1926, 7.

'"So this is jazz"', *ST*, 26 December 1926, 4.

'Poses et mensonges: women who ruined Liszt', *ST*, 24 April 1927, 7.

What to Read on the Evolution of Music (Leeds: Leeds Public Library), 1928.

'Musical history: towards a theory', *ST*, 12 February 1928, 7.

'This Schönberg case', *ST*, 19 February 1928, 7.

'A problem of musical criticism: The composer and his period', *ST*, 18 March 1928, 7.

'Oedipus Rex', *ST*, 20 May 1928, 7.

'A chance for a millionaire', *ST*, 10 June 1928, 7.

'Dr Terry's Bach', *ST*, 2 September 1928, 5.

'A physiology of criticism', *ST*, 20 January 1929, 7; 10 February, 7; 17 February, 7.

'New light on Wagner?', *ST*, 26 May, 1929, 7.

'The last laps', *ST*, 5 May 1929, 7.

'Another illusion shattered', *ST*, 17 November 1929, 7.

'Thoughts on the present discontents VI', *ST*, 12 January 1930, 5.

'Some Covent Garden errors', *ST*, 6 July 1930, 5.

'A new work about Wagner', *ST*, 16 February 1930, 7.

'Fiction about Wagner II', *ST*, 23 February 1930, 7.

'Fiction about Wagner III', *ST*, 2 March 1930, 7.

Fact and Fiction about Wagner (London: Cassell and Company), 1931.

'Acting in opera', *ST*, 10 May 1931, 7.

'Miming in opera', *ST*, 17 May 1931, 5.

The Sibelius Society *Newsletters* vols. 1–6, *c.* 1932.

'The week in music', *MG*, 18 January 1932, 5.

'Mr Bernard Shaw as Musical Critic', *ST*, 26 June 1932, 7.

'Generalise in haste ...', *ST*, 25 September 1932, 7.

'Jazz and Dionysis', *ST*, 23 October 1932, 5.

The Life of Richard Wagner vol. I, 1813–1848. (New York: Alfred A. Knopf), 1933.

'Wireless and the time factor', *ST*, 26 February 1933, 7.

'Bach and his orchestra', *ST*, 12 March 1933, 7.

'New light on Liszt', *ST*, 23 April 1933, 7.

'Acting in opera: the eternal feminine', *ST*, 7 May 1933, 7.

'Ecrasons l'infâme!', *ST*, 11 June 1933, 7.

'The sins of Covent Garden: repentance and salvation', *ST*, 18 June 1933, 7.

'Biographies of musicians', *ST*, 10 December 1933, 7.

The Man Liszt: A study of the tragi-comedy of a soul divided against itself (London: Cassell), 1934, (New York: Charles Scribner), 1935, (London: Victor Gollancz Ltd), 1970.

'Delius', *ST*, 17 June 1934, 7.

'Acting in opera: how might it be improved', *ST*, 23 June 1935, 7.

'Delius and the opera', *ST*, 29 September 1935, 5.

'Appreciation', in John M. Robertson, *A History of Freethought Ancient and Modern, to the Period of the French Revolution*, vol. 2, 4th edn (London: Dawsons of Pall Mall, 1969): xxii. Original publication 1936.

'Progress in musicology: law in musical history', *ST*, 19 April 1936, 7.

'Some aspects of 18th-century music, Dr Balet's generalisations', *ST*, 26 April 1936, 7.

'The Germans and the "Beggar's Opera"', *ST*, 3 May 1936, 7.

The Life of Richard Wagner vol. 2, 1848–1860. (New York: Alfred A. Knopf), 1937.

'Covent Garden's problems: English opera audiences', *ST*, 4 July 1937, 7.

'More about conducting: Schenker on notation', *ST*, 24 October 1937, 5.

'In the service of ideology: Wagner and the Boers', *ST*, 26 March 1939, 5.

'Regimentation of German thought', *ST*, 24 September 1939, 7.

'Wagner and the Germans', *ST*, 5 May 1940, 3.

'Schenker and the composer', *ST*, 15 December 1940, 3.

The Life of Richard Wagner vol. 3, 1859–1886. (New York: Alfred A. Knopf), 1941.

'The nations and their music', *ST*, 5 January 1941, 3.

'Audiences old and new', *ST*, 9 January 1944, 2.

'Walton today', *ST*, 5 April 1942, 2.

'Our music and our epoch', *ST*, 12 March 1944, 2.

'A job for a dictator', *ST*, 2 July 1944, 2.

'The truth about Wagner', *ST*, 20 May 1945, 2.

'The truth about Wagner II', *ST*, 27 May 1945, 2.

The Life of Richard Wagner vol. 4, 1866–1883. (New York: Alfred A. Knopf), 1946.

'Schönberg once more', *ST*, 10 August 1947, 2.

'"Wozzeck"', 27 March 1949, 2.

'Covent Garden', *ST*, 27 November 1949, 2.

'The "garden" again', *ST*, 22 January 1950, 2.

'Holst today', *ST*, 11 March 1951, 2.

'Bayreuth revisited', *ST*, 5 August 1951, 2.

'Bayreuth revisited II', *ST*, 10 August 1930, 5.

'Büchner and Berg', *ST*, 13 January 1952, 2.

'Berg and Wozzeck', *ST*, 20 January 1952, 2.

'"Wozzeck"', *ST*, 27 January 1952, 2.

'Thoughts on television', *ST*, 21 June 1953, 9.

'Television opera', *ST*, 16 August 1953, 4.

'Shenkerism', *ST*, 14 November 1954, 11.

'Troilus and Cressida', *ST*, 5 December 1954, 11.

'Two Beethovens', *ST*, 23 January 1955, 11.

'Music as language', *ST*, 26 May 1957, 22.

'The Trojans', *ST*, 9 June 1957, 21.

'On the Trojans', *ST*, 16 June 1957, 22.

'The Trojans: A final word', *ST*, 29 June 1957, 8.

SELECTED SECONDARY SOURCES
UNSIGNED ARTICLES

Advertisement for *Pseudo-Philosophy*, in *UMFR* 11 (1899), 405. Extracted from Unsigned, 'An indictment of latter-day irrationalism' [Review of *Pesudo-Philosophy at the end of the Nineteenth Century*], *Literary Guide*, 1 April 1897, 147–8.

'Ernest Newman's World of Music: Our critic retires after 38 years', *ST*, 9 November 1958.

'Mr Ernest Newman', *MH*, 1 May 1912, 131–4.

'Musical taste in England, and the influence of the gramophone', *Bookman*, April 1921, 38–41.

Professor Nietzsche', obituary, the *Times*, 27 August 1900, 4.

'Rex v. Liszt', *MOMTR*, February 1935, 409.

'Wagner as man and artist', *English Review*, July 1914, 566–7.

'Wagner the man', *SR*, 30 May 1914, 706–7.

ARTICLES AND BOOKS

Abert, Hermann. *W.A. Mozart*, trans. Stewart Spencer, ed. Cliff Eisen. New Haven: Yale University Press, 2007 [Leipzig, 1919–21]).

Adams, Byron. '"Thor's Hammer": Sibelius and British Music Critics, 1905–1957', in Daniel M. Grimley (ed.), *Jean Sibelius and his World*. Princeton: Princeton University Press, 2011, 125–57.

Adorno, Theodor W. 'Wagner, Nietzsche and Hitler', *Kenyon Review* 9/1 (1947), 155–62.

—— 'Wagner's Relevance Today' in *Theodor W. Adorno, Can One Live after Auschwitz?: A Philosophical Reader* ed. Rolf Tiedemann. Stanford, CA: Stanford University Press, 203: 314–32.

Aldrich, Richard. 'Ernest Newman on Liszt's loves', *New York Times Book Review*, 17 March 1935, 5.

Algarotti, Francesco. *Saggio dell' Opera in Musica*. Livorno: Coltellini, 1763.

Allen, Grant. *Physiological Aesthetics*. New York: Appleton and Co., 1877.

—— 'The decay of criticism', *FoR*, March 1882, 339–51.

Altick, Richard D. *Lives and Letters: A History of Literary Biography in England and America*. Westport, CT: Greenwood Press, 1965.

Amiel, Henri-Frédéric. *Amiel's Journal*, trans. Mrs Humphrey Ward. London: Macmillan and Co., 1933.

Ampère, Jean-Jacques. *Histoire de la littérature française au moyen âge comparée aux littératures étrangères*. Paris: Tessier, 1841.

Anderson, Robert. 'Liszt tragi-comedy', *MT*, 11/1524 (1 February 1970): 160.

Aprahamian, Felix (ed.). *Essays from the World of Music*. London: J. Calder, 1956.

—— (ed.). *More Essays from the World of Music*. London: J. Calder, 1958.

Archer, William. 'Criticism as an inductive science', *Macmillan's Magazine*, May–October 1886, 45–54.

Arlt, Carl T. 'The Life of Richard Wagner: Volume Four, 1866–1883', *Notes*, September 1946, 359–61.

Arnold, Frank. *The Art of an Accompaniment from a Thorough Bass*, 2 vols. London: Oxford University Press, 1931.

Arnold, Matthew. 'The function of criticism at the present time', *National Review* 2/1 (1864): 280–307. Reproduced in *Arnold: Culture and Anarchy and other Writings* ed. Stefan Collini. Cambridge: Cambridge University Press, 1993, 26–52.

—— *Essays in Criticism*. London and Cambridge: Macmillan and Co., 1865.

—— *Essays in Criticism*. 2nd series. London and New York: Macmillan and Co., 1888, 300–31.

Arrandale, Karen. *Edward J. Dent: A Life of Music and Words*. Woodbridge: The Boydell Press, 2017.

Arteaga, Stefano. *Le Rivoluzioni del Teatro Musicale Italiano dalla sua origine fino al presente*, 3 vols. Bologna: per la stamperia di Carlo Trenti all'insegna di Sant' Antonio, 1783–8.

Bahners, Patrick. '"A place among the English classics": Ranke's *History of the Popes* and its British readers', in Benedikt Stuchtey and Peter Wende (eds), *British and German Historiography, 1750–1950: Traditions, Perceptions and Transfers*. Oxford: Oxford University Press, 2000, 123–57.

Balfour, A.J. *The Foundations of Belief, Being Notes Introductory to the Study of Theology*. London, New York, Bombay: Longmans, Green, and Co., 1895.

Ball, W.P. 'Weismann's views', *NR*, 25 June 1893, 403–4.

—— 'Weismann's views', *NR*, 16 July 1893, 35–6.

—— 'Weismann's views', *NR*, 23 July 1893, 60–1.

Barzun, Jacques. *Berlioz and the Romantic Century*. Boston: Little Brown, 1950.

—— *Clio and the Doctors: Psycho-history, Quanto-history and History*. Chicago and London: University of Chicago Press, 1974.

Bassnett, Susan. *Comparative Literature: A Critical Introduction*. Oxford: Blackwell, 1993.

Bauer, Karin. 'Adorno's Wagner: History and the potential of the artwork', *Cultural Critique* 60 (2005): 68–91.

Beckson, Karl. *London in the 1890s: A Cultural History*. New York: W.W. Norton, 1992.

Beeson, W. 'Ernest Newman's departure from Birmingham', *MT*, 60/95 (1 May 1919): 215.

Bekker, Paul. 'Liszt and his Critics', *MQ*, 22/3 (1936): 277–83.

Bentley, Michael. *Modern Historiography: An Introduction*. London: Routledge, 1999.

Berman, David. *A History of Atheism in Britain: From Hobbes to Russell*. London: Croom Helm, 1988.

Bledsoe, Robert. *Henry Fothergill Chorley: Victorian Journalist*. Aldershot: Ashgate, 1998.

Blissett, William. 'Ernest Newman and English Wagnerism', *ML*, 40/10 (1959): 311–23.

Blom, J.M. and F.J.M. Blom. 'Bertram Dobell and Samuel Bradbury: The literary friendship between a bookseller and an industrial chemist', *English Studies* 79/5 (1998): 447–61.

Bock, Kenneth E. 'The comparative method of anthropology', *Comparative Studies in Society and History* 8/3 (1966), 269–80.

Bohannan, Paul (ed. and abr.). *Researches into the Early History of Mankind*. Chicago: University of Chicago Press, 1964.

Bradbury, S. *Bertram Dobell: Bookseller and Man of Letters*. London: Bertram Dobell, 1909.

Bradlaugh, Charles. 'A plea for atheism', in *Theological Essays*. London: Freethought Publishing Company, 1898, n.p.

Bradley, A.C. *Aristotle and the State*. London: Abbott Hellenica, 1898.

—— *Commentary on Tennyson's 'In memoriam'*. London: Macmillan and Co., 1901.

——*Shakespearean Tragedy: Lectures on Hamlet, Othello, King Lear and Macbeth*. London: Macmillan and Co., 1904.

Brooke, John Hedley. 'Darwin and Victorian Christianity', in Jonathan Hodge and Gregory Radick (eds), *The Cambridge Companion to Darwin*. Cambridge: Cambridge University Press, 2003, 192–213.

Brooke, Tucke (ed.). *Two Essays of James Russell Lowell, On a Certain Condescension in Foreigners and Democracy*. New York: H. Holt & Co., 1927.

Brookes, Christopher. *His Own Man: The Life of Neville Cardus*. London: Methuen, 1985.

Broome, Vincent. *Havelock Ellis: Philosopher of Sex: A Biography*. London: Routledge & Kegan Paul, 1979.

Brown, John. *Letters Upon the Poetry and Music of the Italian Opera*. Edinburgh: Bell and Bradfute and C. Elliot and T. Kay, London, 1789.

Buckle, Henry. *History of Civilisation in England*, 2 vols; vol. I: London: John W. Parker & Son, 1857; vol. II: London: Parker, Son & Bourn, 1861.

Bullock, Philip Ross (ed. and trans.). *The Correspondence of Jean Sibelius and Rosa Newmarch, 1906–1939*. Woodbridge: Boydell Press, 2011.

Bullock, Philip Ross. *Rosa Newmarch and Russian Music in late Nineteenth and Early Twentieth-Century England*. Aldershot: Ashgate, 2009.

Burkhardt, Richard W. 'Introduction', in J.B. Lamarck, *Zoological Philosophy: An Exposition with Regard to the Natural History of Animals*, ed. Richard W. Burkhardt. Chicago: University of Chicago Press, 1984, xv–xxxix.

Burnham, Scott. 'Criticism, faith and the "Idee": A.B. Marx's early reception of Beethoven', *19th-Century Music* 13/3 (1990), 183–92.

Calder-Marshall, Arthur. *Havelock Ellis*. London: Rupert Hart-Davis, 1959.

Calvocoressi, M.D. *Liszt*. Paris: Laurens, 1906.

—— *Glinka: Biographie Critique*. Paris: H. Laurens, 1911.

——'On broadcasting new music', *MT*, 65/976 (1 June 1924): 500–2.

—— *The Principles and Methods of Musical Criticism*. Oxford: Oxford University Press, 1931.

—— 'On Liszt and programme music', *Listener*, 12 September 1934, 437.

Cardus, Neville. *Autobiography*. London: Collins, 1947.

—— 'Ernest Newman', in Herbert van Thal (ed.), *Fanfare for Ernest Newman*. London: Arthur Baker, 1955, 29–37.

—— 'Ernest Newman', *Opera* 10/10 (October 1959), 668–71.

Carpenter, William. *Principles of Mental Physiology*. London: Henry S. King, 1874.

Carr, Jonathan. *The Wager Clan*. London: Faber and Faber, 2007.

Carty, T.J. *A Dictionary of Literary Pseudonyms in the English Language*. London: Mansell Publishing Limited, 1995.

Cecil, Hugh Mortimer. 'The illusion of progress', *Agnostic Annual*, 1898, 29–32.

—— *Pseudo-philosophy at the end of the Nineteenth Century*. Watford: University Press, 1897.

Chadwick, Owen. *The Secularization of the European Mind in the Nineteenth Century*. Cambridge: Cambridge University Press, 1975.

Chamberlain, Houston Stewart. *Richard Wagner*. Munich: Bruckmann, 1895. Trans. G. Ainslie Hight. London: J.M. Dent, Philadelphia: J.P. Lippincott, 1897.

Chantovoine, Jean. *Liszt*. Paris: Libraire Félix Alcan, 1910.

Chorley, Henry F. *Thirty Years' Musical Recollections,* ed. Ernest Newman. New York: Knopf, 1926.

Collini, Stefan. *Public Moralists: Political Thought and Intellectual Life in Britain, 1850–1930*. Oxford: Clarendon, 1991.

Collini, Stefan, Donald Winch and John Burrow (eds), *That Noble Science of Politics: A Study in Nineteenth-Century Intellectual History*. Cambridge: Cambridge University Press, 1983, 207–75.

Collins, Sarah. '"Never out of date and never modern": Aesthetic democracy, radical music criticism and *The Sackbut*', *ML* 95/3 (2014): 404–28.

Combarieu, Jules. 'Les rapports de la musique et de la poésie, considérées au point de vue de l'expression', dissertation, University of Paris (1893).

Comte, Auguste. *General View of Positivism* [being the Preface to Part III of the Second system, *Système de Politique Positive*]. Paris: Republic of the West-Order and Progress, 1848.

Conway, Martin. *The Woodcutters of the Netherlands in the Fifteenth Century*. Cambridge: Cambridge University Press, 1884.

—— *Dawn of Art in the Ancient World: An Archaeological Sketch*. London: Percival, 1891.

Cook, Nicholas. *The Schenker Project: Culture, Race, and Music Theory in fin de siècle Vienna*. Oxford: Oxford University Press, 2007.

Cooke, Bill. *The Gathering of Infidels: A Hundred Years of the Rationalist Press Association*. Amherst, NY: Prometheus Books, 2004.

Corder, Frederick. *Ferencz (François) Liszt*. London: Kegan Paul, Trench, Trubner and Co. Ltd, 1925.

Crook, D.P. *Benjamin Kidd: Portrait of a Social Darwinist*. Cambridge: Cambridge University Press, 1984.

Crowest, Frederick J. *Phases of Musical England*. London: Remington and Co., 1881.

Cummings, Paul. 'The pivotal role of Hans Richter in the London Wagner Festival of 1877', *MQ*, 98/4 (2016): 395–447.

da Sousa Correa, Delia. *George Eliot, Music and Victorian Culture*. London: Palgrave Macmillan, 2003.

de Pourtàles, Guy. *La vie de Franz Liszt: Un homme 'd'amour*. Paris: Gallimard, 1925.

de Törne, Bengt. *Sibelius: A Close-Up*. Boston: Houghton Mifflin Co, 1937.

Daniels, Robin. *Conversations with Cardus*. London: Victor Gollancz, 1976.

Davison, Alan. 'Liszt Among the Degenerates: On the Vagaries on Being a Musical Genius c. 1890–c. 1935', in James Deaville and Michael Saffle (eds), *Liszt Legacies* [Analecta Listziana IV, Franz Liszt Studies No. 15]. Hillside, NY: Pendragon Press, 2014, 236–58

Deathridge, John, *Wagner Beyond Good and Evil*. Berkeley: University of California Press, 2008.

—— 'Waiting for Wagner: Reluctant musicology, radical philosophy, and the rescue of a fraught legacy', *Opera Quarterly* 30/2–3 (2014): 267–85.

Deaville, James. 'Liszt and the Twentieth Century', in Kenneth Hamilton (ed.), *The Cambridge Companion to Liszt*. Cambridge: Cambridge University Press, 2005, 28–56.

Decker, Clarence R. *The Victorian Conscience*. Westport, CT: Greenwood Press, 1952.

Dekkers, Odin. 'Robertson and Shaw: "an unreasonable friendship"', *English Literature in Transition* 39/4 (1996): 431–9.

——*J.M. Robertson: Rationalist and Literary Critic*. Aldershot: Ashgate, 1998.

—— 'Walter Matthew Gallichan: fiction and freethought in the 1890s', *English Studies* 83/5 (2002), 407–22.

Democritus (pseud. Matthew Gallichan). 'Biology with a snuffle', *FR*, 1 July 1896, 337–53.

Dobell, Bertram. *Rosemary and Pansies*. London: Dobell, 1904.

——*Catalogue of Books Printed for Private Circulation*. London: Bertram Dobell, 1906.

—— *The Laureate of Pessimism: A Sketch of the Life and Character of James Thomson ('B.V.') author of 'The City of Dreadful Night'*. London: Dobell, 1910.

Dobell, Percy J. 'Mr Dobell's collection: sale of privately printed books and pamphlets', the *Times*, 29 November 1913, 7.

—— 'In memoriam, Bertram Dobell, 1842–1914'. London: Dobell, 1915.

Dobell, Robert J. 'Bertram Dobell and T.J. Wise', *The Book Collector* 19/3 (1970): 348–55.

Doctor, Jennifer. *The BBC and Ultra-Modern Music, 1922–1936: Shaping a Nation's Taste*. Cambridge: Cambridge University Press, 1999.

Donovan, Robert A. 'The method of Arnold's Essays in Criticism', *Proceedings of the Modern Language Association* 17/5 (1956): 922–31.

Drabkin, William. 'Heinrich Schenker', in Thomas Christensen (ed.), *The Cambridge History of Western Music Theory*. Cambridge: Cambridge University Press, 2002, 812–43.

Drummond, Henry. *The Lowell Lectures on the Ascent of Man*. London: Hodder and Stoughton, 1894.

——*Natural Law in the Spiritual World*. London: Hodder and Stoughton, 1883.

Dyson, A. E. 'The technique of debunking', *Twentieth Century* 157 (1955): 244–56.

Dyson, George. *The Progress of Music*. London: Oxford University Press/ Humphrey Milford, 1932.

E. B. 'The Life of Richard Wagner. Vol. IV: 1866–1883', *ML* 29/2 (1948): 185–7.

Eagleton, Terry. *The Function of Criticism: From 'The Spectator' to Post-Structuralism*. London and New York: Verso, 1996.

Easter, Ruth E. 'Music criticism: a study of the criteria and techniques of the journalistic critic, as seen in the critiques of G.B. Shaw, Ernest Newman, and Neville Cardus', MA thesis, State University College, Potsdam, New York (1972).

Editor's choice. *British Medical Journal* 299 (22 July 1989): n.p.

Ellis, Havelock. *Man and Woman: A Study of Human Secondary Sexual Characteristics*. London: W. Scott, 1894.

Ellis, William Ashton (trans.). *The Life of Richard Wagner*, 6 vols. London: Kegan Paul, Trench, Trübner & Co., 1900–1908.

——*Richard Wagner's Prose Works*. London: Kegan Paul, Trench, Trübner, 1899.

Elsen, Albert, E. *Rodin*. New York: Museum of Modern Art, 1967.

Engel, Carl. 'Views and reviews', *MQ*, 13/4 (October 1927): 646–62.

——'Views and reviews', *MQ*, 21/2 (April 1935): 230–40.

——'Views and reviews', *MQ*, 27/2 (April 1941): 243–8.

Evans, Edwin. 'Objectivity in contemporary criticism', *MT*, 66/990 (1 August 1925): 692–5.

——'The plain man and Wagner', *Musical Mirror and Fanfare*, September 1931, 253–5.

Evans, Richard J. *Cosmopolitan Islanders: British Historians and the European Continent*. Cambridge: Cambridge University Press, 2009.

Farmer, Henry George. *Bernard Shaw's Sister and her Friends: A New Angle on G.B.S.* Leiden: E.J.Brill, 1959.

——'Ernest Newman', *Freethinker*, 16 June 1961, 32.

Fauser, Annegret. 'The scholar behind the medal: Edward J. Dent (1876–1957) and the politics of music history', *Journal of the Royal Musical Association* 139/2 (2014): 235–60.

Fifield, Christopher. *True Artist and Friend: A Biography of Hans Richter*. Oxford: Clarendon, 1993.

Findlater, Richard (ed.). *Author! Author!: A Selection from The Author, the Journal of the Society of Authors since 1890*. London: Faber & Faber, 1984.

Forkel, Johann Nicolas. *Ueber Johann Sebastian Bachs Leben, Kunst und Kunstwerke*. Leipzig: Hoffmeister und Kühnel, 1802.

Forman, Alfred. *Wagner's 'Parsifal' in English Verse*. London: private subscription, 1899.

Franklin, Peter. 'Sibelius in Britain', in Daniel M. Grimley (ed.), *The Cambridge Companion to Sibelius*. Cambridge: Cambridge University Press, 2004, 182–95.

Fuller Maitland, J.A. 'Musical literature', *NQMR*, February 1896, 192–3.

G. A. 'The Life of Richard Wagner. Vol. II: 1848–1860', *ML*, 18/2 (1937): 194–6.

Galloway, W.J. *The Operatic Problem*. London: John Long, 1902.

—— *Musical England*. London: New York, John Lane, 1910.

Gannon, Franklin Reid. *The British Press and Germany 1836–1939*. Oxford: Clarendon, 1971.

Garraty, John A. *The Nature of Biography*. London: Jonathan Cape, 1958.

Gay, Peter. *Freud for Historians*. Oxford: Oxford University Press, 1985.

Gayley, Charles Mill and Fred Newton Scott. *An Introduction to the Methods and Materials of Literary Criticism*. Boston: Ginn & Company, 1899.

Gigante, Denise (ed.). *The Great Age of the English Essay*. New Haven: Yale University Press, 2008.

Goldsmith, Oliver. *A Prospect of Society by Oliver Goldsmith Being the Earliest Form of his Poem from the Traveller*. London: Dobell, 1902.

Gooch, G.P. *History and Historians in the Nineteenth Century*. Boston: Beacon Hill, 1965.

Graves, Charles L. *Hubert Parry: His Life and Works*, 2 vols. London: Macmillan and Co., 1926.

Gray, Cecil. 'The task of criticism', *S* 1/1 (1920): 9–13.

—— 'A critique of pure cant: being an earnest enquiry into the nature of the new man', *S* 1/3 (1920): 112–15.

Graziano, Amy and Julene K. Johnson. 'Richard Wallaschek's nineteenth-century contribution to the psychology of music', *Music Perception* 23/4 (2006): 293–304.

Grew, Eva Mary. '"E.N.": A recollection of his Birmingham days', *MOMTR*, October 1925, 46–8.

—— 'Ernest Newman: English music critic', *S*, November 1928, 113–28.

—— 'Ernest Newman: His life and opinions', *British Musician*, January 1934, 4–6; February 1934, 36–8; March 1934, 54–6; April 1934, 86–8; May 1934, 108–10; June 1934, 126–8; July 1934, 153–4; August 1934, 176–8; September 1934, 203–5; October 1934, 230–1; November 1934, 248–52; December 1934, 275–77.

Grew, Sydney. 'Mr Ernest Newman', *Edgbastonia* 31 (July 1911): 121–30.

—— 'Ernest Newman: Twenty-five years of reading his writings', *British Musician*, July 1931, 154–6; August 1931, 167–8; September 1931, 192–7; October 1931, 208–10; November 1931, 232–4; July 1932, 151–5.

Grey, Thomas S. *Wagner's Musical Prose: Texts and Contexts*. Cambridge: Cambridge University Press, 1995.

Gross, John. *The Rise and Fall of the Man of Letters: Aspects of English Literary Life since 1800*. London: Weidenfeld and Nicolson, 1969.

Grosskurth, Phyllis. *Havelock Ellis: A Biography*. New York: Alfred A. Knopf, 1980.

Gurney, Edmund. *The Power of Sound*. London: Smith, Elder and Co., 1880.

H. D., 'Poetry and music', *NR*, 23 October 1892, 270.

—— 'Poetry and music: a rejoinder', *NR*, 13 November 1892, 309.

H. M. 'A handbook to biography', *Listener*, 24 April 1929, 559.

Hadow, W.H. *Studies in Modern Music*. London: Seeley, 1893.

Hailey, Christopher. 'The Paul Bekker collection in the Yale University Library', *Notes*, second series, 51 (1994): 13–21.

Hanslick, Eduard. *Hanslick's Music Criticisms*, ed. and trans. Henry Pleasants. New York: Dover Publications, Inc., 1978.

Heckert, Deborah. 'Schoenberg, Roger Fry and the Emergence of a Critical Language for the Reception of Musical Modernism in Britain, 1912–1914', in Matthew Riley (ed.), *British Music and Modernism, 1895–1960*. Aldershot: Ashgate, 2010, 49–66.

Hergenham, L.T. 'The reception of George Meredith's early novels', *Nineteenth-Century Fiction* 19/3 (1964): 214.

Hermelink, Heinrich. *Das Christentum in der Menschheitsgeschichte*, vol. II. Stuttgart: Metzlersche Verlagsbuchhandlung, 1955.

Hesketh, Ian. *The Science of History in Victorian Britain: Making the Past Speak*. London: Pickering & Chatto, 2011.

Heyck, T.W. *The Transformation of Intellectual Life in Victorian England*. London: Croom Helm, 1982.

Heyworth, Peter (ed.). *Berlioz, Romantic and Classic: Writings by Ernest Newman*. London: Victor Gollancz Ltd., 1972.

Hight, George Ainslie. *Richard Wagner*, 2 vols. London: Arrowsmith, 1925.

Hill, Ralph. 'On Wagner, Hanslick, and Mr Newman', *S*, October 1931, 18–24.

—— *Reflected Music and Other Essays*. London: Methuen, 1930.

Hiller, H. Croft. *Against Dogma and Free-Will and for Weismann*. London: Williams and Norgate, c. 1893.

—— 'Spencer or Weismann?', *NR*, 30 April 1893, 277–9.

—— 'Weismannism and its adversaries', *NR*, 28 May 1883, 339–41.

—— 'Weismannism and sociology: a reply', *NR*, 18 June 1893, 388–90.

—— 'Weismannism and sociology: a further reply', *NR*, 2 July 1893, 10–11.

—— 'Weismannism and sociology: a further reply', *NR*, 23 July 1893, 58–9.

Hobson, Harold, Phillip Knightley and Leonard Russell, *The Pearl of Days: An Intimate Memoir of The Sunday Times, 1822–1972*. London: Hamish Hamilton, 1972.

Hollinrake, Roger. 'Nietzsche, Wagner and Ernest Newman', *ML*, 41/3 (1960): 245–55.

Holloway, John. *The Victorian Sage: Studies in Argument,* 2nd edn. New York: W.W. Norton, 1965.

Hope-Wallace, Philip. 'E.N.', *MT*, 104/1450 (1 December 1963): 870–1.

Howes, Frank. *The English Musical Renaissance.* London: Secker & Warburg, 1966.

Hueffer, Francis. *Richard Wagner and the Music of the Future.* London: Chapman and Hall, 1874.

—— George Bernard Shaw, *The Perfect Wagnerite.* London: Grant Richards, 1898.

Huneker, James. *Franz Liszt.* New York: Charles Scribner's, 1924.

Hurn, Philip Dutton. 'Wagner's "Mein Leben"' [Letter to the editor], *ST*, 2 June 1929, 7.

—— 'Mein Leben', *ST*, 16 June 1929, 7.

Hurn, Philip Dutton and Waverley Lewis Root, *The Truth About Wagner.* London: Cassell and Company Ltd., 1930.

Huxley, Aldous. 'Music and machinery', *Weekly Westminster Gazette*, 29 April 1922. Reproduced in Michael Allis (ed.), *Temporaries and Eternals: The Music Criticism of Aldous Huxley, 1922–1923.* Newcastle: Cambridge Scholars Publishing, 2013, 71–3.

Iggers, Georg G. *The German Conception of History.* Middletown, CT: Wesleyan University Press, 1966.

—— *Historiography in the Twentieth Century: From Scientific Objectivity to the Postmodern Challenge.* Hanover: University Press of New England, 1997.

Irvine, David. *'Parsifal' and Wagner's Christianity.* London: H. Grevel and Co,. 1899.

Jackson, Holbrook. *The Eighteen Nineties: A Review of Art and Ideas at the Close of the Nineteenth Century.* London: Cresset, 1988 [1913].

Jacobs, Robert L. 'The Life of Richard Wagner, Vol. 4', *MT*, 89/1259 (1 January 1948): 16, 19.

Jahn, Otto. *The Life of Mozart,* trans. Pauline D. Townsend, 3 vols. London: Novello, 1992 [Leipzig, 1856–59].

Johnson, George H. 'The comparative method of study', *Science* 21/529 (March 1893): 155–6.

Jones, Greta. *Social Darwinism and English Thought: The Interaction between Biological and Social Theory.* Brighton: Harvester Press, 1980.

Kapp, Julius. *Franz Liszt: Eine Biographie.* Berlin: Newman, Schuster & Loeffler, 1909.

—— *Richard Wagner: Eine Biographie.* Berlin: Newman, Schuster & Loeffler, 1910.

Karnes, Kevin C. *Music, Criticism, and the Challenge of History: Shaping Modern Musical Thought in Late Nineteenth-Century Vienna.* Oxford: Oxford University Press, 2008.

Katz, Israel J. *Henry George Farmer and the First International Congress of Arab Music (Cairo 1932).* Leiden: Brill, 2015.

Kendall, Paul Murray. *The Art of Biography*. London: George Allen & Unwin Ltd., 1965.

Kennedy, Kate and Trudi Tate. 'Literature and music of the First World War', *First World War Studies* 2/1 (2011): 1–6.

Kenyon, John. *The History Men: The Historical Profession in England since the Renaissance*. London: Weidenfeld and Nicolson, 1983.

Kerman, Joseph. *Musicology*. London: Fontana, 1985.

Kidd, Benjamin. *Social Evolution*. London and New York: Macmillan and Co., 1894.

Klein, Hermann. *The Golden Age of Opera*. London: George Routledge & Sons, 1933.

Korsten, Frans. '"An heretical bookworm": Bertram Dobell's life and career', *English Studies* 81/4 (2000): 305–27.

La Mara [Marie Lipsius] (ed.) *Franz Liszt's Briefe*, 2nd edn. Leipzig: Breitkopf & Härtel, 1900.

—— *Liszt und die Frauen*. Leipzig: Breitkopf & Härtel, 1911.

Lamarck, J.B. *Zoological Philosophy: An Exposition with Regard to the Natural History of Animals* (1809), ed. Richard W. Burkhardt. Chicago: University of Chicago Press, 1984.

Lambert, Constant. 'Heads I win, tails you lose', *New Statesman and Nation*, 12 January 1935, 46–7.

Landormy, Paul. *A History of Music*, trans. Frederick H. Martens. New York: Charles Scribner's, 1927.

Lang, Paul H. 'Mr Newman tries to Debunk Liszt', *SR*, 25 May 1935, 18.

Langlois, Ch. V. and Ch. Seignobos, *Introduction to the Study of History*, trans. G.G. Berry. London: Duckworth & Co., 1925.

Laurence, Dan H. (ed.). *Shaw's Music: The Complete Musical Criticism of Bernard Shaw vol. III: 1893–1950*. London: The Bodley Head, 1981.

Le Gallienne, Richard. *Rudyard Kipling: A Criticism*. London and New York: John Lane, The Bodley Head, 1900.

Legány, Dezső. 'Some problems in Liszt research', *Journal of the American Liszt Society* 7 (1980): 17–34.

—— 'New directions in Liszt research', *Journal of the American Liszt Society* 20 (1986): 125–37.

Lenrow, Elbert. Review of *The Man Liszt* in *Journal of Nervous & Mental Disease* 82/6 (1935): 693–5.

Leroy, L. Archier. *Wagner's Music Drama of the Ring*. London: Noel Douglas, 1924.

Linton, E. Lynn. 'Professor Henry Drummond's Discovery', *CR*, September 1894, 448–57.

Lodge, Oliver. *Past Years: An Autobiography*. London: Hodder and Stoughton, 1931.

Lorimer, Rowland. 'The socioeconomy of scholarly and cultural book publishing', *Media, Culture and Society*, April 1993, 203–16.

Lucas, John. *Thomas Beecham: An Obsession with Music*. Woodbridge: Boydell Press, 2008.

Lynch, Arthur. *Human Documents: Character-Sketches of Representative Men and Women of the Time*. London: Bertram Dobell, 1896.

MacCunn, John. *Six Radical Thinkers*. London: Edward Arnold, 1907.

Macintosh, Robert. *From Comte to Benjamin Kidd: The Appeal to Biology of Evolution for Human Guidance*. London: Macmillan and Co., Limited, 1899.

MacKillop, Ian. *The British Ethical Societies*. Cambridge: Cambridge University Press, 1986.

Maine, Basil. 'Personalities among Musical Critics. IX: Ernest Newman', *MT*, 68/1007 (1 January 1927): 27–8.

—— *Behold These Daniels, Being Studies of Contemporary Music Critics*. London: H. and W. Brown, 1928.

Makari, George. *Revolution in Mind: The Creation of Psychoanalysis*. Melbourne: Melbourne University Press, 2008.

Mallett, Phillip (ed.). *Kipling Considered*. London: The Macmillan Press Ltd, 1989.

Mann, William. 'Review of books', *ML*, 6/4 (October 1925): 371–3.

Marsh, Joss Lutz. '"Bibliolatry" and "bible-smashing": G.W. Foote, George Meredith, and the heretic trope of the book', *Victorian Studies* 34/3 (1991): 315–36.

Marx, Adolph Bernhard. *Gluck und die Oper*, 2 vols. Berlin: O. Janke, 1863.

Maurois, André. *Aspects de la biographie*. Paris: B. Grasset, 1928.

—— *Aspects of Biography*, translated by S.C. Roberts. Cambridge: Cambridge University Press, 1929.

McCabe, Joseph. *Modern Rationalism: Being a Sketch of the Progress of the Rationalistic Spirit in the Nineteenth Century*. London: Watts and Co., 1909.

McColl, Sandra. *Music Criticism in Vienna 1896–1897: Critically Moving Forms*. Oxford: Clarendon Press, 1996.

McDonnell, Siobhan. 'Ernest Newman's philosophy of music criticism', MA thesis, McMaster University (1989).

Melody. 'Poetry and music', *NR*, 20 November 1892, 362.

Miles, Paul. 'Beethoven sketches', *Gramophone*, 29 October 1929, 12.

Mill, John Stuart. *On Liberty*. London: John W. Parker, 1859.

Moore, Gregory. 'Art and evolution: Nietzsche's physiological aesthetics', *British Journal for the History of Philosophy* 10/1 (2002): 109–26.

Morton, Peter. *The Vital Science: Biology and the Literary Imagination, 1860–1900*. London, Boston: Allen & Unwin, 1984.

Mugglestone, Erica. 'Adler's "The scope, method, and aim of musicology" (1885): an English translation with an historico-analytical commentary', *Yearbook for Traditional Music* 13 (1981): 1–21.

Muir, Stephen. '"About as wild and barbaric as well could be imagined …": The critical reception of Rimsky-Korsakov in nineteenth-century England', *ML*, 93/4 (2012): 513–42.

Nash, David S. *Secularism, Art and Freedom*. Leicester; New York: Leicester University Press, 1992.

Newman, Vera. *Ernest Newman: A Memoir by his Wife*. London: Putnam, 1963.

Nicolson, Harold. *The Development of English Biography*, 3rd edn. London: The Hogarth Press, 1947.

Nordau, Max. *Entartung*. Berlin: C. Duncker, 1892. English translation *Degeneration*, trans. George L. Moss. New York: Howard Fertig, 1968.

Offer, John. 'An examination of Spencer's sociology of music and its impact on music historiography in Britain', *International Review of the Aesthetics and Sociology of Music*, 14/1 (June 1983): 33–52.

Oldroyd, D.R. *Darwinian Impacts: An Introduction to the Darwinian Revolution*. Sydney: University of New South Wales Press, 1980.

Parry, Hubert. *The Evolution of the Art of Music*. London: Kegan Paul, Trench, Trübner, 1896.

Passmore, John. *A Hundred Years of Philosophy*. London: Gerald Duckworth & Co., 1966.

Pater, Walter. *The Renaissance: Studies in Art and Poetry*. London: Macmillan and Co. Ltd, 1910 [1873].

Pekacz, Jolanta. 'Memory, history and meaning: musical biography and its discontents', *Journal of Musicological Research* 23/1 (2004): 39–80.

—— (ed.). *Musical Biography: Towards New Paradigms*. Aldershot: Ashgate, 2006.

Peterson, Linda H. 'Sage writing', in Herbert F. Tucker (ed.), *A Companion to Victorian Literature and Culture*. Oxford: Blackwell, 1999, 373–87.

Planelli, Antonio. *Dell' Opera in Musica*. Naples: D. Campo, 1772.

Poplawski, Paul. *English Literature in Context*. New York: Cambridge University Press, 2008.

Posnett, H.M. *Comparative Literature*. London: Kegan Paul, Trench & Co., 1886.

—— 'The science of comparative literature', *CR*, June 1901, 855–72.

Potter, Pamela M. 'Musicology under Hitler: New sources in context', *Journal of the American Musicological Society* 49/1 (Spring 1996): 70–113.

—— *Most German of the Arts: Musicology and Society from the Weimar Republic to the end of Hitler's Reich*. New Haven: Yale University Press, 1998.

Purkis, Charlotte. '"Leader of fashion in musical thought": The importance of Rosa Newmarch in the context of turn-of-the-century British music appreciation', in Peter Horton and Bennett Zon (eds), *Nineteenth-Century British Music Studies* vol. 3. Aldershot: Ashgate, 2003, 4–19.

—— 'Musical writing and Paterian aestheticism, or, the "ravished pen" and the "temperamental critic"'. Conference presentation, Music in Nineteenth-Century Britain, University of Nottingham (8 July 2005).

Raabe, Peter. *Liszts Leben*. Stuttgart: Cotta, 1931.

Ramann, Lina. *Franz Liszt als Künstler und Mensch*, 3 vols. Leipzig, 1880–94.

Raynor, Henry. 'Ernest Newman and the science of criticism', *MMR*, January–February 1960, 19–27.

Rectenwald, Michael. *Nineteenth-Century British Secularism: Science, Religion, and Literature*. Basingstoke, Hants: Palgrave Macmillan, 2016.

Rehding, Alexander. 'Inventing Liszt's Life: Early Biography and Autobiography', in Kenneth Hamilton (ed.), *The Cambridge Companion to Liszt*. Cambridge: Cambridge University Press, 2005, 14–27.

Reid, Charles. *The Music Monster: A Biography of James William Davison*. London: Quartet Books, 1984.

Remak, Henry H. 'Comparative Literature, its Definition and Function', in Newton P. Stallknecht and Horst Frenz (eds), *Comparative Literature: Method and Perspective*. Carbondale: Southern Illinois Press, 1968): 3–37.

Richards, Francis (ed.). *At Scotland Yard: Being the Experiences during Twenty-Seven Years' Service of John Sweeney*. London: Grant Richards, 1904.

Roberts, James B. and Alexander G. Skutt. *The Boxing Register*. London: McBooks Press, 1999.

Roberts, William. *The Book-hunter in London*. London: Elliot Stock, 1895.

Robertson, John M. 'The music of the future', *Progress* 4 (December 1884): 278–84.

—— 'Edgar Allen Poe [part 2]', *Our Corner* 6/4 (October 1885): 204–13.

—— *Essays Towards a Critical Method*. London: T. Fisher Unwin, 1889.

—— 'Literature in 1890', *NR*, 28 December 1890, 402–3.

—— 'Critical chat: the Quintessence of Ibsenism', *NR*, 6 December 1891, 359.

—— 'Tennyson', *NR*, 16 October 1892, 241–2.

—— Editorial note to Melody's 'Poetry and music', *NR*, 20 November 1892, 362.

—— 'Weismannism and sociology', *NR*, 4 June 1893, 353–4.

—— 'Weismannism and sociology', *NR*, 11 June 1893, 371–3.

—— 'Weismann's views', *NR*, 9 July 1893, 20–1.

—— 'Reply to the foregoing', *NR*, 16 July 1893, 36–7.

—— 'Concerning magazines in general and this one in particular', *FR*, October 1893, 1–10.

—— *Buckle and his Critics: A Study in Sociology*. London: Swan Sonnenschein & Co., 1895.

—— 'The problem of publishing', *FR*, May 1895, 97–112.

—— *New Essays Towards a Critical Method*. London: John Lane, 1897.

—— 'Current pseudo-philosophy', *UMFR*, May 1897, 190–6.

—— 'Concerning mares' nests': An open letter, *UMFR*, March 1898, 611–16.

—— 'Concerning musical criticism', *SR*, 28 January 1899, 108–9.

—— *Letters on Reasoning*. London: Watts & Co., 1902.

—— *Did Shakespeare write 'Titus Andronicus'?: A Study in Elizabethan Literature*. London: Watts and Co., 1905.

—— *Rationalism*. London: Constable and Company Ltd, 1912.

—— 'Criticism and science', *North American Review* 209/762 (May 1919): 690–6.

—— *A History of Freethought in the Nineteenth Century*, 2 vols. London: Watts and Co., 1929.

—— *A History of Freethought Ancient and Modern to the Period of the French Revolution*, 4th edn., rev. and expanded, 2 vols. London: Dawsons of Pall Mall, 1969.

Rodmell, Paul. *Opera in the British Isles, 1875–1918*. Aldershot: Ashgate, 2013.

Rolland, Romain. *Vie de Beethoven*. Paris: Hachette, 1927. First published as *Beethoven* in 1903.

Room, Adrian. *A Dictionary of Pseudonyms and their Origins, with Stories of Name Changes*. Chicago: St James Press, 1989.

Rosenthal, Harold. *Two Centuries of Opera at Covent Garden*. London: Putnam, 1958.

Royle, Edward. *Victorian Infidels: the Origins of the British Secularist Movement, 1791–1866*. Manchester: Manchester University Press; Totowa, NJ: Rowman & Littlefield, 1974.

—— *Radicals, Secularists and Republicans: Popular Freethought in Britain, 1866–1915*. Manchester: Manchester University Press; Totowa, NJ: Rowman & Littlefield, 1980.

Runciman, John F. 'The gentle art of musical criticism', *New Review* 12 (January–June 1895), 612–24.

——[signed] J.F.R. 'Gluck', *SR*, 11 January 1896, 36–8.

—— 'Concerning musical criticism', *SR*, 28 January 1899, 108–9.

—— 'After Wagner, books about Wagner', *SR*, 29 July 1899, 132–3.

—— 'Gluck's Orpheus at Cambridge', *SR*, 17 May 1890, 606–7.

—— 'Musical criticism and the critics', *FoR*, August 1894, 170–83.

—— *Richard Wagner: Composer of Operas*. London: G. Bell and Sons, Ltd., 1913.

Russell, John. *The Task of Rationalism*. London: Watts & Co., 1910.

Sackville West, Edward. 'The Task of Egeria', *Spectator*, 7 December 1934, 888.

Saffle, Michael. 'Liszt research since 1936: a bibliographic survey' *Acta Musicologica* 58/2 (1986): 231–81.

—— 'The "Liszt year" 1986 and recent Liszt research', *Acta Musicologcia* 59/3 (1987): 271–99.

Salaman, Charles Kensington 'On musical criticism', *Proceedings of the Musical Association*, second session, 1875–1876, 1–15.

Sampson, George. 'Wagner with a difference,' *Bookman*, July 1914, 172–3.

Sanders, Alan (ed.) *Walter Legge: Words and Music*. London: Duckworth, 1998.

Scaife, Nigel. 'British music criticism in a new era: studies in critical thought, 1894–1945', DPhil thesis, University of Oxford (1994).

Schenker, Heinrich. *Beethovens neunte Sinfonie*. Vienna: Universal Edition, 1912.

Schwarzkopf, Elisabeth. *On and Off the Record: A Memoir of Walter Legge*. London: Faber and Faber, 1982.

Seeger, Charles. 'On the principles of musicology', *MQ*, 10/2 (April 1924): 244–50.

Sessa, Anne Dzamba. *Richard Wagner and the English*. London: Associated University Presses, 1979.

——'At Wagner's Shrine: British and American Wagnerians', in David C. Large and William Weber (eds), *Wagnerism in European Culture and Politics*. Ithaca and London: Cornell University Press, 1984, 246–77.

Sharp, Geoffrey. 'Ernest Newman', *MR* 21/3 (February 1960): 77–8.

Shaw, George Bernard, *Collected Letters*, ed. Dan H. Laurence, 4 vols. London: M. Reinhardt, 1965–88.

——'Italian opera and the French Dickens', *The World*, 20 August 1890, in Dan H. Lawrence (ed.), *Shaw's Music: The Complete Musical Criticism of Bernard Shaw*, 2nd rev. edn. London: The Bodley Head, 1981, vol. II, 151–7, 152–3.

—— *The Perfect Wagnerite: A Commentary on Niblung's Rings*. London: Grant Richards, 1898.

—— 'Some imperfect Wagnerites', *The Critic*, supplement, 28 January 1899, in Dan H. Laurence (ed), *Shaw's Music: The Complete Musical Criticism of Bernard Shaw, vol. III, 1893–1950*, 546–53.

—— *The Quintessence of Ibsenism*, 3rd edn. London: Constable, 1926 [1891].

—— 'Recent Wagner books', *Daily Chronicle*, 8 June 1899, in Dan H. Laurence (ed), *Shaw's Music: The Complete Musical Criticism of Bernard Shaw, vol. III, 1893–1950*. London: The Bodley Head, 1981, 560–9.

——*Shaw's Music: The Complete Musical Criticism of George Bernard Shaw*, ed. Dan H. Laurence, 2nd rev. edn. London: The Bodley Head, 1981.

Shawe-Taylor, Desmond, *Covent Garden*. London: Max Parish and Co. and New York: Chanticleer Press, 1948.

Shelley, P.B., *The Necessity of Atheism* ed. Nicolas Walter. London: G.W. Foote & Co., 1998 [Originally published anonymously in 1811].

—— *Alastor: Or, The Spirit of Solitude: And Other Poems* [The Shelley Society's Publications: Second Series, Number 3]. London: Reeves and Turner, with Dobell, 1885.

Sirius. 'Some reflections on music and its meanings', *NR*, 27 November, 344.

Sitwell, Sacherevell. *Liszt*. London: Faber, 1943.

Sloper, L. A. [untitled], *The Christian Science Monitor Weekly Magazine*, 7 August 1935, 11.

Small, I.C. 'Vernon Lee, association and "impressionist criticism"', *British Journal of Aesthetics* 17/2 (1977): 178–84.

Smith, Goldwin. *Guesses at the Riddle of Existence, and Other Essays in Kindred Subjects*. London and New York: Macmillan, 1897.

Solomon, Maynard. *Beethoven*. New York: Schirmer, 1977.

Spencer, Herbert. *Social Statics or The Conditions Essential to Human Happiness, Specified, and the First of them Developed*. London: John Chapman, 1851.

—— 'The Origin and Function of Music', *Fraser's Magazine* 56, October 1857, 396–408.

—— *First Principles*. London: Williams and Norgate, 1862.

—— *Principles of Biology*, 2 vols. London: Appleton, 1864.

—— *Principles of Psychology*, 2 vols. London: Williams and Norgate, 1870.

—— *Principles of Sociology*, 3 vols. London: Appleton, 1874–5.

—— 'The inadequacy of natural selection', *CR*, February 1893, 153–66, and March 1893, 434–56.

—— 'A rejoinder to Professor Weismann', *CR*, December 1893, 893–912.

—— *Principles of Ethics,* 2 vols. London: Appleton, 1897.

—— *Facts and Comments.* London: Williams & Norgate, 1902.

Spotts, Frederic. *Bayreuth: A History of the Wagner Festival.* New Haven, CT: Yale University Press, 1994.

Stainer, John. 'The principles of musical criticism', *Proceedings of the Royal Musical Association*, seventh session, 1880–1, 35–52.

Stallknecht, Newton P. and Horst Frenz (eds). *Comparative Literature: Method and Perspective.* Carbondale: Southern Illinois Press, 1961.

Stanford, C.V. 'Some aspects of musical criticism in England', *FoR*, June 1894, 826–31.

Stannard, David E. *Shrinking History: On Freud and the Failure of Psychohistory.* New York and Oxford: Oxford University Press, 1980.

Steane, John B. 'English opera criticism between the wars 3: Newman of "The Sunday Times"', *Opera*, February 1982, 126–31; April 1982, 369–75; June 1982, 582–9.

Stocking, George W. *Victorian Anthropology.* New York and London: The Free Press, 1987.

Stricker, Salomon. *Du langage et de la musique.* Paris: Félix Alcan, 1885.

Stuart, Charles. 'Fifty Years of Music Criticism', *Tempo* 19 (1951): 12–18.

The Sunday Times: A Pictorial Biography of One of the World's Great Newspapers. London: Thomson House, 1961.

Taine, Hippolyte. *On Intelligence,* trans. T.D. Haye. London: L. Reeve, 1871.

—— *History of English Literature,* trans. H. Van Laun, 2nd edn. Edinburgh: Edmonston and Douglas, 1972 [1864].

Taylor, Stainton de B. *Two Centuries of Music in Liverpool: A Scrap-book of Information Concerning Musical Activities both Professional and Amateur.* Liverpool: Rockliff Brothers Limited, c. 1974.

Taylor, Timothy D. 'The commodification of music at the dawn of the era of "mechanical music"', *Ethnomusicology* 51/2 (2007): 281–305.

Tellenbach, Marie-Elisabeth. 'Psychoanalysis and the historiocritical method: On Maynard Solomon's image of Beethoven', *Beethoven Newsletter* vols 8 and 9 (1993–4): 84–92; 119–27.

Terry, Charles Sanford. *Bach: A Biography,* 2nd rev. edn. Oxford: Oxford University Press, 1933.

Thayer, A.W. *Ludwig van Beethovens Leben,* 3 vols. Berlin: Schneider, 1866; Weber, 1872–79.

Tribe, David. *100 Years of Freethought.* London: Elek Books Limited, 1967.

Trollope, Anthony. *An Autobiography* with an introduction by Charles Morgan. London: Williams and Norgate Ltd., 1946 [1883].

Turing, Penelope. *New Bayreuth.* London: St Ann's Press, 1969.

Turner, W.J. *Musical Meanderings.* London: Methuen & Co. Ltd, 1928.

Tylor, Edward B. *Anthropology: An Introduction to the Study of Man and Civilization,* ed. A.C. Haddon. London: Watts and Co., 1930 [1881].

—— *Primitive Culture: Researches into the Development of Mythology, Philosophy, Religion, Art, and Customs,* 2 vols. London: John Murray, 1871.

—— *Researches into the Early History of Mankind and the Development of Civilization.* London: John Murray, 1865.

Upton, George, *Woman in Music.* Chicago: A.C. McClurg, 1886.

Vaget, Hans Rudolph. 'The importance of Ernest Newman', *Wagner Journal* 1/3 (2007): 19–34.

van Thal, Herbert (ed.). *Fanfare for Ernest Newman.* London: Arthur Baker, 1955.

—— *Testament of Music: Essays and Papers by Ernest Newman.* London: Putnam, 1962.

Villemain, Abel-François. *Cours de littérature française: Tableau de la littérature au moyen âge en France, en Italie, en Espagne et en Angleterre* (2 vols). Paris: Pichon et Didier, 1830.

von Hofsten, N. 'From Cuvier to Darwin', *Isis* 24/2 (1936): 361–6.

von Rodenbeck, John. 'Bernard Shaw's revolt against rationalism', *Victorian Studies* 15/4 (June 1972): 409–37.

W.M., 'Reviews of books', *ML,* 6/4 (1925): 371–3.

W.M.G. 'Gluck and the opera', *FR,* 1 January 1896, 432–5.

Walker, Alan (ed.), *Franz Liszt: The Man and his Music.* London: Barrie & Jenkins, 1970.

—— *Franz Liszt,* 3 vols. Vols I and II: London: Faber & Faber, 1983–89; vol. III: New York: Knopf, 1996. Rev. edn. Ithaca, NY: Cornell University Press, 1997.

Walkley, A.B. *Dramatic Criticism: Three Lectures Delivered at the Royal Institution.* London: John Murray, 1903.

Wallace, William. *Wagner, As He Lived.* London: Kegan Paul, Trench, Trubner & Co. Ltd., 1925.

—— *Liszt, Wagner and the Princess.* London: Kegan, Trench, Trubner and Co. Ltd, 1927.

Wallaschek, Richard. 'Über die Bedeutung der Aphasie für den musikalischen Ausdruck' [On the significance of aphasia in musical expression], *Vierteljahrsschrift für Musikwissenschaft* 7 (1891): 53–73.

Watson, Derek, *Liszt.* New York: Schirmer Books, 1989.

Watson, Robert W. 'George Meredith's *Sandra Belloni*: The"Philosopher" on the sentimentalists', *English Literary History* 24/4 (1957): 321–35.

Watt, Paul 'The catalogue of Ernest Newman's library: Revelations about his intellectual life in the 1890s', *Script and Print* 31/2 (2007): 81–103.

—— 'A "gigantic and popular place of entertainment": Granville Bantock and music-making at the New Brighton Tower in the late 1890s', *Royal Musical Association Research Chronicle* 42 (2009): 109–64.

—— 'The intellectual life of Ernest Newman in the 1890s', PhD thesis, University of Sydney (2009).

—— 'Ernest Newman's draft of a Berlioz biography (1899) and its appropriation of Emile Hennequin's style theory', *Nineteenth-Century Music Review* 1/1 (2013): 151–68.

—— 'Critics', in Helen Greenwald (ed.), *The Oxford Handbook of Opera*. New York: Oxford University Press, 2014, 881–98.

—— 'A "Nationalist in art": Holbrooke's *Contemporary British Composers*' in Paul Watt and Anne-Marie Forbes (eds), *Joseph Holbrooke: Composer, Critic, and Musical Patriot*. Lanham, MD: Rowman and Littlefield, 2015, 153–74.

—— 'Musical and literary networks in the *Weekly Critical Review*, Paris, 1903–1904', *Nineteenth-Century Music Review*, 14/1 (2017), 33–50.

Weismann, August, *The Germ-Plasm: A Theory of Heredity*. London: Charles Scribner's, 1893.

—— 'All sufficiency of natural selection', *CR*, September 1893, 309–38 and October 1893, 596–610.

Weisstein, Ulrich. *Comparative Literature and Literary Theory*. Bloomington: Indiana University Press, 1973.

Wellek, René and Austin Warren. *Theory of Literature: A Seminal Study of the Nature and Function of Literature in all its Contexts*. Harmondsworth, Middlesex: Penguin, 1986 [1949].

Wells, G.A. *J.M. Robertson (1856–1933): Liberal, Rationalist, and Scholar*. London: Pemberton, 1987.

West, Henry R. (ed.). *The Blackwell Guide to Mill's Utilitarianism*. Maldon, MA: Blackwell, 2006.

Williams, Francis. *Dangerous Estate: The Anatomy of Newspapers*. London: Longmans, Green and Co., 1957.

Williams, Simon. 'Ibsen and the theatre 1877–1900', in James McFarlane (ed.), *The Cambridge Companion to Ibsen*. Cambridge: Cambridge University Press, 1994, 165–82.

Zon, Bennett. *Music and Metaphor in Nineteenth-Century British Musicology*. Aldershot: Ashgate, 2000.

Index

New titles published under the series title
Music in Britain, 1600–2000
ISSN 2053-3217

Hamilton Harty: Musical Polymath
Jeremy Dibble

Thomas Morley: Elizabethan Music Publisher
Tessa Murray

*The Advancement of Music in Enlightenment England:
Benjamin Cooke and the Academy of Ancient Music*
Tim Eggington

George Smart and Nineteenth-Century London Concert Life
John Carnelley

The Lives of George Frideric Handel
David Hunter

*Musicians of Bath and Beyond:
Edward Loder (1809–1865) and his Family*
Edited by Nicholas Temperley

Conductors in Britain, 1870-1914
Fiona M. Palmer